# TRANSGRAMMAR

# TRANSGRAMMAR

## English Structure, Style, and Dialects

Jean Malmstrom • Constance Weaver
Western Michigan University

Scott, Foresman and Company
Glenview, Illinois    Brighton, England

*For Val
and John*

ACKNOWLEDGMENTS

Excerpt from *Our Language Today*, Book 6 by David A. Conlin
and Neil C. Thompson. Copyright © 1967 American Book Company. Reprinted by permission.    "Evictions Mount in CBL
Struggle" by Sheryl Butler in *Chicago Daily Defender* (May 5,
1970). Reprinted by permission.    "Evict 14 S. Side Families"
from *Chicago Sun-Times* (May 5, 1970). Reprinted with permission from the Chicago Sun-Times.    Excerpt from "Of
Apollo and Dionysus" copyright © 1970 Christian Century
Foundation. Reprinted by permission from the November 4,
1970 issue of *The Christian Century*.    "Between the World
and Me" from *White Man, Listen!* by Richard Wright. Text copy-
right © 1957 by Richard Wright. Reprinted by permission of
Doubleday & Company, Inc., and Paul R. Reynolds, Inc., 599
Fifth Avenue, New York, N.Y. 10017.    "First Fig" from *Col-
lected Poems*, Harper & Row. Copyright 1922, 1950 by Edna
St. Vincent Millay. Reprinted by permission of Norma Millay
Ellis, Literary Executor.    "Catch Her in the Oatmeal" and
"A Farewell to Porridge" reprinted by permission of Esquire
Magazine, © 1958 by Esquire, Inc.    Excerpt from pages 165–
166 of *Building the American Nation* by Jerome R. Reich and
Edward L. Biller. Copyright © 1968 by Harcourt Brace Jovano-
vich, Inc. Reprinted by permission of the publisher.    Excerpts from "the cambridge ladies," "The hours rise up putting
off stars," and "somewhere i have never travelled" by E. E.
Cummings from *Poems 1923–1954*. Reprinted by permission of
Harcourt Brace Jovanovich, Inc., and Granada Publishing Limited.    "The Harbor" from *Chicago Poems* by Carl Sandburg,
copyright, 1916, by Holt, Rinehart and Winston, Inc.; renewed,
1944 by Carl Sandburg. Reprinted by permission of Harcourt
Brace Jovanovich, Inc.    "wherelings whenlings" and "anyone lived in a pretty how town" copyright, 1940, by E. E. Cummings; renewed, 1968, by Marion Morehouse Cummings. Reprinted from *Complete Poems 1913–1962* by E. E. Cummings
by permission of Harcourt Brace Jovanovich, Inc., and Granada

# PREFACE

We intend this book primarily for use in introductory courses in the English language, courses for the prospective teacher of English as well as the non-teaching major or minor. Our book has two major aims. The first is to foster the attitudes and abilities needed in studying the structure of language. Since no grammatical theory or description is universally accepted or permanently established, anyone interested in studying language must be able to ask his own questions and draw his own generalizations about language structure. To this end, the "For Further Exploration" sections in each chapter contain reading suggestions, arranged in order of increasing difficulty, to stimulate individual thought and study. The "Working with" sections, also found in each chapter, generally proceed from relatively easy exercises to challenging discovery questions, questions to which there is no "right" answer. These discovery questions are designed to stimulate students and teachers to decide for themselves various questions about language structure and to examine and criticize linguists' aims, assumptions, and hypotheses, as well as their grammatical descriptions.

The second major aim of the book is to convince the reader that a knowledge of the structure of English can increase his appreciation of writing style and his respect for dialects other than his own. Chapters 7 and 8 are particularly directed toward this aim.

We wish to thank our teachers, Robert B. Lees and Owen Thomas, who first brought us to an understanding of transformational-generative grammar. We thank also our colleagues and students at Western Michigan University who tried out earlier versions of this book and offered valuable suggestions for its improvement. We particularly thank those students whose work we have drawn upon or quoted: Gail Barley, Ruby Johnson, Alice Park, Susan Silverthorn, and Joseph Woodworth. We thank also our researchers and typists, who worked unflaggingly to meet deadlines: Philip Kabza, Susan Holaday, Joal Sowers, and Cheri Lumbard. We thank too our editors, Richard Welna, David R. Ebbitt, and Nancy Godlewski, the production editor, Mary Helfrich, and the designer, Bronwyn Rex Moore, for their invaluable assistance in getting the book into print. Finally, we thank our husbands, Vincent F. Malmstrom and James F. Weaver, for their unremitting encouragement and support. They let us work.

J. M.
C. W.

# OVERVIEW

# CONTENTS

Chapter 2
THE SOUND SYSTEM
44

# transformational theory:
# the basic model
58

Chapter 3
THE BASICS OF TRANSFORMATIONAL GRAMMAR
60

Chapter 4
TRANSFORMING  THE  BASIC  SENTENCE:
SOME  SINGULARY  TRANSFORMATIONS
109

# PART III

## transformational theory:
## expanding and revising the model
170

Chapter 6
CURRENT TRENDS IN TRANSFORMATIONAL THEORY
254

# PART IV

## grammatical theory:
## practical applications
282

Chapter 7
THE STRUCTURE OF STYLE
284

Chapter 8
THE STRUCTURE OF DIALECTS
338

Appendix I
THE FORMS OF *HAVE* AND *BE*
385

Appendix II
SOME LATIN AND SOME GREEK PREFIXES AND ROOTS
387

Appendix III
PHONOLOGICALLY CONDITIONED INFLECTIONS
390

# INTRODUCTION

The first three parts of this book introduce readers to the structure of English. This study of structure provides a foundation for Part IV, which is concerned with style in writing and with dialects in speech.

Every textbook that describes the structure of English has behind its description some *theory* of how English is structured, or even some theory about the nature of language. We will describe the structure of English according to two grammatical theories, structural and transformational. We give heavier emphasis to transformational theory because it has been more influential in recent years. But both theories have had considerable impact in the United States, stimulating the development of other theories of language structure, affecting other disciplines, and influencing the education of our children.

The use of literary passages throughout the chapters on grammatical theory suggests various ways in which a knowledge of the structure of English can increase one's understanding and appreciation of literature. The style chapter in Part IV shows how choices in word and sentence patterns create different styles in writing, and the last chapter discusses dialects as structured systems, thus making use of one's knowledge of sound patterns and grammatical patterns.

In 1933, Leonard Bloomfield, the father of structural linguistics, wrote that "It is only within the last century or so that language has been studied in a scientific way, by careful and comprehensive observation. . . . Linguistics, *the study of language, is only in its beginnings.*" *

The structural approach to language study insists that in making generalizations about language structure, we must restrict ourselves to describing externally observable data. Until the rise of transformational grammar in the late 1950s and 1960s, the structural approach dominated American linguistics. Part I of this book describes the structural approach in some detail and discusses its valuable insights into the structure of English.

* Leonard Bloomfield, Language (New York: Holt, Rinehart and Winston, Inc., 1933), p. 3.

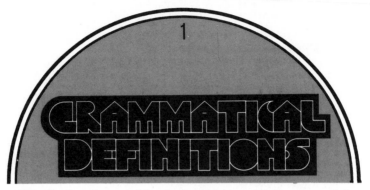

The first section of this chapter gives a brief survey of the study of English grammar. The second presents traditional schoolroom definitions of parts of speech, explaining the primary objection of structural linguists to these definitions; it then discusses at some length the structuralists' definitions of parts of speech and applies these definitions in studying a poem.

## THE STUDY OF ENGLISH GRAMMAR

Underlying any understanding of a language is an analysis of its grammar, which can be defined as the rules by which it operates. The grammar of English was first discussed in books which appeared in the seventeenth century, when the language was becoming a respectable subject of study. Previously, throughout the Middle Ages, Latin grammar had been the only grammar studied in schools; and it continued to exert a powerful influence. Where English differed from Latin, seventeenth-century grammarians felt obliged to force English to follow Latin rules. This habit created misfits because certain English structures did not occur in Latin and vice versa. Such misfits are still reflected in some of our English grammar books today, as in the Latin-based rule, "Do not split an infinitive." [1]

In the late eighteenth century the Industrial Revolution created a class of newly rich whose education did not equal their wealth and who wanted to speak and write so that their language would not betray their lack of background and educa-

---

[1] *A Latin infinitive is a single indivisible word* (explicare, *to explain*), *but an English infinitive consists of two words, which can be split by a modifying adverb* (to clearly explain).

tion. They created a demand for a prescriptive grammar, based on Latin grammar, which dictated rules of correctness. When Latin lacked a particular usage, grammarians made up a rule to cover it. These eighteenth century grammars are the ancestors of the conventional grammar textbooks still found in some classrooms.

Paralleling this development were the comparative and historical studies of languages also begun in the eighteenth century. Linguists compared different languages and discovered relationships among them. They simultaneously examined languages through time and noted how all had changed through the centuries. These comparative and historical studies resulted in massive compilations of data on modern English by such linguists as Otto Jespersen and Henry Sweet. These linguists examined the English language and endeavored to elicit its patterns of organization from their data. They described grammatical facts; they did not prescribe correctness of usage. This contrast between description and prescription is one key difference between these traditional scholarly grammarians and the traditional schoolbook grammarians.

In the United States in the early twentieth century, linguists worked with anthropologists to unlock Indian cultures through their languages. Edward Sapir and Leonard Bloomfield, for example, were themselves anthropological linguists. In order to describe Indian languages, they developed new techniques which they later applied to the analysis of English. From this seedbed developed United States structural linguistics, which in the 1950s began to have its impact upon language study in United States colleges. In 1951 there appeared *An Outline of English Structure,* by George L. Trager and Henry Lee Smith, Jr. It was followed in 1952 by Charles C. Fries' *The Structure of English.* These two books profoundly influenced linguistics in the United States. They were followed by many other structural linguistic books, written chiefly as textbooks for colleges and high schools.

Structural linguistics dominated the field in the United States until 1957, when Noam Chomsky's *Syntactic Structures* was published at The Hague in the Netherlands. Almost overnight this small book—which no American publisher had been interested in—revolutionized linguistics throughout the world.

 FOR FURTHER EXPLORATION

Paul Roberts, *Understanding Grammar.* New York: Harper and Row, Inc., 1954. Roberts' first book, preceding his later structural and transformational volumes. He offers

lucid explanations of traditional assumptions and definitions and describes how traditional grammarians arrived
at them.

Ralph B. Long, *The Sentence and Its Parts: A Grammar
of Contemporary English.* Chicago: The University of Chicago Press, 1961. A modern scholarly traditional grammar, illuminated by many interesting examples. Long
seeks to describe standard American English by careful
attention to both written and spoken language.

Ralph B. Long and Dorothy R. Long, *The System of
English Grammar.* Glenview, Ill.: Scott, Foresman and
Company, 1971. A later, less complete, more pedagogical
presentation of Long's scholarly traditional theory. Closer
to European scholarly grammars of English than to traditional schoolroom grammars.

Otto Jespersen, *Essentials of English Grammar.* University, Alabama: The University of Alabama Press, 1964.
A reissue of a classic that was originally published in
London in 1933. Jespersen here synthesizes the principles elaborated in his seven-volume *Modern English
Grammar,* in which he attempted to present a complete
grammar of English. His definitions and attitudes contrast
interestingly with those of traditional schoolroom grammarians. The book is more useful for reference than for
reading.

# THE STRUCTURALISTS' GRAMMATICAL
# DEFINITIONS

Traditionally, a noun is defined as a word that names a person, place, thing, or idea. For example, the bold-faced words
below function as names:

the electrical **short** caused a fire [2]
his **sleep** was disturbed by bats
their **side** won
he crashed into the **back** of the truck

---

[2] *Following Transformational Grammar convention, all sample sentences in the book
will be set without initial capital letters or final periods.*

A verb is traditionally defined as a word that expresses action or a state of being or becoming. When the bold-faced words above express actions, they are traditionally called verbs:

the storm could **short** the connection
I must **sleep** eight hours every night
he will **side** with his wife
can you **back** into that parking place?

An adjective is traditionally defined as a word that modifies a noun. When the bold-faced words above modify nouns, they are traditionally said to perform adjective functions:

he took a **short** trip
he drank a beer as a **sleep** inducer
we went in the **side** door
she climbed over the **back** fence

By traditional definition, an adverb is a word that modifies a verb or adjective or adverb. When the bold-faced words above modify a verb, they are traditionally said to function as adverbs. Adverbs can be created by the addition of a prefix (*he took her* **aside,** *she was taken* **aback**) or by the addition of a suffix (*he will leave* **shortly,** *she glanced* **sideways,** *he fell* **backwards**). *Back* can function adverbially without a suffix (*he looked* **back**); *sleep* first adds the adjective ending *-y* (*sleepy*) and then, to form an adverb from *sleepy,* changes the *-y* to *-i* and adds *-ly* (*she yawned* **sleepily**).

The structural linguists objected to these definitions primarily because the definitions relied heavily upon meaning. Structuralists had the same objection to the traditional schoolbook definition of a sentence as "a group of words containing a subject and a predicate and expressing a complete thought."

In 1952, after examining more than two hundred different definitions of the sentence, the structural linguist Charles C. Fries adopted the definition originally formulated by Leonard Bloomfield in 1933:

Each sentence is an independent linguistic form, not included by virtue of any grammatical construction in any larger linguistic form.[3]

---

[3] *Leonard Bloomfield,* Language *(New York: Holt, Rinehart and Winston, Inc., 1933), p. 170. Quoted in Charles C. Fries,* The Structure of English *(New York: Harcourt Brace Jovanovich, Inc., 1952), p. 21.*

*Webster's Third New International Dictionary,* published in 1961, offers a similar, though more detailed, definition of the sentence:

> A grammatically self-contained unit consisting of a word or a syntactically related group of words that expresses an assertion, a question, a command, a wish, or an exclamation, that in writing usually begins with a capital letter and concludes with appropriate end punctuation, and that in speech is phonetically distinguished by various patterns of stress, pitch, and pauses.

In defining the sentence, structuralists avoided the idea of a complete thought. They defined the sentence in terms of its grammatical structure, its punctuation in writing, and its intonation in speech. Their aversion to the use of meaning as a basis for definition derives from a famous statement by Leonard Bloomfield:

> The statement of meanings is . . . the weak point in language-study, and will remain so until human knowledge advances very far beyond its present state.[4]

Besides rejecting traditional meaning-based definitions, the structuralists refused to use Latin grammar as a model for English grammar, insisting that each language must be described in terms of its own individual patterns. Structuralists prided themselves on being "scientific," using objective and precise criteria to establish the facts of grammar. They were empiricists who used inductive methods to reach generalizations based on observable evidence, as a chemist might in his laboratory. Any other chemist performing the same experiment under the same conditions should reach the same conclusions. Similarly, structuralists believed that every linguist armed with their structural definitions ought to reach the same conclusions about how to segment and classify the parts of any given sentence.

Structuralists based their definitions on two distinct criteria: *form* and *function.* That is, they noted 1) a word's affixes, and 2) how it is used in its context.

The following sections show how structuralists defined English parts of speech.

---

[4] *Bloomfield,* Language, *p. 140.*

## RECOGNIZING NOUNS AND NOMINALS

The form of a word is determined by the affixes it takes. An **affix** is a meaning bearing element added at the beginning or end of a word. When added at the beginning, an affix is called a **prefix** (*endanger, ahead, inopportune*); when added at the end, it is called a **suffix** (*communist, glassy, stabilize*). Many English words are marked by a suffix that identifies their part of speech. These suffixes add grammatical meaning, usually (though not always) changing the part of speech of the base to which they are attached. Thus, the verb *agree* becomes the noun *agreement* by the addition of the suffix *-ment,* and the adjective *bold* becomes the noun *boldness* by the addition of the suffix *-ness.* Such suffixes are called **derivational suffixes.** All prefixes are derivational as well. (See Appendix II for some Latin and Greek prefixes and roots.)

The derivational suffixes may have more than one spelling and/or pronunciation. For example, one such suffix may be spelled either *-ance* or *-ence* (*contrivance, correspondence*) and may be pronounced /əns, ənts, ins/ etc.[5] In some words— like *carpenter, theism,* and *linguist*—the stem is not an independent word but a bound base (*carpent-, the-, ling-*). A **bound base** is a word stem that never stands alone as a word but must always have an affix attached to it. If it can stand alone, it is a **free base,** a word. Bases and affixes alike are technically called **morphemes.**

The following list includes some common derivational noun suffixes, with illustrative examples: [6]

Suffixes added to verbs to form nouns:

| | |
|---|---|
| *-age* | demurrage, breakage |
| *-ance* | conveyance, reference |
| *-er* | boiler, sailor, liar, sawyer |
| *-ee* | payee, employee, draftee |
| *-ment* | payment, agreement, argument |

Suffixes added to adjectives to form nouns:

| | |
|---|---|
| *-ce* | abundance, convenience, compliance, independence |
| *-cy* | consistency, relevancy, intricacy |
| *-ity* | facility, hostility |
| *-ness* | happiness, boldness, friendliness, hopelessness |
| *-ster* | youngster, oldster |

---

[5] *The symbol / ə /, called schwa, is pronounced like the* a *in above; /ɨ/ is pronounced like the* e *of ages. The other symbols are self-explanatory. Chapter Two discusses such phonetic transcriptions in detail.*
[6] *The material on derivational suffixes is adapted from W. Nelson Francis,* The Structure of American English *(New York: The Ronald Press Company, 1958), Chapter 5.*

Suffixes added to other nouns:

| | |
|---|---|
| *-cy* | advocacy, democracy, captaincy |
| *-er* | lifer, liner, outfielder |
| *-ian* | mathematician, librarian |
| *-ism* | Methodism, monarchism, gangsterism |
| *-ist* | physicist, violinist, Jansenist |
| *-ship* | friendship, professorship |
| *-ster* | gangster, roadster, dopester |

Suffixes added to bound stems to form nouns:

| | |
|---|---|
| *-er* | carpenter, tailor, porter |
| *-ism* | monism, polytheism, hypnotism, fascism |
| *-ist* | monist, hypnotist, fascist |
| *-ity* | depravity, debility, felicity |

Other noun suffixes are called **inflectional suffixes**. These differ from derivational suffixes in never changing the part-of-speech class to which they are attached. Noun inflectional suffixes are *-s* or *-es*, meaning "plural," and *-'s* or *-s'*, meaning "possessive." Thus, a noun is a word inflected like *man* or *boy*; that is, a noun is any word that fits into an inflectional series that is built on either or both of the contrasts between singular and plural numbers (*man, men* or *boy, boys*) and/or between common and genitive (possessive) case (*man, man's; men, men's* or *boy, boy's; boys, boys'*):

| | |
|---|---|
| I saw a *man* | I saw the *man's* dog |
| I saw three *men* | I saw the *men's* dog |
| I saw a *boy* | I saw the *boy's* dog |
| I saw three *boys* | I saw the *boys'* dog |

Turning now to the structural linguists' second method for identifying English nouns, we can consider the functions of nouns in English sentences. Structuralists devised the test frame below for identifying nouns. A **test frame** is a sentence with a blank space to be filled by the word being tested. Not all nouns (that is, words inflected like *boy* or *man* or otherwise showing at least one of the two contrasts above) will fit into this test frame.[7] However, any single word that does fit into this test frame is a noun.

---

[7] *Parentheses indicate that the item enclosed may or may not be needed in the test frame. Braces mean that one of the options must be used in the test frame.*

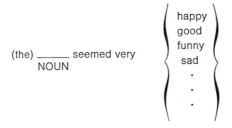

Any word or group of words that functions like a noun can be said to be a **nominal**, a nounlike construction. Nominals have several basic functions in sentences: subject, direct object, predicate nominative, object of preposition, and indirect object.

When a nominal is functioning as a **subject**, it normally stands at the beginning of its **clause**, which is a group of words with a subject and a predicate:

> **anteaters** look amusing
> **the anteater's snout** looks amusing

*The anteater's snout* is a **phrase**, a group of words lacking a subject-plus-predicate construction and functioning the way a single-word part of speech normally functions. This phrase is an expansion of the **head** noun, *snout*. The first example below shows the head noun *anteater* modified by a clause; the second example has a clause as subject:

> **the anteater which was born yesterday** looks amusing
> **that the anteater will become a nuisance** is obvious

Every clause has a subject, by definition, and every subject is a nominal:

> I think [that **the anteater** is amusing]
> I like the anteater [**which** was born yesterday]
> I will bring out the anteater [when **Mom** leaves]

In the first sentence above, *I* is the subject of the main clause: *I think. . . . Think* has a nominal clause after it, and *the anteater* is the subject of this clause. *I* is again the subject of the main clause in the second sentence. This sentence contains an adjectival (adjectivelike) clause, *which was born yesterday*; the word *which* is the subject of this clause. In the third sentence, *I* is once again the subject of the main clause; *Mom* is the subject of the adverbial (adverblike) clause *when Mom leaves*.

Thus there are basically two kinds of clauses, **main** or **independent**, and **dependent** or **subordinate**. Main clauses are the only ones which can stand alone as sentences. Nominal, adjectival, and adverbial clauses are subordinate clauses.

As **direct objects**, nominals normally stand immediately following their verb. Here is a set of examples:

> I like **anteaters**
> I like **the anteaters**
> I like **the anteater which was born yesterday**
> I think **that the anteater is amusing**

As **predicate nominatives**, nominals follow a linking verb. These nominals have the same referent as the subject; they refer to the same person, place, thing, or concept, with the verb serving as a link between the two:

> those animals are **anteaters**
> the anteater became **a nuisance**
> my idea is **that the anteaters should all go**

A construction consisting of a preposition plus a nominal is called a **prepositional phrase**; the nominal is called the **object of the preposition**:

> he gave some termites to **these baby anteaters**
> she gave a birthday party for **Joan**

As **indirect objects**, nouns precede direct objects, and indicate the person to whom or for whom something is given, said, or done:

> he gave **these baby anteaters** some termites
> he gave **them** some termites
> she gave **Joan** a birthday party

WORKING WITH NOUNS AND NOMINALS

In the following poems, identify the nominals. What signals make identification possible?

## Colours

When your face
appeared over my crumpled life
at first I understood
only the poverty of what I have.
5    Then its particular light
on woods, on rivers, on the sea,
became my beginning in the coloured world
in which I had not yet had my beginning.
I am so frightened, I am so frightened,
10   of the unexpected sunrise finishing,
of revelations
and tears and the excitement finishing,
I don't fight it, my love is this fear,
I nourish it who can nourish nothing,
15   love's slipshod watchman.
Fear hems me in.
I am conscious that these minutes are short
and that the colours in my eyes will vanish
when your face sets.[8]

> —Yevgeny Yevtushenko, translated by
> Robin Milner-Gulland and Peter Levi

## To an Athlete Dying Young

The time you won your town the race
We chaired you through the market-place;
Man and boy stood cheering by,
And home we brought you shoulder-high.

5   To-day, the road all runners come,
Shoulder-high we bring you home,
And set you at your threshold down,
Townsman of a stiller town.

Smart lad, to slip betimes away
10   From fields where glory does not stay
And early though the laurel grows
It withers quicker than the rose.

---

[8] *Yevgeny Yevtushenko,* Selected Poems of Yevtushenko, *trans. Robin Milner-Gulland and Peter Levi (Baltimore, Md.: Penguin Books, 1970), p. 77.*

Eyes the shady night has shut
Cannot see the record cut,
15      And silence sounds no worse than cheers
After earth has stopped the ears:

Now you will not swell the rout
Of lads that wore their honours out,
Runners whom renown outran
20      And the name died before the man.

So set, before its echoes fade,
The fleet foot on the sill of shade,
And hold to the low lintel up
The still-defended challenge-cup.

25      And round that early-laurelled head
Will flock to gaze the strengthless dead,
And find unwithered on its curls
The garland briefer than a girl's.[9]

—A. E. Housman

## RECOGNIZING VERBS AND VERBALS

Verbs too can be identified by their form and their function. First, they have their characteristic derivational suffixes. Some are attached to full words and others to bound bases. The following list contains almost all the derivational suffixes found on verbs:

*-ate:*   added to bound bases and a few nouns: *implicate, operate, salivate.* (Note that some *-ate* words, like *duplicate* and *syndicate,* can be verbs, nouns, or adjectives. How does their pronunciation differ according to their part-of-speech class?)

*-ize:*   added to bound bases, nouns, and adjectives: *utilize, idolize, socialize.* (These verbs have related nouns ending in *-ism, -ation,* or both: *utilization, socialism, socialization.*)

*-fy:*   added to bases, nouns, and adjectives: *liquify, beautify, simplify.* (These verbs have related nouns ending in *-faction* or *-fication: liquefaction, beautification, simplification.*)

[9] A. E. Housman, A Shropshire Lad, *Jubilee ed. (Waterville, Maine: Colby College Library, 1946), pp. 26–27.*

*-ish:*    added to bound bases. *finish, furnish.* (Note that
           adjectives also use *-ish,* added to bound stems or
           nouns: *British, childish.*)

Verbs are words belonging to the inflection system which
patterns like *drive, drives, drove, driven, driving*; or *play, plays,
played, playing.* Verbs like *drive* are called irregular verbs, and
there are a number of different ways in which they can be
"irregular" (compare, for example, the forms of *bring, begin,
do, eat, go,* and *hit*). Verbs which add *-ed* to form the past
tense and past participle are called regular. Here are the forms
of *drive* and *play*:

*Present tense*

*drives, plays*    Used with singular nominals, including
(third singular form)    the personal pronouns *he, she,* and *it* but
                         excluding *I* and *you:*

$$\begin{Bmatrix} \text{this girl} \\ \text{he} \\ \text{she} \\ \text{it} \end{Bmatrix} \begin{Bmatrix} \textit{drives} \\ \textit{plays} \end{Bmatrix} \text{superbly}$$

*drive, play*    Used with all plural nominals and with
                 the personal pronouns *I, we, you, they:*

$$\begin{Bmatrix} \text{those girls} \\ \text{I} \\ \text{we} \\ \text{you} \\ \text{they} \end{Bmatrix} \begin{Bmatrix} \textit{drive} \\ \textit{play} \end{Bmatrix} \text{superbly}$$

*Past tense*

*drove, played*    Used with all nominals:

$$\begin{Bmatrix} \text{they} \\ \text{he} \\ \text{everyone} \end{Bmatrix} \begin{Bmatrix} \textit{drove} \\ \textit{played} \end{Bmatrix} \text{superbly}$$

*Past participle*

*driven, played*    Used after the auxiliary words *have, has, had,*
                    and sometimes *having:*

$$\begin{Bmatrix} \text{they } \textit{have} \\ \text{he } \textit{has} \\ \text{everything } \textit{had} \end{Bmatrix} \begin{Bmatrix} \textit{driven} \\ \textit{played} \end{Bmatrix} \text{superbly}$$

$$\textit{having} \begin{Bmatrix} \textit{driven} \\ \textit{played} \end{Bmatrix} \text{superbly, he was} \\ \text{awarded the prize}$$

*Present participle*
*driving, playing*  Used after the auxiliary words *am, is, are, was,*
*were, been, be:*

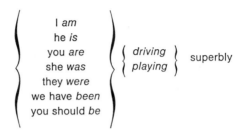

I *am*
he *is*
you *are*
she *was*
they *were*
we have *been*
you should *be*

{ *driving* }
{ *playing* }   superbly

Verbs, like nouns, can be identified by their functions in English sentences. Again, structuralists have devised a test frame. Not all verbs will fit in it comfortably, because some verbs need to be completed by a nominal, adjectival, or adverbial. But any single word that does fit into the following test frame is, by definition, a verb:

they must _____
VERB

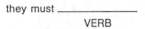

Any word or group of words that functions like a verb can be said to be a **verbal**, a verblike construction. Verbals function as the entire predicate of a sentence, or as part of the predicate:

I **slept** (Entire predicate)
I **have slept** (Entire predicate)
I **may have slept** (Entire predicate)
I **will be driving** the car (Part of predicate)

The head verb, or **main verb**, is always the last verb in a verbal phrase. In the sentences above, *slept* and *driving* are the main verbs. But notice that *may* and *will* are verbs also, because they have past tense forms (*might, would*). And *have* and *be* are verbs, since they have inflected forms: *has, had, having*; *am, is, are, was, were, being, been*. (Henceforth the verb *to have* will be designated as the HAVE verb or auxiliary, or simply as HAVE; the verb *to be* will be designated as the BE verb or auxiliary, or simply as BE. The forms of HAVE and BE are given in Appendix I.) However, in the sentences above, *have, will*, and *be* are acting not as headwords of a verbal phrase, but as **auxiliary** or "helping" verbs. Auxiliaries are function words that work with verbs. A **function word** primarily expresses grammatical relationship, rather than "real-world" meaning.

Main verbs are of three major types: transitive, intransitive, and linking (or copulative). A **transitive verb** has an object:

> Algernon **read** the report
> a bear **ate** the honey

Only transitive verbs have a synonymous passive form, used when the object of the action has become the grammatical subject:

> the report **was read** by Algernon
> the honey **was eaten** by the bear

An **intransitive verb** has no object; it is followed by an adverbial, or nothing:

> they **hiccoughed** constantly
> our group was **singing**

A **linking verb** joins the subject to a noun or adjective in the predicate:

> roses **are** flowers
> everybody **grows** old

The context determines the type of a verb. Verbs can shift type depending on the sentence in which they occur:

| | |
|---|---|
| Transitive: | she **turned** the pancakes |
| Intransitive: | the car **turned** over |
| Linking: | the baby **turned** blue |
| | |
| Transitive: | Mary **sounded** the alarm |
| Intransitive: | the alarm **sounded** |
| Linking: | the music **sounded** lovely |
| | |
| Intransitive: | Joe **was** there |
| Linking: | Joe **was** the boss |
| Linking: | Joe **was** tall |

There are some two-word and even three-word transitive, intransitive, and linking verbs. The verb headword and the adverbial word or words following it convey one single meaning:

| | |
|---|---|
| Transitive: | Elizabeth **called up** ("phoned") her uncle |
| | he was **looked up to** ("respected") by everyone |
| Intransitive: | the sophomore **stood up** ("rose") immediately |
| Linking: | Frank **looked like** ("resembled") an idiot |

## WORKING WITH VERBS AND VERBALS

**1.** Use the verbs listed below in an original sentence. Each verb is to be used as indicated by the verb type given after it.

a.  turn—intransitive
b.  turn—transitive
c.  turn—linking
d.  turn out—intransitive
e.  turn out—transitive
f.  turn out—linking
g.  turn on—transitive
h.  give up—intransitive
i.  give up—transitive
j.  give—intransitive
k.  give—transitive

l.  make—intransitive
m.  think—transitive
n.  think about—transitive
o.  smell—transitive
p.  smell—linking
q.  sound—intransitive
r.  sound—transitive
s.  become—linking
t.  squabble—intransitive
u.  lie—intransitive
v.  seem like—linking

**2.** Locate the verbs in the following lines from "Three Mornings in September," by John Woods.

> I wake in my father's house.
> Autumn smokes from the earth
> As the clock gathers itself, as the sun
> Shoulders up from the river.
> 5    My dog lifts his ears at a neighborly bark,
> Scrabbles off through the arbor.
> The Concords swell, the apples fall
> In light wind. Cows swing heavily.
>
> The first shadow thickens on the wall.
> 10   Now the sun strikes through the window,
> The blind cracked like a blueprint,
> Through the web-woven barn window
> To the searing edge of the scythe.
> The oak leans out of its shadow
> 15   And silently bursts into flame.
> My father tries to cough up the war
> In the shallow trench of his sleep.
> I tie on my sneakers, drift out
> To run awhile with the hounds.[10]

[10] John Woods, The Cutting Edge (Bloomington, Ind.: Indiana University Press, 1966), p. 15.

**3.** Explain Gerard Manley Hopkins' verb use in this excerpt from "As Kingfishers":

> the just man justices

**4.** In the following quotations from *A Reader's Guide to James Joyce*,[11] William York Tindall uses several two-word verbs in an unusual way. Find these two-word verbs and explain why they are unusual. How would they be rephrased to seem more natural to you?

> Not the product of Joyce's imagination,
> these sermons are the product of memory,
> selection, and leafing old sermons through.
>
> Originally his, the theory is Stephen's
> now, serving to show his character forth
> and to advance the plot.
>
> However funny the analogy between Gerty and
> Nausicaa, a great princess, Joyce's parody
> is serious, intended to show man in our
> time forth.

If you substituted a suitable pronoun (*them*, *it*, *him*) for *sermons*, *his character*, and *a man in our time* respectively, what effect would that substitution have on the word order of the sentences?

**5.** Is *present tense* synonymous with *present time*? Is *past tense* synonymous with *past time*? How do we express *future time*? Examine the verbs in the following quotation from *Them*, by Joyce Carol Oates,[12] to arrive at whatever answers to these questions you can.

> I am going to fall in love. Tomorrow
> night I'll see the man I have picked out to love.
> He is already married; he has three children.

[11] *William York Tindall*, A Reader's Guide to James Joyce *(New York: The Noonday Press, A Division of Farrar, Straus, and Giroux, 1959), pp. 71, 95, and 129 respectively.*
[12] *Joyce Carol Oates*, Them *(Greenwich, Conn.: Fawcett Publications, Inc., 1969), pp. 315–316.*

I want him. I want him to marry me. I am going
5                to make this happen and begin my life. We will
have a bedroom together, we will have children,
he will leave his own children behind. I am
telling you these things even though you are
a married woman and would not want any other
10                woman to take your husband from you. But you
are a married woman, I think, who would not mind
taking someone else's husband, so long as it
happened well enough, beautifully enough like
a story. Once in a while, though, I don't
15                believe my life will change. I don't believe
he will marry me or even think of me. I don't
believe something so strange could happen. And
I fall into a sad state and can't get out of it.
I lean forward and my head droops between my
20                shoulders, my bones seem to turn helpless, I
think *Why didn't I die? Why didn't he kill me?*
For thirteen months I was an animal. Ma uses
other words, she says I was "going through a
phase," but I remember it all, I know. Never
25                did I think anything in those months, but pictures
floated through my mind, like a nightmare. Even
when I was awake I was asleep.

## RECOGNIZING ADJECTIVES AND ADJECTIVALS

Adjectives, also, can be identified by their form and function.
First, they are marked by certain derivational suffixes. The following set indicates the most common ones:

| | |
|---|---|
| *-y, -al, -ar, -ary, -ic, -ish, -ous, -ly,* added to nouns and bound stems: | *faulty, leafy, holy; fatal, national, traditional; columnar, popular, spectacular; legendary, literary, contrary; climactic, comic, tragic; childish, lavish, boyish; marvelous, pernicious, delicious; friendly, ugly, ghastly* |
| *-ful, -less,* added to nouns: | *hopeful, useful; hopeless, useless* |
| *-able, -ent* (also spelled *-ant*), *-ive,* added to verbs and bound stems: | *remarkable, understandable, conceivable; abhorrent, convenient, significant; active, native, impulsive* |

An adjective is any word that is or can be compared; that is, any word is an adjective if it fits into an inflectional sequence like *tall* (called the "positive degree"), *taller* (called the "comparative degree"), *tallest* (called the "superlative degree"). We may also consider as an adjective any word that can be modified by *more* or *most*: *more wonderful*, *most wonderful*. Adjectives can add *-er* and *-est* and/or can be modified by *more* and *most*.

Adjectives, like nouns and verbs, can be identified by their functions in English sentences. The structuralists' test frame is useful in identifying adjectives, even though not all adjectives fit into it. Specifically, comparative and superlative adjectives (*taller*, *tallest*, for example) will not fit this test frame. But the positive degree of most adjectives will fit:

$$
(the) \underline{\quad\quad\quad} \underset{\text{ADJECTIVE}}{} \left\{ \begin{array}{l} \text{man} \\ \text{butter} \\ \text{dogs} \\ \text{scissors} \\ \cdot \\ \cdot \\ \cdot \end{array} \right\} \text{seemed very} \underline{\quad\quad\quad} \underset{\text{ADJECTIVE}}{}
$$

Any word or group of words that functions like an adjective can be considered an **adjectival**, an adjectivelike construction.

Adjectivals modify nouns. They may occur before the noun they modify; they may occur after a linking verb and modify the subject; or, particularly if they are phrases or clauses, they may occur immediately after the noun they modify.

Most prenoun adjectivals are adjectives:

> it's a **nice** day today
> that's a **big** house
> she has a **beautiful** coat

All of these words can either add *-er* and *-est*, or be modified by *more* and *most*: *yesterday was a **nicer** day, he has the **biggest** house, she has the **most beautiful** coat*. Also, all of these adjectivals can occur after the intensifier *very*: *the day is **very** nice, that house is **very big**, her coat is **very beautiful***. In short, all of these adjectivally-functioning words are adjectives.

Sometimes, however, a noun can function adjectivally to modify another noun, as in the following sentences:

> it's a **brick** house
> it's a **stone** wall
> it's a **grass** shack

The words *brick*, *stone*, and *grass* inflect like nouns rather than adjectives. For example, we would say *one brick, two bricks*, but not *\*it's a bricker house* or *\*the house is very brick.* (The asterisk designates an ungrammatical construction.) A noun functioning adjectivally to modify another noun is called a **noun adjunct.**

When adjectivals occur after a linking verb, they are called **predicate adjectivals:**

> Ann is **tall**
> Ann seems **taller than Mary**
> Ann is **tallest in her class**
> Ann is **beautiful**

Adjectives following the noun they modify usually occur in a few set phrases like *time **immemorial*** or *mother **dear***, or with a special kind of noun, an indefinite pronoun, in phrases like *something **big***. More frequently, present and past participles occur as postnominal modifiers:

> the nun **singing** is popular
> the jewels **stolen** were in Mason's car

Adverbs can also function adjectivally following a noun:

> the party **yesterday** was a success
> they liked the fence **outside**

Most postnominal modifiers are phrases or clauses rather than single-word adjectivals. The following are some examples:

> the anteater **in the zoo** looked crazy
> the anteater **which is in the zoo** looked crazy

In addition, nominals can function adjectivally following another nominal:

> this is our cat, **Alabaster**, and that's our dog, **Shane**
> Nancy, I'd like you to meet my mother, **Mrs. Williams**
> there's Beverly Jones, **the girl you praised so highly**

In these examples, the bold-faced nominals (**Alabaster, Shane, Mrs. Williams, the girl you praised so highly**) are **appositives**; they modify the preceding noun and are separated from it by a comma. Appositives are said to be *in apposition with* the nominal they modify.

Structural linguists invented the term **determiner** to name the class of adjectivally functioning words that signals the imminent appearance of a noun in an English sentence. Traditional textbook grammar had no separate term for these function words, more often than not classifying them as adjectives. This classification recognizes their function as modifiers of nouns but disregards their differences in form from adjectives.

The four most frequent kinds of determiners are:

**1.   Articles:** definite, *the*; indefinite, *a* or *an.* The articles are an infallible signal that a noun is coming up in a sentence.

> **the** man who ate **the** banana won **the** color TV set
> **a** man without **a** country cannot vote in **an** election

**2.   Demonstratives:** *this, these*; *that, those.* These words function as pronouns when there is no following noun, but they are determiners when they work like *the*:

| *pronouns* | *determiners* |
|---|---|
| **these** are mine | **these** kids are mine |
| **this** is horrible | **this** story is horrible |

**3.   Possessives:** *my, our, your, his, her, its,* and *their.* These words function as determiners when they are immediately followed by a noun:

> **my** husband sold **our** old car to **your** sister after **its** muffler
>   was replaced
> **his** price matched **her** pocketbook and **their** satisfaction with
>   the deal was mutual

English personal pronouns also have a so-called "second possessive" form, which functions as a pronoun. In some cases it matches the possessive determiner, but in other cases it does not. For reference, here is a set of the personal pronoun forms. **First person** refers to the speaker; **second person** refers to the person or persons spoken to; **third person** refers to the person or persons spoken about. **Nominative** refers to forms used in subject position; **accusative** refers to forms used in object position.

|  | Nominative (subject) | Accusative (object) | First Possessive (determiner) | Second Possessive (pronoun) |
|---|---|---|---|---|
| 1st person sg. | I | me | my | mine |
| 2nd person sg./pl. | you | you | your | yours |
| 3rd person sg. | he | him | his | his |
|  | she | her | her | hers |
|  | it | it | its | its |
| 1st person pl. | we | us | our | ours |
| 3rd person pl. | they | them | their | theirs |

**4. Cardinal numbers:** from *one* through *ninety-nine*; after that, the numbers *one* through *ninety-nine* become determiners for the nouns *hundred, thousand, million,* etc. The cardinal numbers can serve also as pronouns:

> he looked at **two** houses and finally bought **one**
>             (determiner)                              (pronoun)

**5.**   Some other determiners are

| | | | |
|---|---|---|---|
| some | every | both | either |
| any | few | much | neither |
| no | each | more | |
| all | several | most | |

## WORKING WITH ADJECTIVES AND ADJECTIVALS

1.   Identify all the adjectivals in "The Yellow Chimney," by William Carlos Williams. State which noun is modified by each adjectival.

> There is a plume
> of fleshpale
> smoke upon the blue
> sky. The silver
>
> 5       rings that
> strap the yellow
> brick stack at

wide intervals shine
in this amber
10    light—not

of the sun not of
the pale sun but
his born brother

the
15    declining season [13]

2.   In his inaugural address of January 1969, President Richard
M. Nixon quoted Archibald MacLeish's comments on the Apollo
astronauts who spoke from the moon to the people of earth on
Christmas Eve, 1968. Identify all of Nixon's and MacLeish's adjectivals, stating which noun is modified by each.

In that moment, their view from the moon moved
poet Archibald MacLeish to write: "To see the
earth as it truly is, small and blue and beautiful
in that eternal silence where it floats, is to see
5    ourselves as riders on the Earth together, brothers
on that bright loveliness in the eternal cold—
brothers who know now they are truly brothers."
In that moment of surpassing technological
triumph, men turned their thoughts toward home
10    and humanity—seeing in that far perspective that
man's destiny on earth is not divisible: telling us
that however far we reach into the cosmos, our
destiny lies not in the stars but here on earth itself,
in our own hands and our own hearts.
15    We have endured a long night of the American
spirit. But as our eyes catch the dimness of the
first rays of dawn, let us not curse the remaining
dark. Let us gather the light.
Our destiny offers, not the cup of despair, but the
20    chalice of opportunity. So let us seize it, not in
fear, but in gladness—and, "riders on the earth
together, let us go forward, firm in our faith, stead-
fast in our purpose, cautious of the dangers: but
sustained by our confidence in the will of God
25    and the promise of man." [14]

[13] William Carlos Williams, Selected Poems (New York: New Directions Books, 1968),
pp. 104–105.
[14] Lester Thonssen, ed., Representative American Speeches: 1968–1969, vol. 41, no.
4 (New York: The H. W. Wilson Company, 1969), p. 120.

**3.** Which of the bold-faced phrases below are adjectivals? In each case, what is the basis for your decision? What is the function of those bold-faced words which are not functioning adjectivally? How do you know?

> he was **determined**
> the outcome was **determined**

> Mr. Higgins will be **dedicated**
> the building will be **dedicated**

> she has been **detached**
> the boxtop has been **detached**

**4.** In the following sentences, identify the determiners and classify them by types: article, demonstrative, possessive, or cardinal number.

- a. this letter seems a crazy idea to her
- b. six watermelons were dropped off that bridge on the boats passing underneath
- c. my mind was sick with all these worries
- d. that is a ridiculous motion and I won't vote for its passage
- e. he was like those graduate students from the university
- f. when does your husband get home from his office?
- g. the heavy edge of an ax bit into the bark of their walnut tree

**5.** What evidence can you think of for or against the idea that each of the bold-faced phrases below is a modifier of the noun that follows it?

- a. he bought **a gallon of** wine
- b. she spilled **a glass of** milk
- c. she spilled **a quart of** milk
- d. she broke **the bottle of** cough medicine
- e. we laughed at **the gaggle of** geese
- f. he ate **a mile of** spaghetti
- g. we watched **a school of** fish
- h. **the pack of** wolves attacked him

## RECOGNIZING ADVERBS AND ADVERBIALS

Like nouns, verbs, and adjectives, adverbs too can be identified by their form and their functions. First, they are marked
regularly by four derivational suffixes:

| | |
|---|---|
| *-ly:* | added to adjectives: *quickly, brightly, strangely* |
| *-wise:* | added to nouns: *sidewise, lengthwise, timewise, cornerwise* |
| *-ward(s):* | added to a few nouns and appearing both with and without *-s: backward(s), forward(s), homeward(s)* |
| *-ways:* | added to a few nouns and adjectives: *sideways, flatways* |

Manner adverbs consist, like *quickly,* of the positive degree
of an adjective, plus the suffix *-ly;* such adverbs cannot be
compared by the addition of the inflectional suffixes *-er* and
*-est.*[15] Adverbs commonly occur under primary stress[16] at the
end of sentences:

> the car left the scene **quickly**
> the apes chattered **wildly**

These manner adverbs tell *how* something is done.
Other adverbs refer to time or place:

> he left **yesterday**
> he goes to the dentist **monthly**

> she stays **home**
> he goes **there**

Any word or group of words functioning like an adverb can
be said to be an **adverbial,** an adverblike construction.
Below is a table showing some types of adverbs and adverbial constructions. The *S* stands for "sentence."

---

[15] *Note that adjectives ending in -ly can be compared:* friendly, friendlier, friendliest; homely, homelier, homeliest; ghastly, ghastlier, ghastliest.
[16] *For a discussion of stress, see p. 51.*

## Some Kinds of Adverbs and Adverbials

### Time

| | | |
|---|---|---|
| point in time | *then*-type word | *yesterday, Friday, monthly* |
| | phrase | *this Friday, two months, five years* |
| | prepositional phrase | *on Friday, in two months, in a year* |

$$\left\{ \begin{array}{l} \textit{before} \\ \textit{after} \\ \textit{since} \\ \textit{until} \\ \textit{till} \\ \textit{when} \end{array} \right\} + S$$

*before he leaves*
*after he has left*
*since time began*
*until he leaves*
*till he leaves*
*when he leaves*

duration
of time

$$\left\{ \begin{array}{l} \textit{when} \\ \textit{while} \\ \textit{as} \end{array} \right\} + S$$

*when he is leaving*
*while he is gone, while he is leaving*
*as he leaves, as he is leaving*

### Place

| | | |
|---|---|---|
| location and direction | *there*-type word | *there, home,* (as in *he is home*) |
| | prepositional phrase | *at home* (location) |
| | | *toward home* (direction) |
| | *where* + S | *where the hogs used to live* (as in *he lives where the hogs used to live*) |

### Manner

| | |
|---|---|
| *thus*-type word | *slow, quick* |
| adjective + *-ly* | *slowly* |
| adverbial phrase | *very quickly, so awfully slowly* |

*Comparison*

| | | |
|---|---|---|
| | as . . . as + S | as blind as a bat is blind |
| | -er than + S | blinder than a bat is blind |
| { more / less } | { . . . than + S } | more stubborn than a mule is stubborn |
| | | less blind than a bat is blind |

*Reason*

prepositional phrase   on account of his death, owing to the emergency, because of him

{ because / since / as / so (that) } + S

because his trombone had been stolen
since it won't do any good
as it is important
so (that) he can go to camp

*Contrast*

prepositional phrase   despite his appearance, contrary to orders

{ though / although / even though } + S

though it might be a possibility
although she is pretty
even though he was very hungry

*Condition*

{ if / unless / whether (or not) } + S

if he can't go
unless it rains
whether or not it rains, whether he's coming

Adverbials function in sentences as modifiers of clauses, verbals, adjectivals, and adverbials.

As clause modifiers, adverbials can occur at the beginning or end of the clause, and sometimes elsewhere. This movability reveals that the modifier does not modify any one word or construction within the clause:

he paid his bill **reluctantly**
**reluctantly,** he paid his bill
he **reluctantly** paid his bill

he paid his bill **yesterday**
**yesterday** he paid his bill

he paid his bill **last month**
**last month** he paid his bill

he paid his bill **in December**
**in December** he paid his bill

he paid his bill **when the electric company threatened to**
   **cut off the power**
**when the electric company threatened to cut off the power,**
   he paid his bill

As modifiers of verbals, adverbials are not normally movable to the front of the clause. In this respect they are unlike clause modifiers:

he runs **rapidly**

To say *rapidly he runs* would be reminiscent of poetry or children's fairy tales, not of normal discourse. The same lack of movability characterizes the following set of examples:

he runs **to town**
the man put the kitten **in a basket**
the baby is sleeping **in his crib**
he lives **where the hogs used to live**

Adverbials also modify adjectivals:

the car is $\left\{ \begin{array}{l} \text{very} \\ \text{extremely} \\ \text{quite} \\ \text{too} \end{array} \right\}$ fast

The adverbial words (*very, extremely, quite, too*) modify adjectives like *fast*. Often such words are called **intensifiers.** Adverbial phrases and clauses modify adjectivals, too:

> I am happy **about it**
> she is **more** stubborn **than a mule**
> I am glad **that he is here**
> they are uncertain **what he should do**

Adverbials also modify adverbs:

$$
\text{he drives}
\begin{Bmatrix}
\text{very} \\
\text{extremely} \\
\text{quite} \\
\text{too}
\end{Bmatrix}
\text{fast}
$$

> the words struck **as** forcefully **as bullets fired close range**
> he drives **so** fast **that he may have an accident**

## RECOGNIZING FUNCTION WORDS

We have already noted two groups of function words—words that primarily express grammatical relationships rather than "real-world" meaning. These groups are determiners, which work with nouns, and auxiliaries, which work with verbs. There are three other major groups of function words—prepositions, subordinators, and coordinating conjunctions. We will discuss each of these in turn.

PREPOSITIONS.  **Prepositions** connect their following nominal with some other word in the sentence. Here is an alphabetic list of the most common English prepositions, with examples of their use. Note that there are one-, two-, and three-word prepositions. According to Charles C. Fries, nine of these prepositions make up ninety-two per cent of all the prepositions used. These nine are *at, by, for, from, in, of, on, to,* and *with.*

| | |
|---|---|
| *aboard* | aboard the ship |
| *about* | about the city, about him, about her painting |
| *above* | above the treetops, above average, above criticism |
| *according to* | according to our data, according to Mary |
| *across* | across the top, across the river |
| *after* | after the party, after Mary |
| *against* | against the window, against the truth |

| | |
|---|---|
| *ahead of* | ahead of his time, ahead of time |
| *along* | along the river, along the road |
| *among* | among the three of us |
| *around* | around her waist, around town |
| *as* | as president, as student |
| *as far as* | as far as the church, as far as Chicago |
| *at* | at school, at once, at our suggestion |
| *back of* | back of the door, back of the book, back of the idea |
| *because of* | because of the flood, because of his wish |
| *before* | before the winter, before the congregation, before answering |
| *behind* | behind the screen, behind the suggestion |
| *below* | below our house, below our expectations |
| *beneath* | beneath the ocean, beneath him |
| *beside* | beside the lake, beside the question, beside myself |
| *besides* | besides me, no one besides Bill |
| *between* | between Toledo and Cleveland, between joy and sorrow |
| *beyond* | beyond the gas station, beyond hope |
| *by* | by the house, by the army, by rights, by day |
| *concerning* | concerning my petition, concerning our vote |
| *down* | down the river, down the hill, down the list |
| *due to* | due to a mistake, due to illness |
| *during* | during the wedding, during the past century |
| *except* | except the old folks, except apologies |
| *for* | for Joe, for reward, for the nation |
| *from* | from the kitchen, from Europe, from desperation |
| *in* | in the city, in the room, in Shakespeare, in need |
| *in place of* | in place of his old coat, in place of his brother |
| *inside* or *inside of* | inside (of) the cottage, inside (of) five years |
| *in spite of* | in spite of the rule, in spite of his opinion |
| *into* | into the car, into the argument |
| *like* | like a hurricane, like a clown |
| *near* | near the table, near the bottom, near death |
| *of* | of Maine, of a similar shade, of his party, of the teacher |
| *off* | off the aircraft, off the stage |
| *on* | on the cuff, on the trip |
| *on account of* | on account of the rain, on account of his beliefs |
| *onto* | onto the beach, onto the ship |
| *opposite* | opposite the station |
| *out* | out the door |
| *over* | over the river, over the mountains, over his head |
| *owing to* | owing to her illness, owing to his energy |
| *past* | past all hope, past the school |
| *per* | per year, per ton |

| | |
|---|---|
| *round* | round the world, round town |
| *since* | since his arrival, since the olden times |
| *through* | through the window, through the years |
| *throughout* | throughout his life, throughout the world |
| *till* | till nightfall, till the end |
| *to* | to Kalamazoo, to the mountains, to Frank, to the point |
| *toward* | toward Lansing, toward bedtime, toward belief |
| *under* | under the hill, under cover, under the rainbow |
| *until* | until death, until seven tonight |
| *up* | up the slope, up the scale |
| *upon* | upon the windowsill, upon further questioning |
| *up to* | up to this position |
| *via* | via American Air Lines |
| *with* | with his friends, with care, with the negative |
| *within* | within reason, within the town, within a month |
| *without* | without a country, without argument |

SUBORDINATORS.   There is a relatively small group of function words that structural linguists call **subordinators** (or **includers**). They introduce adverbial clauses. Here is a list of the most common subordinators.

| | |
|---|---|
| *after* | you'll have to do the dishes after he has left |
| *although* | she is unpopular, although she is pretty |
| *as* | I'll ask him as he is leaving; I'll ask him, as it is important |
| *as . . . as* | he seems to be as blind as a bat is blind |
| *as if* | he looked as if he wanted to sing |
| *because* | he was unhappy because his trombone had been stolen |
| *before* | we'll see him before he leaves |
| *-er than* | he seems to be blinder than a bat is blind |
| *even though* | she is unpopular, even though she is pretty |
| *if* | I plan to stay home if he can't go |
| *more . . . than* | he is more stubborn than a mule is stubborn |
| *since* | that has been true since time began; let's not complain, since it won't do any good |
| *so (that)* | he is saving his money so (that) he can go to camp |
| *though* | she is unpopular, though she is pretty |
| *till, until* | we can wait till he leaves, we can wait until he leaves |
| *when* | don't stop him when he leaves |
| *where* | he lives where the hogs used to live |
| *whether (or not)* | we'll play golf whether or not it rains, I wonder whether he's coming |
| *while* | ask him while he is leaving |

Note that a few words can function either as prepositions or as subordinators, depending on whether they are followed by a nominal or a clause:

| *prepositions* | *subordinators* |
| --- | --- |
| after lunch | after lunch was over |
| as chairman | as he became chairman |
| before the meeting | before the meeting began |
| since his arrival | since he arrived |
| till the show | till the show ends |
| until his victory | until he won the victory |

COORDINATING CONJUNCTIONS. **Coordinating conjunctions** form a very small group of function words. They link together parts of sentences that have coordinate grammatical status, equal grammatical weight:

| | |
| --- | --- |
| *and* | John and Mary, soft and easy, quickly and smoothly, in the morning and in the night, Bill went to school and Mary stayed home |
| *but* | Bill went to school but Mary stayed home |
| *yet* | he said he would come, yet he hadn't been heard from by six o'clock |
| (*either*) . . . *or* | either you or I must go, he needs an operation or a long rest |
| *neither* . . . *nor* | he needs neither an operation nor a long rest |

## WORKING WITH GRAMMATICAL DEFINITIONS

1.  The following sentences are adapted from a short story, "The Day of the Rabbit," by Robert La Rue.[17] In the first blank to the left of the sentences, tell how each of the bold-faced words or groups of words is functioning: as *nominal*, as *verbal*, as *adjectival*, or as *adverbial*. In the second blank, tell more specifically how the word or group of words is functioning. The following is a list of these more specific functions:

[17] *Robert La Rue, "The Day of the Rabbit,"* Arizona Quarterly, *19 (Autumn 1963),* 211–228.

*Nominal*

Subject of a clause
Direct object of verb
Predicate nominative
Object of preposition
Indirect object of verb

*Verbal*

Entire predicate
Part of predicate

*Adjectival*

Prenoun modifier
Predicate adjectival
Postnoun modifier

*Adverbial*

Clause modifier
Modifier of verb
Modifier of adjectival
Modifier of adverbial

_____ _____ 1. [1]**When the pain subsided,** he wheezed a sigh of relief.
_____ _____ 2. He could see the open mouths [2]**that ringed him with laughter.**
_____ _____ 3. There was the soft sound of [3]**female** laughter from the outside of the circle, but the men were quiet,
_____ _____ 4. [4]**staring down at the boy.**
_____ _____ 5. [5]**The vision of the frightened boy** caused him to chuckle.
_____ _____ 6. Sometimes he [6]**would spit** into one of the furrows.
_____ _____ 7. The others sifted back into [7]**the spectral light.**
_____ _____ 8. [8]**Finding none,** he spoke louder.
_____ _____ 9. He suspected [9]**that the Indian sometimes ate rats.**
_____ _____ 10. The boy moved forward [10]**cautiously.**
_____ _____ 11. His corn flourished [11]**in his own powdery soil.**
_____ _____ 12. His hat fell off and the bandanna slid down to his chin, [12]**revealing his bruised cheekbones and forehead.**
_____ _____ 13. "Yes, he [13]**was beaten**
_____ _____ 14. because he was [14]**a foolish boy."**
_____ _____ 15. In mute agreement with the sergeant, he put his foot in the stirrup once more and boosted himself into the saddle [15]**with a grunt.**
_____ _____ 16. We heard the other horse galloping away, [16]**its rider piping like a child.**
_____ _____ 17. It was nearly [17]**dusk** when the men finished.
_____ _____ 18. But [18]**he had been** lucky in his choice, picking the boy,
_____ _____ 19. [19]**the slim one.**
_____ _____ 20. I [20]**can get** water in a short time.

**2.** Identify each of the bold-faced phrases in this passage from *Macbeth* in the same way you identified the bold-faced phrases in the preceding exercise:

\_\_\_\_ \_\_\_\_\_ *1.* She should have died [1]**hereafter;**
\_\_\_\_ \_\_\_\_\_ *2.* There would have been a time for [2]**such a word.**
\_\_\_\_ \_\_\_\_\_ *3.* [3]**To-morrow, and to-morrow, and to-morrow,**
\_\_\_\_ \_\_\_\_\_ *4.* Creeps in this petty pace [4]**from day to day**
\_\_\_\_ \_\_\_\_\_ *5.* [5]**To the last syllable of recorded time,**
\_\_\_\_ \_\_\_\_\_ *6.* And [6]**all our yesterdays** [7]**have lighted** [8]**fools**
\_\_\_\_ \_\_\_\_\_ *7.*
\_\_\_\_ \_\_\_\_\_ *8.*
\_\_\_\_ \_\_\_\_\_ *9.* [9]**The way to dusty death.** Out, out, brief candle!
\_\_\_\_ \_\_\_\_\_ *10.* Life's but [10]**a walking shadow,** a poor player
\_\_\_\_ \_\_\_\_\_ *11.* That struts and frets [11]**his hour** upon the stage
\_\_\_\_ \_\_\_\_\_ *12.* And then [12]**is heard** no more: it is a tale
\_\_\_\_ \_\_\_\_\_ *13.* [13]**Told by an idiot,** full of sound and fury,
\_\_\_\_ \_\_\_\_\_ *14.* [14]**Signifying nothing.**

**3.** Classify the suffixes in the bold-faced words below as to whether they are derivational or inflectional. In each case, explain the basis for your decision.

     a.  she's a good **teacher**
     b.  the grass is **greener** on the other side
     c.  that's a very **interesting** book
     d.  the salesman was **interesting** them in buying a car
     e.  the snake **fascinated** her
     f.  the **fascinated** woman stared in disbelief
     g.  she was **fascinated** by the snake

**4.** Analyze the following nonsense sentences, identifying nouns, verbs, adjectives, and adverbs and stating how you did so. Note that although the bases have no lexical meaning in English, the signals of form and grammatical context are present to give information.

     a.  Karombees zumched fedimently on one lacomping rattener
     b.  coripingly, Fatozin nampled that grinkling hoochment
     c.  the neckser straw an esslinget down and rickled up some hellerweg
     d.  after all wothens are grupped, his sentagation will kettang my chorhood
     e.  without any stumpletion, several crumpy facultoms have to kipple their mooshy hildersnatches

**5.** Do the two sentences below mean the same? How can you explain the difference, if there is any?

> the artist sketched deer in the forest
> in the forest, the artist sketched deer

**6.** For each of the three sentences below, tell how the bold-faced part is functioning in the sentence:

> the girl knows **where he used to live**
> the house **where he used to live** is being torn down
> he isn't **where he used to live**

**7.** For each of the five sentences below, discuss how the word or phrase following the verb is functioning in the sentence. Explain the structural similarities and differences between the sentences.

> a.  the clown was lonely
> b.  the clown was an expert performer
> c.  the clown was in the arena
> d.  the clown was in disgrace
> e.  the clown was at home

**8.** Some of the following words are adjectives and others are adverbs, even though all end with the derivational suffix that most often signals "adverb." Separate the adjectives from the adverbs and explain how you reached your decisions. How is *bodily* different from all the other words in the list?

> | | |
> |---|---|
> | friendly | sweetly |
> | quietly | bodily |
> | comely | decidedly |
> | lovely | homely |
> | naturally | frantically |

**9 a.** Do the bold-faced adverbials below fit comfortably into one of our categories: manner, time, place, etc.? Discuss.

> I baked a cake **for Jim**
> she tore the cloth **into three strips**
> I got this recipe **from a cookbook**
> the play lasted **for only an hour**

b. Do the bold-faced adverbials below seem to be manner adverbials? In what ways are these adverbials all similar? What differences are there between them?

> he walked **with a limp**
> he cut himself **with a knife**
> He went **with his uncle**
> he greeted us **with a smile**

 ## FOR FURTHER EXPLORATION

Paul Roberts, *Patterns of English.* New York: Harcourt Brace Jovanovich, Inc., 1956. The first classroom text based on structuralist theory. It has had wide impact on American education, and many of its pedagogical techniques are still viable. Especially effective on the relationships between intonation and punctuation.

Harold Whitehall, *Structural Essentials of English.* New York: Harcourt Brace Jovanovich, Inc., 1956. A very brief, compact treatment of structural linguistics, differing in some ways from Roberts'.

James Sledd, *A Short Introduction to English Grammar.* Glenview, Ill.: Scott, Foresman and Company, Inc., 1959. Sledd's view of structural grammar is tempered by his own special insights, resulting in a balanced compromise between traditional and structural theories. Comparing Sledd's with Roberts' and Whitehall's views adds depth to one's understanding of structural theory.

Leonard Bloomfield, *Language.* New York: Holt, Rinehart and Winston, 1933. The starting point of modern linguistic thinking in the United States. This book presents a comprehensive view of the field in the 1930s and is still respected by both structuralists and transformationalists, although each school would revise, elaborate, or eliminate some of Bloomfield's statements.

# PUTTING GRAMMAR TO WORK
# IN ANALYZING POETRY

A poet often exercises "poetic license" by inventing new words and structures, but we can understand his grammar if we can determine how he has violated the normal grammatical rules of English. For example, examine "anyone lived in a pretty how town," in which E. E. Cummings stretches the grammar of English. Here is the poem:

```
            anyone lived in a pretty how town
            (with up so floating many bells down)
            spring summer autumn winter
            he sang his didn't he danced his did.

5           Women and men (both little and small)
            cared for anyone not at all
            they sowed their isn't they reaped their same
            sun moon stars rain

            children guessed (but only a few
10          and down they forgot as up they grew
            autumn winter spring summer)
            that noone loved him more by more

            when by now and tree by leaf
            she laughed his joy she cried his grief
15          bird by snow and stir by still
            anyone's any was all to her

            someones married their everyones
            laughed their cryings and did their dance
            (sleep wake hope and then) they
20          said their nevers they slept their dream

            stars rain sun moon
            (and only the snow can begin to explain
            how children are apt to forget to remember
            with up so floating many bells down)

25          one day anyone died i guess
            (and noone stooped to kiss his face)
            busy folk buried them side by side
            little by little and was by was
```

all by all and deep by deep
30        and more by more they dream their sleep
noone and anyone earth by april
wish by spirit and if by yes.

Women and men (both dong and ding)
summer autumn winter spring
35        reaped their sowing and went their came
sun moon stars rain [18]

We can understand the syntax of the poem by reading the various grammatical signals that Cummings has given us. To begin with, the indefinite pronouns in this poem do not behave normally. *Any* does not usually function as the subject of a sentence, yet Cummings says "anyone's any was all to her"; here, *any* apparently functions as a nonanimate noun. *Anyone* is referred to by *he,* and *noone* is referred to by *she,* indicating that these indefinite pronouns are functioning as animate nouns; the lack of an article before these nouns suggests that they are proper nouns. *Anyone* and *noone* are contrasted with the rest of the people, the *someones* and the *everyones;* the indefinite pronouns *someone* and *everyone* have been made into plural nouns by the addition of *-s.*

*Didn't, did, isn't,* and *came* are marked as nouns by the determiners *his* or *their,* which immediately precede them: *his didn't, his did, their isn't, their came.* In the poem, the noun function of these verb forms is further signaled by the sentence structure:

he sang his didn't            they sowed their isn't
he danced his did             they went their came

All these suggest the familiar subject-verb-object word order most typical of English sentences. Compare, for instance:

he sang his didn't, he sang his song, he rang his gong
they sowed their isn't, they sowed their seed, they mowed
    their mead
he danced his did, he danced his dance, he hoofed his jig

*They went their came* is more interesting because *went* is normally an intransitive verb, working without an object. It is customarily followed by an adverbial or by nothing, as in

they went upstairs, they went gladly, they went

[18] E.E. Cummings, 50 Poems (New York: Grosset and Dunlap, 1940), poem 29.

Thus Cummings asks us to assume that *went* has moved over into the transitive verb class and is working like the three transitives *sang, danced,* and *sowed.* The fact that *they went their came* is the fourth in the series and that it immediately follows *they reaped their sowing*—a normal transitive in subject-verb-object order—predisposes us to accept it as a transitive verb.

The same signals—determiner, and object position in the sentence—inform us that *cryings* and *nevers* are nouns in

> laughed their cryings
> said their nevers

In addition they carry the inflectional noun suffix *-s,* meaning plural. Clearly, Cummings wishes them to be read as nouns.

Cummings gives unmistakeable signals, too, that *how* in line one is an adjective. Its position between *pretty* and *town* is a typical position for adjectives, even though here *pretty* is semantically ambiguous. It can mean *rather* and be working as an adverb of the intensifier type, or it can be an adjective meaning *beautiful,* in which case it is one of two adjectives modifying *town.* Comparably, we might say "It's a pretty dull town" or "It's a pretty, dull town." But in either case *how* is functioning as an adjective.

Another interesting line in the poem is the second:

> (with up so floating many bells down)

Changing the word order clarifies the line:

> with so many bells floating up (and) down

The fact that *up* and *down* are adverbs is signaled by the order of the words. If they were prepositions (as in *up the river* and *down the hill*), they would be followed by nouns. The adverbial information is reinforced in line ten:

> and down they forgot as up they grew

In both lines the adverbial function will draw strongest stress to *up* and *down,* a normal situation for adverbials.

Looking now at Cummings' fourteen uses of the preposition *by,* we can start with the ordinary *side by side* and *little by little,* so common as to be practically clichés. We note that *by* appears between identical words in these two phrases—as it does also in some of Cummings' parallel inventions: *more by more* (twice), *was by was, all by all,* and *deep by deep.* Three *by* phrases concern nature: *tree by leaf, bird by snow, earth by april.* Two others concern abstractions: *wish by spirit* and *if by yes.* Cummings is paralleling his pairs somehow. Generally, these *by* phrases depict the increasing intensity of anyone's and noone's lives.

You might wish to apply the above techniques to two other Cummings poems, "what if a much of a which of a wind" and "wherelings whenlings."

what if a much of a which of a wind
gives the truth to summer's lie;
bloodies with dizzying leaves the sun
and yanks immortal stars awry?
5      Blow king to beggar and queen to seem
(blow friend to fiend:blow space to time)
—when skies are hanged and oceans drowned,
the single secret will still be man

what if a keen of a lean wind flays
10     screaming hills with sleet and snow:
strangles valleys by ropes of thing
and stifles forests in white ago?
Blow hope to terror;blow seeing to blind
(blow pity to envy and soul to mind)
15     —whose hearts are mountains,roots are trees,
it's they shall cry hello to the spring

what if a dawn of a doom of a dream
bites this universe in two,
peels forever out of his grave
20     and sprinkles nowhere with me and you?
Blow soon to never and never to twice
(blow life to isn't:blow death to was)
—all nothing's only our hugest home;
the most who die,the more we live [19]

—E. E. Cummings

wherelings whenlings
(daughters of ifbut offspring of hopefear
sons of unless and children of almost)
never shall guess the dimension of

5      him whose
each
foot likes the
here of this earth

[19] *E.E. Cummings, 1 x 1 (New York: Harcourt Brace Jovanovich, Inc., 1944), poem xx.*

whose both
10          eyes
            love
            this now of the sky

            —endings of isn't
            shall never
15          begin
            to begin to

            imagine how (only are shall be were
            dawn dark rain snow rain
            — bow +
20          a [20]

                              —E. E. Cummings

[20] *E.E. Cummings, 50 Poems, poem 26.*

2

THE SOUND
SYSTEM

One especially important contribution of structural linguistics is the Trager-Smith system for transcribing sounds. The complexities of English spelling had long focused attention on the need for a set of writing symbols with a closer correlation to English sounds than the standard alphabet offered. Interest in phonetic transcription extended from Orm in the early thirteenth century through William Bullokar in the sixteenth century, John Wilkins in the seventeenth century, Benjamin Franklin in the eighteenth century, to Henry Sweet in the late nineteenth century. In 1886 Sweet's Broad Romic Alphabet was the basis of the International Phonetic Alphabet (IPA) adopted by the International Phonetic Association, a group of European phoneticians. The IPA is still widely used today.

In the 1950s, two American structural linguists, George L. Trager and Henry Lee Smith, Jr., formulated a shorter alphabet which, they believed, was more suitable for transcribing American English. Either alphabet is suitable for our purposes in transcribing vowels and consonants. However, the Trager-Smith system is the only one that offers symbols for transcribing intonation patterns, the rhythm and music of our language. We will distinguish the two alphabets by enclosing IPA symbols between square brackets and the Trager-Smith symbols between slashes.

In **phonetic** alphabets like the IPA each distinctive sound feature is represented by a separate symbol. In other words, phonetic alphabets seek a consistent one-to-one correlation between sound and symbol. The Trager-Smith alphabet is actually **phonemic** rather than phonetic. Each symbol in a phonemic alphabet represents not a single distinctive feature of sound but a bundle of features representing place and manner of articulation. The consonant and vowel sounds are called **segmental phonemes;** the intonation patterns (patterns of pitch,

stress, and pause) are called **suprasegmental phonemes.** We
will discuss each of these in turn.


## CONSONANT AND VOWEL SOUNDS


Figure 2-1 shows the human speech organs. The chart presents the consonant sounds of American English, along with
the technical names of these sounds. The accompanying lists
illustrate the sounds.

In articulatory phonetics, English consonant sounds may be
defined by four variables: 1) modification by the vocal cords,
2) articulator, 3) point of articulation, and 4) type of breath
release.

First there is **modification by the vocal cords.** Air, which
issues from the lungs as breath, passes through the **glottis,**
which is the space between the **vocal cords** (or **bands** or **lips**)
in the **larynx,** or voice box, which is immediately behind the
Adam's apple. When we swallow, the glottis is covered by the
**epiglottis,** a thin plate of elastic cartilege.

The vocal cords may be relaxed and open; then the breath
passes through without causing vibration, and the resulting
sound is **voiceless** (or **unvoiced**). Conversely, the vocal cords
may be drawn together and under tension; then the breath
passing through causes them to vibrate, and the resulting
sound is **voiced.** To feel the voicing, place your thumb and
forefinger on your Adam's apple and pronounce the pair *pit*
and *bit* several times; notice the difference felt by your fingers.
The contrast is the voicing of the /b/ as compared with the
unvoiced /p/. Or plug your ears tightly with your fingers and
pronounce the same pair, listening for the vibration caused by
*bit* and comparing it to the lack of vibration in *pit.* All English
sounds are either voiced or voiceless.

The **articulators** are the lips, teeth, and tongue. The upper
lip articulates /p, b, m, w/. The upper teeth form the articulator
for /f/ and /v/. The **apex** (tip) of the tongue is involved in the
articulation of /θ, ð, t, d, s, z, č, ǰ, n, r, l/. The front of the tongue
helps form /š, ž, y/, and the back of the tongue is used in
articulating /k, g, ŋ/.

The **point of articulation** is the lower lip for /p, b, m, w, f, v/,
the teeth for /θ, ð/, the **alveolar ridge** for /t, d, s, z, č, ǰ, n, r, l/,
the **palate** for /š, ž, y/ and the **velum** for /k, g, ŋ/.

The **breath release** may be **unimpeded** or **impeded.** In the
production of a **stop,** the articulator is brought against the point
of articulation, momentarily cutting off the air flow completely;
this articulation characterizes the consonants /p, b, t, d, k, g/.

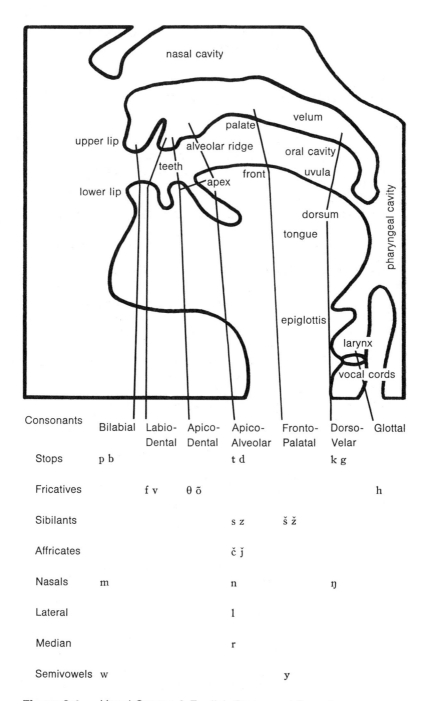

**Figure 2-1**   Vocal Organs & English Consonent Sounds

## Table 2-A

| Consonants | International Phonetic Alphabet (IPA) | | Trager-Smith Phonemic Alphabet |
|---|---|---|---|
| voiceless bilabial stop | [p] | pot | /p/ |
| voiced bilabial stop | [b] | bought | /b/ |
| voiceless apico-alveolar stop | [t] | tot | /t/ |
| voiced apico-alveolar stop | [d] | dot | /d/ |
| voiceless dorso-velar stop | [k] | cot | /k/ |
| voiced dorso-velar stop | [g] | got | /g/ |
| voiceless labio-dental fricative | [f] | fan | /f/ |
| voiced labio-dental fricative | [v] | van | /v/ |
| voiceless apico-dental fricative | [θ] | thistle | /θ/ "theta" |
| voiced apico-dental fricative | [ð] | this'll | /ð/ "crossed d" |
| voiceless apico-alveolar sibilant | [s] | sip | /s/ |
| voiced apico-alveolar sibilant | [z] | zip | /z/ |
| voiceless fronto-palatal sibilant | [ʃ] | ship, dilution | /š/ |
| voiced fronto-palatal sibilant | [ʒ] | azure, delusion | /ž/ |
| voiceless apico-alveolar affricate | [tʃ] | chip | /č/ |
| voiced apico-alveolar affricate | [dʒ] | gyp, jam | /ǰ/ |
| voiced bilabial nasal | [m] | might | /m/ |
| **voiced apico-alveolar nasal** | [n] | night, sin | /n/ |
| voiced dorso-velar nasal | [ŋ] | sing | /ŋ/ "eng" |
| voiced apico-alveolar lateral | [l] | led | /l/ |
| voiced apico-alveolar median | [r] | red | /r/ |
| voiced fronto-palatal semivowel | [j] | yet, you | /y/ |
| voiced bilabial semivowel | [w] | wet, woo | /w/ |
| voiceless glottal semivowel | [h] | hot, who | /h/ |

In the production of a **fricative,** the articulator is brought close to the point of articulation, causing the breath to issue with a friction noise; this articulation characterizes /f, v, θ, ð, s, z, š, ž/. The **affricates,** /č/ and /ǰ/, start out like stops, the breath flow being completely cut off for just an instant; then the tongue moves backwards slightly and the sounds end as fricatives.

Stops, fricatives, and affricates are made with the velum raised to block off the nasal cavity so that the breath issues through the mouth; all these sounds are **oral.** However, three English consonants are made with the velum lowered and the breath exiting through the nasal cavity: /m/ with the mouth cavity blocked by the two lips, /n/ with the mouth cavity blocked by the apex of the tongue, and /ŋ/ with the mouth cavity blocked by the dorsum of the tongue. These three consonants are **nasals.**

There are only two consonant sounds made without the flow of breath being impeded: the **lateral** /l/ and the **median** /r/. In the production of /l/, the breath stream is released along the sides of the oral cavity as the apex of the tongue touches some part of the alveolar ridge and one or both sides of the tongue lower to provide an opening for the breath stream. The median /r/ is produced with the breath escaping through an opening down the middle of the mouth cavity as the sides of the tongue press against the sides of the palate.

**Semivowels** are half vowels and half consonants, according to the Trager-Smith phonemic analysis. When they precede a vowel, they function like consonants; when they follow a vowel, they function like vowels to produce the so-called "long vowels" or "complex vowel nuclei" of English. The semivowel /y/ means a glide to a higher and fronter tongue position; the semivowel /w/ represents a glide to a higher and backer tongue position; and the semivowel /h/ represents a glide to a more central tongue position.

In order to understand the semivowels, we need to consider the **vowels** of English. Table 2-B presents the simple vowels and complex vowel nuclei. According to the Trager-Smith system, the simple vowels can be represented in a "vowel quadrangle" (Figure 2-2) symbolizing the mouth cavity, the resonating chamber in which all vowels are produced. Its divisions are defined on the vertical dimension as *high, mid, low,* and on the horizontal dimension as *front, central, back.*

|  | Front | Central | Back |
|---|---|---|---|
| High | /i/ (b**i**t) | /ɨ/ (j**u**st-Adverb) "barred i" | /u/ (b**oo**k) |
| Mid | /e/ (b**e**t) | /ə/ (b**u**t) "schwa" | /o/ (no example of short [o] in American English) |
| Low | /æ/ (b**a**t) "asch" | /a/ (f**a**ther) | /ɔ/ (**aw**e) "open o" |

**Figure 2-2**    Vowel Quadrangle

## Table 2-B

| Vowels | IPA | | Trager-Smith |
|---|---|---|---|
| high front vowel | [ɪ] | b*i*t, *i*t, s*i*t | /i/ |
| mid front vowel | [ɛ] | bet, set, net | /e/ |
| low front vowel | [æ] | bat, sat, gnat | /æ/ "asch" |
| high central vowel | [ɨ] | j*u*st (adverb), ag*e*s | /ɨ/ "barred i" |
| mid central vowel | | | |
| unstressed | [ə] | above, even, rob*i*n, lemon, circ*u*s | /ə/ "schwa" |
| stressed | [ʌ] | b*u*t, j*u*t, n*u*t | /ə/ |
| low central vowel | [ɑ] | father | /a/ |
| high back vowel | [ʊ] | book, p*u*t | /u/ |
| mid back vowel | [o] | no example; in American English, /o/ occurs only as part of a diphthong | /o/ |
| low back vowel | [ɔ] | *awe* | /ɔ/ "open o" |
| *intermediate "a" | [a] | ask, path, a*u*nt | no equivalent |

| Dipthongs | IPA | | Trager-Smith |
|---|---|---|---|
| | [i] | b*ea*t, m*ea*t, m*ee*t | /iy/ |
| | [ɛɪ] | b*ai*t, mate, we*i*ght | /ey/ |
| | [aɪ]* | b*i*te, m*i*te, m*i*ght | /ay/ |
| | [ɔɪ] | boy, bo*i*l, toy | /ɔy/ |
| | [u] | boot, mood, lewd | /uw/ |
| | [oʊ] | boat, *oa*k, m*oa*t, mote | /ow/ |
| | [aʊ]* | b*ou*t, how, now | /aw/ |
| | [ɛh] | yeah | /eh/ |

| Diphthongs before /r/ | IPA | | Trager-Smith |
|---|---|---|---|
| | [ɪɚ] | fear, dear, near | /ihr/ |
| | [ɛɚ] | care, bear, hair | /ehr/ |
| | [oɚ] | for, tore, bore | /ohr/ |
| | [ʊɚ] | lure, tour | /uhr/ |
| | [aɚ]* | far, tar, par | /ahr/ |

* This [a] is called an "intermediate a." It is made lower and slightly farther back than the [æ] sound. Some people use this sound in words like "ask," "path," and "aunt."

Henry Lee Smith, Jr. offers the words *ye, woo,* and *hah* as "excellent examples of our semivowels *y, w,* and *h* used in both initial and final positions, that is, both preceding and following a simple vowel." [1] He points out that when saying *ye* we start at a very high position and drop to /i/ and then return by gliding to the higher and fronter original position. In *woo,* we hear and feel a very high back sound followed by a vowel close to the simple vowel of *book,* followed by a gliding return to the very high sound. The Trager-Smith analysis of the /h/ semivowel is somewhat controversial; we quote Smith's explanation:

Now for a quick rundown on the complex nuclei with *h.* The *h,* we remember, represents a glide to the center from one of our simple vowel positions. In *hah,* we note that the initial sound has some friction noise along with it, and it starts off without the vocal cords vibrating (or, to use the technical term, "voiceless"). The sound represented by the final *h,* however, is accompanied by no friction noise and is "voiced" all the way through. We have all learned to associate the friction noise, which characterizes *initial h's* in English, with the letter symbol *h,* and so it comes as a slight shock to see the symbol used to represent the semivowel glide to the center after a simple vowel. In other words, *hah, ah, pa,* and *ma* all rhyme; all end in *h* though the final *h* is seldom represented in our writing system. It takes only a little careful listening, however, to realize that the initial *h's* in *he* and in *hot,* though noticeably different in tongue position, are actually starting *nearer the center* of the mouth than the simple vowels that follow them. Even more easily can we notice the gliding to the center from the simple vowel position when *h* follows, as in *idea, poor* and *law.* [2]

[1] *Henry Lee Smith, Jr.,* Linguistic Science and the Teaching of English *(Cambridge, Mass.: Harvard University Press, 1956), pp. 28–29.*
[2] *Smith,* Linguistic Science, *pp. 32–33.*

## INTONATION PATTERNS

Trager and Smith also formulated a system for recording the **intonation** of American English speech. They specified twelve **suprasegmental phonemes:** four stresses, four pitches, and four junctures, or pauses. These ride on top of the vowels and consonants—the **segmental phonemes.**

According to this system, every speaker of American English uses four contrasting degrees of **stress** or emphasis: primary, secondary, tertiary, and weak, indicated respectively by the symbols /ˊ ˄ ˎ ˬ/. Every isolated English word carries primary stress, and every phrase has only one primary stress. The location of this stress often determines the meaning of the phrase. For example, it shows orally that *Énglĭsh teàchĕr* means "teacher of English," whereas *Énglĭsh teáchĕr* means "teacher from England." The first is a compound noun like *blackbird* while the second is an adjective plus a noun like *black bird.* In writing and out of context, *English teacher* is ambiguous; in speech the stress contrasts prevent ambiguity.

In sentences, stress works along with four contrasting **pitches**—/1, 2, 3, 4/, numbered from lowest to highest—to organize the words into larger structures. Thus normally, say the structuralists, we start our declarative sentences on pitch /2/, rise to pitch /3/ concurrently with primary sentence stress, and drop to pitch /1/ at the end of the sentence. Unless the sentence is a question beginning with a word like *who, what, when, where, why,* or *how,* the American English listener automatically reacts to this pattern as meaning "statement," if it is combined with a particular kind of final pause: double-cross juncture.

Pauses, or **junctures,** to use the structuralists' technical term, are also of four kinds. **Double-cross juncture,** symbolized by /#/, is a complex of pause, slight drop in pitch, and gradual fading of sound to silence. **Double-bar juncture,** symbolized by /‖/, is a complex of pause, slight rise in pitch, and abrupt cut-off of sound. This type of juncture combines with pitch /3/ at the end of a sentence to signal a question asking for a "yes" or "no" answer. For example, the yes/no question *is he here?* would be transcribed thus:

/²ĭz hìy ³híyr³ ‖/

By means of this intonation pattern any English sentence can be made into a question. In addition, English has another type of question, the WH question, which begins with a "WH word," such as *who, what, when, where, why, how,* and calls for more than a yes/no answer; it asks for additional information and uses the intonation pattern /231#/, the same pattern as English statements:

| | |
|---|---|
| why has he left? | /²wây hǽz hìy ³léft¹ #/ |
| how does she feel? | /²hâw dɔ̌z šìy ³fíyl¹ #/ |

**Single-bar** juncture, symbolized by / | /, does not occur at the ends of sentences but instead divides long sentences into breath groups. It is a complex of pause with level pitch and no complete cessation of sound across the pause. For example, a single-bar juncture before *up* in *he looked up the street* signals that *up the street* is an adverbial telling in what direction he looked, whereas a single-bar juncture after *up* signals that he was locating the street on a map. Double-cross, double-bar, and single-bar junctures are all called **terminal junctures.** Their function is to organize words into breath groups, each breath group containing one, and only one, primary stress. The fourth juncture serves a different function. It is **plus juncture,** symbolized by /+/, and it separates phonetic words. It makes possible the following contrasts:

| | | |
|---|---|---|
| /ays + kriym | : | ay + skriym / |
| /grey + treyn | : | greyt + reyn / |
| /naytreyt | : | nayt + reyt/ |

With these suprasegmental phonemes structuralists can give a "full phonemic transcription" of sentences. Here are a few from Trager and Smith's *An Outline of English Structure.*[3]

(By convention, weak stresses are unmarked.)

how do they study?
/²hǽw + də + ðèy + ³stɔ́diy¹ #/
how do they study now we've got their books?
/²hǽw + də + ðèy + ³stɔ́diy²|
²nǽw + wìyv + gât + ðèhr + ³búks¹ #/
are you reading Macaulay?
/²àhr + yə + rîydiŋ + mə ³kóhliy³ ||/
are you reading, Macaulay?
/²àhr + yə + ³riydiŋ³| ³məkóhliy ³||/

[3] *George L. Trager and Henry Lee Smith, Jr.,* An Outline of English Structure *(Norman, Okla.: Battenburg Press, 1951), pp. 50–51.*

## WORKING WITH THE SOUND SYSTEM

**1.** Read the following limericks and jingles aloud; then write them in standard orthography.[4] The suprasegmental features have not been marked; conventional punctuation is therefore used as an aid to the reader.

ə fliy ən ə flay in ə fluw
wər imprizind, sow wət kud ðey duw?
   sed ðə flay, "let əs fliy,"
   sed ðə fliy, "let əs flay,"
sow ðey fluw θruw ə flɔh in ðə fluw.

ðər wəz a yəŋ felə neymd hɔl
huw fel in ðə spriŋ in ðə fɔl.
   twud əv bin ə sæd θiŋ
   if iyd dayd in ðə spriŋ,
bət iy didint, hiy dayd in ðə fɔl.

hirz tə ðə čigər ðits nat eniy bigər
ðin ðə hed əv ə veriy smɔl pin,
   bət ðə ləmp ðit iy reyziz
   ičiz layk bleyziz,
ən ðæts wer ðə rəb kəmz in.

betiy hæd ə bit əv bitər bətər
wič meyd ər bætər bitər.
šiy gat ə bit əv betər bətər
ən meyd ər bitər bætər betər.

ðə reyn it reyniθ an ðə ǰəst
ən ɔlsow an ðə ənǰəst felə.
bət čiyfliy an ðə ǰəst, bikəz
ðə ənǰəst stiylz ðə ǰəsts əmbrelə.

flow wəz fand əv ebiniyzər,
eb fər šohrt šiy kɔld ər bow.
tɔk əv taydz əv ləv, greyt siyzər!
yuw šud siy əm, eb ən flow.

[4] Adapted from Henry Allan Gleason, Jr., Workbook in Descriptive Linguistics (New York: Holt, Rinehart and Winston, Inc., 1955), p. 14.

**2.** Write the following words in Trager-Smith symbols. Be careful not to confuse letters with *sounds.*

| | | |
|---|---|---|
| bank | gnat | rare |
| beauty | guile | scar |
| call | Gwendolyn | scene |
| chain | have | screen |
| character | human | shrink |
| chrome | jewel | sphere |
| city | khaki | squeal |
| clean | knife | step |
| cube | kraft | stews |
| czar | let | sugar |
| dangle | lute | then |
| dream | mute | thin |
| dune | nature | think |
| euphemism | new | three |
| fine | once | tune |
| frock | paddle | two |
| gag | philosophy | use (noun) |
| gem | pneumonia | who |
| ghost | psychology | which |
| glean | quest | witch |

**3.** Transcribe the following pairs of words. What differences between consonant and/or vowel pronunciations do you find between the two words in the pairs of each set?

| | | | |
|---|---|---|---|
| a. | medicate | : | medicine |
| | critical | : | criticize |
| b. | resident | : | residential |
| | expedite | : | expedition |
| c. | prodigal | : | prodigious |
| | sagacity | : | sage |
| d. | sign | : | signal |
| | grade | : | gradual |
| | mode | : | model |

**4.** Transcribe the following poem into Trager-Smith notation. Be prepared to discuss how the sounds of the poem seem to *reinforce the content.* For example, the fact that /d/ is a voiced stop is relevant to the kind of poetic effect Sandburg creates in the first part of the poem.

## The Harbor

Passing through huddled and ugly walls,
by doorways where women
Looked from their hunger-deep eyes,
Haunted with shadows of hunger-hands,
Out from the huddled and ugly walls,
I came sudden, at the city's edge,
On a blue burst of lake,
Long lake waves breaking under the sun
On a spray-flung curve of shore;
And a fluttering storm of gulls,
Masses of great gray wings
And flying white bellies
Veering and wheeling free in the open.[5]

—Carl Sandburg

**5.** The following set of sound symbols is from a sixth grade text. What advantages and/or disadvantages might it have for these students as compared with a set of dictionary pronunciation symbols or the IPA or the Trager-Smith symbols?

| | | | | |
|---|---|---|---|---|
| \a\ | bad | \g\ | get, bigger, guest |
| \ä\ | hot, father, heart | \h\ | hot, who |
| \ā\ | mane, main, may, steak | \j\ | joke, gem, ledge, soldier |
| \e\ | bed, head, said, any, again | \k\ | kick, cat |
| | | \l\ | lull |
| \ē\ | me, feet, feat, field | \m\ | maim, hammer |
| \i\ | bid, busy, build, been | \n\ | neat, sunny |
| \ī\ | bite, tie, my, buy | \ng\ | ring, think, angry |
| \ō\ | hope, coat, flow, doe | \p\ | pup, puppy |
| \o\ | moth, tall, bawl, laud | \r\ | river, hurry, rhyme |
| \ə\ | bud, son, rough, blood | \s\ | seal, hoss, kiss, cent, scene, quartz |
| \ü\ | rule, rue, boot, you, few, lose, fruit | \sh\ | shine, sugar, issue, session, nation, machine |
| \u̇\ | full, wool, wolf | | |
| \au̇\ | now, loud | \t\ | top, little, dropped |
| \oi\ | boy, coin | \th\ | then, though |
| \b\ | bib, robber | \th\ | thin, thaw |
| \ch\ | chain, latch | \v\ | van, of, flivver |
| \d\ | did, ladder, grinned | \z\ | zeal, buzz, prison, dessert [6] |
| \f\ | fan, waffle, phone, laugh | | |

[5] Carl Sandburg, The Complete Poems of Carl Sandburg, rev. ed. (New York: Harcourt Brace Jovanovich, Inc., 1969), p. 5.
[6] David A. Conlin and Neil C. Thompson, Our Language Today, Book 6 (New York: American Book Company, 1967), p. 23.

**6.**   Leo Rosten in *The Joys of Yiddish* comments on how much
we "are aided, in telling a joke, by tonal variations and strategic
gestures; by artful pauses and inflections; by the deliberate
camouflage of chuckles, dismay, smiles, murmurs." His example is the following story:

       During a gigantic celebration in Red Square,
after Trotsky had been sent into exile, Stalin, on
Lenin's great tomb, suddenly and excitedly raised
his hand to still the acclamations: "Comrades,
comrades! A most historic event! A cablegram—
of congratulations—from Trotsky!"

       The hordes cheered and chortled and cheered
again, and Stalin read the historic cable aloud:

       JOSEPH  STALIN
       KREMLIN
       MOSCOW
       YOU WERE RIGHT AND I WAS WRONG.
       YOU ARE THE TRUE HEIR OF LENIN.
       I SHOULD APOLOGIZE.
                        TROTSKY

       You can imagine what a roar, what an
explosion of astonishment and triumph erupted in
Red Square now!

       But in the front row, below the podium, a little
tailor called, "Pst! Pst! Comrade Stalin."

       Stalin leaned down.

       The tailor said, "Such a message, Comrade
Stalin. For the ages! But you read it without the
right *feeling*!"

       Whereupon Stalin raised his hand and stilled
the throng once more. "Comrades! Here is a simple
worker, a loyal Communist, who says I haven't read
the message from Trotsky with enough feeling!
Come, Comrade Worker! Up here! *You* read this
historic communication!"

       So the little tailor went up to the reviewing stand
and took the cablegram from Stalin and read:

       JOSEPH  STALIN
       KREMLIN
       MOSCOW

       Then he cleared his throat, and sang out:
       YOU WERE RIGHT AND I WAS *WRONG?*
       *YOU* ARE THE TRUE HEIR OF LENIN?
       *I* SHOULD APOLOGIZE??!! . .
                        TROTSKY![7]

Lines: 5, 10, 15, 20, 25, 30, 35, 40

---

[7] *Leo Rosten,* The Joys of Yiddish *(New York: Pocket Books, 1970), pp. xxiv–xxv.*

If the first version of the message is transcribed as follows, in Trager-Smith notation, how would the second version be transcribed?

/ ³yúw + wer + râyt ² | ²ænd + ay + wəz + rɔ̂ŋ¹ #
²yùw + ar + ðə + trùw + êhr + ev + ³lénìn¹ #
²ày + šud + ə³páləjâyz¹ # /

 FOR FURTHER EXPLORATION

Cynthia D. Buchanan, *A Programed Introduction to Linguistics: Phonetics and Phonemics.* Boston: D. C. Heath and Company, 1963. A self-teaching presentation of the Trager-Smith system; useful also for learning about articulatory phonetics. Detailed and clear.

Neal D. Houston and John J. Quinn, *Phonetikon: A Visual Aid to Phonetic Study.* Glenview, Ill.: Scott Foresman and Company, Inc., 1970. A wheel of IPA symbols, providing a key word, transcription, and phonetic definition. The information provided by this wheel is more detailed than that given in our book.

Kreidler, Charles W., "Teaching English Spelling and Pronunciation," *TESOL Quarterly,* 6 (March 1972), 3–12. A useful overview of correspondences between English spelling and pronunciation, showing that, though complicated, English spelling is more patterned and consistent than commonly supposed.

Venezky, Richard L., "English Orthography: Its Graphical Structure and Its Relations to Sound," *Reading Research Quarterly,* 2 (Spring 1967), 75–105. More difficult and more complete than Kreidler's article, this discussion of English spelling presents and organizes sets of orthographic patterns based on an analysis of the spellings and pronunciations of the 20,000 most common English words.

Carol Chomsky, "Reading, Writing, and Phonology," *Harvard Educational Review,* 40 (May 1970), 287–309. Presents interesting insights from transformational generative phonology about relationships between spelling and the underlying sound structure of English. The implications of this view for the teaching of reading and spelling are seminal. The entire issue, subtitled *Illiteracy in America,* is relevant to this chapter.

In 1968 Noam Chomsky, the father of transformational linguistics, classified the maturing discipline of linguistics as a branch of cognitive psychology and predicted that "the major contribution of the study of language will lie in the understanding it can provide as to the character of mental processes and the structures they form and manipulate." *

In contrast to the structural approach, the transformational approach to language study insists that in making generalizations about language structure we must not limit ourselves to describing externally observable data but must, of necessity, rely upon our intuition as to what is grammatical and what is not.

Transformational grammar has been influential in recent years, and it will probably continue to be influential for some time to come. It has laid some of the foundations upon which other grammatical theories have been constructed; it has stimulated a revival of rationalism in philosophy and of antibehavioralism in psychology; it has been influential in the development of psycholinguistics, a hybrid discipline which

# PART

## transformational theory: the basic model

*is providing valuable insights into the process of language acquisition and into the nature of the reading process; and it has stimulated the writing of new transformationally oriented textbooks for use in the schools...*

*This second part of the book discusses the basics of transformational grammar. Chapter 3 discusses first the linguistic reasons for the rise of transformational grammar and then its method of generating basic sentences. Chapter 4 describes some ways of transforming basic sentences. Part III will be concerned with ways of expanding basic sentences and with current trends in transformational theory.*

\* *Noam Chomsky, Language and Mind (New York: Harcourt Brace Jovanovich, Inc., 1968), pp. 1 and 76; the quote is from p. 59.*

# 3

# THE BASICS OF TRANSFORMATIONAL GRAMMAR

This chapter begins with a discussion of the why of transformational grammar. The second section discusses the major part of a transformational grammar, the syntactic component, which is concerned with the structure of sentences. Following that section is a discussion of the transformational lexicon, a dictionary of sorts. The chapter ends with another discussion of the why of transformational grammar, this time on a more theoretical level.

## THE WHY OF TRANSFORMATIONAL GRAMMAR: A SYNTACTIC VIEW

Transformational grammar grew out of a linguist's concern with what he called "deep" structure. To understand this concern, let us examine the three sentences below. They have essentially the same kind of surface structure (the same parts of speech in the same order), but one sentence reflects a different underlying structure—or deep structure—than the other two. See if you can determine which sentence has a different kind of underlying structure:

> the picture was painted by a new student
> the picture was painted by a new method
> the recipe was devised by a new chef

In the first sentence, the student did the painting; we could paraphrase the sentence as *a new student painted the picture.* In the second sentence, did the method do the painting? Did the chef do the devising, in the third? If we try paraphrasing these sentences in the same way that the first sentence was paraphrased, we see it is the second sentence that has an underlying structure different from what the other two sentences have. That is, there is a different relationship between certain constructions within the sentence. In the second sentence, the prepositional phrase (*by a new method*) tells *how* the painting was done; the prepositional phrases in the other sentences tell *by whom.* The prepositional phrase in sentence two has a different relationship with its verb than the prepositional phrases in the other two sentences.

Which of the following three sentences has a different kind of underlying structure than the other two?

> Jon wanted the guest to eat
> Jon wanted the baby to eat
> Jon wanted the hamburger to eat

In the third sentence, *hamburger* is the logical object of *eat*; Jon wanted to eat the hamburger. But in the other sentences, the nouns occurring in the same sentence position as *hamburger*—the nouns *guest* and *baby*—are logically the subjects of the verb *eat*; Jon wanted the guest and the baby to eat something. (Of course if Jon is a cannibal, the three sentences all have the same kind of underlying structure.)

The structuralists' major contribution to sentence-level analysis was a cutting and labeling procedure called **immediate constituent analysis.** Usually this involved first cutting a sentence between the subject and predicate, then cutting off the modifiers of the subject noun and the main verb, until at last each word was isolated and labeled as to part of speech. Applying such a procedure to *the picture was painted by a new student* and *the picture was painted by a new technique,* we would get something like the following:

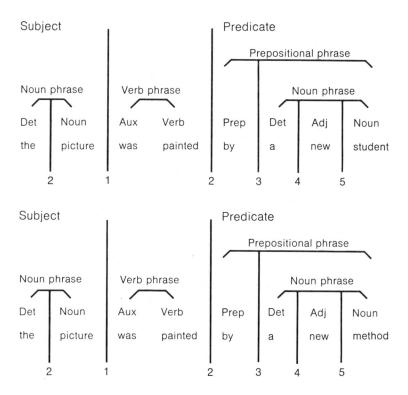

An immediate constituent analysis of the sentences shows them to be exactly alike in structure. But such an analysis of surface structure overlooks the fact that the prepositional phrases *by a new student* and *by a new method* have different functions in their respective sentences. The two sentences have the same kind of surface structure—the same parts of speech in the same order. But they have a different kind of deep structure, as revealed by the differing functions of *student* and *method* in the two sentences.

Immediate constituent analysis did not uncover such discrepancies between surface structure and deep structure, since the structuralists were not particularly interested in the fact that sentences with the same kind of surface structure may have different underlying deep structures. However, this fact did interest Noam Chomsky, a linguist who, in the mid-1950s, began to challenge the structuralists' conception of language structure.

Chomsky was also interested in the fact that a sentence might be structurally ambiguous, that it might have more than one kind of underlying structure. *Visiting relatives can be a nuisance*, for example, might be interpreted as "relatives who are visiting can be a nuisance" or as "to visit relatives can be a nuisance"; in the former case, relatives are doing the visiting, whereas in the latter case, relatives are being visited. Somewhat similarly, *the committee's appointment surprised me* might mean "I was surprised that someone appointed the committee" or "I was surprised that the committee appointed someone." (Can you think of any other meanings the sentence might have?)

Still another aspect of syntax which particularly interested Chomsky was the fact that two or in some cases more than two sentence structures may be employed to say essentially the same thing. One example would be *a new student painted the picture* and its passive counterpart, *the picture was painted by a new student*. Another pair of synonymous sentences is *our grocer sells melons which are mouldy* and *our grocer sells mouldy melons;* the first sentence's restrictive relative clause means the same as the prenoun adjective *mouldy* in the second sentence. As we shall see in subsequent chapters, there are various other sets of syntactic structures which can be employed to say basically the same thing.

Chomsky thought that a grammar, a grammatical theory, ought to be able to account explicitly for 1) the fact that two sentences may have the same kind of surface structure but a different kind of deep underlying structure (*the picture was painted by a new student* versus *the picture was painted by a new method*); 2) the fact that a sentence may be structurally ambiguous, that it may represent more than one underlying structure (*visiting relatives can be a nuisance*); and 3) the fact that sometimes two or more syntactic structures may be used to say the same thing (*a new student painted the picture, the picture was painted by a new student*). It was partly his interest in these aspects of syntax which structuralists generally had shown little interest in that prompted Chomsky to formulate a new theory of language structure. Chomsky's **transformational-generative** theory (the terms will be explained later) has come to be known simply as **transformational** grammar.

Chomsky first presented his theory in 1957, in a book called *Syntactic Structures.* In this book he says "Syntactic investigation of a given language has as its goal the construction of a grammar that can be viewed as a device of some sort for producing the sentences of the language under analysis." [1]

A transformational grammar has three major kinds of rules: syntactic rules, which specify the deep structure of the sentence and then transform that deep structure into a surface structure; semantic rules, which provide an interpretation for the sentence; and phonological rules, which specify information necessary in pronouncing the sentence. Although the interrela-

[1] *Noam Chomsky,* Syntactic Structures *(The Hague: Mouton & Company, N.V. Publishers, 1957), p. 11.*

tionship of these rules will be discussed later, we are concerned almost exclusively with the syntactic rules, which are the core of Chomsky's transformational grammar. Syntactic rules deal primarily with word order (subject-verb-object, for example), agreement (*these are* rather than *these is*, and *he goes* rather than *he go,* in standard English), and word inflection (*the boys wanted it, he wants to go*).

In the following sections of this chapter, we will present and discuss a highly simplified model of the syntactic component of a grammar, a model which will produce strings of words very much like English sentences. Our model grammar has two **major parts: 1)** a set of phrase structure rules, plus a lexicon; and 2) a set of transformational rules. The phrase structure rules and lexicon provide the **deep structure** of a sentence, a string of words and symbols joined by plus signs. The transformational rules manipulate these words and symbols in various ways in order to produce a **surface structure**, a string ready to be pronounced or written as an actual sentence.

Chomsky found it necessary to postulate a deep level and a surface level of language structure in order to account for the types of syntactic phenomena we have already discussed. For example, the deep structure underlying both *a new student painted the picture* and *the picture was painted by a new student* would be essentially like

a + new + student + paint + PAST + the + picture

This deep structure (here slightly simplified) would ultimately become either *a new student painted the picture* or, if the passive transformation was applied, *the picture was painted by a new student.* By deriving both sentences from the same deep structure, a transformational grammar "explains" the fact that the sentences are synonymous even though their surface structures differ.

 FOR FURTHER EXPLORATION

Arthur A. Stern, "Spatial and Temporal Grammar," *English Journal,* 57 (September 1968), 880–883, 888. Clarifies a basic distinction between structural grammar and transformational grammar. Easy to read.

John Algeo, "Linguistics: Where Do We Go From Here?" *English Journal,* 58 (January 1969), 102–112. Discusses various approaches to the study of grammar and describes the history of the teaching of grammar. An informative article; enjoyable to read.

# THE SYNTACTIC COMPONENT OF
# A TRANSFORMATIONAL GRAMMAR

Here we will discuss in some detail the nature of the syntactic component, the basic part of the grammar. We will discuss first the phrase structure rules and the lexicon, which specify the deep structure of a sentence, and then the transformational rules, which alter the deep structure to produce the surface structure of the sentence.

## PHRASE STRUCTURE RULES AND LEXICON

If we wanted to divide the sentence *the astronaut can walk* into two parts, where would it seem most logical to divide it? Probably between *astronaut* and *can*:

> the astronaut | can walk

Each of these two parts could, of course, be further divided:

> the | astronaut
> can | walk

The following diagram shows the division of *the astronaut can walk* into its constituent parts:

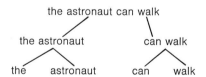

*The astronaut can walk* is, of course, a sentence. *The astronaut* is a noun phrase consisting of the determiner *the,* plus the noun *astronaut; can walk* is a verb phrase made up of the auxiliary *can,* plus the verb *walk.*[2] Thus the constituents of *the astronaut can walk* may be represented abstractly as follows:

---

[2] *The term "noun phrase" is roughly equivalent to the structuralists' term "nominal phrase." The structuralists' term "verbal phrase" refers to the auxiliary plus the main verb; the transformationalists' term "verb phrase" includes also any noun phrase or adjective phrase that might follow the main verb. In this and subsequent chapters we will use the term* **main verb phrase** *to refer to the auxiliary plus the main verb;* **verbal phrase** *will be used to refer to the main verb plus any noun phrase or adjective phrase that follows it.*

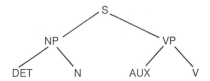

That is, the sentence is basically made up of a noun phrase plus a verb phrase; the noun phrase consists of a determiner plus a noun; and the verb phrase consists of an auxiliary plus a verb.

We have broken down the sentence *the astronaut can walk* into its constituent parts and have labeled the parts. That is, we have done an immediate constituent analysis of the sentence. The phrase structure rules of a transformational grammar do just the opposite: they build up sentences by specifying the basic parts in increasingly greater detail. For example, the first three phrase structure rules of a simplified transformational grammar might look like this:

PS 1     S → NP + VP
PS 2     NP → DET + N
PS 3     VP → AUX + V

The arrow means "consists of"; thus S → NP + VP means that a sentence basically consists of a noun phrase plus a verb phrase. The arrow in these rules can also be interpreted to mean "rewrite as"; thus S → NP + VP means "rewrite S as NP + VP." We can do this rewriting in the form of a "tree" diagram:

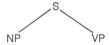

After we have rewritten NP as DET + N in accordance with rule PS 2, the tree will have two more branches:

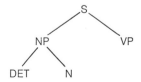

Finally, application of rule PS 3 will give DET + N + AUX + V:

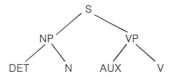

Since there are no more phrase structure rules in our simplified grammar, we are ready to insert words from the lexicon, which is something like a dictionary. Here is a highly abbreviated and simplified lexicon (for convenience, it is arranged by part of speech rather than alphabetically):

| | |
|---|---|
| DET: | the |
| N: | anteater, astronaut, cow, dog, girl, man |
| AUX: | can, may, shall, will |
| V: | play, run, walk |

By choosing different combinations of words from the lexicon, we can produce as many as seventy-two different sentences, all having the structure DET + N + AUX + V. One possibility, of course, is the sentence we broke down into its constituent parts: *the astronaut can walk.* What are some of the other possibilities?

## TRANSFORMATIONS AND THE STRUCTURE OF THE AUXILIARY

So far, we have not looked at that part of a transformational grammar which gives the grammar its name: the transformations. Before doing this, we need to look at the structure of the auxiliary, since a thorough grasp of the English auxiliary structure is needed in order to understand many of the transformations that are basic to a transformational grammar.

THE STRUCTURE OF THE AUXILIARY.   The auxiliary word and the following verb are bold-faced in these sentences:

> someone **has eaten** the garlic toast
> the roaches **have taken** my lunch
> Lady Godiva **had ridden** through the streets before

In each sentence, the auxiliary word is a form of the verb *to have,* henceforth designated as the HAVE auxiliary or verb, or simply as HAVE. (See Appendix I, p. 385, for a list of the forms of HAVE.) In each case, the HAVE auxiliary is followed by a past participle form.

The past participle of many "irregular" or "strong" verbs has a distinctive form. Compare, for example, the past tense and past participle forms in the following sentences:

|  |  |
|---:|:---|
| past | the child **began** to cry |
| past participle | the child has **begun** to cry |
|  |  |
| past | the cowboys **rode** beyond the horizon |
| past participle | the cowboys have **ridden** beyond the horizon |
|  |  |
| past | Grover **knew** it was wrong |
| past participle | Grover had **known** it was wrong |

In each of these pairs of sentences, the past tense form differs from the past participle form, the form that is used after the HAVE auxiliary.

For some irregular verbs and all "regular" or "weak" verbs, there is no distinction between the past tense form and the form used after HAVE:

|  |  |
|---:|:---|
| past | Sebastian **cut** his knee |
| past participle | Sebastian has **cut** himself often |
|  |  |
| past | Kevin and Mary **fed** the horses |
| past participle | they have **fed** the horses often |
|  |  |
| past | Herbert **won** the game |
| past participle | he had **won** often |
|  |  |
| past | Cinderella **scrubbed** the floor |
| past participle | she has **scrubbed** the floor often |
|  |  |
| past | Roger and Cheryl **walked** through Central Park |
| past participle | they have **walked** there a lot lately |
|  |  |
| past | Socrates **waited** patiently |
| past participle | he had **waited** for two years already |

In each of the above cases, the form used after the HAVE auxiliary is the same as the past tense form, though their functions are different.

For those verbs with a past participle form that is distinct from the past tense form (*eaten, given, taken,* etc.), it is always the past participle form that occurs after the HAVE auxiliary. Linguists therefore sometimes say that the HAVE auxiliary is followed by the past participle form. But since there is no distinctive past participle form for many verbs, it would be more accurate to say that the past participle of a verb is that form which occurs after the HAVE auxiliary. For example, *kissed* in *he has kissed her before* is a past participle just because it is preceded by the auxiliary word *has.*

But what happens if the HAVE auxiliary is followed by another auxiliary word rather than by a main verb? The following sentences illustrate this situation:

> someone **has been** eating the garlic toast
> the roaches **have been** taking my lunch
> Lady Godiva **had been** riding through the streets

In each case, the HAVE auxiliary is immediately followed by the auxiliary word *been,* which is the past participle form of the verb *to be,* henceforth designated as the BE auxiliary or verb, or simply as BE. (See Appendix I, p. 386, for a list of the forms of BE.) Thus the generalization holds: the HAVE auxiliary is always followed by a past participle. Since many of the distinctive past participle forms end in *-en* or *-n* (*eaten, written, known,* etc.), we will use the symbol EN to represent the concept of past participle.

In the preceding set of examples, the main verb was always in the present participle form, the form ending in *-ing*; in each case, this present participle was preceded by *been.* Apparently the auxiliary *been* is always followed by a present participle (except in passive sentences: *the pizza has been eaten*). This fact, however, is only one part of a broader generalization. In the following sentences, notice what precedes the present participle:

> I **am dreaming**
> he **is dreaming**
> we **are dreaming**
> she **was dreaming**
> you **were dreaming**
> they **have been dreaming**
> he **is being** silly
> they **were being** silly

In each of these cases the main verb is in the present participle form, and the present participle is immediately preceded by a form of BE. Thus it seems that a present participle main verb is always preceded by a form of BE functioning as an auxiliary, and that, conversely, a form of BE occurring as an auxiliary is followed by a verb in the present participle form. The first part of this generalization is always valid; the second part does not hold when the sentence is passive, as we shall see in the next chapter.

One major kind of auxiliary word remains to be discussed: the modal auxiliary. The following sentences illustrate the nine basic modal forms:

> John **can** play the piano well
> yes, John **can** go to the concert
>
> John **could** have gone
> it **could** rain today
> John **could** go tomorrow
>
> I **shall** be glad to do it
> he **shall** do the work
>
> he **should** do the work
> they **should** win easily
> I **should** like to visit you
>
> I **will** be glad to do it
> he **will** do the work
>
> he **would** do his work, occasionally
> I **would** like to visit you
> I **would** do the work, if I were you
>
> yes, John **may** go to the concert
> it **may** rain today
>
> it **might** rain today
>
> he **must** do the work
> he **must** like spinach, since he eats it so often [3]

It is difficult to specify the meaning or meanings of the modal forms. Do you see any meaning relationship between *can* and *could*? Between *shall* and *should*? *Will* and *would*? *May* and *might?* The first word in each of these pairs is considered a present tense form and the second is considered the past tense form corresponding to it. Thus the present tense modals and their corresponding past tense forms are as follows:

---

[3] *Many Southern speakers use, at least occasionally, such double modals as* may can, may could, might can, might could, might ought, *and* might would; *all these are negativized by adding* n't *to the second modal:* may can't, may couldn't, *and so forth. Double modals are commonly used also by some black speakers in the North.*

| *present* | *past* |
|-----------|--------|
| can | could |
| shall | should |
| will | would |
| may | might |
| must | ——— |

As the table indicates, *must* has no past tense form.

It should be emphasized that the past tense forms do not necessarily have a past meaning; indeed, they often refer to the future, as in *John could go tomorrow, they should win easily, I would like to visit you,* and *it might rain today.* Nevertheless, the modals *could, should, would,* and *might* are customarily designated as past tense forms.[4]

This discrepancy between form and meaning (here, a past tense form with a future meaning) is not uncommon in English. In the following sentences, for example, the verb is present tense in form but does not refer to present time:

> John **works** hard all the time
> John **leaves** tomorrow
> yesterday this man **walks** up to me and **says** . . . .

In the first sentence, *works* has a habitual meaning; if we wanted to indicate that the action is presently occurring, we would say *John is working hard.* The sentence *John leaves tomorrow* clearly indicates a future time. And *walks* and *says* in the third example refer to past time; these sentences illustrate the **historical present**: the use of present tense forms to indicate past time.

If you look back at the example sentences in this chapter (and at all the other sentences in the book), you will see that in each case, the first word of the verb phrase is in either the present or the past tense. The following sentences also illustrate this fact:

> he **may** leave today
> they **may** leave today
> they **might** leave today
>
> he **has** seen the TV show
> we **have** seen the TV show
> he **had** seen the TV show

---

[4] *For an interesting discussion of the historical origin of the modal auxiliaries, see Samuel Moore's* Historical Outlines of English Sounds and Inflections *(Ann Arbor, Mich.: George Wahr Publishing Company, 1951; revised by Albert H. Marckwardt and republished in 1964), pp. 171–174.*

I **am** playing the guitar
she **is** playing the guitar
you **are** playing the guitar
I **was** playing the guitar
they **were** playing the guitar

I **play** the guitar
she **plays** the guitar
they **played** the guitar

In each case the first auxiliary word is in the present or the past tense; when there is no auxiliary word, as in the last three sentences, the main verb is in the present or the past tense. Note that the modal auxiliaries have only one present tense form; they differ in this respect from all other verbs and auxiliaries. Also, they have no present or past participle form.

Clearly, **tense** and **time** are not the same. There are only two tenses, present and past. Future time is usually indicated by an adverb or a modal auxiliary, or both:

John leaves **tomorrow**
John **will** be leaving
John **will** leave **tomorrow**

Study the following sentences to see how present time and past time are indicated, and to see also what kinds of time relationships are generally indicated by the various tense and auxiliary combinations (excluding the modals, which have already been discussed). What difference in meaning do you notice between the bold-faced phrases in each of the following pairs of sentences?

John **drives** a Toronado
John **is driving** a Toronado

John **drove** a Toronado
John **was driving** a Toronado

Bob **barbecued** the steaks
Bob **has barbecued** the steaks, and so we're ready to eat

Bob **barbecued** the steaks
when Bob **had barbecued** the steaks, we were ready to eat

Can you see why phrases containing a present tense form of BE plus a present participle (*am going, is going, are going*) have traditionally been called **present progressive aspect?**

What, then, would be the logical term for phrases containing a *past* tense form of BE plus a present participle (*was going, were going*)? Can you see why phrases containing a present tense form of HAVE plus a past participle (*has eaten, have eaten*) have traditionally been called **present perfect aspect?** ("Perfect" expresses the idea of completion.) What, then, would be the term for a phrase containing a *past* tense form of HAVE plus a past participle (*had eaten*)?

There is one more important fact about the structure of the auxiliary in English: the order of the auxiliary words. Consider the following sentences:

> he **will have eaten** by then
> he **will be leaving** by 3:00
> he **has been thinking**
> he **should have been thinking** harder

If two or more auxiliary words occur together, in what order must they occur? Try ordering the auxiliaries in alternate ways to demonstrate that your conclusion is valid.

THE TRANSFORMATIONALISTS' CONTRIBUTION. From the previous discussion and examples, four important generalizations can be formulated about the basic structure of the English auxiliary:

1.   The first auxiliary word is always in the present or the past tense form. (If there is no auxiliary word, the main verb is in either the present or the past tense form.)

2.   If a form of HAVE occurs in the auxiliary, the next word will always be in the past participle form.

3.   If a form of BE occurs in the auxiliary, the next word will be in the present participle form. (Certain exceptions will be noted in the next section of this chapter and in the next chapter, where passives will be discussed.)

4.   The order of the auxiliary words is invariable: the modal comes first, then the HAVE auxiliary, and last the BE auxiliary.

Noam Chomsky was not the first linguist to notice these facts about the auxiliary structure of English, but his revolutionary *Syntactic Structures* provided a more revealing explanation of the structure than had previously been offered.[5] We have noted before that the HAVE auxiliary is always followed by a past participle; conversely, a past participle in a main verb phrase is always preceded by a HAVE auxiliary (in nonpassive sentences). Thus HAVE and EN form a single unit, logically. However, they are separated in the surface structure of sentences; it is the word following HAVE which is in the past participle

---

[5] See Chomsky, Syntactic Structure, *pp. 39–40.*

form: *we have eaten lunch, the president has spoken.* The same sort of relationship exists between the BE auxiliary and the present participle: BE and ING form a single unit logically, yet in actual sentences they are separated: *we are eating lunch, the president is speaking.* It was to account for these facts, as well as many others, that Chomsky postulated a *deep* structure level of language and a *surface* structure, the two being related by transformations. On the deep level, the structure of the auxiliary is expressed by a phrase structure rule:

$$AUX \rightarrow T + (M) + (HAVE + EN) + (BE + ING)$$

This rule says that the auxiliary consists of an obligatory tense marker, plus optionally a modal (parentheses indicate that an item is optional), plus optionally HAVE + EN, plus optionally BE + ING. (We will explain below why the tense marker is part of the auxiliary.)

To see how this deep structure would be transformed into a surface structure, let us assume 1) that we have chosen all the optional elements; 2) that the tense is past; 3) that the modal is *shall*; and 4) that the main verb following this auxiliary is *walk.* Thus we have the string

PAST + shall + HAVE + EN + BE + ING + walk

In the surface structure, each affix symbol (PAST, EN, ING) goes with the element that follows it: we want the past tense form of *shall,* the past participle of BE, and the present participle of *walk.* Usually the affix symbol simply represents the addition of a suffix to the base form of a word; for example, the present participle *walking* is derived by adding *-ing* to the base form *walk.* Similarly, the past tense and past participle forms of regular verbs are derived by adding *-ed* to the base form (*I walked, I have walked*) and the third singular form is derived by the addition of final *-s* or *-es* (*she walks, he misses her*). Therefore it seems desirable to have a rule which will move the affix symbols to a position following the word to which they apply. The arrows in the example below indicate how the affix transformation would move the affix symbols in our string:

PAST + shall + HAVE + EN + BE + ING + walk

The affix transformation (which will be formulated later) moves these symbols as indicated to give

shall + PAST # HAVE # BE + EN # walk + ING #

(The double cross symbol, #, is used to separate word units. In addition to the affix transformation, a word boundary transformation has been applied here so that the word units will be clearer.) *Shall* + PAST gives *should*; HAVE ends up simply as the base form *have*, since no affix is added to it; BE + EN gives *been*, which is the past participle of BE; and *walk* + *ING* gives *walking:*

should have been walking

Thus the phrase structure rule

AUX → T + (M) + (HAVE + EN) + (BE + ING)

describes the *deep* structure of the auxiliary, in which HAVE and EN go together, and BE and ING go together. Later an affix transformation separates EN from HAVE and ING from BE, giving the *surface* structure of the auxiliary.

This auxiliary rewrite rule and the affix transformation also account for the fact that the first word in the verb phrase is always in the present or past tense form. If the verb phrase has one or more auxiliary words, the first auxiliary word is in the present or the past tense form; or, if there is no auxiliary word, the main verb is in the present or the past.

Let us look again at the structure underlying *should have been walking:*

PAST + shall + HAVE + EN + BE + ING + walk

The affix transformation will move each affix to a position following the word it precedes in the deep structure; the arrows indicate the positions to which the affixes will be moved. Note that the first auxiliary word, *shall*, ends up as the past tense form *should*. Now suppose that we have the same deep structure, except that the optional modal has not been chosen. Then we would have

PAST        + HAVE + EN + BE + ING + walk

This will produce *had been walking*: again, the first auxiliary word is in the past. Now let us eliminate the HAVE + EN element as well as the modal:

PAST        + BE + ING + walk

This will give *was walking* or *were walking,* depending on the subject of the verb phrase; here, too, the first auxiliary word is in the past tense. If all the *optional* auxiliary elements are eliminated, the only remaining auxiliary element is the tense marker, PAST:

PAST                    + walk

This produces *walked*; here, the main verb is in the past tense because there is no auxiliary word to carry the tense indicator.

## WORKING WITH THE AUXILIARY

**1.** Apply the affix transformation to each of the following strings (or use arrows to indicate the positions to which the affixes will be moved). The symbol ES indicates that we want the third singular present, the form which is used with *he, she, it,* and other singular nominals (excluding the singular pronoun *I* and the singular *you*); this third singular form is usually derived by adding *-s* or *-es* to the base form: *she walks, he misses her.* The symbol Ø (zero-with-a-slash) is used here to indicate that we want the present tense form which agrees with *I, we, you, they,* and plural nominals; this is the base form of the verb, the form that "adds nothing": *I walk, they miss her.*

The first three of the following strings are worked out. (Note that the modals do not add *-s* or *-es* in the third singular; in this case the ES has no surface representation.)

        a.   ES + will + walk

              will + ES # walk
              will walk

        b.   Ø + will + walk

              will + Ø # walk
              will walk

        c.   PAST + will + walk

              will + PAST # walk
              would walk

        d.   ES + HAVE + EN + drive
        e.   Ø + HAVE + EN + drive
        f.   PAST + HAVE + EN + drive
        g.   ES + may + HAVE + EN + walk
        h.   Ø + may + HAVE + EN + walk

i.   PAST + may + HAVE + EN + walk
j.   PAST + shall + BE + ING + eat
k.   ES + HAVE + EN + BE + ING + eat
l.   Ø + HAVE + EN + BE + ING + eat
m.  ES + walk
n.  Ø + walk
o.  PAST + walk

**2.** Why do you suppose phrases with BE as the first auxiliary word were excluded from the preceding exercise? Examples of such strings are

PAST + BE + ING + walk
Ø + BE + ING + walk
ES + BE + ING + walk

**3.** Examine the sentences below. Do you find any evidence suggesting that *dare* and *need* are modal auxiliaries? In your opinion, should they or should they not be considered regular modals? What evidence is there to support your opinion?

he dare not go      he need not go
dare he go?         need he go?

**4.** a. How do you pronounce *have* and *has* in the following sentences?

we have two runs     he has two runs
we have to run       he has to run

How do you pronounce *used* in the following sentences?

we used two brushes
we used to use two brushes

How do you pronounce *going* plus *to* in the following sentences?

I'm going to the store
I'm going to go to the store

How do you pronounce *got* plus *to* and *ought* plus *to* in the following sentences?

I've got to study
I ought to study

b. Does your pronunciation of the second sentence in each of the first three sets above and both sentences of the last set provide evidence for assuming that *HAVE to* (*have to, has to, had to*), *used to, going to, got to,* and *ought to* function as two-word auxiliary elements? Can you think of any reasons why these phrases should *not* be considered as two-word auxiliary elements?

**5.** The following new rule for specifying the auxiliary is an expansion of the basic rule:

$$AUX \rightarrow T + (M) + (HAVE + EN) + (BE + ING)$$

This expanded rule includes the two-word auxiliaries mentioned in the previous two exercises, plus some other new items:

$$AUX \rightarrow T + \left\{ \begin{array}{l} \left\{ \begin{array}{l} M \\ ought + to \\ BE + going + to \\ (had) + better \end{array} \right\} + (HAVE + EN) + (BE + ING) \\ \\ (used + to) + (HAVE + to) + (BE + ING) \\ \\ (be + (supposed) + to) + (HAVE + EN) \end{array} \right\}$$

Parentheses indicate optionality. Thus we can choose only the tense marker, T, if we wish. Braces indicate that one must choose the items on the top line, or the second line, or the third, or . . . . A simple example is the rule

$$T \rightarrow \left\{ \begin{array}{l} PRES \\ PAST \end{array} \right\}$$

which means that T must be rewritten as either PRES or PAST. In the expanded auxiliary rule, there are three basic lines to choose from. There are four options for the first element in the first line.

The following is an example of an expanded auxiliary (*go* has been added as the main verb):

$$PAST + ought + to + HAVE + EN + go$$

The affix transformation and the word boundary transformation will give

$$ought + PAST \# to \# HAVE \# go + EN \#$$

which reads out as *ought to have gone.* Phonological rules—rules providing the information needed for pronunciation—will have to specify that *ought + PAST* produces *ought* and also that *ought + ES* and *ought + Ø* produce *ought.* There will have to be similar rules for *(had) better* and for *used*, which are also invariable in form. An alternative solution would be a rule which deletes the tense marker before the auxiliary elements *ought, (had) better*, and *used.*

The following are some of the other auxiliary possibilities, again with *go* provided as the main verb:

PAST + used + to + HAVE + to + go

used to have to go

PAST + BE + supposed + to + HAVE + EN + go

$\left\{ \begin{array}{l} \text{was} \\ \text{were} \end{array} \right\}$ supposed to have gone

Now try your hand at creating a variety of expanded auxiliaries.

**6.** After working with the expanded auxiliary rule, would you recommend any particular changes in it? Are there any items you think should be omitted or added? For example, should

(M) + (GET + to)

be added as a fourth basic option, to allow for such sentences as *he will get to go, he gets to go, he got to go*? Or how about expanding the element (BE + ING) to include the verb *to get* as an alternative to BE:

$$\left( \left\{ \begin{array}{l} \text{BE} \\ \text{GET} \end{array} \right\} + \text{ING} \right)$$

Should the expanded auxiliary rule incorporate either or both of these additions?

A MODEL GRAMMAR
(SYNTACTIC COMPONENT)

The following is a highly simplified model of the syntactic component of a transformational grammar. The symbols and rules are explained in the discussion which follows the model grammar.

*Phrase Structure Rules*

PS 1     S → NP + VP
PS 2     VP → AUX + VBP
PS 3     AUX → T + (M) + (HAVE + EN) + (BE + ING)

PS 4     T →     $\left\{ \begin{array}{c} \text{PRES} \\ \text{PAST} \end{array} \right\}$

PS 5     VBP → $\left\{ \begin{array}{l} V_i \\ V_t + NP \\ V_l + ADJ \end{array} \right\}$

PS 6     NP → $\left\{ \begin{array}{l} \text{PRO} \\ \\ \text{DET} + N + \left\{ \begin{array}{c} \text{SG} \\ \text{PL} \end{array} \right\} \end{array} \right\}$

*Lexicon*

| | |
|---|---|
| DET: | the |
| M: | may, shall, will |
| PRO: | I, we, you, he, she, it, they |
| N: | anteater, astronaut, cow, dog, girl, man |
| $V_i$: | play, run, walk |
| $V_t$: | encounter, see, watch |
| $V_l$: | appear, look, seem [6] |
| ADJ: | funny, lonesome, patient, tipsy |

---

[6] *Most of these nine verbs have more than one verbal function. For example,* play *can be transitive as well as intransitive (she played the piano);* watch *can be intransitive as well as transitive (we watched cautiously); and* appear *can be intransitive as well as linking (he appeared suddenly).*

*Transformational Rules*

T1

$$V_t + \begin{bmatrix} \text{I} \\ \text{we} \\ \text{he} \\ \text{she} \\ \text{they} \end{bmatrix} \Rightarrow V_t + \begin{bmatrix} \text{me} \\ \text{us} \\ \text{him} \\ \text{her} \\ \text{them} \end{bmatrix}$$

T2 I + PRES + BE $\Rightarrow$ I + $PRES_1$ + BE

T3 $\begin{bmatrix} \text{he, she, it, SG} \\ \text{I, we, you, they, PL} \end{bmatrix} + \text{PRES} \Rightarrow \begin{bmatrix} \text{he, she, it, SG} \\ \text{I, we, you, they, PL} \end{bmatrix} + \begin{bmatrix} \text{ES} \\ \text{Ø} \end{bmatrix}$

T4 $\begin{bmatrix} \text{I, he, she, it, SG} \\ \text{we, you, they, PL} \end{bmatrix} + \text{PAST} + \text{BE} \Rightarrow$

$$\begin{bmatrix} \text{I, he, she, it, SG} \\ \text{we, you, they, PL} \end{bmatrix} + \begin{bmatrix} PAST_{sg} \\ PAST_{pl} \end{bmatrix} + \text{BE}$$

T5 Af + v $\Rightarrow$ v + Af # where Af = $PRES_1$, ES, Ø, $PAST_{sg}$, $PAST_{pl}$, PAST, EN, or ING and v = any M, HAVE, BE, $V_i$, $V_t$, or $V_l$

T6 X + Y $\Rightarrow$ X # Y where X + Y is not a N + $\begin{Bmatrix} \text{SG} \\ \text{PL} \end{Bmatrix}$ combination or a v + Af combination

To generate a sentence with this model grammar, we must begin with the first phrase structure rule, S → NP + VP:

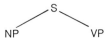

We now have two **nodes** from which branches can be further extended, an NP node and a VP node: that is, we can apply PS 6 to further specify the noun phrase and PS 2 to further specify the verb phrase. Rule PS 2 is slightly different from our earlier rule for rewriting the verb phrase, VP → AUX + V. The new rule replaces the earlier symbol V, "verb," with VBP, "verbal phrase"; the latter is more inclusive, as rule PS 5 indicates. Let us arbitrarily choose to apply rule PS 2 now, rather than rule PS 6:

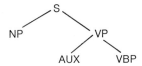

The rule specifying the noun phrase is still applicable, of course, and now we can also apply PS 3 to specify the auxiliary or PS 5 to specify the verbal phrase. Let us arbitrarily choose to rewrite AUX next. In so doing, we can elect one or more of the optional elements. Again arbitrarily, we will choose BE + ING in addition to the obligatory tense marker, T:

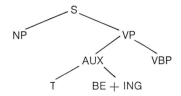

Let us further specify the tense as PRES, by rule PS 4:

At this point we can further specify either the noun phrase, NP, or the verbal phrase, VBP. In specifying the verbal phrase, we can choose an intransitive verb, $V_i$; a transitive verb plus a noun phrase, $V_t + NP$; or a linking verb plus an adjective, $V_l + ADJ$. Let us arbitrarily choose $V_t + NP$:

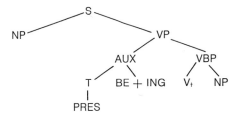

Now the only elements which can be rewritten are the two NP's; there is no PS rule which further specifies any of the other symbols at the bottom of the branches of this tree. Let us rewrite the first NP as PRO, for pronoun (rule PS 6):

And let us specify the second NP as consisting of a determiner plus a noun plus a symbol indicating that the noun is to be singular rather than plural:

Now that we have applied all the phrase structure rules, it is advisable to take the terminal symbols from the tree and write them linearly:

$$PRO + PRES + BE + ING + V_t + DET + N + SG$$

We are now ready to choose from the lexicon a pronoun, PRO; a transitive verb, $V_t$; a determiner, DET; and a noun, N. One possible string would be

$$I + PRES + BE + ING + watch + the + cow + SG$$

At last we are ready for the transformational rules. Not all of them will be applicable to every sentence, but we must check each rule in turn to see if it does apply. The transformational rules must be applied in the order in which they are listed; otherwise an ungrammatical sentence may result.

Whenever a pronoun follows a transitive verb (or occurs as the object of a preposition) the pronoun must be in the objective form: we say *I saw him,* not *\*I saw he.* Thus in our simple grammar we need rule T 1 to change subject pronouns into object pronouns after transitive verbs:

$$V_t + \begin{bmatrix} I \\ we \\ he \\ she \\ they \end{bmatrix} \Longrightarrow V_t + \begin{bmatrix} me \\ us \\ him \\ her \\ them \end{bmatrix}$$

The double arrow, $\Longrightarrow$, indicates that this is a transformational rule rather than a phrase structure rule. Unlike a phrase structure rule, this rule is **context-sensitive**; it changes a nominative pronoun (subject form) into an accusative pronoun (object form) only when the pronoun follows a transitive verb. If the context were not specified, we might erroneously produce *\*me saw him.* This first rule is obligatory, when applicable. But it is not applicable to our string

$$I + PRES + BE + ING + watch + the + cow + SG$$

because the transitive verb, *watch,* is not followed by a pronoun. (Notice that we must still have available to us the information presented in our phrase structure tree. In this case, we must know whether or not *watch* is a transitive verb; if it were not, we would not need to check further to see whether it is followed by a pronoun.)

Rule T 2 is needed to handle an "exception." Usually the pronoun *I* takes the same present tense verb forms that plural pronouns take: *I watch her, we watch her, they watch her.* But *I* has its own special present tense form of the BE verb: *I am watching her,* not *\*I are watching her.* In a transformational grammar one typically accounts for exceptions before making broad generalizations, in order to avoid producing ungrammati-

cal sentences. In this case, we are kept from producing *I are....
by rule T 2:

I + PRES + BE =⟩ I + PRES₁ + BE

This rule says PRES should be rewritten as PRES₁ ("present
sub-one"; the "1" is an arbitrary designation) when the subject
is *I* and the tense marker PRES is immediately followed by BE.
This second transformational rule must be applied to our string.
We will then have

I + PRES₁ + BE + ING + watch + the + cow + SG

Rule T 3 applies to all strings in which the tense marker is
PRES (just PRES, not PRES₁). The rule is as follows:

$$\begin{bmatrix} \text{he, she, it, SG} \\ \text{I, we, you, they, PL} \end{bmatrix} + \text{PRES} =\rangle \begin{bmatrix} \text{he, she, it, SG} \\ \text{I, we, you, they, PL} \end{bmatrix} + \begin{bmatrix} \text{ES} \\ \varnothing \end{bmatrix}$$

This rule says that PRES is to be rewritten as ES whenever the
subject is *he, she, it,* or a singular noun (as indicated by the
symbol SG); PRES is to be rewritten as Ø whenever the subject
is *I, we, you, they,* or a plural noun. This third transformational
rule does not apply to our string, since PRES has already been
rewritten as PRES₁ by the application of rule T 2.

Rule T 4 handles a second exception. The BE verb is the
only verb in English that has two past tense forms, *was* and
*were.* This rule says that whenever PAST is immediately followed by BE, PAST is to be rewritten as PAST$_{sg}$ if the subject is
*I, he, she, it,* or a singular noun; if the subject is *we, you, they,*
or a plural noun, PAST is to be rewritten as PAST$_{pl}$.

This fourth transformational rule does not apply to our string
either, since this string has a present tense marker.

At this point our string is as follows:

I + PRES₁ + BE + ING + watch + the + cow + SG

The affix transformation, rule T 5, now applies to give

I + BE + PRES₁ # watch + ING # the + cow + SG

Our model grammar has been designed so that the affix transformation applies at least once in the derivation of every
sentence.

Finally, the word boundary transformation, T 6, replaces all
plus symbols with word boundary symbols except when the
plus joins two elements which must go together to form a word.
Thus we have

I # BE + PRES₁ # watch + ING # the # cow + SG

which will ultimately turn out to be the sentence

I am watching the cow

According to Chomsky, this process we have just gone through is a model of what native speakers of the language do instantaneously, without conscious thought, in producing sentences.

Now that we have worked through the derivation of one sentence step by step, it should not be difficult to produce other sentences. Let us begin once again with S. The phrase structure rules are listed on page 80. Applying PS 1, we have

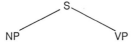

This time, we will rewrite the noun phrase first, arbitrarily choosing DET + N + PL (by rule PS 6):

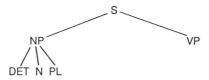

Now we must rewrite the VP as AUX + VBP:

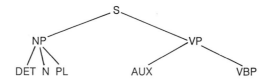

Let us further specify the auxiliary element, arbitrarily choosing some but not all of the optional elements (rule PS 3):

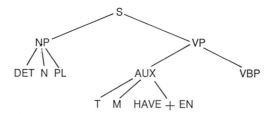

The tense we shall specify as PAST (rule PS 4):

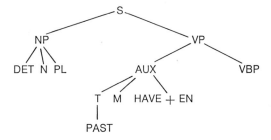

Finally, let us choose to rewrite VBP as $V_1$ + ADJ (by PS 5):

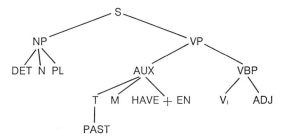

There are now no more symbols which can be rewritten (no symbols which occur to the left of the arrow in a PS rule), so we are ready to write the terminal symbols linearly:

DET + N + PL + PAST + M + HAVE + EN + $V_i$ + ADJ

The specification of appropriate words from the lexicon might produce a string such as

the + astronaut + PL + PAST + may + HAVE + EN + appear + tipsy

Now we must work our way through the transformational rules, applying in turn each rule that is relevant to our string. The transformational rules are listed on page 81.

T 1     does not apply: we do not have a transitive verb.
T 2     does not apply: we do not have the pronoun / followed by PRES.
T 3     does not apply: our string does not include the symbol PRES.
T 4     does not apply: we do not have PAST followed by BE.
T 5     (the verb affix transformation) always applies at least once in The derivation of every sentence. It applies twice in our string, moving PAST to a position following *may* and EN to a position following *appear:*

the + astronaut + PL + may + PAST # HAVE + appear + EN # tipsy

T 6     (the word boundary transformation) also applies at least once
        in the derivation of every sentence. In this case, the result is

> the # astronaut + PL # may + PAST # HAVE #
> appear + EN # tipsy

From this string we will get the sentence

> the astronauts might have appeared tipsy

One more illustration may prove helpful. This time instead of
building our phrase structure tree up (or down) step by step, we
will simply present another tree which can be produced by the
phrase structure rules. You can check for yourself to see what
rule has been applied in further specifying each element:

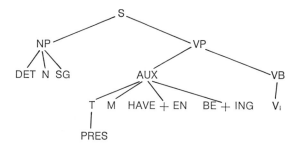

Taking the terminal symbols off the tree, we have

> DET + N + SG + PRES + M + HAVE + EN + BE + ING + V$_i$

The substitution of words from the lexicon might produce

> the + anteater + SG + PRES + may + HAVE + EN +
> BE + ING + play

Now for the transformational rules:

T 1     is not applicable.
T 2     is not applicable.
T 3     specifies PRES as ES (in this case) to produce
        > the + anteater + SG + ES + may + HAVE + EN +
        > BE + ING + play
T 4     is not applicable.
T 5     (the affix transformation) moves the three verb affixes
        (ES, EN, and ING) to produce
        > the + anteater + SG + may + ES # HAVE + BE + EN
        > # play + ING #

T 6    adds word boundaries where appropriate:

> the # anteater + SG # may + ES # HAVE # BE + EN
> # play + ING #

This string finally yields

> the anteater may have been playing

Now try your hand at producing some sentences with the phrase structure rules, lexical items, and transformational rules provided in this chapter. This simple grammar will produce over 43,000 different sentences.

 FOR FURTHER EXPLORATION

Owen Thomas, *Transformational Grammar and the Teacher of English.* 1st ed. New York: Holt, Rinehart and Winston, Inc., 1965. Chapters 2 and 3, pp. 21–73. These chapters discuss in a slightly different manner some of the same matters discussed here. This book was the first popularization of transformational grammar, describing its first stage, from 1957 to approximately 1964. The revised edition of Thomas' book (in press) treats transformational grammar historically, with a long section on the first stage of transformational grammar.

Noam Chomsky, *Syntactic Structures.* The Hague, Mouton & Company, N.V. Publishers, 1957. This was the pioneering work of transformational grammar. It was intended for linguists rather than for students of English, and it is difficult reading.

Roderick A. Jacobs and Peter S. Rosenbaum, *English Transformational Grammar.* Waltham, Mass.: Blaisdell Publishing Company, 1968. Chapters 14 through 16 (pp. 108–135) discuss auxiliary elements. Jacobs and Rosenbaum's description of the auxiliary is more advanced, in transformational terms, than the description given here. To understand Jacobs and Rosenbaum's description, it would probably be necessary to read their preceding chapters, or at least to read the next section of the present book, "The Lexicon in Detail." *English Transformational Grammar* is more difficult to read than the Thomas book, but less difficult than *Syntactic Structures.* It is a clear description of the second stage of transformational grammar, dating approximately from 1964 to 1967.

## THE LEXICON IN DETAIL

The lexicon of a transformational grammar is much more complex than simply a list of words like the list provided in our model syntactic component. Each word in the lexicon has three sets of features: syntactic features, needed by the syntactic component; semantic features, needed by the semantic component; and phonological features, needed by the phonological component. (The functions of and the relationships among these components will be discussed in the next major section of this chapter.)

### PHONOLOGICAL MATRICES

The phonological **matrix** (set of features) for a word indicates, in sequence, how each consonant and/or vowel is pronounced. For example, the matrix for the word *man* would indicate 1) that the first sound is a bilabial nasal consonant, a sound made by completely closing the lips and lowering the velum to expel the air entirely through the nose; 2) that the second distinguishable sound is a vowel sound made low in the front part of the mouth; and 3) that the last sound is an apico-alveolar nasal consonant, a sound made by using the tip (apex) of the tongue to stop the air flow at the alveolar ridge and by again lowering the velum to expel the air through the nasal passages. The phonological matrix for *man* would also indicate that all three of these sounds are voiced; that is, the vocal chords are constricted and vibrating. Since the phonological matrix for *man* would look much more complicated than even this detailed explanation implies, we will not attempt to represent the phonological matrix graphically.

### SYNTACTIC MATRICES

Ideally, a grammar ought to be able to explain why the following sentences will seem ungrammatical to a native speaker of English:

> *he wiped up stubbornness
> *I ate a spinach
> *he liked idea
> *the lightning frightened the rocket
> *the mare mumbled incoherently
> *my nephew wrecked her own car

The sentence *he wiped up stubbornness* is ungrammatical because one cannot wipe up a quality, like stubbornness; the object of *wipe up* must be a concrete entity, something which can be perceived by the senses (though, of course, the sentences could receive a metaphorical interpretation). *I ate a spinach* is ungrammatical because we do not use the indefinite article before noncount nouns. (A count noun is a noun which can take the cardinal numbers as determiners: *one idea, two ideas,* but not *one spinach, *two spinaches.*) *He liked idea* is ungrammatical because the count noun *idea* is being used in its singular form without a determiner word (compare with *he liked spinach,* the word *spinach* being a singular noncount noun). *The lightning frightened the rocket* is ungrammatical because one cannot frighten inanimate objects (except metaphorically). *The mare mumbled incoherently* is also ungrammatical, because nonhumans are not normally said to mumble (though again the sentence might be given a metaphorical interpretation.) Finally, *my nephew wrecked her own car* is ungrammatical because we don't use feminine pronoun forms like *her* to refer to masculine nouns like *nephew.*[7]

To prevent our grammar from producing sentences which are ungrammatical in the ways just mentioned, we need to specify certain syntactic features in the lexical entry of nouns, and we also need to specify certain contextual restrictions for verbs.

It is clear from the preceding discussion that there are at least five syntactic features which are needed in the marking of nouns:

**1.** All nouns are either **noncount** or **count.** That is, either they cannot take the cardinal numbers as determiners (**one stubbornness,* *one spinach*), or they can (*one idea, two rockets, three mares, four nephews*).

**2 a.** All noncount nouns are either **nonconcrete (abstract)** or **concrete.** For example, *stubborness* is an abstract noncount noun, since stubbornness is not an entity which can be seen, heard, smelled, tasted, or touched. *Spinach* is a concrete non-

---

[7] Note that her would not be interpreted as referring to nephew if the intensive pronoun own had been omitted. In my nephew wrecked her car, the pronoun her is interpreted as referring to someone not specified in the sentence.

count noun, a **mass** noun referring to something which can be apprehended by the senses.[8]

b.   All count nouns are either nonconcrete (abstract) or concrete. *Idea* is an abstract count noun; *rocket, mare,* and *nephew* are concrete count nouns.

**3.**   All concrete nouns are either **inanimate** or **animate.** For example, *rocket* is an inanimate noun, since it does not designate a living thing; *mare* and *nephew* are animate because they are designations for living things.

**4.**   All animate nouns are either **nonhuman** (*mare*) or **human** (*nephew*).

**5** a.   All nonconcrete nouns (*stubbornness, idea*) are syntactically **neuter.** (Syntactic gender is discussed in the next section of this chapter, the section on semantic matrices.)

b.   All concrete nouns are syntactically either neuter (*rocket*) or **feminine** (*mare*) or **masculine** (*nephew*).[9]

The following syntactic feature matrices illustrate various combinations of noun features:

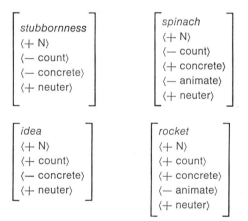

$$\begin{bmatrix} stubbornness \\ \langle + N \rangle \\ \langle - \text{count} \rangle \\ \langle - \text{concrete} \rangle \\ \langle + \text{neuter} \rangle \end{bmatrix} \quad \begin{bmatrix} spinach \\ \langle + N \rangle \\ \langle - \text{count} \rangle \\ \langle + \text{concrete} \rangle \\ \langle - \text{animate} \rangle \\ \langle + \text{neuter} \rangle \end{bmatrix}$$

$$\begin{bmatrix} idea \\ \langle + N \rangle \\ \langle + \text{count} \rangle \\ \langle - \text{concrete} \rangle \\ \langle + \text{neuter} \rangle \end{bmatrix} \quad \begin{bmatrix} rocket \\ \langle + N \rangle \\ \langle + \text{count} \rangle \\ \langle + \text{concrete} \rangle \\ \langle - \text{animate} \rangle \\ \langle + \text{neuter} \rangle \end{bmatrix}$$

[8] *Grammar books usually mention the distinction between "common" nouns and "proper" nouns. Proper nouns are defined as the names of unique places or things* (Harlem, The Hague, Hoover Dam, the Girl Scouts), *or unique animals* (Lassie, Man-O'-War), *or unique persons* (Abraham Lincoln, Bill Cosby). *It seems to us that proper nouns are inherently noncount. When a capitalized noun is pluralized or is modified by a cardinal number, an indefinite determiner, or a restrictive adjectival clause or phrase, the noun loses the idea of uniqueness that is supposed to characterize proper nouns. In other words, the noun is not a proper noun, even though it is capitalized. The following sentences include capitalized nouns which seem to be functioning as common nouns:* he writes about two Harlems, the Harlem of his youth and the Harlem of today; there is an Abraham Lincoln living down the street from us; the Louise who lives downstairs is my best friend. *These examples suggest that not all capitalized nouns refer to a unique entity. Proper nouns seem to be, by definition, noncount nouns.*

[9] *Some nouns have more than one syntactic gender.* Mare, *for example, is syntactically neuter as well as feminine, because we can use neuter pronouns* (it, its, itself) *to refer to the noun* mare: the mare broke its leg. *But for simplicity, and because we more commonly use the feminine pronouns* (she, her, hers, herself) *to refer to a* mare, *we will here mark the noun* mare *only as* ⟨+feminine⟩. *See the next section, on semantic matrices, for a fuller description of syntactic gender versus semantic gender.*

$$
\begin{bmatrix}
\textit{mare} \\
\langle + \text{N} \rangle \\
\langle + \text{count} \rangle \\
\langle + \text{concrete} \rangle \\
\langle + \text{animate} \rangle \\
\langle - \text{human} \rangle \\
\langle + \text{feminine} \rangle
\end{bmatrix}
\qquad
\begin{bmatrix}
\textit{nephew} \\
\langle + \text{N} \rangle \\
\langle + \text{count} \rangle \\
\langle + \text{concrete} \rangle \\
\langle + \text{animate} \rangle \\
\langle + \text{human} \rangle \\
\langle + \text{masculine} \rangle
\end{bmatrix}
$$

The symbol $\langle +\text{N} \rangle$ indicates that the word is a noun. The other plus signs indicate the presence of a given feature, while minus signs indicate the absence of the feature indicated. For example, $\langle + \text{count} \rangle$ means that the noun is a count noun, whereas $\langle - \text{count} \rangle$ indicates that the noun is noncount.

These feature matrices can be simplified in certain ways:

**1.** Since most nouns are neuter, we can conventionally omit the $\langle + \text{neuter} \rangle$ marking and simply mark the non-neuter nouns. Then masculine nouns can be marked $\langle + \text{masculine} \rangle$ and feminine nouns can be marked $\langle - \text{masculine.} \rangle$

**2.** Since all human nouns are animate and concrete, the $\langle + \text{animate} \rangle$ and $\langle + \text{concrete} \rangle$ markings can be conventionally omitted for all nouns for which the feature $\langle \text{human} \rangle$ is relevant. (Can the $\langle + \text{count} \rangle$ marking be eliminated also? Why or why not?)

**3.** Since all animate nouns are concrete, the $\langle + \text{concrete} \rangle$ marking can be conventionally omitted for all nouns for which the feature $\langle \text{animate} \rangle$ is relevant.

These conventions for marking nouns will allow considerable simplification of some of the matrices previously given. For example, the simplified matrices for *rocket* and *nephew* will be:

$$
\begin{bmatrix}
\textit{rocket} \\
\langle + \text{N} \rangle \\
\langle + \text{count} \rangle \\
\langle - \text{animate} \rangle
\end{bmatrix}
\qquad
\begin{bmatrix}
\textit{nephew} \\
\langle + \text{N} \rangle \\
\langle + \text{count} \rangle \\
\langle + \text{human} \rangle \\
\langle + \text{masculine} \rangle
\end{bmatrix}
$$

Different kinds of features need to be specified for other parts of speech. Linguists have discovered various similarities between verbs and adjectives. For example, some verbs and adjectives can occur in imperative sentences (see the next chapter for a discussion of imperatives), while other verbs and adjectives cannot occur in imperatives:

*drive* carefully
*open* the door
be *careful*
be *alert*

\**resemble* your mother
\**own* a car
\*be *short*
\*be *old*

The verbs and adjectives in the first group can be preceded by the auxiliary BE + ING, but the verbs and adjectives in the second group cannot:

she is driving carefully
I am opening the door
he is being careful
she is being alert

\*she is resembling her mother
\*he is owning a car
\*the woman is being short
\*the men were being old

The verbs and adjectives in the first group are sometimes called **action** words; they have the feature ⟨+ action⟩. In contrast, the verbs and adjectives in the second group are ⟨− action⟩.

These and various other similarities between verbs and adjectives suggest that together they form a larger class, a class of what we might call **verbals.** Thus verbs will have the features ⟨+ VB⟩ and ⟨+V⟩, while adjectives will have the features ⟨+ VB⟩ and ⟨− V⟩.

To see what other kinds of feature markings are needed for verbs, let us examine the following sentences:

\*he snored the night
\*he endorsed
\*he seemed slowly

In the first sentence, the intransitive verb *snore* has been used as if it were a transitive; we would have to change the noun phrase *the night* into an adverbial phrase (such as *all night long*) for the sentence to be grammatical. The second sentence uses a transitive verb, *endorse*, as if it were an intransitive; transitive verbs must have a following noun phrase, a direct object. The third sentence is ungrammatical because the linking verb *seem* must be followed by an adjectival or a noun phrase; it cannot be followed by a manner adverbial.

To prevent a grammar from generating ungrammatical sentences like these, we can mark verbs according to the syntactic context which must follow them. The feature $\langle +$ ____$\rangle$ for a verb indicates that the verb can occur with nothing following it in the verbal phrase; this marking is given to potential intransitive verbs. (Intransitive verbs may, of course, have adverbial modifiers, such as *loudly* in *he snored loudly.* But such adverbial modifiers are not obligatory.) Potential transitive verbs are given the feature $\langle +$ ____ NP$\rangle$ to indicate that they must have a following noun phrase. And most potential linking verbs are given the feature $\langle +$ ____ ADJ$\rangle$ to show that they must be followed by an adjectival, though some potential linking verbs (in particular, *become, stay,* and *remain*) will be marked $<+$ ____ $\left\{ {ADJ \atop NP} \right\} >$ to show that they can be followed by either an adjectival or a noun phrase (*he became sick, he became a doctor*). If verbs are marked with these **strict subcategorization features,** we no longer need to specify verb types in the phrase structure rules. We can replace the rule

$$VBP \rightarrow \left\{ {V_i \atop {V_t + NP \atop V_l + ADJ}} \right\}$$

with the rule

$$VBP \rightarrow V + \left( \left\{ {NP \atop ADJ} \right\} \right)$$

**Selectional restrictions** must also be marked for some verbs to indicate that the verb's subject and/or its direct object must have a certain syntactic feature. Let us look at the following ungrammatical sentences:

*the table snored
*the mare mumbled incoherently
*the lightning frightened the rocket
*the minister married the skunks
*the skunk married the minister

The verb *snore* takes an animate subject. We can indicate this requirement by marking the verb $\langle + \langle +$ animate$\rangle$ ____$\rangle$; this says that in the deep structure the verb must be preceded by a word which has the feature $\langle +$ animate$\rangle$. *Mumbled* takes a subject which is not merely animate, but human; this is indicated by marking *mumble* with the feature $\langle + \langle +$ human$\rangle$ ____$\rangle$. *Frighten* must be marked $\langle +$ ____ $\langle +$ animate$\rangle\rangle$ to indicate that it takes an animate object when it functions transitively. *Marry* must be marked ⟨+ _____ ⟨+ human⟩⟩ to indicate that it takes a human object when it functions transitively; it must be marked ⟨+ ⟨+ human⟩_____⟩ also, to indicate that it takes a human subject. (Regardless of whether the minister is being married *to* the skunk or *by* the skunk in the last example above, the sentence is ungrammatical.)

Thus the four verbs just discussed would have at least the following syntactic features:

$$\begin{bmatrix} snore \\ \langle + \text{VB} \rangle \\ \langle + \text{V} \rangle \\ \langle + \text{\_\_\_\_} \rangle \\ \langle + \langle + \text{animate} \rangle \rangle \end{bmatrix} \qquad \begin{bmatrix} mumble \\ \langle + \text{VB} \rangle \\ \langle + \text{V} \rangle \\ \langle + \text{\_\_\_\_ (NP)} \rangle \\ \langle + \langle + \text{human} \rangle \text{\_\_\_\_} \rangle \end{bmatrix}$$

$$\begin{bmatrix} frighten \\ \langle + \text{VB} \rangle \\ \langle + \text{V} \rangle \\ \langle + \text{\_\_\_\_ (NP)} \rangle \\ \langle + \text{\_\_\_\_} \langle + \text{animate} \rangle \text{\_\_\_\_} \rangle \end{bmatrix} \qquad \begin{bmatrix} marry \\ \langle + \text{VB} \rangle \\ \langle + \text{V} \rangle \\ \langle + \text{\_\_\_\_ (NP)} \rangle \\ \langle + \langle + \text{human} \rangle \text{\_\_\_\_} \rangle \\ \langle + \text{\_\_\_\_} \langle + \text{human} \rangle \rangle \end{bmatrix}$$

The feature ⟨+ _____ (NP)⟩ for the verb *mumble* means that the following NP is optional: the verb can function either intransitively (*he mumbled incoherently*) or transitively (*he mumbled his apologies*); as indicated, *frighten* and *marry* are likewise intransitive as well as transitive (*they frighten easily, they married*).

Thus far, linguists are not sure how the rules of a transformational grammar must operate to prevent the production of such ungrammatical sentences as those discussed here, or to designate such sentences as ungrammatical. But by determining some of the major syntactic features which must be indicated for words, they have at least made a solid beginning.

## SEMANTIC MATRICES

Semantic matrices indicate the meaning or meanings of a word. It is not possible to make a rigid distinction between syntactic features and semantic features because many features which are considered semantic have what seem to be syntactic consequences. For example, the following sentences probably do not seem sensible or logical:

she drank the spinach hurriedly
he navigated the waters of the Atlantic in his rocket
mares are chartreuse
my nephew is my sister's father

The first sentence seems odd because spinach is too solid to be drinkable. The second sentence is odd because rockets (the kind used for transportation) are designed for travel through space, not for ocean travel. Since mares are not chartreuse, except perhaps in works of literature or in toy shops, the third sentence does not seem normal either. And finally, one's nephew cannot be the father of one's sister.

We might attempt to indicate these restrictions by describing *spinach* as ⟨+ solid⟩; *rocket* as ⟨+ space travel⟩; *mare* as ⟨+ brown⟩ or whatever (the basic color possibilities for mares would have to be listed as alternative features); and *nephew* as ⟨+ child of one's brother or sister⟩. Since the feature ⟨+ solid⟩ applies to a number of nouns, the distinction between solids, liquids, and gases should probably be indicated by syntactic features. The other features just mentioned determine the way certain nouns are used in sentences, but they are not relevant to the subclassification of very many nouns. It is largely for this reason that such features are considered semantic rather than syntactic.

A semantic matrix would look something like the following matrix for *nephew*:

$$\begin{bmatrix} \textit{nephew} \\ \langle + \text{N} \rangle \\ \langle + \text{count} \rangle \\ \langle + \text{human} \rangle \\ \langle + \text{male} \rangle \\ \left\{ \begin{array}{l} \langle + \text{the child of one's brother or sister} \rangle \\ \langle + \text{the child of one's brother-in-law or sister-in-law} \rangle \\ \langle + \text{an illegitimate child} \rangle \end{array} \right\} \end{bmatrix}$$

*Nephew* is marked as ⟨+ N⟩, ⟨+ count⟩, and ⟨+ human⟩ in the semantic matrix as well as in the syntactic matrix; these features are part of the meaning of the word. However, the semantic feature ⟨+ male⟩ is not quite the same as the syntactic feature ⟨+ masculine⟩. (Sometimes there are other discrepancies between the basic syntactic and semantic features, too.) The syntactic gender of a noun is determined by observing what pronouns are normally used in referring to the noun: nouns referred to by *it, its,* and *itself* are considered syntactically neuter; nouns referred to by *he, him, his,* and *himself* are considered syntactically masculine; and nouns referred to by *she, her, hers,* and *herself* are considered syntactically feminine. (Nouns do not reveal any syntactic gender in their plural form, since plural nouns are referred to by *they, them, their, theirs,* and *themselves,* or by the first or second person plural pronouns.) It is true, of course, that most semantically neutral nouns are syntactically neuter, most male nouns are syntactically masculine, and most female nouns are feminine. But there are some exceptions:

> the old ship lost **its** way in the fog
> or
> the old ship lost **her** way in the fog

> the sun **itself** could not have defrosted her
> or
> the sun **himself** could not have defrosted her

> the hen abandoned **her** own chicks
> or
> the hen abandoned **its** own chicks

> the bull fell to **his** knees
> or
> the bull fell to **its** knees

*Ship* is semantically neutral but syntactically either neuter or feminine; *sun* is semantically neutral but syntactically neuter or masculine; *hen* is semantically female but syntactically feminine or neuter; and *bull* is semantically male but syntactically masculine or neuter.

Another possible discrepancy between semantic features and syntactic features is illustrated by the sentence *my dog Fido, who had really become a member of the family, got run over yesterday.* Here, the semantically nonhuman dog Fido is referred to by *who,* indicating that Fido is syntactically ⟨+ human⟩.

The most important way in which the semantic matrix for *nephew* differs from the usual dictionary entry is in what linguists call the "atomization" of meaning, the analysis of a word into its components of meaning. Instead of saying that a *nephew* is the *son* of one's brother or sister (or of one's brother-in-law or sister-in-law), we mark *nephew* as ⟨+ male⟩ and define nephew as the *child* of one's brother or sister. Thus instead of having a full semantic entry for the noun *niece,* we could somehow indicate that *niece* has the same features as nephew except that niece is ⟨− male⟩ rather than ⟨+ male⟩. There are, of course, other pairs related in this same way: *brother, sister; uncle, aunt; stallion, mare; bull, cow; rooster, hen;* and so forth. Somewhat similarly, *come* can be described as having the features of *go,* plus the feature ⟨+ direction toward⟩; the same relationship holds between *bring* and *take,* *buy* and *sell, learn* and *teach.* Of course this kind of economy in semantic descriptions may not be possible for large numbers of words, but many linguists are concerned with this aspect of semantics. They want to determine the components of the meanings of words in order to find out to what extent there is a universal semantics, a set of meanings common to all human languages.

## WORKING WITH THE LEXICON

**1.** Devise a feature matrix for each of the following nouns. Some nouns will have more than one distinct meaning and hence two (or more) submatrices (for example, the features of *justice* in *we should seek justice for all* are not the same as the features of *justice* in *there are nine justices on the Supreme Court.*)

| | | | |
|---|---|---|---|
| a. | child | f. | right | k. | gopher |
| b. | coffee | g. | news | l. | pants |
| c. | pool | h. | sinner | m. | ugliness |
| d. | dishwasher | i. | love | n. | physicist |
| e. | smirk | j. | television | o. | dust |

**2.** Reread footnote 8, page 92. Then decide whether each of the capitalized nouns in the following sentences is or is not functioning as a proper noun, a noun which names a unique entity.

a. I bought a Ford LTD
b. can you come over next Tuesday?
c. I've never met a Russian
d. the Russians are coming
e. are you visiting The Hague?
f. will you hand me some Kleenex?
g. he's in Christ Hospital
h. I shop at the Harding's grocery which is in Oshtemo
i. he drank three Budweisers
j. he thinks he's a Romeo
k. for once, the Americans are in agreement
l. she'll be arriving on May 8, 1978

**3.** Pronouns could be considered a special type of noun, and the rewrite rule for NP could then be simplified to read

$$NP \rightarrow (DET) + N + \left\{ \begin{matrix} SG \\ PL \end{matrix} \right\}$$

What strict subcategorization feature would pronouns need in order to keep the grammar from producing such nonsentences as *the she ran* and *the they played*? What about proper nouns?

**4.** Construct syntactic feature matrices for the personal pronouns.

**5.** In addition to the features discussed, are there any others you can think of that ought to be considered syntactic? Consider, for example, the following:

a. Those nouns which designate human beings (*man, actor, duchess, teacher*) are marked with the syntactic feature ⟨+ human⟩. However, there are many nouns which do not designate human beings but which nevertheless connote humanness: *personality, sorrow, widowhood*, for example. Similarly, other nouns which do not designate animals nevertheless connote animateness: *muscle, sinew, paw.* Should such connotations be considered syntactic and be indicated in syntactic feature matrices? Why or why not?

b. Should inanimate concrete nouns be further divided into ⟨− plant⟩ and ⟨+ plant⟩, the latter feature applying to *tree, bush, flower*, and so forth? Also, should words describing the "lower" animals (*flea, fly, worm*, and so forth) have some syntactic feature distinguishing them from the "higher" animals?

**6.** Metaphorical expressions (including metaphors, personifications, similes, and various other figurative devices) often seem to involve syntactic feature violation. That is, they couple two nouns having one or more contradictory syntactic features (*happiness is a warm puppy*) or they couple a noun with a verb or an adjective whose syntactic features are not entirely compatible with the syntactic features of the noun (*the incinerator burped, the incinerator had been greedy*). (Sometimes, of course, the metaphorical equation is less explicit, syntactically, as in *socialism has developed middle-aged spread*.)

In each of the following metaphorical expressions, a noun is coupled with another noun that has one or more contradictory syntactic features, or else a noun is coupled with a verb or adjective whose syntactic features are not entirely compatible with the syntactic features of the noun. Describe each of these "ungrammatical" couplings.

a.  "The mailbox bloomed"—John Woods, "The Murder"
b.  she chafed under the harness of housewifery
c.  "nobody,not even the rain,has such small hands"
    —E. E. Cummings, "somewhere i have never travelled"
d.  contentment is waffles on Sunday
e.  love is rainbow sweat in the early morning sun
f.  the sink has bad breath
g.  "the hours rise up putting off stars"
    —E. E. Cummings, "the hours rise up"
h.  I was appalled by the jello of his intellect
i.  "the blind sword of patriotism"—Norman Mailer,
    *Miami and the Siege of Chicago*
j.  "a hippo of a four-motor plane"—Mailer, *Miami*
k.  "pools of irritability were swabbed up immediately"
    —Mailer, *Miami*
l.  "the subtle rubber of his own [Richard Nixon's] credibility"
    —Mailer, *Miami*
m.  "sagging brassieres of flesh"—Mailer, *Miami*

**7.**  Write a paper discussing the structure of the metaphorical expressions in one of the following poems, explaining how the expressions group together to reveal the theme of the poem. Make use of what you have learned about the syntactic features of words, but write so that your paper can be understood by people with no formal linguistic background.

### *Vale* from Carthage (Spring, 1944)

I, now at Carthage. He, shot dead at Rome.
Shipmates last May. "And what if one of us,"
I asked last May, in fun, in gentleness,
"Wears doom, like dungarees, and doesn't know?"
5    He laughed, *"Not see Times Square again?"* The
        foam,
Feathering across that deck a year ago,
Swept those five words—like seeds—beyond the
        seas
        Into his future. There they grew like trees;
        And as he passed them there next spring, they
            laid
10        Upon his road of fire their sudden shade.
Though he had always scraped his mess-kit pure
And scrubbed redeemingly his barracks floor,
Though all his buttons glowed their ritual-hymn
Like cloudless moons to intercede for him,
15    No furlough fluttered from the sky. He will

Not see Times Square—he will not see—he will
Not see Times
                 change; at Carthage (while my friend,
Living those words at Rome, screamed in the end)
20          I saw an ancient Roman's tomb and read
*"Vale"* in stone. Here two wars mix their dead:
      Roman, my shipmate's dream walks hand in
          hand
      With yours tonight ("New York again" and
          "Rome"),
      Like widowed sisters bearing water home
25      On tired heads through hot Tunisian sand
      In good cool urns, and says, "I understand."
Roman, you'll see your Forum Square no more;
What's left but this to say of any war? [10]

—Peter Viereck

## Modern Love (I)

By this he knew she wept with waking eyes:
That, at his hand's light quiver by her head,
The strange low sobs that shook their common bed,
Were called into her with a sharp surprise,
5      And strangled mute, like little gaping snakes,
Dreadfully venomous to him. She lay
Stone-still, and the long darkness flowed away
With muffled pulses. Then, as midnight makes
Her giant heart of Memory and Tears
10    Drink the pale drug of silence, and so beat
Sleep's heavy measure, they from head to feet
Were moveless, looking through their dead black
      years,
By vain regret scrawled over the blank wall.
Like sculptured effigies they might be seen
15    Upon their marriage-tomb, the sword between;
Each wishing for the sword that severs all.[11]

—George Meredith

[10] *Peter Viereck,* Terror and Decorum: Poems: 1940–1948 *(New York: Charles Scrib-ner's Sons, 1949), p. 92.*
[11] *E. K. Brown and J. O. Bailey, eds.,* Victorian Poetry, *2nd ed. (New York: The Ronald Press Company, 1962), pp. 551–552.*

## Santa Claus

Somewhere on his travels the strange Child
Picked up with this overstuffed confidence man,
Affection's inverted thief, who climbs at night
Down chimneys, into dreams, with this world's
    goods.
5      Bringing all the benevolence of money,
He teaches the innocent to want, thus keeps
Our fat world rolling. His prescribed costume,
White flannel beard, red belly of cotton waste,
Conceals the thinness of essential hunger,
10    An appetite that feeds on satisfaction;
Or, pregnant with possessions, he brings forth
Vanity and the void. His name itself
Is corrupted, and even Saint Nicholas, in his turn,
Gives off a faint and reminiscent stench,
15    The merest soupçon, of brimstone and the pit.

Now, at the season when the Child is born
To suffer for the world, suffer the world,
His bloated Other, jovial satellite
And sycophant, makes his appearance also
20    In a glitter of goodies, in a rock candy glare.
Played at the better stores by bums, for money,
This annual savior of the economy
Speaks in the parables of the dollar sign:
Suffer the little children to come to Him.

25    At Easter, he's anonymous again,
Just one of the crowd lunching on Calvary.[12]

—Howard Nemerov

**8.** Should nouns be inserted into deep structure strings before verbs are inserted, or should verbs be inserted before nouns? When should adjectives be inserted? Discuss.

 FOR FURTHER EXPLORATION

Bruce L. Liles, *An Introductory Transformational Grammar*. Englewood Cliffs, N.J.: Prentice-Hall, 1971. Chapter 4, pp. 27–40. This chapter treats lexical features in much

---

[12] *Howard Nemerov*, The Next Room of the Dream *(Chicago: The University of Chicago Press, 1962), p. 5.*

the same way as they are treated here. An interesting complement to the present discussion. Fairly easy to understand.

D. Terence Langendoen, *The Study of Syntax: The Generative-Transformational Approach to the Structure of American English.* New York: Holt, Rinehart and Winston, Inc., 1969. Chapter 4, "The Nature of Semantics," pp. 34–51. Discusses semantic features and the method by which the meanings of individual words are combined to provide the meanings of larger units. Very interesting; readable.

Roderick A. Jacobs and Peter S. Rosenbaum, *English Transformational Grammar.* Waltham, Mass.: Blaisdell Publishing Company, 1968. Chapter 9, "Features, Lexical Items, and Deep Structures," pp. 59–69; pp. 92–93; pp. 153–155; p. 220. Discusses features of nouns, verbs, adjectives, pronouns, and WH words (words like *who, what, when*). Interesting and not difficult to understand.

Thomas G. Bever and Peter S. Rosenbaum, "Some Lexical Structures and their Empirical Validity," *Readings in English Transformational Grammar,* ed. Roderick A. Jacobs and Peter S. Rosenbaum. Waltham, Mass.: Ginn and Company, 1970, pp. 3–19. Discusses syntactic features and hierarchies of meaning. Of medium difficulty.

Noam Chomsky, *Aspects of the Theory of Syntax.* Cambridge, Mass.: M.I.T. Press, 1965. Discusses subcategorization and selectional rules and their place in a transformational grammar (pp. 90–105, 113–127, 148–160). Historically important, but very difficult reading; definitely not for beginners.

Owen Thomas, *Metaphor and Related Subjects.* New York: Random House, 1969. Presents a linguistic definition of metaphor and discusses the need for metaphor and the uses of metaphor. Easy to read.

# THE COMPONENTS OF
# A TRANSFORMATIONAL GRAMMAR:
# AN OVERVIEW

So far, we have examined only the syntactic component of a transformational grammar. The other components will not be discussed in detail, but we need to see how the syntactic component combines with the others if we are to fully understand how the syntactic component operates.

The major parts of a transformational grammar are these:

> Syntactic component
>> Base
>>> Phrase structure rules
>>> Lexicon
>> Transformational rules
> Semantic component
> Phonological component

In generating a sentence, first the phrase structure rules specify the underlying syntactic structure. The output of the phrase structure rules is a string of terminal symbols (a terminal string) such as

$$DET + N + SG + PRES + V_i + ADJ$$

Next, words are supplied from the lexicon:

the + man + SG + PRES + seem + honest

This string represents the deep structure of what ultimately becomes *the man seems honest*. (The word *honest* was not included in the simplified lexicon of our model grammar, but of course it is part of the total lexicon of English.)

In a complete grammar, a string would be sent to the semantic component for interpretation at this point instead of being immediately processed by the transformational rules. Linguists do not know precisely how to formulate the rules of the semantic component, but somehow this component combines the meanings for the individual words in a string (these meanings are provided in the lexicon) to provide an appropriate interpretation or interpretations for the sentence as a whole. For

the + man + SG + PRES + seem + honest

there would be at least two appropriate interpretations: "the man seems truthful" and "the man seems trustworthy." However, the semantic component probably should rule out the interpretation "the man seems chaste," since the "chaste" meaning of *honest* is usually applied only to women (and even so, this interpretation of *honest* is archaic; people no longer use the expression *she's an honest woman* in praising a woman's virtue).

After the semantic component has provided the meaning or meanings for a string, the string is modified by the transformational rules. Clearly the transformational rules must not change the meaning of a string, since one or more interpretations have already been provided by the semantic component. In the case of the string we have been working with, the first relevant transformation (T 3 in our model syntactic component) specifies PRES as ES because the subject is a singular noun, as the symbol SG indicates. Finally the affix transformation (T 5) and the word boundary transformation (T 6) operate to give

the # man + SG # seem + ES # honest

Now that the transformational rules have provided the surface structure, the string is ready for the phonological component, which specifies information essential in pronouncing the string. The basic pronunciation for each word is given in the lexicon, but the phonological component must provide the information essential in pronouncing the particular combinations of words that are specified by the transformational rules. One thing the phonological component must do is indicate how word affixes are to be pronounced in the given context. *Man +* *SG* is of course just *man;* the affix is not pronounced. But *seem + ES* is *seems* rather than *seem.* The phonological component will indicate that in this case the third singular ending, indicated by the symbol ES, will be pronounced with a /z/ sound. (In other cases ES might turn out to be /s/, as in *walks,* or /ɨz/, as in *kisses.*) Another thing the phonological component must do is specify stress, pitch, and juncture. For example, the syllable *hon-* in *the man seems honest* will normally receive greater stress than any other syllable in the sentence; also, *hon-* will be at a higher pitch level than any other syllable. If there is a major juncture (what we hear as a pause), that juncture will occur after *man,* separating the subject from the predicate; however, in a short sentence like *the man seems honest,* a speaker might not pause any longer between the subject and predicate than between any other two words or word groups. (Some other syllable besides *hon-* could, of course, receive the greatest stress and be at the highest pitch level. One might choose to stress *seems,* for example, in which case the major juncture would occur after *seems.*)

The phonological component's final output for a string is a rather complicated set of features and markings which provide the information essential for pronouncing the given sentence.

The following diagram shows the path that a sentence takes from the initial symbol S to the final phonetic representation:

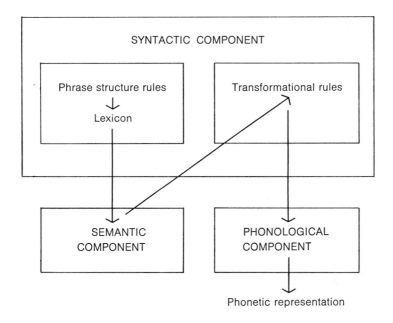

Phonetic representation

## THE WHY OF TRANSFORMATIONAL
## GRAMMAR: A COMPETENCE MODEL

The preceding sections of this chapter have undoubtedly given the impression that a transformational grammar is a device for producing sentences. Indeed, we have explicitly said this and quoted Chomsky to this effect. But Chomsky did not want to construct merely "a device of some sort for producing the sentences of the language under analysis." [13] When he said that a grammar should "generate" all the grammatical sequences of a language,[14] he apparently did not mean that the grammar should "produce" sentences in some mechanical way; rather, he meant that the grammar should be able to provide a description of the structure of all the sequences which a native speaker of the language would consider grammatical. As Chomsky explained in his 1965 book, *Aspects of the Theory of Syntax,* "by a generative grammar I mean simply a system of rules that in some explicit and well-defined way assigns structural

[13] *Chomsky,* Syntactic Structures, *p. 11.*
[14] *Chomsky,* Syntactic Structures, *p. 13.*

descriptions to sentences." [15] Not all generative grammars are transformational; that is, not all generative grammars have transformations that alter deep structures to produce surface structures.

Transformationalists insist that a transformational grammar is not a **performance model**: it is not a model of how a speaker perceives sentences (a perceptual model) or a model of how a speaker produces sentences (a speech production model). Thus a transformational grammar does not enable a speaker to either decode messages or encode them. Rather, it is a **competence model**: an attempt to describe a native speaker's ability to form grammatical sentences and to distinguish between grammatical and ungrammatical sentences or sequences.

Chomsky suggested that native speakers of English will consider the sentence *colorless green ideas sleep furiously* to be in some sense grammatical, but they will consider *furiously sleep ideas green colorless* to be ungrammatical.[16] We can even recognize degrees of grammaticality. Try, for example, to rank the following "sentences" from the least grammatical to the most grammatical:

> *the hippopotamus lapped up tenacity
> *hippopotamus the friend is my
> *the hippopotamus lapped up the capitalize

Probably all native speakers of English would agree that the second sentence is the least grammatical; the words are not in the right order. In the third sentence the words seem to be in the right order, but the verb *capitalize* is occupying the position of a noun. The first sentence seems most grammatical because the words are in the right order and no part of speech occurs in a position it could not normally fill; the problem with the first sentence is that the abstract noun *tenacity* occurs after a verb which requires a concrete object.

Clearly a grammar will have to be far more complex than the model syntactic component presented earlier in this chapter if it is to account for our grammatical **competence**, our ability to distinguish grammatical sequences from nongrammatical ones and to determine degrees of grammaticality. The section on the lexicon and the overview section should give some idea of how complex a grammar must be if it is to describe a language accurately and adequately.

---

[15] *Noam Chomsky,* Aspects of the Theory of Syntax *(Cambridge, Mass.: M.I.T. Press, 1965), p. 8. Chomsky continued by saying "Obviously every speaker of a language has mastered and internalized a generative grammar that expresses his knowledge of his language. This is not to say that he is aware of the rules of the grammar or even that he can become aware of them, or that his statements about his intuitive knowledge of the language are necessarily accurate."*
[16] *Chomsky,* Syntactic Structures, *p. 15.*

# 4

# TRANSFORMING THE BASIC SENTENCE: SOME SINGULARY TRANSFORMATIONS

The first major section of this chapter is concerned with transformations that are triggered by an element in the deep structure. The second major section is concerned with transformations that produce stylistic variants.

## TRANSFORMATIONS TRIGGERED BY
## A DEEP STRUCTURE ELEMENT

One of the things that prompted Noam Chomsky to formulate a new grammatical theory was his concern with apparently regular processes of sentence formation, processes which had been virtually ignored by the structuralists. Five of these processes are illustrated in the sets of sentences below. Try to determine how the sentences in each set are different in structure from the kinds of sentences produced by our first model grammar:

Jimmie will not like the tricycle
Frank has not broken his arm
Ebenezer is not wiggling his toes
Charles had not been weeding the garden

will Jimmie like the tricycle?
has Frank broken his arm?
is Ebenezer wiggling his toes?
had Charles been weeding the garden?

how will the janitor smoke a cigar?
when will the janitor smoke a cigar?
where will the janitor smoke a cigar?
why will the janitor smoke a cigar?

what will the janitor smoke?
who will the janitor smoke a cigar with?
who will smoke a cigar?
what cigar will the janitor smoke?
which cigar will the janitor smoke?
whose cigar will the janitor smoke?


Jim **will** cut the grass
Jim **has** cut the grass
Jim **is** cutting the grass
Jim **should** be cutting the grass


behave yourself
scrub the floor
close the door
be quiet


The sentences in the first group are obviously negatives. The sentences in the second group are yes/no questions. A yes/no question is a question which invites the answer "yes" or the answer "no" and which has a somewhat different word order than a declarative sentence. (Compare the yes/no question *is Ebenezer wiggling his toes?* with the echo question *Ebenezer is wiggling his toes?* The latter sentence has the same word order as a statement; the fact that the sentence is a question rather than a statement is signaled by a question mark when the sentence is written, or by the intonation pattern when the sentence is spoken.) The sentences in the third set are WH questions. A WH question asks for more information than a simple "yes" or "no" and begins with a so-called "WH word" —in Modern English, *who* (and its accusative form, *whom*), *what, which, whose, when, where, why, how,* or one of the related compounds ending in *-ever: whoever* (*whomever*), *whatever, whichever, whosoever, whenever,* and so forth.

The sentences in the fourth group are emphatic sentences; the first auxiliary word is stressed. The sentences in the last of the five groups are imperatives. Imperatives are interpreted as commands or requests and differ somewhat in structure from declarative sentences and questions.

The first major section of this chapter will be primarily concerned with the transformations whose results are illustrated in the five sets of sentences above: the **negative transformation,** the **question transformation,** the **WH-word transformation,** the **emphasis transformation,** and the **imperative transformation.** These transformations are all **singulary:** they involve only one "sentence," one deep structure S.

## THE NEGATIVE TRANSFORMATION

Make the following sentences negative by adding *not* (or *n't*) where appropriate:

> Bob should write a satire
> Bob has written a satire
> Bob is writing a satire
> Bob should have written a satire
> Bob had been writing a satire
> Bob should have been writing a satire

Now try to draw a generalization about where the *not* or *n't* is located in negative sentences having one or more auxiliary words.

We have not yet constructed present-day English negatives from sentences which have a tense marker as the only auxiliary element in the deep structure. Before doing so, let us examine the structure of this kind of negative in some sentences from Shakespeare's *Romeo and Juliet*: [1]

> Venus smiles not in a house of tears (IV. i. 8)
> he speaks not true (III. i. 175)
> Therefore he that cannot lick his fingers/goes not with me
>    (IV. ii. 7–8)
> you know/not how to choose a man (II. v. 38–39)
> You know not what you do (I. i. 62)
> I would [wish] I knew not why it should be slowed (IV. i. 16)

In each case, where does the *not* occur?

Now make the following sentences into Modern English negatives:

> Venus smiles
> you know how
> I knew why

How does the structure of these present-day English negatives differ from the structure of the negatives taken from *Romeo and*

---

[1] *These and subsequent examples from* Romeo and Juliet *were taken from* William Shakespeare: The Complete Works, *gen. ed. Alfred Harbage (Baltimore, Md.: Penguin Books, 1969). This Pelican edition of Shakespeare uses as its primary source for* Romeo and Juliet *the quarto version printed in 1599.*

*Juliet?* [2] In addition to the *not* or *n't,* what must be added to make these sentences into present-day English negatives?

There is a special case which must yet be mentioned. You have observed that if the deep structure auxiliary consists of only a tense marker, a form of DO (*does, do, did*) must be added to make a sentence negative: *Venus does not smile, you do not know how, I did not know why.* What happens, though, if a form of BE is the main verb and the tense marker is the only deep structure auxiliary element? To find out, make the following sentences into negatives:

> I am sleepy
> the circus is noisy
> the workmen are lazy
> Napoleon was powerful
> the gods were angry

Clearly, in standard English we do not add a form of DO to make such sentences negative: we add *not* or *n't* after the BE verb. That is, when a form of BE occurs as a main verb with no auxiliary word preceding it, the BE form is treated as if it were a first auxiliary word.[3]

---

[2] *In* Romeo and Juliet *(which was first printed in 1597), two kinds of negative constructions occur when there is only the tense marker in the deep structure: there are negatives which have* not *after the main verb, as in the examples here, and there are negatives constructed as in present-day English:* You say you do not know the lady's mind *(IV. i. 4). The same is true of yes/no questions and WH questions when there is only the tense marker in the deep structure: along with the older sentence patterns (which will be illustrated in the next two sections of this chapter), one finds questions constructed in the present-day English manner.*

[3] *We did not provide for BE as a main verb in our model grammar in Chapter 3. We wish now to suggest that in sentences where BE is the main verb and is followed by an adjectival, this BE verb does not add any meaning to the sentence: it serves merely to carry the tense marker and to perform the grammatical function of linking the subject with the adjectival. For example, we think that the meaning of* the lion is hungry *is fully expressed by the deep structure string* the + lion + SG + PRES + hungry; *a BE form must be present in the final sentence only because a verb is needed to carry the tense marker. If BE adds no meaning when it occurs as a main verb before adjectivals, then in such cases BE can be introduced by a transformation. First, however, we must revise our earlier rewrite rule for the verbal phrase (p. 80) to allow one to choose just ADJ:*

$$VBP \rightarrow \left\{ \begin{matrix} V \\ \\ ADJ \end{matrix} \ + \ \left( \left\{ \begin{matrix} NP \\ ADJ \end{matrix} \right\} \right) \right\}$$

*This rule allows for four possibilities: V (turn), V + NP (turn the pancakes), V + ADJ (turn blue), or just ADJ (blue). The choice of just ADJ will activate a transformation which introduces BE when the auxiliary (whatever it might be) is immediately followed by ADJ:*

AUX + ADJ $\Rightarrow$ AUX + BE + ADJ

*Thus the BE-addition transformation would convert*

the + man + SG + PAST + blue

*to*

the + man + SG + PAST + BE + blue

*We will not attempt to account formally for sentences in which BE is the main verb and is followed by a noun phrase (as in* lions are mammals*) or by an adverbial phrase (as in* the lion is in the zoo*).*

We have been discussing how affirmative *sentences* are regularly made into negatives, but actually all transformations operate on *strings of words and symbols* specified by the phrase structure rules and the lexicon, rather than on actual sentences. The negative transformation is no exception.

Clearly, a negative sentence like *Ebenezer is not wiggling his toes* does not have entirely the same meaning as its affirmative counterpart, *Ebenezer is wiggling his toes*. This difference in meaning must be specified by the phrase structure rules. Since a string has already been interpreted by the semantic component by the time it reaches the transformational rules, transformations cannot be allowed to change meaning. Thus the negative transformation must somehow be triggered by an optional element allowed for in a phrase structure rule. We will use the symbol NEG to trigger the negative transformation and will revise the first phrase structure rule to include this optional NEG:

$$S \rightarrow (NEG) + NP + VP$$

If we choose NEG, this symbol will guarantee a negative interpretation for the sentence and will automatically trigger the negative transformation.

This negative transformation might be formulated as follows:

$$NEG + X + \begin{bmatrix} T + M \\ T + HAVE_{AUX} \\ T + BE \\ T \end{bmatrix} + Y =\rangle X \# \begin{bmatrix} T + M \\ T + HAVE_{AUX} \\ T + BE \\ T \end{bmatrix} \# \ not + Y$$

In this and all other transformational rules, the symbols X and Y represent "anything" (and in some cases this "anything" might be null, or nothing at all); in other words, it is not important, here, to know what comes between NEG and the bracketed elements or what comes after the bracketed elements in the left-hand part of the rule, nor is it important to know what comes before the first word boundary symbol or what comes after *not* in the right-hand part of the rule. As will be explained below, the word boundary symbols are needed to trigger a DO transformation when there is no deep structure auxiliary element to carry the tense marker. The NEG symbol is present to trigger the negative transformation, as explained; it shows up as *not* in the transformed string. A negative contraction transformation is needed to reduce *not* to *n't* and to attach it to the appropriate word, after deleting the preceding word boundary symbol.[4]

The negative transformation says, in effect, that when the tense marker (any tense marker: PRES₁, ES, Ø, PAST_sg, PAST_pl, or PAST) is immediately followed by a modal, *not* is added after the modal; when the tense marker is immediately followed by a form of HAVE that is functioning as an auxiliary (a HAVE dominated by AUX), the *not* is added after the HAVE auxiliary form; or when the tense marker is immediately followed by a form of BE, the *not* is added after the BE form. When none of these conditions prevail (the rule is ordered from top to bottom, and all these preceding possibilities must be checked first), the *not* is added immediately after the tense marker; in this situation the *not* will immediately precede a V: an intransitive, transitive, or linking verb.

In other words, the negative transformation says that *not* goes after the first auxiliary word, if there *is* one (or more) in the deep structure; if there is no deep structure auxiliary word, *not* goes between the tense marker and the main verb. The one exception to this generalization is that when a form of BE occurs as a main verb with no preceding deep structure auxiliary word, the BE verb is treated as if it were a first auxiliary. Thus for example we will produce *he is not hungry* rather than *\*he doesn't be hungry,* since the latter is ungrammatical in standard English.[5]

To be sure you understand how the negative transformation operates, perform this transformation on the following strings:

NEG + he + SG + PAST + shall + write + a + satire + SG
NEG + he + SG + ES + HAVE + EN + write + a +
  satire + SG
NEG + he + SG + ES + BE + ING + write + a + satire + SG
NEG + he + SG + PAST + shall + HAVE + EN + write +
  a + satire + SG
NEG + he + SG + PAST + HAVE + EN + BE + ING +
  write + a + satire + SG
NEG + he + SG + PAST + shall + HAVE + EN + BE +
  ING + write + a + satire + SG

---

[4] *Although we will not formalize a negative contraction transformation, it should be noted that this contraction transformation would be obligatory in negative questions, when* not *is followed by a noun phrase. We would want to produce* didn't Bob write a satire?, isn't he going?, *and* hasn't he gone? *rather than* \*did not Bob write a satire?, is not he going?, *and* \*has not he gone?.

[5] *As presently formulated, our rule will not account for such sentences as* he hasn't any money *and* you haven't the time, *sentences in which there is no DO form despite the fact that the deep structure contains no auxiliary word. When a form of HAVE is the main verb and there is no preceding deep structure auxiliary word, we can sometimes negate the sentence either by treating the HAVE form as if it were a first auxiliary* (he hasn't any money) *or by treating it like an ordinary main verb and adding a form of DO* (he doesn't have any money). *Our model grammar allows for only the latter kind of construction.*

Your resulting strings should be as follows (note the addition of the word boundary symbols before the tense marker and after the first auxiliary word):

he + SG # PAST + shall # not + write + a + satire + SG

he + SG # ES + HAVE # not + EN + write + a +
satire + SG

he + SG # ES + BE # not + ING + write + a + satire + SG

he + SG # PAST + shall # not + HAVE + EN + write +
a + satire + SG

he + SG # PAST + HAVE # not + EN + BE + ING + write +
a + satire + SG

he + SG # PAST + shall # not + HAVE + EN + BE + ING +
write + a + satire + SG

After the affix transformation and the word boundary transformation have been applied, we will ultimately produce

he should not write a satire

he has not written a satire

he is not writing a satire

he should not have written a satire

he had not been writing a satire

he should not have been writing a satire

Now apply the negative transformation to the strings below, in which there is no auxiliary word. Don't forget the word boundary symbols.

NEG + he + SG + ES + play + the + cello + SG

NEG + they + PL + Ø + play + the + cello + SG

NEG + she + SG + PAST + play + the + cello + SG

After applying the negative transformation, you should have

he + SG # ES # not + play + the + cello + SG

they + PL # Ø # not + play + the + cello + SG

she + SG # PAST # not + play + the + cello + SG

This time the tense markers are not only preceded by a word boundary symbol, but are immediately followed by one. Obviously we need something else here: ES, Ø, and PAST cannot remain isolated between word boundaries. Sentences like *Venus does not smile, you do not know how,* and *I did not know why* (our earlier examples) suggest that DO needs to be added.

We will add DO after the tense marker rather than before, since the affix transformation is yet to be applied:

he + SG # ES + DO # not + play + the + cello + SG
they + PL # Ø + DO # not + play + the + cello + SG
she + SG # PAST + DO # not + play + the + cello + SG

The affix transformation will move the tense markers to a position following DO, and we will ultimately get

he does not play the cello
they do not play the cello
she did not play the cello

We can formulate the DO transformation as follows:

$$\# \ T \ \# \ \Rightarrow \ \# \ T + DO \ \#$$

This rule says that whenever a tense marker—any tense marker—is isolated between word boundary symbols, DO must be added after the tense marker. As we shall see, this rule is needed in formulating questions and certain kinds of emphatic sentences as well as in formulating negatives, whenever there is no deep structure auxiliary word.

It should be apparent that not all semantically negative sentences can be created or described by the negative transformation discussed here. For example, *Maria dislikes him* means essentially the same as *Maria does not like him,* but only the latter sentence can be described in terms of the negative transformation. (Indeed, the former sentence can yet undergo the negative transformation: *Maria does not dislike him.*) Somewhat similarly, the sentence *teenagers want to be independent* means basically the same as *teenagers do not want to be dependent,* yet again only the latter sentence can be accounted for by the negative transformation. The sentences *Joan is uncomfortable* and *Joan is not comfortable* are related to each other in essentially the same manner as the previous two sets of sentences. Do you think a grammar ought to be able to account for the similarity between pairs of sentences which are related the way these three pairs are? If so, can you offer any suggestions as to how a transformational grammar might account for this similarity?

Can you think of other kinds of negatives which are not accounted for by the negative transformation presented here?

## THE QUESTION TRANSFORMATION

Make the following sentences into yes/no questions, questions structured like *will Jimmie like the tricycle?* and *is Ebenezer wiggling his toes?*:

Bob should write a satire
Bob has written a satire
Bob is writing a satire
Bob should have written a satire
Bob had been writing a satire
Bob should have been writing a satire

Now draw a generalization about what element is moved to the front of the sentence.

The question transformation may be temporarily formulated as follows:

$$Q + X + \begin{bmatrix} T + M \\ T + HAVE_{AUX} \\ T + BE \\ T \end{bmatrix} + Y \Longrightarrow \# \begin{bmatrix} T + M \\ T + HAVE_{AUX} \\ T + BE \\ T \end{bmatrix} \# X + Y$$

Again X and Y are cover symbols representing "anything." Also, the word boundary symbols in the transformed string will again be needed to trigger the DO transformation when there is no deep structure auxiliary word. The Q (which should be allowed for by the first phrase structure rule, as we shall explain) insures that the semantic component will interpret the sentence as a question; the Q also serves to trigger the question transformation. The transformation says, in effect, that the tense marker (whatever it may be) and the first auxiliary word (modal, HAVE, or BE) are to be moved to the beginning of the sentence. If there is no auxiliary word, then just the tense marker will be moved. Again the one exception is that when a form of BE occurs as a main verb with no preceding deep structure auxiliary word, the BE verb is treated as if it were a first auxiliary. Thus we will produce, for example, *is he hungry?* rather than *\*does he be hungry?* [6]

[6] *The question transformation formulated here will not account for such sentences as* has he any money? *and* have you the time? *When a form of HAVE is the main verb and there is no preceding deep structure auxiliary word, we can sometimes make a yes/no question either by treating the HAVE form as if it were a first auxiliary (has he any money?) or by treating it like an ordinary main verb and adding DO (does he have any money?). Our model grammar allows for only the latter kind of construction.*

Try performing the question transformation on the following strings (don't forget the word boundary symbols), and then determine what sentences would ultimately result after the affix transformation and the word boundary transformation have been applied:

Q + she + SG + ES + must + bake + a + cake + SG
Q + he + SG + ES + HAVE + EN + mow + the + lawn + SG
Q + he + SG + ES + BE + ING + polish + the +
    teapot + SG
Q + they + PL + ES + HAVE + EN + BE + ING + snore
Q + they + PL + PAST + shall + HAVE + EN + BE +
    ING + sleep

Now let us apply the question transformation to the following strings, in which there is no auxiliary word:

Q + he + SG + ES + mow + the + lawn + SG
Q + they + PL + Ø + snore
Q + they + PAST + sleep

We should get the following results:

# ES # he + SG + mow + the + lawn + SG
# Ø # they + PL + snore
# PAST # they + PL + sleep

Once again, we have tense markers isolated between word boundary symbols, and the DO transformation must therefore be applied to add DO after the isolated tense marker:

# ES + DO # he + SG + mow + the + lawn + SG
# Ø + DO # they + PL + snore
# PAST + DO # they + PL + sleep

After the affix transformation and the word boundary transformation have been applied, we will ultimately get

does he mow the lawn?
do they snore?
did they sleep?

In Shakespeare's time, yes/no questions were not always structured in this way when there was no auxiliary word in the deep structure. For example, in *Romeo and Juliet* we find

Saw you him to-day? (I. i. 114)
Need you my help? (IV. iii. 6)
And weep ye now . . . ? (IV. v. 73)

How would these sentences read in present-day English? Assuming that this is the only structural difference between Middle English questions and present-day English questions, can you devise a question transformation for Middle English?

## THE *WH*-WORD TRANSFORMATION

A WH-word transformation is needed to produce WH questions, relative clauses, and certain types of nominalizations (the term "nominalization" will be explained in the next chapter). These three functions are illustrated in the following sentences:

> where was he living?
> I liked the place where he was living
> I knew where he was living

The first sentence is a WH question, a question beginning with a WH word rather than with an auxiliary. In the second sentence, the phrase *where he was living* is functioning adjectivally; it tells what place it was that I liked. In the third sentence, *where he was living* tells what I knew; it is the direct object of *knew.* In all three of these cases, the WH word *where* has been moved from its initial position at the end of the clause

he + SG + PAST + BE + ING + live + WHERE

to a position at the beginning of the clause. (In the deep structure, all adverbials—including the WH adverbs *when, where, why,* and *how*—are located at the end of the string.) [7]

We are concerned here with the WH-word transformation as it applies in the formation of WH questions. Since transformations cannot be allowed to change the basic meaning of a sentence, the WH word in a WH question must be present in the deep structure. That is, we cannot take a string like

Q + the + janitor + SG + ES + will + smoke + a +
cigar + SG + behind + the + furnace + SG

and replace the adverbial phrase *behind + the + furnace + SG* with the interrogative adverb *where* to produce *where will the janitor smoke a cigar?.* We cannot transformationally replace

---

[7] *We have already introduced into our deep structure strings several lexical items not provided in our simple model grammar. Here, for the first time, we are introducing a kind of element not previously introduced: adverbs. In our section on the adverb placement transformation, we will indicate how the first phrase structure rule can be expanded to allow for optional adverbials.*

a specific, definite adverbial phrase with an indefinite WH word because in so doing we would be changing the meaning of the sentence: the adverbial phrase *behind the furnace* is obviously not recoverable from the sentence *where will the janitor smoke a cigar?* If in generating WH questions we could replace specific adverbial phrases (or noun phrases or articles) with WH words, there would be numerous possible sources for *where* in *where will the janitor smoke a cigar?* Since transformations cannot be allowed to change the basic meaning of a string by deleting irrecoverable items (or by doing anything else to the string), in order to generate *where will the janitor smoke a cigar?* we must select *where* from the lexicon to function as an adverbial in the underlying string:

> Q + the + janitor + SG + ES + will + smoke + a +
> cigar + SG + WHERE

(The WH word WHERE is capitalized here to call attention to the fact that it will trigger the WH-word transformation.)

The lexical entry for the interrogative pronouns *who* and *what* must indicate that they (like all other pronouns) do not occur with a determiner: we say *who is there?*, not *\*the who is there?*. The lexical entry for the pronouns *who* and *what* must also indicate that they (like most other pronouns) are syntactically singular rather than plural: we say *who is there?* rather than *\*who are there?*, and *who is coming?* rather than *\*who are coming?*. It is true that sometimes *who* and *what* are followed by plural verb forms, as in *who are the culprits?* and *what are your preferences?*. In such cases as these, however, *who* and *what* are not the deep structure subjects; they are predicate nominatives in the deep structure. Thus the deep structures for these two examples are:

> Q + the + culprit + PL + PRES + BE + WHO
> Q + your + preference + PL + PRES + BE + WHAT

In the former case, the BE verb is made to agree with *culprits*; in the latter case, with *preferences.* (This means, of course, that the agreement transformations must precede the WH-word transformation.) Since *who* and *what* do not take determiners, they must have the subcategorization feature ⟨-DET _____⟩, and since they are not syntactically plural, they must be marked ⟨-_____PL⟩. Thus *who* or *what* can occur in a string if and only if the NP has been specified as N + SG. (Our revised rule for rewriting the NP

$$NP \rightarrow (DET) + N + \begin{Bmatrix} SG \\ PL \end{Bmatrix}$$

will allow for the exclusion of a determiner. See p. 100 for a discussion of this revised rule.)

In the lexicon, the syntactic matrices for the basic interrogative pronouns, articles, and adverbs might be represented as follows:

$$
\begin{bmatrix}
who \\
\langle + \text{N} \rangle \\
\langle + \text{pronoun} \rangle \\
\langle + \text{human} \rangle \\
\langle - \text{accusative} \rangle \\
\langle + \text{WH} \rangle \\
\langle - \text{DET} \underline{\quad} \rangle \\
\langle - \underline{\quad} \text{PL} \rangle
\end{bmatrix}
\qquad
\begin{bmatrix}
what \\
\langle + \text{N} \rangle \\
\langle + \text{pronoun} \rangle \\
\langle - \text{human} \rangle \\
\langle + \text{WH} \rangle \\
\langle - \text{DET} \underline{\quad} \rangle \\
\langle - \underline{\quad} \text{PL} \rangle
\end{bmatrix}
$$

$$
\begin{bmatrix}
what \\
\langle + \text{ART} \rangle \\
\langle - \text{DEF} \rangle \\
\langle + \text{WH} \rangle
\end{bmatrix}
\qquad
\begin{bmatrix}
which \\
\langle + \text{ART} \rangle \\
\langle + \text{DEF} \rangle \\
\langle + \text{WH} \rangle
\end{bmatrix}
\qquad
\begin{bmatrix}
whose \\
\langle + \text{ART} \rangle \\
\langle + \text{DEF} \rangle \\
\langle + \text{possessive} \rangle \\
\langle + \text{WH} \rangle
\end{bmatrix}
$$

$$
\begin{bmatrix}
when \\
\langle + \text{ADV} \rangle \\
\langle + \text{time} \rangle \\
\langle + \text{WH} \rangle
\end{bmatrix}
\quad
\begin{bmatrix}
where \\
\langle + \text{ADV} \rangle \\
\left\{ \begin{matrix} \langle + \text{location} \rangle \\ \langle + \text{direction} \rangle \end{matrix} \right\} \\
\langle + \text{WH} \rangle
\end{bmatrix}
\quad
\begin{bmatrix}
why \\
\langle + \text{ADV} \rangle \\
\langle + \text{reason} \rangle \\
\langle + \text{WH} \rangle
\end{bmatrix}
\quad
\begin{bmatrix}
how \\
\langle + \text{ADV} \rangle \\
\langle + \text{manner} \rangle \\
\langle + \text{WH} \rangle
\end{bmatrix}
$$

The $\langle - \text{accusative} \rangle$ marking for *who* indicates that *who* is the subject (or nominative) form rather than the object (or accusative) form: an accusative transformation will charge $\langle - \text{accusative} \rangle$ to $\langle + \text{accusative} \rangle$ when the form *whom* is needed.[8] The interrogative article *what* seems to be indefinite, in contrast to the definite interrogative article *which;* compare, for example, *what girl would wear such an outlandish outfit?* with *which girl would wear such an outlandish outfit?*

Let us now produce some WH questions, working from the following strings:

Q + the + janitor + SG + ES + will + smoke + a + cigar + SG + HOW

Q + the + janitor + SG + ES + will + smoke + a + cigar + SG + WHEN

---

[8] *Now that we have introduced the notion of semantic features, we can revise our accusative transformation (our first transformational rule) so that all object pronoun forms (me, him, her, us, them, whom, and their compounds) will be derived from subject forms by changing the subject form's $\langle - \text{accusative} \rangle$ marking to $\langle + \text{accusative} \rangle$.*

Q + the + janitor + SG + ES + will + smoke + a +
cigar + SG + WHERE
Q + the + janitor + SG + ES + will + smoke + a +
cigar + SG + WHY

The WH-word transformation moves the WH word to the front of the string, uncapitalizing it in the process:

how + Q + the + janitor + SG + ES + will + smoke +
a + cigar + SG
when + Q + the + janitor + SG + ES + will + smoke +
a + cigar + SG
where + Q + the + janitor + SG + ES + will + smoke +
a + cigar + SG
why + Q + the + janitor + SG + ES + will + smoke +
a + cigar + SG

The question transformation will have to be reformulated to move the tense marker plus the first auxiliary word (if there is one) to a position immediately *following* any WH constituent occurring at the beginning of a string. (When there is no WH constituent, the question transformation will move the tense marker and first auxiliary word to the very front of the string, as before.) The symbol Q will be eliminated in the process, as before, and word boundaries will be added before the tense marker and after the first auxiliary word. After performing the question transformation on the preceding strings, we will get:

how # ES + will # the + janitor + SG + smoke + a +
cigar + SG
when # ES + will # the + janitor + SG + smoke + a +
cigar + SG
where # ES + will # the + janitor + SG + smoke + a +
cigar + SG
why # ES + will # the + janitor + SG + smoke + a +
cigar + SG

The affix transformation and the word boundary transformation must yet be applied to give, ultimately,

how will the janitor smoke a cigar?
when will the janitor smoke a cigar?
where will the janitor smoke a cigar?
why will the janitor smoke a cigar?

As explained previously, the interrogative pronouns *who* and *what* must always be followed by SG in the deep structure. The WH-word transformation moves this SG to the front of a string

along with the *who* or *what.* The SG will be deleted by a phonological rule, not specified here. When the WH word is one of
the WH articles *what, which,* or *whose,* the WH-word transformation must move the following noun and number indicator
as well as the WH article itself. The following strings illustrate
these situations:

Q + WHO + SG + ES + will + smoke + a + cigar + SG
Q + the + janitor + SG + ES + will + smoke + WHAT + SG
Q + the + janitor + SG + ES + will + smoke + a +
  cigar + SG + with + WHO + SG

Q + the + janitor + SG + ES + will + smoke + WHAT +
  cigar + SG
Q + the + janitor + SG + ES + will + smoke + WHICH +
  cigar + SG
Q + the + janitor + SG + ES + will + smoke + WHOSE +
  cigar + PL

The WH-word transformation will convert these strings into

who + SG + Q + ES + will + smoke + a + cigar + SG
what + SG + Q + the + janitor + SG + ES + will + smoke
who + SG + Q + the + janitor + SG + ES + will +
  smoke + a + cigar + SG + with

what + cigar + SG + Q + the + janitor + SG + ES +
  will + smoke
which + cigar + SG + Q + the + janitor + SG + ES +
  will + smoke
whose + cigar + PL + Q + the + janitor + SG + ES +
  will + smoke

Now the question transformation moves the tense marker, ES,
plus the first (and only) auxiliary word to a position immediately
following the WH constituent. Q is eliminated in the process,
and word boundaries are added before the tense marker and
after the first auxiliary:

who + SG # ES + will # smoke + a + cigar + SG
what + SG # ES + will # the + janitor + SG + smoke
who + SG # ES + will # the + janitor + SG + smoke +
  a + cigar + SG + with
what + cigar + SG # ES + will # the + janitor + SG + smoke
which + cigar + SG # ES + will # the + janitor + SG + smoke
whose + cigar + PL # ES + will # the + janitor + SG + smoke

Finally we will get

who will smoke a cigar?
what will the janitor smoke?
who will the janitor smoke a cigar with?
what cigar will the janitor smoke?
which cigar will the janitor smoke?
whose cigars will the janitor smoke?

In formal English, *with* in the third sentence would have to be moved to the front of the underlying string and *who* would have to be converted to *whom* by an accusative transformation (see footnote 8, Chapter 4) to give *with whom will the janitor smoke a cigar.*

The movement of WH words is rather complicated, as we have seen. If the WH word is an adverb, just the WH word is moved to the front of the string; if the WH word is *who* or *what,* the following SG must also be moved to the front; and if the WH word is an article, the following noun and number indicator must both be moved along with the WH word. But though all these various situations must be accounted for by the WH-word transformation, the transformation itself can be formulated rather simply. Whenever a noun phrase contains a WH article or noun, the entire noun phrase acquires the $\langle + \text{WH} \rangle$ feature of that WH word. Therefore the WH-word transformation can be formulated as

$$X + \langle + \text{WH} \rangle + Y \implies \langle + \text{WH} \rangle + X + Y$$

This transformation will move any WH-word constituent—either adverb or noun phrase—to the front of its string.

This rule illustrates the generative power of a transformational grammar: with a simple generalization, it is able to account for a complex set of phenomena.

The question transformation must now be reformulated so that it will move the tense marker and the first auxiliary word (if there is one) to the front of a string, except when the string begins with a WH constituent; in this case the tense marker and first auxiliary word will be moved to a position immediately following the WH constituent. The question transformation will thus read as follows:

$$(\langle + \text{WH} \rangle) + Q + X + \begin{bmatrix} T + M \\ T + \text{HAVE}_{\text{AUX}} \\ T + \text{BE} \\ T \end{bmatrix} + Y \implies$$

$$(\langle + \text{WH} \rangle) \, \# \begin{bmatrix} T + M \\ T + \text{HAVE}_{\text{AUX}} \\ T + \text{BE} \\ T \end{bmatrix} \# X + Y$$

The parentheses around the ⟨+ WH⟩ constituent indicate its optionality.

As presently formulated, the question transformation creates difficulties in the derivation of WH questions when the WH word is the deep structure subject, or part of it, and there is no deep structure auxiliary word. Consider, for example, the following strings:

Q + WHO + SG + PRES + sing
Q + WHAT + SG + PAST + happen
Q + WHICH + boy + SG + PAST + fall

The question transformation will add word boundaries before and after the tense marker, thus calling the DO transformation into operation. Ultimately, we will get the following sentences:

who does sing?
what did happen?
which boy did fall?

The DO form in these questions makes them emphatic. The simple WH questions corresponding to the above strings would be *who sings?*, *what happened?*, and *which boy fell?* A more complete and more precise grammar would have to allow for the latter outputs, and only these, from the strings above. Can you suggest a way in which our present grammar could be modified to do this?

Returning from symbols and rules to sentences, let us briefly look at some WH questions from *Romeo and Juliet:*

How stands your disposition to be married? (I. iii. 65)
wherefore weep I then? (III. ii. 107)
Why call you for a sword? (I. i. 74)
What say you? (I. iii. 79)
Whence come you? (III. iii. 78)

What do the WH words *wherefore* and *whence* mean? What does *stands* mean, in this context? How would these questions be structured in present-day English?

## THE EMPHASIS TRANSFORMATION

The emphasis transformation assigns primary stress to the first auxiliary word in a sentence; if there is no auxiliary word, the emphasis transformation calls the DO transformation into operation, thus providing a form of DO to carry the stress. For example, one might answer the question *has Jim cut their grass?* by saying

> no, but he **will** cut it, tomorrow
> yes, he **has** cut it
> he **is** cutting it, right now
> no, but he **should** be cutting it
> no, but he **does** cut it, sometimes
> no, but he **did** trim the hedges

The bold type here indicates that the bold-faced word receives greater stress than any other syllable in the sentence.

The emphasis transformation can be formulated as follows:

$$EMP + X + \begin{bmatrix} T + M \\ T + HAVE_{AUX} \\ T + BE \\ T \end{bmatrix} + Y =\rangle$$

$$X \# \begin{bmatrix} T + M \\ T + HAVE_{AUX} \\ T + BE \\ T \end{bmatrix} \# STRESS\ 1 + Y$$

The emphasis transformation is triggered by EMP, an optional element allowed for by the first phrase structure rule. The symbol *STRESS 1* stands for primary stress, which will be assigned to the preceding auxiliary word. When there is no deep structure auxiliary word or no BE form functioning as main verb without a preceding deep structure auxiliary, the emphasis transformation isolates the tense marker between word boundary symbols to trigger the DO transformation; in this case primary stress will be added to the DO form. (It is not logical to have a word boundary symbol before STRESS 1 in this transformation, because the stress is assigned to the preceding auxiliary; in this simple grammar, however, we see no easy way of avoiding this undesirable consequence.)

It is, of course, possible to emphasize any word in a sentence:

> **Jim** has cut their grass (Ralph didn't cut it)
> Jim **has** cut their grass (so you can stop reminding him to do it)
> Jim has **cut** their grass (but he hasn't watered it)
> Jim has cut **their** grass (but he hasn't cut ours)
> Jim has cut their **grass** (but he hasn't cut the weeds too)

As formulated here, the emphasis transformation accounts for the stress in only the second of these sentences: *Jim **has** cut their grass.*

## THE IMPERATIVE TRANSFORMATION

At the beginning of this chapter, we gave the following examples of imperatives:

> behave yourself
> scrub the floor
> close the door
> be quiet

What does the deep structure subject of these sentences seem to be? The answer seems to us an obvious one: the understood subject is *you.* From a speaker's vantage point, the person being addressed is a *you.* Thus we would not command or request someone to do something by saying

> *behave myself
> *behave himself
> *behave herself
> *behave itself
> *behave ourselves
> *behave themselves

Rather, we would say

> behave yourself
> or
> behave yourselves

The existence of *you* as the deep structure subject of imperatives is verified by the fact that *yourself* and *yourselves* are the only reflexive pronouns which can occur in imperatives: without *you* as the underlying subject, *yourself* or *yourselves* could not function as the direct object.

Sentences like the following provide further evidence that *you* is the deep subject of imperatives:

> behave yourself, will you?
> behave yourself, won't you?
> behave yourself, would you?
>
> scrub the floor, will you?
> scrub the floor, won't you?
> scrub the floor, would you?

The pronoun *you* would not occur in these "tag" questions if it were not the subject in the deep structure.

Many tranformationalists consider tag questions like these to be evidence that imperatives also have an underlying *will* as auxiliary. Thus the imperative transformation can be said to operate on a string having *you* as the subject and *will* as an auxiliary (perhaps the only auxiliary, perhaps not). The imperative transformation can be formulated as follows:

$$\text{IMP} + \text{you} + \text{T} + \text{will} + \begin{bmatrix} \text{BE} \\ \text{V} \end{bmatrix} + \text{X} \Rightarrow (\text{you}) + \begin{bmatrix} \text{BE} \\ \text{V} \end{bmatrix} + \text{X}$$

As formulated here, the imperative transformation (triggered by an optional IMP element provided in the first phrase structure rule) will produce imperatives with or without *you* in the surface structure:

> you behave yourself
> behave yourself
> you scrub the floor
> scrub the floor

In addition to imperatives like these, where the first verb phrase element is a V (an intransitive, transitive, or linking verb other than BE), this transformation will also produce imperatives in which the verb phrase element is the word *be,* the base form of the BE verb:

> be quiet
> be a man
> be there
> be working on it
> be thinking about it

In the first three sentences, *be* is a main verb; in the last two, be is an auxiliary.

Obviously we do not always use imperative structures like these exemplified here in commanding or requesting someone to do something. We can say *will you please behave?, won't you behave, please?, I expect you to behave yourself, you must behave, you've got to behave, you'd better behave,* and so forth; all these sentences, said with appropriate intonation, would be interpreted as requests or (in most cases more likely) as commands. Alternatively, we might say just *you will behave,* perhaps stressing one of the words to indicate that we mean the sentence as a command. With appropriate intonation, the question *will you behave?* could also be interpreted as a command. Still another possibility would be to use a sentence which, in transformational terminology, has undergone both an imperative transformation and a tag question transformation: *behave yourself, will you? behave yourself, won't you?, behave yourself, would you?* (In the second example, the tag has obviously undergone a negative transformation.) Clearly, then, the imperative transformation will not account for all the kinds of structures one might use in making requests or giving commands.

Earlier, we revised our first phrase structure rule to include the optional symbol NEG, which will trigger the negative transformation. However, we have not yet formally revised this rule to allow for Q, which will trigger the question transformation; to allow for EMP, which will trigger the emphasis transformation; or to allow for IMP, which will trigger the imperative transformation. It should be fairly obvious that a sentence cannot simultaneously be structured as a question and as an imperative, so our rule must prevent us from choosing both Q and IMP. But we should be able to choose EMP and NEG and Q all together, since there certainly are emphatic negative questions:

> **won't** you go with me?
> **aren't** you done yet?
> **hasn't** he left?
> **didn't** they want it?

There are also emphatic imperatives, negative imperatives, and emphatic negative imperatives:

> **be** a fool
> **do** it

> don't be a fool
> don't do it

> **don't** you do it
> **don't** give up the ship

Therefore we ought also to be able to choose EMP and NEG and IMP all together. However, we will not account for negative imperatives (or emphatic negative imperatives) in our revised rule, because the transformational rules needed to generate negative imperatives would be rather complicated. Thus we will revise our first phrase structure rule to read

$$S \rightarrow (EMP) + \begin{Bmatrix} (NEG) + (Q) \\ (IMP) \end{Bmatrix} + NP + VP$$

WORKING WITH TRANSFORMATIONS
TRIGGERED BY A DEEP STRUCTURE
ELEMENT

**1.** Transform the following strings into questions structured like the examples from *Romeo and Juliet.* Then transform these same strings into present-day English questions.

    a.   Q + he + SG + ES + sleep + fitfully
    b.   Q + they + PL + Ø + stand + there
    c.   Q + he + SG + PAST + kill + the + rabbit + SG +
        yesterday

    d.   Q + WHO + SG + ES + sleep + fitfully
    e.   Q + he + SG + ES + sleep + HOW
    f.   Q + they + PL + Ø + stand + WHERE

    g.   Q + he + SG + PAST + kill + WHAT + SG + yesterday
    h.   Q + he + SG + PAST + kill + the + rabbit + SG +
        WHEN

**2 a.** Make the following sentences into negatives. In each case, where does the *not* or *n't* go? Is there any deep structure auxiliary word or words preceding the *not* or *n't,* or do you have to add a form of DO before the *not* or *n't?*

           he ought to go
           he used to go
           he is going to go
           he is supposed to go
           he had better go
           he has to go
           he has got to go

    b.   Make the same sentences into yes/no questions. Are the auxiliary elements you move to the front of the sentences the same ones that preceded *not* or *n't* in the negatives just formulated? Do you add a form of DO to the same sentences as previously?

    c.   Do you now think we should expand the auxiliary to include any of the elements below? If so, which one or ones? Before deciding, refer to exercises 4 and 5, Chapter 3, pp. 77–78.

ought + to
used + to
BE + going + to
BE + supposed + to
had + better
HAVE + to
HAVE + got + to

3. The examples below indicate that strings containing certain "preverbs" cannot undergo the negative transformation. We say

$$
he \begin{Bmatrix} barely \\ scarcely \\ rarely \\ seldom \end{Bmatrix} \text{knew what he was doing}
$$

but not (at least not in formal standard English)

$$
he\ didn't \begin{Bmatrix} barely \\ scarcely \\ rarely \\ seldom \end{Bmatrix} \text{know what he was doing}
$$

Why do you suppose sentences with such preverbs do not undergo the negative transformation in formal standard English? Is *he didn't* **hardly** *know what he was doing* acceptable in formal standard English?

4. Does *I don't think he's going to leave* mean the same as *I think he isn't going to leave*? What about *I don't think I'm going to go* versus *I think I'm not going to go*? Should a grammar account for the similarity between such pairs of sentences? How might a transformational grammar account for this similarity?

5. Should a grammar allow for such negative sentences as the following, in which the subject occurs between a first auxiliary and the word *not*? Discuss.

has he not left yet?
is he not going?
did he not do it?

6. Judging from the following sets, how can we negate sentences that include either the determiner word *some* or the prefix *some-*?

Sally felt some pain
Sally didn't feel any pain
Sally felt no pain

Roger loves somebody
Roger doesn't love anybody
Roger loves nobody

Francine remembered something about him
Francine didn't remember anything about him
Francine remembered nothing about him

that path leads somewhere
that path doesn't lead anywhere
that path leads nowhere

**7.** Can the sentence *the scout leader expects some of the girls to go to camp* be negated in both of the following ways? If so, why? If not, why not?

the scout leader doesn't expect some of the girls to go to camp
the scout leader doesn't expect any of the girls to go to camp

**8.** In Robert Frost's "The Death of the Hired Man," Mary defines "home" by saying

"I should have called it
Something you somehow haven't to deserve"

Does the phrase *haven't to deserve* sound ungrammatical to you? What might account for its occurrence in this line from "The Death of the Hired Man"?

**9.** Do some of the sentences below seem less acceptable to you than the others? If so, why do you suppose they seem less acceptable?

Roger hasn't any money
Roger hasn't a friend in the world
Roger hasn't a chance
Roger hasn't a dime
Roger hasn't the money
Roger hasn't the time
Roger hasn't bronchitis
Roger hadn't acne

**10.** How might we explain the generation of such WH questions as the following:

how many roads must a man walk down?
how far does he have to go?
how long will it take?
how much will it cost?
how deep is the ocean?
how important is it?


**11.** How might we explain the generation of such WH exclamations as the following:

what a mess you've made!
what a bore he is!


how tired I am!
how thin she is!
how expensive this roast is!


**12.** Imperatives beginning with *be not* were common in earlier English, as the following examples from the King James Bible illustrate:

be not afraid (Matt. 14:27)
Be not wise in your own conceits (Rom. 12:16)
Be not hasty in thy spirit to be angry (Eccles. 7:9)
Be not righteous overmuch (Eccles. 7:16)
Be not overmuch wicked (Eccles. 7:17)


What would be the present-day English equivalents of these imperatives?


**13.** The following is a stanza from Gerard Manley Hopkins' "The Loss of the Eurydice." The speaker imagines that people are saying to God

"And the prayer thou hearst me making
Have, at the awful overtaking,
    Heard, have heard and granted
Grace that day grace was wanted." [9]


[9] W. H. Gardner, ed., Poems and Prose of Gerard Manley Hopkins *(Baltimore, Md.: Penguin Books, 1953), p. 37.*

Try to rephrase this stanza in your own words. Is *have heard* an imperative? (If so, it is not accounted for by the imperative transformation as formulated here. Should it be?)

**14.** What poetic function is performed by the imperatives in the following poem?

### A Poem

Another man has died.
Give away his clothing to relatives.
Lying in wait beneath the oil furnace.
Under the cellar steps
5    Cowering from sight behind the
shower curtain.
Give his money away,
To the casketmaker;
To the priest;
10   To the garbageman;
To the slut in his bedroom.
Sell his house and his land.
To the church . . . looks good on
the record book.
15   Sell his children into slavery,
Claim his wife;
Fire up the ovens for his body,
And bury his soul in the ashes.[10]

—Charles Franklin

**15.** Do the sentences in the following sets seem to be requests, commands, or neither? Can they be accounted for by the imperative transformation? Should they be? Discuss.

nobody move
none of you move

everybody get out
everyone of you get out

somebody turn out the lights
someone among you turn out the lights

let's look at these sentences
let's get a pizza
let's go swimming

God help us
God save the king

[10] *Stephen M. Joseph, ed.,* The Me Nobody Knows: Children's Voices from the Ghetto *(New York: Avon Books, 1969), p. 140.*

# TRANSFORMATIONS PRODUCING
# STYLISTIC VARIANTS

We have mentioned several times the fact that transformations cannot be allowed to change the basic meaning of a string because the semantic component will already have assigned one or ₍more interpretations to the string before the string reaches the transformational rules. It seems desirable, however, to allow transformations to determine what we might call the **surface meaning** of sentences. For example, we would say that *the picture was painted by a new student* has the same basic meaning as its active counterpart, *a new student painted the picture;* therefore the two sentences ought to have the same deep structure. The surface structure difference would then be accounted for by an optional passive transformation.

Transformations which determine surface structure often focus attention on some specific element of a sentence. For example, *what the mongoose ate was the cobra* means basically the same as *the mongoose ate the cobra,* but *the cobra* receives emphatic focus only in the former sentence. There is also another difference in surface meaning: the first sentence presupposes that the mongoose ate something, whereas the second involves no such presupposition. The sentence *what ate the cobra was the mongoose* has the reverse focus and presupposition: *the mongoose* now receives emphatic focus, and the presupposition is that something ate the cobra.

This second major section of Chapter 4 will be concerned with five singulary transformations that determine the surface meaning of sentences: the **passive transformation**, the **WHAT-cleft transformation**, the **IT-cleft transformation**, the **THERE transformation**, and the **adverb placement transformation**. These transformations are all optional.

## THE PASSIVE TRANSFORMATION

The following two passages describe the same historical events but are somewhat different in style: [11]

---

[11] *The idea for this comparison comes from Richard Ohmann, "Mentalism in the Study of Literary Language." In* Proceedings of the Conference on Language and Language Behavior, *ed. Eric M. Zale (New York: Appleton-Century-Crofts, 1968), pp. 191–195.*

I

The expulsion of the daemons from the bodies of
those unhappy persons whom they had been
permitted to torment was considered as a signal
though ordinary triumph of religion, and is
repeatedly alleged by the ancient apologists as the
most convincing evidence of the truth of
Christianity. The awful ceremony was usually
performed in a public manner, and in the presence
of a great number of spectators; the patient was
relieved by the power or skill of the exorcist,
and the vanquished daemon was heard to confess
that he was one of the fabled gods of antiquity,
who had impiously usurped the adoration of
mankind. But the miraculous cure of diseases of
the most inveterate or even preternatural kind can
no longer occasion any surprise, when we recollect
that in the days of Irenaeus, about the end of the
second century, the resurrection of the dead was
very far from being esteemed an uncommon event;
that the miracle was frequently performed on
necessary occasions, by great fasting and the joint
supplication of the church of the place, and that
the persons thus restored to their prayers had lived
afterwards among them many years.

II

The early Christians considered as a signal though
ordinary triumph of religion the expulsion of the
daemons from the bodies of those unhappy
persons whom God had permitted them to torment,
and the ancient apologists repeatedly allege this
expulsion to be the most convincing evidence of
the truth of Christianity. The early Christians usually
performed the awful ceremony in a public manner,
and in the presence of a great number of
spectators; the power or skill of the exorcist
relieved the patient, and the spectators heard the
vanquished daemon confess that he was one of
the fabled gods of antiquity, who had impiously
usurped the adoration of mankind. But the
miraculous cure of diseases of the most inveterate
or even preternatural kind can no longer occasion
any surprise, when we recollect that in the days of
Irenaeus, about the end of the second century,

20          people did not consider the resurrection of the
            dead an uncommon event; that they frequently
            performed the miracle on necessary occasions by
            great fasting and the joint supplication of the
            church of the place, and that the persons they thus
            restored to their prayers had lived afterwards
25          among them many years.

Which of these versions do you like better? Which is easier to
understand? In which version does the style seem more appropriate to the subject?

As you probably realized, many of the verbal phrases in the
first version are passive. To see what the passive transformation does, let us compare the pairs of sentences below. The
first sentence in each pair is active and the second is its passive counterpart:

the roaches eat the crackers
the crackers are eaten by the roaches

the roaches ate the crackers
the crackers were eaten by the roaches

the roaches will eat the crackers
the crackers will be eaten by the roaches

the roaches have eaten the crackers
the crackers have been eaten by the roaches

the roaches are eating the crackers
the crackers are being eaten by the roaches

the roaches will have eaten the crackers
the crackers will have been eaten by the roaches

In the active sentences, *the roaches* is the subject; in the passive sentences, *the roaches* occurs at the end of the sentence,
with *by* before it: *by the roaches. The crackers* occurs as the
direct object of the verb in the active sentences; in the passive
sentences, *the crackers* occurs as the subject. In each case,
the verbal phrase is different, too: in the passive sentences,
the main verb is always in the past participle form (*eaten*) and
this main verb is always preceded by a form of BE, a form
which is not present in the active sentences. In the active sentences, past participle verb forms are preceded by a form of
HAVE, and BE auxiliaries are followed by a present participle

verb. (Note that the passive counterpart of *are eating* is *are be-ing eaten;* the active phrase has one BE form and the passive phrase has two. Somewhat similarly, the active phrase *have eaten* has one past participle, whereas its passive counterpart has two: *have been eaten*.)

The passive transformation, which accounts for these surface structure differences, can be formulated as follows:

$$NP_1 + AUX + V + NP_2 \Rightarrow NP_2 + AUX + BE + EN + V + by + NP_1$$

This transformation adds *by* at the end of the underlying string and then moves the subject of this string (here designated $NP_1$ for convenient reference) to a position following *by*. The direct object of the underlying string (designated $NP_2$) becomes the new subject. The passive transformation then adds BE + EN before the main verb.

To see the passive transformation in action, let us work with the following deep structure strings:

> the + roach + PL + PRES + eat + the + cracker + PL
> the + roach + PL + PAST + eat + the + cracker + PL
> the + roach + PL + PRES + will + eat + the + cracker + PL
> the + roach + PL + PRES + HAVE + EN + eat + the + cracker + PL
> the + roach + PL + PRES + BE + ING + eat + the + cracker + PL
> the + roach + PL + PRES + will + HAVE + EN + eat + the + cracker + PL

After the passive transformation has been applied, we will have:

> the + cracker + PL + PRES + BE + EN + eat + by + the + roach + PL
> the + cracker + PL + PAST + BE + EN + eat + by + the + roach + PL
> the + cracker + PL + PRES + will + BE + EN + eat + by + the + roach + PL
> the + cracker + PL + PRES + HAVE + EN + BE + EN + eat + by + the + roach + PL
> the + cracker + PL + PRES + BE + ING + BE + EN + eat + by + the + roach + PL
> the + cracker + PL + PRES + will + HAVE + EN + BE + EN + eat + by + the + roach + PL

Since the subject of each string is plural, the symbol PRES must be further specified as Ø, and PAST before BE must be specified as $PAST_{pl}$. After performing these agreement operations and after also applying the affix transformation and the word boundary transformation, we will have strings with the following verbal phrases:

BE + Ø # eat + EN #
BE + $PAST_{pl}$ # eat + EN #
will + Ø # BE # eat + EN #
HAVE + Ø # BE + EN # eat + EN #
BE + Ø # BE + ING # eat + EN #
will + Ø # HAVE # BE + EN # eat + EN #

Ultimately, we will get the following sentences:

the crackers are eaten by the roaches
the crackers were eaten by the roaches
the crackers will be eaten by the roaches
the crackers have been eaten by the roaches
the crackers are being eaten by the roaches
the crackers will have been eaten by the roaches

If the subject of the underlying string is an indefinite *someone* or *something,* the agent phrase (*by someone, by something*) resulting from the passive transformation can optionally be deleted. For example, we could passivize

someone + SG + PAST + commend + the + sergeant + SG

to eventually produce either *the sergeant was commended by someone* or *the sergeant was commended.* Similarly, we could passivize

someone + SG + PAST + eat + the + cracker + PL

to ultimately produce either *the crackers were eaten by someone* or *the crackers were eaten.* Note, however, that *the crackers were eaten* could result also from

something + SG + PAST + eat + the + cracker + PL

That is, *the crackers were eaten* is ambiguous in that we do not know whether some*one* ate the crackers, or some*thing.* Such structural ambiguity is always the result when an irrecoverable item is deleted from the deep structure.

We might note, briefly, that the passive transformation verifies the existence of two-word and three-word verbs. For example, the string

the + girl + SG + PAST + cut + up + the + onion + PL

would be passivized as

the + onion + PL + PAST + BE + EN + cut + up +
    by + the + girl + SG

The fact that the string can be passivized indicates that *up the
onions* is not an adverbial prepositional phrase. This seems
obvious enough; possibly no one trying to analyze the structure
of this sentence would assume that *up the onions* is an adverbial. To take a less obvious example, then, how would you
analyze *someone was talking about Leo?* Does it seem grammatical to say *Leo was being talked about?* If so, then *talk
about* must be a two-word verb. Similarly, the passive sentence
*he was looked up to by everyone* indicates that *look up to* is a
three-word verb.

We have seen that in passive sentences, the main verb is
in the past participle form and is immediately preceded by a
form of BE. The following are some examples of active verbal
phrases with their corresponding passives:

| *Actives* | *Passives* |
|---|---|
| drives | is driven |
| should drive | should be driven |
| has driven | has been driven |
| are driving | are being driven |
| should have driven | should have been driven |
| | |
| walks | is walked |
| should walk | should be walked |
| have walked | have been walked |
| is walking | is being walked |
| should have walked | should have been walked |

It should not be difficult to distinguish passive verbal phrases
from actives. Distinguishing passives from BE + adjectival combinations often is not difficult either. Consider the following
pairs of sentences:

he was determined
the outcome was determined

Mr. Higgins will be dedicated
the building will be dedicated

she has been detached
the boxtop has been detached

In the first sentence of each of these pairs, the *-ed* word seems to be indicating a quality attributed to the subject; in each case, *very* fits before the *-ed* word:

he was very determined
Mr. Higgins will be very dedicated
she has been very detached

It would not sound grammatical, however, to put *very* before the *-ed* word in the other sentences:

*the outcome was very determined
*the building will be very dedicated
*the boxtop has been very detached

On the other hand, each sentence which does not accept *very* before the *-ed* word does seem to have an implied agent phrase, whereas the other sentences do not:

the outcome was determined by $\begin{Bmatrix} \text{someone} \\ \text{something} \end{Bmatrix}$
the building will be dedicated by someone
the boxtop has been detached by someone

but not, ordinarily,

*he was determined by $\begin{Bmatrix} \text{someone} \\ \text{something} \end{Bmatrix}$
*Mr. Higgins will be dedicated by someone
*she has been detached by someone

In the sentences which can take *very* before the *-ed* word, the *-ed* word is functioning adjectivally; the BE form is the main verb and the *-ed* word is an adjectival. The sentences which can take an agent phrase are passives with the original *by*-phrase deleted; the BE form is an auxiliary and the *-ed* word is the main verb.

It is not always this easy to tell whether a word which looks like the past participle form of a verb is functioning adjectivally after the main verb BE or whether it is functioning as a main verb after a BE auxiliary; nevertheless, the *very* test and the agent phrase test will often resolve the issue.

## THE CLEFT TRANSFORMATION

Compare the sentences in the following sets:

the mongoose ate the cobra
what the mongoose ate was the cobra
what ate the cobra was the mongoose

Jean's new car crashed into the stop sign
what Jean's new car crashed into was the stop sign
what crashed into the stop sign was Jean's new car

Jean's new car was crumpled by the stop sign
what Jean's new car was crumpled by was the stop sign
what was crumpled by the stop sign was Jean's new car

the soprano likes beer
what the soprano likes is beer
but not    *what likes beer is the soprano

Sharon hates having to do dishes
what Sharon hates is having to do dishes
but not    *what hates having to do dishes is Sharon

his having left so early annoyed her
what annoyed her was his having left so early
but not    *what his having left so early annoyed was her

These sets of sentences suggest that by performing three simple operations, one can focus attention on almost any construction functioning as a noun phrase, except for those noun phrases having a ⟨+ human⟩ noun as head. The three operations are: 1) place *what* at the front of the sentence; 2) add *is* or *was* (whichever is appropriate) at the end of the sentence; and 3) move to the end of the sentence the noun phrase to be emphasized. As an example, let us follow this process in changing *the tornado razed the house* to focus attention first on *the house* and then on *the tornado.* Placing *what* at the beginning of the sentence, we have

*what the tornado razed the house

Next we add *was* at the end of the sentence:

*what the tornado razed the house was

Last, we move to the end of the sentence the noun phrase we want to emphasize. There are two nonhuman noun phrases and hence two possible results:

> what the tornado razed was the house
> what razed the house was the tornado

Notice that *what the tornado razed was the house* presupposes that the tornado razed something, whereas *what razed the house was the tornado* presupposes that something razed the house.

Constructions like *what the tornado razed was the house* and *what razed the house was the tornado* are called *cleft* sentences: "cleft" because the basic sentence is cleft, or split, by the introduction of *is* or *was*. We can call such sentences *WHAT-clefts,* to distinguish them from another kind of cleft sentence; the transformation producing WHAT-cleft sentences might then be called the WHAT-cleft transformation.

We will formulate this WHAT-cleft transformation in two parts. The first is as follows:

$$X + NP_{\langle - \text{ human}\rangle} + Y \Rightarrow \text{what} + X + Y + T +$$

$$BE + NP_{\langle - \text{ human}\rangle}$$

This first part of the transformation adds *what* at the beginning of the string, adds $T + BE$ at the end, and then moves to the end of the sentence some nonhuman noun phrase. The nonhumanness of the noun phrase is indicated here by the $\langle - \text{ human}\rangle$ subscript attached to the NP (the entire noun phrase acquires the $\langle - \text{ human}\rangle$ marking of the head noun, if there is a head noun—and, of course, if this head noun is $\langle - \text{ human}\rangle$).

The second part of the WHAT-cleft transformation guarantees that the added BE form will become *is* if the auxiliary in the original string specifies a present tense affix, *was* if the original auxiliary specifies a past tense affix: [12]

$$\begin{bmatrix} PRES \\ PAST \end{bmatrix} + Z + T + BE \Rightarrow \begin{bmatrix} PRES \\ PAST \end{bmatrix} + Z + \begin{bmatrix} ES \\ PAST_{sg} \end{bmatrix} + BE$$

Like X and Y, Z is a cover symbol representing "anything." $ES + BE$ will eventually become *is,* and $PAST_{sg} + BE$ will eventually become *was.*

---

[12] *A more precise grammar would have to provide for the plural forms* are *and* were. *As formulated here, the WHAT-cleft transformation will produce such ungrammatical sentences as* \*what were outside was some burglars *and* \*what are outside is some burglars.

The WHAT-cleft transformation will operate on a string like the following, to which any relevant agreement transformation must already have been applied:

the + house + PAST$_{sg}$ + BE + EN + raze + by + the + tornado + SG

Performing the WHAT-cleft transformation on the string, we will get either of the following strings:

what + the + house + PAST$_{sg}$ + BE + EN + raze + by + PAST$_{sg}$ + BE + the + tornado + SG
what + PAST$_{sg}$ + BE + EN + raze + by + the + tornado + SG + PAST$_{sg}$ + BE + the + house + SG

Both parts of the WHAT-cleft transformation have been applied to these strings. The resulting sentence will be either of the following, depending on which noun phrase is moved to the end of the string:

what the house was razed by was the tornado
what was razed by the tornado was the house

These passive WHAT-clefts may seem clumsy, but they are nevertheless grammatical: a string can undergo both the passive transformation and the WHAT-cleft transformation. So that the passive transformation will not be unnecessarily complicated, it should be placed before the WHAT-cleft transformation in the block of transformational rules.

You may have realized that WHAT-cleft sentences can be inverted without changing the focus or presupposition of the sentence. Below are three WHAT-clefts, each followed by its inverted counterpart:

what the mongoose ate was the cobra
the cobra was what the mongoose ate

what the soprano likes is beer
beer is what the soprano likes

what Sharon hates is having to do dishes
having to do dishes is what Sharon hates

As these examples show, an inversion transformation can shift the emphasized noun phrase into subject position while shifting into predicate nominal position the noun phrase that formerly was the subject. (In both the uninverted and the inverted

WHAT-cleft sentences, the main verb is the *is* or *was* added by the WHAT-cleft transformation.)

Rather than formalize this inversion transformation, which applies to some other kinds of sentences besides WHAT-clefts, we will discuss another kind of cleft transformation: the *IT-cleft.* Let us examine the following sets of sentences:

> the mongoose ate the cobra
> what the mongoose ate was the cobra
> it was the cobra that the mongoose ate
>
> Jean's new car crashed into the stop sign
> what crashed into the stop sign was Jean's new car
> it was Jean's new car that crashed into the stop sign
>
> his having left so early annoyed her
> what annoyed her was his having left so early
> it was his having left so early that annoyed her
>
> that she was unreliable was unfortunate
> what was unfortunate was that she was unreliable
> it was that she was unreliable that was unfortunate

The third sentence in each set is an IT-cleft. The IT-clefts focus upon the same noun phrase as the related WHAT-clefts, and the presupposition seems also to be the same. In fact, the simplest way of generating IT-clefts is to derive them from strings that have undergone the WHAT-cleft transformation.[13] The process is fairly simple. First, *it* is added to the left of the BE form inserted by the WHAT-cleft transformation. Then everything preceding this *it* is moved to the end of the sentence, and the *what* added by the WHAT-cleft transformation is replaced with *that:*

> what ate the cobra was the mongoose
> what ate the cobra *it* was the mongoose
> it was the mongoose what ate the cobra
> it was the mongoose that ate the cobra

The second string is possible in very informal English speech, with a pause before *it*. The third string, *it was the mongoose **what** ate the cobra,* is a nonstandard variant of the formal standard IT-cleft sentence *it was the mongoose **that** ate the cobra.*

[13]*For this idea and for many of the other ideas underlying our discussion of cleft sentences, we are indebted to Robert P. Stockwell, Paul Schachter, and Barbara Hall Partee,* Integration of Transformational Theories on English Syntax *(Los Angeles, Calif.: University of California at Los Angeles, 1968), Vol. 2, pp. 799–840. Stockwell et al. mention on pages 839–840 several reasons for deriving IT-clefts from strings which have undergone the WHAT-cleft transformation; they also mention several difficulties that arise if one attempts to produce IT-clefts in this manner.*

*We should note that Stockwell et al. apparently think the strings underlying two source sentences must be combined in generating a WHAT-cleft or an IT-cleft sentence. While admitting the validity of the arguments for such an analysis, we consider the simpler analysis presented here to be adequate for our pedagogical purposes.*

The IT-cleft transformation can be formulated as follows:

$$\text{what} + \text{X} + \begin{bmatrix} \text{ES} \\ \text{PAST}_{sg} \end{bmatrix} + \text{BE} + \text{NP}_{\langle - \text{ human} \rangle} =\rangle$$

$$\text{it} + \begin{bmatrix} \text{ES} \\ \text{PAST}_{sg} \end{bmatrix} + \text{BE} + \text{NP}_{\langle - \text{ human} \rangle} + \text{that} + \text{X}$$

Notice that the tense of the BE verb will already have been specified by the second part of the WHAT-cleft transformation.

To see in more detail how the IT-cleft transformation functions, let us work with three strings which have already undergone the WHAT-cleft transformation:

what + the + tornado + SG + PAST + raze + PAST$_{sg}$ +
BE + the + house + SG
what + PAST$_{sg}$ + raze + the + house + SG + PAST$_{sg}$ +
BE + the + tornado + SG
what + PAST$_{sg}$ + BE + EN + raze + by + the + tornado +
SG + PAST$_{sg}$ + BE + the + house + SG

The IT-cleft transformation will change these strings into

it + PAST$_{sg}$ + BE + the + house + SG + that + the +
tornado + SG + PAST$_{sg}$ + raze
it + PAST$_{sg}$ + BE + the + tornado + SG + that + PAST$_{sg}$ +
raze + the + house + SG
it + PAST$_{sg}$ + BE + the + house + SG + that + PAST$_{sg}$ +
BE + EN + raze + by + the + tornado + SG

After the affix transformation and the word boundary transformation have been applied, we will ultimately get

it was the house that the tornado razed
it was the tornado that razed the house
it was the house that was razed by the tornado

In the next chapter we will discuss what is sometimes called the **IT-inversion transformation.** Sentences which have resulted from this IT-inversion transformation do not have the same structure as IT-cleft sentences. For example, from the same string which underlies that she was unreliable was unfortunate

one could optionally produce

it was unfortunate that she was unreliable

which has undergone the IT-inversion transformation. Another alternative would be to apply the WHAT-cleft transformation and then apply the IT-cleft transformation, to produce first the string underlying

what was unfortunate was that she was unreliable

and finally the sentence

it was that she was unreliable that was unfortunate

The sentence *it was unfortunate that she was unreliable* seems to focus attention on the unfortunateness of her unreliability. The awkward IT-cleft sentence, on the other hand, focuses attention on her unreliability and presupposes that something was unfortunate. (As we will explain in the next chapter, the IT-cleft sentence could and probably should have *the fact* before the first *that* to make it less awkward: *it was the fact that she was unreliable that was unfortunate.*)


## THE *THERE* TRANSFORMATION


To see how the THERE transformation operates, examine the following sets of sentences:

a mouse was in the house
there was a mouse in the house

some mice have been in the house
there have been some mice in the house

no mouse is in the pancake flour yet
there is no mouse in the pancake flour yet
                    or
there isn't any mouse in the pancake flour yet

mice are running around everywhere
there are mice running around everywhere

many mice have been getting into the oatmeal
there have been many mice getting into the oatmeal

four mice were eaten by our cat
there were four mice eaten by our cat

The second sentence in each pair begins with *there.* In these sentences, the word *there* has no semantic meaning. The following sentences illustrate the difference between this "expletive" *there* and the place adverb *there:*

some mice were there
there were some mice there

The *there* in the first sentence indicates where the mice were. Although the second *there* in the second sentence performs this same function, the first *there* does not function adverbially; it simply serves as the surface structure subject.

You may have noticed that each sentence in the above sets has a BE functioning either as the main verb (in the first three sets) or as the auxiliary (in the last three sets of sentences). Generally a string will not undergo the THERE transformation unless it contains a form of BE. The transformation moves the BE and the auxiliary element or elements preceding it to the beginning of the string, then adds *there* before the auxiliary element(s) and the BE form. (There will always be at least one auxiliary element: the tense marker.)

We will formalize the THERE transformation as follows:

NP + X + BE + Y $=$) there + X + BE + NP + Y

As usual, X and Y represent "anything." But at this point in a derivation, only auxiliary elements could occur between an NP and a following BE form. Thus the X in this rule actually stands for whatever auxiliary element or elements precede the BE form.

To see how this rule operates, let us work with the following strings, to which any relevant agreement transformation must already have been applied: [14]

a + mouse + SG + $PAST_{sg}$ + BE + in + the + house + SG
many + mouse + PL + $\emptyset$ + HAVE + EN + BE + ING +
get + into + the + oatmeal + SG
four + mouse + PL + $PAST_{pl}$ + BE + EN + eat + by +
our + cat + SG

---

[14] *The agreement transformations must apply before the THERE transformation moves the subject to a position after the tense marker. Apparently the cleft transformations should apply after the THERE transformation so that one can generate such sentences as* what there was outside was a burglar *and (more awkwardly)* it was a burglar that there was outside. *Even if we do not want to be able to generate such sentences as these, it seems necessary for the THERE transformation to precede the cleft transformations so that the THERE transformation will not be unduly complicated.*

The THERE transformation will change these strings into

there + PAST$_{sg}$ + BE + a + mouse + SG + in + the +
house + SG

there + Ø + HAVE + EN + BE + many + mouse + PL +
ING + get + into + the + oatmeal + SG

there + PAST$_{pl}$ + BE + four + mouse + PL + EN + eat +
by + our + cat + SG

Note that in the second and third strings, where BE functions as an auxiliary, the deep structure subject of the sentence now separates the BE auxiliary from the affix which originally followed it. The affix immediately precedes the main verb, to which it will be attached. After the affix transformation and the word boundary transformation have been applied, we will ultimately get

there was a mouse in the house
there have been many mice getting into the oatmeal
there were four mice eaten by our cat

## THE ADVERB PLACEMENT TRANSFORMATION

Many sentences (that is, many NP + VP constructions) can be modified by a manner adverbial,[15] and almost all sentences can be modified by an adverbial of time and/or an adverbial of location. (Adverbials of location are a subcategory of place adverbials: some place adverbials indicate direction, as in *he went to town,* and some indicate location, as in *he lived in town.*) We can provide for these optional "sentence" modifiers (actually they are clause modifiers) in the first phrase structure rule, which will now read

$$S \rightarrow (EMP) + \begin{Bmatrix} (NEG) + (Q) \\ (IMP) \end{Bmatrix} + NP + VP + (ADVP_{\langle + man \rangle}) +$$

$$(ADVP_{\langle + loc \rangle}) + (ADVP_{\langle + tm \rangle})$$

As the rule suggests, a manner adverbial will usually precede a locative and/or a time adverbial, if they both or all occur at the end of a sentence; also, a locative adverbial will usually precede a time adverbial if both occur at the end.

---

[15] *The BE verb, certain kinds of linking verbs, and certain kinds of intransitive verbs cannot take manner adverbials: we do not say* *he was tall happily,* *he smelled good pleasantly, or* *the toy cost $50 expensively. If a verb cannot be followed by a manner adverbial, this fact will have to be indicated by a subcategorization feature in its syntactic matrix.*

The following sentences illustrate the three types of adverbials provided for by this rule:

> he paid his bill **reluctantly**
> he paid his bill **yesterday**
> he paid his bill **in December**
> he paid his bill **last month**
> he paid his bill **when the electric company threatened to
>     cut off the power** [16]
> he paid his bill **downtown**
> he paid his bill **at the electric company office**
> he paid his bill **where he had been told to pay his bills**
> he paid his bill **reluctantly / last month**
> he paid his bill **downtown / yesterday**
> he paid his bill **at the electric company office / last month**
> he paid his bill **where he had been told to pay his bills, / when
>     the electric company threatened to cut off the power**

Manner adverbials are more freely movable than the other kinds of sentence adverbials, as the following examples indicate:

> he had paid his bill **reluctantly**
> **reluctantly,** he had paid his bill
> he had **reluctantly** paid his bill
> he had **reluctantly** been paying his bills
> he **reluctantly** had been paying his bills
> he had been **reluctantly** paying his bills

Usually manner adverbials can be moved from their deep structure position after the verbal phrase to one of four other positions: 1) the front of the sentence; 2) immediately after the first auxiliary word, if there is one; 3) immediately before the first auxiliary word, if there is one; and 4) immediately before the main verb. The basic meaning of the sentence seems to be the same, regardless of where the manner adverbial occurs.

Time adverbials are freely movable to the front of the sentence:

> **yesterday** he paid his bill
> **in December** he paid his bill
> **last month** he paid his bill
> **when the electric company threatened to cut off the power,**
>     he paid his bill

---

[16] *Adverbially-functioning constructions consisting of a subordinator plus a sentence (constructions such as* when the electric company threatened to cut off the power) *are called adverbializations. Although we have not yet discussed how adverbializations are generated, the present discussion will include several adverbializations as examples of sentence-modifying adverbials.*

Locative adverbials are not so freely movable as time adverbials. Locatives often seem more awkward in initial position, and moving them sometimes causes a slight change in the meaning of the sentence. Still, the *basic* meaning of the sentence usually seems to be the same, as in the following pairs of sentences:

> he paid his bill **downtown**
> **downtown** he paid his bill

> he paid his bill **at the electric company office**
> **at the electric company office** he paid his bill

Before formalizing this adverb placement transformation, we should mention three other types of sentence adverbials: adverbials of **reason, contrast,** and **condition.** These adverbials can usually be moved from their original postverbal-phrase position to the front of the sentence. Here are some examples:

*Adverbials of reason*

> we ran the stop sign, **because of the emergency**
> **because of the emergency,** we ran the stop sign

> you might as well not explain, **since it won't do any good**
> **since it won't do any good,** you might as well not explain

*Adverbials of contrast*

> he charged ahead, **contrary to orders**
> **contrary to orders,** he charged ahead

> he wouldn't eat his supper, **even though he was hungry**
> **even though he was hungry,** he wouldn't eat his supper

*Adverbials of condition*

> I won't go **if he can't go**
> **if he can't go** I won't go

> I won't go **unless he can go**
> **unless he can go** I won't go

For simplicity, we have formulated the first phrase structure rule in our second model grammar (p. 163) so as to allow for only three types of sentence adverbials: manner, location, and time. Furthermore, the rule rewriting ADVP (one rule will take care of all three types of adverbials) will allow only for single word adverbials like *carefully, inquisitively; here, there; today, tomorrow.* A more complete grammar would of course allow for adverbials of reason, condition, and contrast (plus some others) and might specify ADVP as follows:

$$\text{ADVP} \rightarrow \begin{Bmatrix} \text{ADV} \\ \text{(PREP)} + \text{NP} \\ \text{SUB} + \text{S} \end{Bmatrix}$$

This rule says that an adverbial phrase can be specified as a single word adverb or adverbial (*carefully, here*); as a prepositional phrase (*in the city, at home*); as a noun phrase (*last month,* or *home* in a sentence like *he went home*); or as a subordinator plus a sentence (*when the electric company threatened to cut off the power*).

The following sentences illustrate some of the combinations of sentence adverbials that might be generated by a grammar providing for all the kinds of adverbials we have discussed:

> he paid his bill **reluctantly / in the electric company office /
> yesterday** (manner, location, time)
> he paid his bill **yesterday / because he was afraid the electric
> company would cut off the power** (time, reason)
> he pays his bill **downtown, / unless he can't get a taxi**
> (location, condition)
> he pays his bill **reluctantly / every month, / even though
> he has plenty of money** (manner, time, contrast)
> he will pay his bill **if he has to, / even though he doesn't have
> much money** (condition, contrast)
> he won't pay his bill **unless he is forced to, / because he
> doesn't have much money** (condition, reason)

Often it seems stylistically preferable to move only one sentence adverbial to the front of a sentence, even though there is more than one adverbial which could be moved. For this reason, and for simplicity, we will formulate the adverb placement transformation as follows:

$$\text{X} + \text{ADVP} + \text{Y} \Rightarrow \text{ADVP} + \text{X} + \text{Y}$$

This optional rule will move one sentence adverbial—any adverbial—to the front of its string.

We will not attempt to formalize a rule that will move manner adverbials to any of the other positions they might occupy.

## WORKING WITH TRANSFORMATIONS THAT
## PRODUCE STYLISTIC VARIANTS

1 a.   For each of the strings below, tell whether the resulting phrase will be active or passive, assuming that the passive transformation has already been applied if it is going to be. Put an A in the blank if the phrase will be active, a P if it will be passive. Since the affix transformation has not yet been applied to these strings, a resulting phrase will be passive if and only if the string contains BE immediately *followed* by EN. (How would an EN *preceding* BE have come into the string?)

   b.   After telling whether each of the resulting phrases will be active or passive, perform the affix and word boundary transformations on the strings below and determine specifically what each of the resulting phrases will be.

_____  *1.*   ES + will + run
_____  *2.*   ES + will + BE + EN + run
_____  *3.*   Ø + may + HAVE + EN + drive
_____  *4.*   Ø + may + HAVE + EN + BE + EN + drive
_____  *5.*   PAST + HAVE + EN + hit
_____  *6.*   PAST + HAVE + EN + BE + EN + hit
_____  *7.*   Ø + BE + ING + BE + EN + hit
_____  *8.*   ES + BE + ING + hit
_____  *9.*   Ø + BE + EN + hit
_____  *10.*   PAST + may + HAVE + EN + BE + EN + buy
_____  *11.*   PAST + may + BE + EN + buy
_____  *12.*   Ø + BE + ING + BE + EN + drive + out
_____  *13.*   PAST + HAVE + EN + think
_____  *14.*   PAST + HAVE + EN + BE + EN + wash
_____  *15.*   ES + may + BE + EN + wash
_____  *16.*   ES + BE + ING + BE + EN + think + about

2.   Change the following active sentences into their corresponding passives. Remember that in making a sentence passive, you always add a form of BE, even if the original sentence already contains a BE. In order to passivize these sentences correctly, you might find it helpful to break the main verb phrase down into its constituent parts, add BE + EN before the main verb, and recombine the auxiliary and main verb constituents by performing the affix transformation. The first sentence has been passivized in this manner as an example:

a.   my husband has wrecked our new car

Breaking down the main verb phrase, we have

PRES + HAVE + EN + wreck

(The tense should be indicated as PRES rather than ES because the agreement transformation will have to apply after the passive transformation to assure proper subject-verb agreement for some passives.) Adding BE + EN before the main verb, we get

PRES + HAVE + EN + BE + EN + wreck

An agreement transformation specifies PRES as ES, and the affix transformation then gives

HAVE + ES # BE + EN # wreck + EN #

The main verb phrase will thus be

has been wrecked

The entire passive sentence will be

our new car has been wrecked by my husband

b.   her little girl ruined the rug
c.   they examine the eggs
d.   Ralph can drive the bus
e.   Johnny has shut the refrigerator
f.   the workers have pulled down the fence
g.   the chefs were frying mushrooms
h.   he is cutting the grass
i.   someone should stop him
j.   someone ought to chill the wine
k.   something knocked over the garbage

**3.**   In each of the following sentences, how is the bold-faced word functioning: as an adjectival, or as the main verb? In each case, what is the basis for your decision?

a.   the door is **locked**
b.   the toy was **broken**
c.   the woman was **annoyed**
d.   the drawings were **detailed**
e.   they are **finished** with the work
f.   they are **gone**

g.   I am **done**
h.   the Lord is **risen**

**4.**   Locate all of the main verb phrases in the two passages at the beginning of the section on the passive transformation (pp. 136–137); then determine whether each phrase is active or passive. The first version is from Gibbon's *The Decline and Fall of the Roman Empire;* [17] the second is our rewriting of Gibbon's passage. Notice that in changing Gibbon's passive phrases to actives, we often had to supply a grammatical subject that could only be inferred from the original; compare, for instance, the first sentence of our version with Gibbon's first sentence. Why do you suppose Gibbon used so many passives? Do you suppose he used them consciously, or not?

**5.**   Underline each main verb phrase in the following passage and then determine whether the phrase is active or passive. Approximately what percent of the phrases are passive? Judging by the percentage of passives, what do you think the narrator must be like as a person? Does the passage offer any other evidence to support this impression?

Whether I shall turn out to be the hero of my
own life, or whether that station will be held
by anybody else, these pages must show. To
begin my life with the beginning of my life, I
5   record that I was born (as I have been informed
and believe) on a Friday, at twelve o'clock at
night. It was remarked that the clock began to
strike, and I began to cry, simultaneously.
In consideration of the day and hour of my
10   birth, it was declared by the nurse, and by some
sage women in the neighbourhood who had taken
a lively interest in me several months before there
was any possibility of our becoming personally
acquainted, first, that I was destined to be unlucky
15   in life; and secondly, that I was privileged to
see ghosts and spirits; both these gifts inevitably
attaching, as they believed, to all unlucky infants
of either gender, born towards the small hours
on a Friday night.
20   I need say nothing here on the first head,
because nothing can show better than my history
whether that prediction was verified or falsified
by the result. [18]

---

[17] *Edward Gibbon,* The Decline and Fall of the Roman Empire *(New York: E. P. Dutton & Company, Inc., 1910), Vol. 1, 458–459.*
[18] *These are the opening sentences of Charles Dickens'* David Copperfield. *We are quoting from the Oxford reprint edition (London: Oxford University Press, 1966), p. 1.*

**6.** Locate all the passives in the following excerpts from a newspaper article. Are very many of them followed by an agent phrase (*by so-and-so*) specifying the deep structure subject? What function or functions do the passives serve in this article?


### Mass Murder Graves Found


YUBA CITY, Calif. (UPI)—A stocky farm labor
contractor was arrested early today and charged
with the mass murder of nine men whose bodies
were found buried near the Feather River.
5          The suspect, identified as Juan V. Corona,
37-year-old father of four, was arrested without
resistance at his residence in a quiet middle-class
neighborhood and booked on nine counts of
homicide.
10         Clad in gray work pants, green sweater and
cowboy boots, the suspect was brought to the
county jail early today.
           He was picked up within hours of the discovery
of the bodies buried in an orchard and nearby
15         riverbank undergrowth on the big James Sullivan
ranch about five miles north of Yuba City.
           Rain and exhaustion forced an end to the
search for a few hours, but it was to resume today.
There were at least two more dug-up areas which
20         could be graves, deputies reported. . . .
           He [the sheriff] said each of the victims had been
hacked severely in the back of the head, that
some had heavy facial lacerations, and that
most had been stabbed in the chest.
25         All were buried three to five feet beneath the
ground, lying on their backs with their arms
extended above their heads and their shirts pulled
up over their bloody heads.
           Two of the graves found near the river appeared
30         to be fresh, "probably dug within the past 48
hours," the sheriff said. The rest seemed to be
a little older, maybe as far back as five or six
weeks, he said.
           The graves along the Feather River were found
35         in heavy brush and wild grapevine about a
dozen feet from the stream. Three bodies were
unearthed a few feet apart, two others were
discovered nearby and another pair were found
a quarter mile away.

40      Sheriff Whiteaker ordered an inch-by-inch search
        of the region after foreman Ray Duron of the
        Sullivan Ranch reported the second body Tuesday
        morning.
                It was found in the orchard about a quarter
45      of a mile from the grave where Whitacre's remains
        were discovered last Thursday. The sheriff also
        said a farmer reported finding an empty grave
        a month ago in the field 400 yards from Whitacre's
        grave. The man filled it in a week later and didn't
50      report it to police until after the first body was
        dug up.
                All the victims were clothed except one man
        who was wearing only a shirt.
                Some of the bodies had two pairs of pants and
55      two shirts, indicating the victims were transient
        laborers, investigators said. The orchards are
        being thinned at this time of year.[19]

**7.**   Sometimes sentences are made passive by the addition of
GET + EN rather than BE + EN. For example, we might say
*he gets reelected every time* rather than *he is reelected every
time, they get eaten up by mosquitoes every summer* rather
than *they are eaten up by mosquitoes every summer, he
got killed* rather than *he was killed,* and so forth. Do you sense
any difference in surface meaning between the GET passives
and the BE passives?

**8.**   Which verbal phrases are passive in the following quotes?

a.   "he [Robert Cohn] came out of Princeton
     with painful self-consciousness and the
     flattened nose, and was married by the first
     girl who was nice to him. He was married
     five years."

                —Ernest Hemingway, *The Sun Also Rises*

b.   "the Joe Christmases get lynched, the Lena
     Groveses get husbands."

                —Irving Howe, *William Faulkner*

**9.**   Is *got engaged* passive in either or both of the following
sentences?   Discuss.

[19] Kalamazoo Gazette, *26 May, 1971, pp. 1–2.*

a.   she got engaged by her father's employer
b.   she got engaged to her father's employer

**10.**   Does either of the two sentences in the following pairs have a passive main verb phrase? Explain.

a.   the fact that he arrived surprised me
     I was surprised by the fact that he arrived
b.   that he arrived surprised me
     I was surprised that he arrived
c.   how promptly he arrived surprised me
     I was surprised by how promptly he arrived
d.   his arriving so promptly surprised me
     I was surprised at his arriving so promptly

**11.**   In the following passage, Leopold Bloom is thinking about what must have happened earlier in the day when his wife Molly was visited by her lover, "Blazes" Boylan. Bloom considers

> the natural grammatical transition by inversion
> involving no alteration of sense of an aorist
> preterite proposition (parsed as masculine subject,
> monosyllabic onomatopoeic transitive verb with
> 5     direct feminine object) from the active voice
> into its correlative aorist preterite proposition
> (parsed as feminine subject, auxiliary verb and
> quasimonosyllabic onomatopoeic past participle
> with complementary masculine agent) [20]

What grammatical transformation is Bloom describing? Why do you suppose he thinks about this act of adultery in grammatical terms?

**12.**   Do the sentences below seem to be WHAT-clefts? How do they differ in structure from sentences produced by the WHAT-cleft transformation presented in this chapter? Try to formulate a transformation which would account for such sentences as these:

a.   what the baby did was giggle
b.   what the boy did was break the window
c.   what the drowning man did was turn blue
d.   what the kitten does is play
e.   what little boys do is get into trouble
f.   what the law student hopes to do is become a judge
g.   what you must do is be brave

[20] *James Joyce,* Ulysses *(New York: The Modern Library, 1961), p. 734.*

**13.** Do all or most of the sentences below sound grammatical to you? If so, try to formulate a generalization which will explain how the sentences you consider grammatical can be derived from noncleft strings.

    a.   when I last saw him was yesterday
    b.   where he lived was in the ghetto
    c.   why he drinks beer is because he likes the taste
    d.   how he cut off his toe was with an axe
    e.   who hates having to do dishes is Sharon
    f.   $\begin{Bmatrix} \text{what} \\ \text{which} \end{Bmatrix}$ house they are buying is the house next to the Johnsons'
    g.   whose house they are buying is the Johnsons' house

**14.** Should we be able to derive *it wasn't Alfred that was eating the steak* and *it wasn't the steak that Alfred was eating* from a deep structure string identical to the one that underlies *Alfred wasn't eating the steak?* Why or why not?

**15.** As presently formulated, our THERE transformation will produce such ungrammatical sentences as the following:

    *there was one mouse obnoxious
    *there are some couches sofa beds

What needs to be added to these sentences to make them grammatical? Try to formulate a transformation which would do this. Under what conditions would it apply?

**16.** Why do you suppose the first sentence in the sets below is ungrammatical, while the corresponding THERE version is grammatical? In other words, what is it about the strings underlying these sentences that makes the THERE transformation obligatory?

    a.   *ghosts are
        there are ghosts
    b.   *no life after death is
        there is no life after death
    c.   *no God is
        there is no God
    d.   *no possibility of his being on time is
        there is no possibility of his being on time
    e.   *a problem appeared to be
        there appeared to be a problem

(But compare *God is* with *there is God,* the latter sentence being grammatical only if *there* is interpreted as a place adverbial. What accounts for the ungrammaticality of *there is God?*)

**17.** Can you offer any suggestions as to what grammatical conditions must prevail if the basic THERE transformation is to be performed on strings that have no BE form? The sets of sentences below provide some examples:

   a.   a time came when he had to act
       there came a time when he had to act
   b.   a ghost appeared at the door
       there appeared a ghost at the door
   c.   one question remains in my mind
       there remains one question in my mind
   d.   a glory hath past away from the earth
       "there hath past away a glory from the earth"
          —William Wordsworth, *Ode: Intimations of*
            *Immortality from Recollections of Early*
            *Childhood*
   e.   a serious accident occurred
       there occurred a serious accident

**18** a.   Do any (or all) of the THERE sentences below seem ungrammatical to you? Do the sentences which have undergone the THERE transformation seem in each case to mean the same as their untransformed counterparts, or not?

       the mouse was in the house
       there was the mouse in the house

       this mouse was in the house
       there was this mouse in the house

       his mouse was in the house
       there was his mouse in the house

   b.   Do your answers to the questions above suggest that there is a restriction on the kind of determiner that the subject of a string can have if the string is to undergo the THERE transformation? If so, what does this restriction seem to be? (Compare the sentences here with the examples on pp. 147–148.)

**19** a.   What interesting peculiarities do you notice about the structure of the following lines from Sir Walter Scott's *The Lay of the Last Minstrel, Canto 6?*

       Breathes there the man, with soul so dead,
       Who never to himself hath said,
         This is my own, my native land!

b.   Why do you suppose many people remember the first of these lines as *Breathes there a man, with soul so dead?*

**20.**   Should our grammar have a THERE transformation which will produce the *b* sentences below from strings underlying the *a* sentences? Discuss.

   a.   an old man died yesterday
   b.   there was an old man who died yesterday

   a.   a man caught a million fish
   b.   there was a man who caught a million fish

   a.   a little girl is singing outside
   b.   there is a little girl (who is) singing outside

**21.**   We have seen that the THERE transformation moves a BE form and the auxiliary element(s) preceding it to the beginning of a string, then adds *there* before the auxiliary and the BE. But we have not yet examined strings in which there are two BE forms. The following sentences illustrate this situation:

> some crackers were being eaten
> there were some crackers being eaten
> *there were being eaten some crackers

> some mice were being obnoxious
> there were some mice being obnoxious
> *there were being some mice obnoxious

Apparently only the first BE is moved to the front, accompanied by the preceding auxiliary element or elements. (In these two examples, the tense marker is the only preceding auxiliary element.) How might we revise our THERE transformation so that only the first of two BE forms is moved to the front of a string?

**22.**   What does *in the saloon* modify in *he threatened to kill all the politicians in the saloon?*

**23.**   One type of sentence adverbial we have not mentioned is illustrated in the following sentences:

> **certainly** he should be awarded the prize
> he is **probably** competent enough
> it is time to leave, **definitely**

> **unfortunately** he didn't know what to do
> he was **luckily** there at the right time
> he didn't know the answer, **surprisingly**

Do you think such sentence adverbials should be accounted for in the same way as other sentence adverbials? If not, can you suggest a better way of accounting for them?

**24.** See how many of the following transformations can be applied, separately, to the sentences below (sometimes the DO transformation will have to be applied also).

> passive
> imperative
> THERE
> WHAT-cleft
> IT-cleft (applies to the output of the WHAT-cleft transformation)
> question
> negative
> emphasis
> adverb placement

The first sentence is transformed for you as an example:

> a. one puppy was making all that noise
>    Passive: all that noise was being made by one puppy
>    Imperative: not applicable
>    THERE: there was one puppy making all that noise
>    WHAT-cleft: what was making all that noise was one
>        puppy
>    IT-cleft: it was one puppy that was making all that noise
>    Question: was one puppy making all that noise?
>    Negative: one puppy wasn't making all that noise
>    Emphasis: one puppy **was** making all that noise
>    Adverb placement: not applicable
> b. he wanted a puppy
> c. a wasp is in the house
> d. you will polish the furniture
> e. mustard was all over the sink
> f. an old woman lived in a shoe
> g. the child swallowed a tack yesterday

## SECOND MODEL GRAMMAR

In this section we will attempt to incorporate the transformations presented in this chapter into our earlier model syntactic component. As we have mentioned before, transformational rules are ordered rules; that is, each rule must be checked in turn to see whether it *must* be applied (if the rule is obligatory) or whether it *may* be applied (if the rule is optional). Our major purpose here is to indicate how the transformational rules developed in this chapter might be (and often must be) ordered with respect to each other and with respect to the basic transformations presented in Chapter 3.

The numbers in parentheses to the right of a rule indicate the earlier page or pages where the rule is listed or the formulation of the rule is discussed.

## PHRASE STRUCTURE RULES

Now that syntactic features have been introduced, we can simplify our original phrase structure rules rewriting VBP and NP (see pp. 95 and 100). The only other changes in and additions to our original phrase structure rules are those required by the transformations introduced in this chapter.

PS 1    $S \rightarrow (EMP) + \begin{Bmatrix} (NEG) + (Q) \\ (IMP) \end{Bmatrix} + NP + VP +$

$(ADVP_{\langle + man \rangle}) + (ADVP_{\langle + loc \rangle}) + (ADVP_{\langle + tm \rangle})$

(pp. 66, 80, 113, 129, 149)

PS 2    $VP \rightarrow AUX + VBP$ (pp. 66, 80, 82; old PS 3)

PS 3    $AUX \rightarrow T + (M) + (HAVE + EN) + (BE + ING)$
        (pp. 74, 78, 80; old PS 4)

PS 4    $T \rightarrow \begin{Bmatrix} PRES \\ PAST \end{Bmatrix}$ (pp. 78, 80; old PS 5)

PS 5    $VBP \rightarrow \begin{Bmatrix} V + \left( \begin{Bmatrix} NP \\ ADJ \end{Bmatrix} \right) \\ ADJ \end{Bmatrix}$ (pp. 80, 83, 95, 112 *fn.*)

PS 6    $ADVP \rightarrow ADV$ (p. 152)

PS 7    $NP \rightarrow (DET) + N + \begin{Bmatrix} SG \\ PL \end{Bmatrix}$ (pp. 66, 80, 83, 100)

*LEXICON*

DET:    the
        what, which, whose
M:      may, shall, will
N:      anteater, astronaut, cow, dog, girl, man
        I, we, you, he, she, it, they
        who, what
V:      play, run, walk
        encounter, see, watch
        appear, look, seem
ADJ:    funny, lonesome, patient, tipsy
ADV:    carefully, inquisitively
        here, there
        now, today, tomorrow, yesterday
        how, when, where, why

This lexicon looks somewhat different from the lexicon in our earlier model grammar. We are assuming that each lexical item has a syntactic, a semantic, and a phonological feature matrix. Therefore it is unnecessary to list pronouns as a separate category; they can simply be listed as nouns with the subcategorization feature $\langle- \text{DET} \_\_\_\_\rangle$, which indicates that they cannot occur after a determiner. Similarly, we do not need to separate the verbs into intransitive, transitive, and linking, because they can simply be listed as verbs and their subcategory can be indicated with the appropriate subcategorization feature: $\langle+ \_\_\_\_\rangle$ to indicate that a verb can function intransitively, $\langle+ \_\_\_\_ \text{NP}\rangle$ to indicate that it can function transitively, and

$\langle+ \_\_\_\_ \text{ADJ}\rangle$ or $\langle+ \_\_\_\_ \begin{Bmatrix} \text{ADJ} \\ \text{NP} \end{Bmatrix}\rangle$ to indicate that it can func-

tion as a linking verb (see pp. 100 and 95 respectively).

Another difference between this lexicon and our previous one is that WH articles, nouns, and adverbs have been included so that we can generate WH questions. In addition to the WH adverbs, we have added some adverbs of manner, location, and time.

We suggest that you supply syntactic feature matrices for the lexical items given here and perhaps add some lexical items of your own. If you do add lexical items and then try producing some sentences with this grammar, you will quickly discover some of the problems involved in constructing even a simple grammar. What kind of problem will arise, for example, if you add *a* with its variant *an* to the determiner category?

## TRANSFORMATIONAL RULES

T 1     *Passive* (optional) (p. 138)

$NP_1 + AUX + V + NP_2 =\rangle NP_2 + AUX + BE + EN + V +$ $by + NP_1$

T 2     *BE-addition (p. 112 fn.)*

$AUX + ADJ =\rangle AUX + BE + ADJ$

Since transformations cannot change basic meaning, this transformation implicitly claims that when BE occurs as a main verb before an adjectival, the BE verb does not add any meaning to the sentence. It serves merely to carry the tense marker and to perform the grammatical function of linking the subject with the adjectival. For a fuller discussion of this transformation, see footnote 3.

T 3     *Imperative* (p. 128)

$$IMP + you + T + will + \begin{bmatrix} BE \\ V \end{bmatrix} + X =\rangle (you) + \begin{bmatrix} BE \\ V \end{bmatrix} + X$$

T 4     *Agreement* (BE verb with *I* as subject) (pp. 81, 84–85)

$$I + PL + \begin{bmatrix} PRES \\ PAST \end{bmatrix} + BE = I + PL + \begin{bmatrix} PRES_1 \\ PAST_{sg} \end{bmatrix} + BE$$

This is similar to old T 2, except that this rule accounts for the *past* tense of BE as well as the present tense when the subject is *I*. The symbol PL after the *I* indicates that this pronoun is syntactically plural, as a rule.

T 5     *Agreement* (present tense) (pp. 81, 85)

$$\begin{bmatrix} SG \\ PL \end{bmatrix} + PRES =\rangle \begin{bmatrix} SG + ES \\ PL + \emptyset \end{bmatrix}$$

This rule is a simplification of the old T 3. Now that all pronouns will be followed by SG or PL, we do not have to list the pronouns in the rule.

T 6     *Agreement* (past tense of BE) (pp. 81, 85)

$$\begin{bmatrix} SG \\ PL \end{bmatrix} + PAST + BE =\rangle \begin{bmatrix} SG + PAST_{sg} \\ PL + PAST_{pl} \end{bmatrix} + BE$$

This is the same as old T 4, but the pronouns are not listed in the rule; they will all be followed by either SG or PL. Also, *I was* has already been guaranteed by rule T 4. *You* is always followed by PL because *you* always takes a "plural" verb form, even when semantically singular.

T 7     THERE (optional) (p. 148)

$NP + X + BE + Y =\rangle there + X + BE + NP + Y$

T 8     *WHAT-cleft* (two-part rule, optional) (p. 143)

PART I

$X + NP_{\langle - human \rangle} + Y =\rangle$

$what + X + Y + T + BE + NP_{\langle - human \rangle}$

PART II

$$\begin{bmatrix} PRES \\ PAST \end{bmatrix} + Z + T + BE =\rangle \begin{bmatrix} PRES \\ PAST \end{bmatrix} + Z + \begin{bmatrix} ES \\ PAST_{sg} \end{bmatrix} + BE$$

T 9     *IT-cleft* (optional; can be applied only if WHAT-cleft has
        been applied) (p. 146)

$$\text{what} + X + \begin{bmatrix} ES \\ PAST_{sg} \end{bmatrix} + BE + NP_{\langle - \text{ human} \rangle} \quad =\rangle$$

$$\text{it} + \begin{bmatrix} ES \\ PAST_{sg} \end{bmatrix} + BE + NP_{\langle - \text{ human} \rangle} \quad + \text{that} + X$$

T 10    *WH-word* (p. 124)

$$X + \langle + WH \rangle + Y =\rangle \langle + WH \rangle + X + Y$$

T 11    *Question* (pp. 117, 124)

$$(\langle + WH \rangle) + Q + X + \begin{bmatrix} T + M \\ T + HAVE_{AUX} \\ T + BE \\ T \end{bmatrix} + Y =\rangle$$

$$(\langle + WH \rangle) \ \# \begin{bmatrix} T + M \\ T + HAVE_{AUX} \\ T + BE \\ T \end{bmatrix} \# X + Y$$

T 12    *Accusative* (pp. 81, 84, 121 *fn.*)

$$\begin{bmatrix} V \\ by \end{bmatrix} + \langle - \text{ accusative} \rangle =\rangle \begin{bmatrix} V \\ by \end{bmatrix} + \langle + \text{ accusative} \rangle$$

Whenever a word with the feature ⟨— accusative⟩ is
immediately preceded by a verb or the preposition *by,*
this transformation changes the ⟨— accusative⟩ to
⟨+ accusative⟩. This transformation (old T 1, revised) is
needed to provide the proper forms of certain pronouns
whenever they occur immediately after a verb or after *by*;
in our model grammar, the latter situation will occur only
when the passive transformation has added *by* at the end
of a string and moved the deep structure subject to a
position after *by.*

T 13    *Negative* (p. 113)

$$NEG + X + \begin{bmatrix} T + M \\ T + HAVE_{AUX} \\ T + BE \\ T \end{bmatrix} + Y =\rangle$$

$$X \ \# \begin{bmatrix} T + M \\ T + HAVE_{AUX} \\ T + BE \\ T \end{bmatrix} \# \text{not} + Y$$

T 14    *Emphasis* (p. 126)

$$EMP + X + \begin{bmatrix} T + M \\ T + HAVE_{AUX} \\ T + BE \\ T \end{bmatrix} + Y =\rangle$$

$$X \ \# \begin{bmatrix} T + M \\ T + HAVE_{AUX} \\ T + BE \\ T \end{bmatrix} \# \text{STRESS } 1 + Y$$

T 15   *Adverb Placement* (optional) (p. 152)
$$X + ADVP + Y \Rightarrow ADVP + X + Y$$

T 16   *DO* (p. 116)
$$\# T \# \Rightarrow \# T + DO \#$$

T 17   *Affix* (pp. 74–75, 81; old T 5)
$$Af + v \Rightarrow v + Af \# \quad \text{where } Af = PRES_1, ES, \emptyset,$$
$$PAST_{sg}, PAST_{pl}, PAST$$
$$EN, \text{ or } ING$$
$$\text{and } v = \text{any M, HAVE, BE, or V}$$

T 18   *Word boundary* (pp. 81, 85)
$$X + Y \Rightarrow X \# Y \quad \text{where } X + Y \text{ is not a}$$
$$N + \begin{Bmatrix} SG \\ PL \end{Bmatrix} \text{ combination or}$$
$$\text{a } v + Af \text{ combination}$$

Here are some questions to ask yourself as you study and work with these transformations:

1. What will happen if you perform the passive transformation on a string containing IMP, the symbol that triggers the imperative transformation?

2. Is there any good reason for putting the BE-addition transformation
   a. before the imperative transformation
   b. before the THERE transformation

3. Why are the agreement transformations placed
   a. after the passive transformation
   b. after the imperative transformation
   c. before the THERE transformation
   d. before the question transformation

4. Why are the cleft transformations placed
   a. before the question and the WH-word transformations
   b. before the negative transformation

5. Why is the adverb placement transformation placed
   a. after the THERE transformaiton
   b. after the cleft transformation
   c. after the question transformations

6. Is there any reason for putting the accusative transformation after the WH-word transformation?

If you try to generate sentences with this model grammar, you will doubtless discover some of the inadequacies of the transformations, as we have formulated and combined them. As you become aware of some of the limitations of this model grammar, try to determine how these limitations can be overcome.

# FOR FURTHER EXPLORATION

Albert B. Cook III, *Introduction to the English Language: Structure and History.* New York: The Ronald Press Company, 1969. See pp. 197–199 and 202–204 for a discussion of the negative, question, and imperative transformations in Shakespeare's *Henry IV, Part I.* Approximately same level of difficulty as the present book.

Roderick A. Jacobs, "Focus and Presupposition: Transformations and Meaning," *College Composition and Communication,* 20 (October, 1969), 187–190. This article is interesting and easy to read.

Owen Thomas, *Transformational Grammar and the Teacher of English,* 1st ed. New York: Holt, Rinehart and Winston, Inc., 1965. Chapter 7, "Rearranging the Basic Sentence," pp. 177–204, discusses some of the same singulary transformations as the present chapter, plus some others. About the same level of difficulty as the present book.

Bruce L. Liles, *An Introductory Transformational Grammar.* Englewood Cliffs, N.J.: Prentice-Hall, Inc., 1971. Part Two, "Transformations I," pp. 41–72. Like the Thomas chapter, this part of Liles' book discusses some of the same singulary transformations as the present chapter, plus some others. About the same level of difficulty as the present book.

Noam Chomsky, *Syntactic Structures.* The Hague: Mouton & Company, N.V. Publishers, 1957. This is difficult to read, but it should prove interesting to compare Chomsky's original formulation of certain transformations (see Chapter 7, pp. 61–84, and Appendix II, pp. 111–113) with our formulation of them.

Part II of this book was concerned with the basics of transformational grammar: the linguistic reasons for its coming into being, and its method of generating basic sentences. Here in Part III we describe the linguistic and philosophical growth of transformational grammar. Concerned with the major ways of expanding basic sentences, Chapter 5 incidentally indicates some of the relatively recent concerns and procedures of transformationalists. Chapter 6 is more theoretical, describing the major debates current among transformational theorists.

Our simple-to-complex approach is also roughly historical. Chapters 3 and 4 were concerned primarily with the first two stages of transformational grammar (from 1957 until approximately 1967), the stages which have provided the syntactic core of the theory. Chapter 5 is anchored in the first two stages but indicates some of the concerns of the third; Chapter 6 is concerned almost exclusively with the third stage of transformational grammar.

# transformational theory:
# expanding and revising the model

5

# EXPANDING THE BASIC SENTENCE: SOME EMBEDDING TRANSFORMATIONS

This chapter is concerned with transformations that "embed" one sentence into another. To get some idea of what this process involves, let us look at the following three sentences, each illustrating the effects of a different kind of embedding:

> the man **that bought the cobra** must be crazy
> he spent lots of money **so that he might win the election**
> I thought **that he was making a mistake**

In the first example, there are two separate "ideas" and two underlying predications, two separate deep structure "sentences," each consisting of an NP plus a VP: *the man must be crazy* and *the man bought the cobra*. By making *the man bought the cobra* into a modifier of *the man* in the first example, we get *the man who bought the cobra must be crazy* or (replacing *who* with *that*) *the man **that** bought the cobra must be crazy*.

The second of the examples above is likewise composed of two separate underlying predications, two deep structure sentences: *he spent lots of money* and *he might win the election*. By putting the subordinator *so that* in front of the second of these sentences, we make it into an adverbial modifier of the first: *he spent lots of money so that he might win the election* or, putting the adverbial clause at the front, *so that he might win the election, he spent lots of money*. The third of the examples above is likewise derived from two underlying sentences, but in this case the second underlying sentence seems to fill a hole in the first:

I thought SOMETHING
↓
(that) he was making a mistake

*That he was making a mistake* functions as the direct object of *thought.*

A deep structure "sentence" is a string of words and symbols representing a subject-plus-predicate construction. Deep structure sentences can become independent clauses, or they can be transformed into a subordinate construction of some sort. In this chapter we will be concerned with transformations that take deep structure sentences and make them into adjectival modifiers of nouns (*that bought the cobra*); into adverbial modifiers, usually modifiers of other sentences (*so that he might win the election*); or into nominals that function as subjects, predicate nominatives, direct objects, and objects of prepositions. These transformed strings can be termed **adjectivalizations, adverbializations,** and **nominalizations,** respectively, to distinguish them from those adjectivals, adverbials, and nominals which are not derived from underlying strings containing a subject and a predicate.

The transformations which make subject-plus-predicate strings into adjectivalizations, adverbializations, and nominalizations are called **embedding** transformations; they embed one deep structure sentence into another. Generally we will use the terms *adjectivalization, adverbialization,* and *nominalization* to refer to the transformational processes involved; in referring to the results of these processes, we will usually use, for convenience, the shorter terms *adjectival, adverbial,* and *nominal.*

The other kind of construction discussed in this chapter is the **absolute.** The two basic types of absolutes are illustrated in the following sentences:

the boy suddenly appeared in the door way, **his lips moving unintelligibly**
she could not see very well, **the light being out**

As we shall explain, there are two basic processes of **absolutization:** one process creates absolutes which resemble reduced nonrestrictive clauses (as in the first example), and the other process creates absolutes which resemble adverbializations (as in the second example).

The general nature of transformational rules should be apparent from the preceding two chapters. Therefore the transformations discussed in this chapter will not be expressed in formal rules.

## RESTRICTIVE ADJECTIVALIZATIONS

The explanatory power of transformational grammar is clearly revealed in the way it accounts for prenoun adjectivals. We will begin this section by discussing alternative methods of accounting for such adjectivals, giving emphasis to the transformationalists' method. We will then discuss various kinds of restrictive adjectivalizations.

### MAKING INFINITE USE OF FINITE MEANS

Notice the wealth of adjectivals in this passage from William Faulkner's *Light in August:*

        Memory believes before knowing remembers.
        Believes longer than recollects, longer than
        knowing even wonders. Knows remembers believes
        a corridor in a big long garbled cold echoing
5      building of dark red brick soot-bleakened by more
        chimneys than its own, set in a grassless
        cinderstrewnpacked compound surrounded by
        smoking factory purlieus and enclosed by a ten
        foot steel-and-wire fence like a penitentiary or a
10     zoo, where in random erratic surges, with sparrow-
        like childtrembilng, orphans in identical and
        uniform blue denim in and out of remembering
        but in knowing constant as the bleak walls,
        the bleak windows where in rain soot from the
15     yearly adjacenting chimneys streaked like black
        tears.[1]

It is not often that a writer uses as many adjectivals before a single noun as Faulkner has used before the noun *building* in this passage. But let us, as an illustration, use an even longer series of adjectivals to describe a house. The house is huge; it's ugly; it's dirty; it's old; it's dilapidated; it's deserted; it's yellow. We can describe the house more concisely as a

---

[1] *William Faulkner,* Light in August *(New York: Random House, Modern Library College Edition, 1959), p. 111.*

huge, ugly, dirty, old, dilapidated, deserted, yellow house

This phrase seems awkward with seven adjectivals before the noun *house.* But where would we draw the line, if we were to limit the number of adjectivals occurring before a noun? Any decision must necessarily be arbitrary; theoretically, there is no limit to the number of adjectivals that can occur before a noun. Our grammar must allow for this theoretical possibility, even though in most cases, one would not want to use very many adjectivals before any given noun.

It would be rather simple to expand our phrase structure rules so that they would allow for a potentially infinite number of prenoun adjectives:

$$NP \rightarrow (DET) + (ADJP) + N + \begin{Bmatrix} SG \\ PL \end{Bmatrix}$$

$$ADJP \rightarrow ADJ + (ADJP)$$

The first of these two rules is our regular noun phrase rewrite rule, expanded to include an optional adjectival phrase. The second rule says that an adjectival phrase consists of an adjective, ADJ, which can optionally be followed by an adjectival phrase, ADJP. This second rule is what linguists call a **recursive** rule: since the rewriting of ADJP can optionally include another ADJP, the rule provides for a potentially infinite set of structures.

Let us see how these two phrase structure rules would operate in deriving

the huge, ugly, dirty, old, dilapidated, deserted, yellow house

Starting with NP, we would rewrite it as

DET + ADJP + N + SG

Rewriting ADJP as ADJ + ADJP, we would get

DET + ADJ + ADJP + N + SG

ADJP can once again be rewritten as ADJ + ADJP, to give

DET + ADJ + ADJ + ADJP + N + SG

To provide for seven adjectivals, we would need to rewrite ADJP as ADJ + ADJP four more times

DET + ADJ + ADJ + ADJ + ADJ + ADJ + ADJ + ADJP +
N + SG

and then we would rewrite the remaining ADJP as just ADJ, this time ignoring the optional ADJP:

DET + ADJ + ADJ + ADJ + ADJ + ADJ + ADJ + ADJ +
N + SG

Since no rewrite rule applies to any of the symbols in this string, we are now ready to supply words from the lexicon:

the + huge + ugly + dirty + old + dilapidated + deserted
+ yellow + house + SG

After adding commas to separate the coordinate prenoun adjectivals, we will finally get

the huge, ugly, dirty, old, dilapidated, deserted, yellow house

A potentially infinite number of prenoun adjectives can be provided for rather simply, then, by expanding the NP rewrite rule to include an optional adjectival phrase and by making the ADJP rewrite rule recursive. This is not, however, the method transformationalists have adopted for introducing prenoun adjectivals.

## GENERATING PRENOUN ADJECTIVALS

To see why transformationalists have not adopted the above method of accounting for prenoun adjectivals, let us examine the following sets of sentences. For each set, try to determine whether the second sentence is closer to the first in meaning or closer to the third:

our grocer sells melons which are mouldy
our grocer sells mouldy melons
our grocer sells melons, which are mouldy

the policeman who was drowsy was on the corner
the drowsy policeman was on the corner
the policeman, who was drowsy, was on the corner

they ate all the candy which was half-melted
they ate all the half-melted candy
they ate all the candy, which was half-melted

Are your conclusions consistent? That is, does the second sentence always seem closer to the first in meaning, or always seem closer to the third?

The third sentence in each of these sets contains a **nonrestrictive** relative clause; a nonrestrictive clause (or **appositive** clause) is an adjectival clause that is immediately preceded by a comma. **Restrictive** relative clauses are adjectival clauses that are not immediately preceded by a comma, as illustrated in the first sentences of the above sets. Transformationalists have generally agreed that a prenoun adjectival, such as *mouldy* in *mouldy melons,* means essentially the same as a postnominal restrictive relative clause containing that same word functioning as the verbal phrase of the clause: *which are mouldy,* in the noun phrase *melons which are mouldy.* (*Mouldy* is the only constituent of the verbal phrase of the clause; the BE form is transformationally added between the auxiliary and the verbal phrase. See Chapter 4, footnote 3.) In other words, transformationalists would argue that the second sentences in the above sets mean essentially the same as the first sentences; the third sentences, they would argue, have a somewhat different meaning. (Linguists, grammarians, and rhetoricians all generally consider the two types of clauses to have somewhat different implications.)

As we explained in Chapter 3, one of the primary concerns of transformationalists has been to account for paraphrase relationships between two or more kinds of constructions by deriving them from the same deep structure. Therefore, in order to account for the paraphrase relationship between prenoun adjectivals and postnominal restrictive relative clauses, transformationalists derive the former from the latter. Although the relevant transformations actually operate on strings, the process can be illustrated with the following sentences:

> our grocer sells melons
> melons are mouldy

First we will place the second sentence after the nominal *melons* in the first sentence, since *melons* is the nominal to be modified:

> our grocer sells melons   [melons are mouldy]

We use square brackets in a nontechnical way here, to indicate that the enclosed sentence, *melons are mouldy,* is to be embedded into the other sentence; specifically it is to become a modifier of *melons.* The sentence which is to be embedded into another sentence is usually called the **constituent** sentence (Chomsky's term) or the **insert** sentence; the sentence into which this sentence is inserted is usually called the **matrix** sentence (Chomsky's term) or the **receiver** sentence. We will adopt the two shorter terms, **insert** and **matrix.**

In order to make one sentence into a modifier of a nominal in another sentence, the two sentences must include the same nominal. Specifically, we cannot make a sentence into a modifier of *melons* in *our grocer sells melons* unless the potential insert sentence also contains the nominal *melons*. Since the condition for adjectivalization is met by the potential insert *melons are mouldy,* we can proceed to make this sentence into a restrictive relative clause modifying *melons* in *our grocer sells melons*. First, we replace the nonhuman nominal *melons* in the insert with the nonhuman relative pronoun *which*:

> which
> our grocer sells **melons**   [melons are mouldy]

The next step in the adjectivalization process is to apply the WH-word transformation, which moves a WH word (*which* in this case, *who* if the replaced nominal is ⟨+ human⟩) to the front of the sentence of which it is immediately a part. In this case the WH-word transformation has no effect (applies vacuously) because the WH word is already at the front of the insert sentence. We now have three options: 1) we can leave the sentence as it is; 2) we can replace the WH word with *that*; or 3) we can transform the relative clause into a prenoun adjectival. To do the latter, we first delete the WH word and the BE verb, to give

> our grocer sells melons   [mouldy]

Then we move the adjective *mouldy* into prenoun position:

> our grocer sells mouldy melons

This last operation is usually obligatory when deletion of the WH word and the BE verb leaves only one word. If we had not chosen to reduce the relative clause, we would have produced *our grocer sells melons which are mouldy.* Since the relative pronoun *that* can replace either *who* or *which* introducing a restrictive clause, we could get, alternatively, *our grocer sells melons that are mouldy.*

It may seem that there is something odd about saying the adjectivalization *which are mouldy* comes from the sentence *melons are mouldy.* The fact that "our grocer sells mouldy melons" (if or when it *is* a fact) does not mean that all melons are mouldy, which is what the sentence *melons are mouldy* seems to imply. Also, *our grocer sells mouldy melons* does not necessarily mean "our grocer sells all kinds of melons," though this is one possible interpretation of the matrix *our grocer sells melons*. To take care of problems of this sort, which occur frequently, we will stipulate that the article of the matrix nominal to be modified and also the article of the insert nominal identical to this matrix nominal must both be marked ⟨+ specific⟩. Then if *melons* in *melons are mouldy* is preceded by a zero article [2] having the feature ⟨+ specific⟩, the sentence means something like "certain melons are mouldy," even though *certain* is not actually present in the underlying string. Similarly, *our grocer sells melons* must mean something like "our grocer sells certain melons" if the zero article preceding *melons* in this sentence is marked ⟨+ specific⟩. With these meanings for the insert and matrix sentences, it no longer seems illogical to derive *our grocer sells melons which are mouldy* from *our grocer sells melons* (matrix) and *melons are mouldy* (insert).

Our NP rewrite rule has not yet been modified to allow for sentences that will be transformed into adjectivalizations. We will revise the NP rule to read

$$NP \rightarrow NOM + (S + (and + S)^*)$$

This rule says that a noun phrase consists of a nominal, NOM, plus, optionally, one or more sentences; each embedded sentence except the first is preceded by *and*. The asterisk indicates that the first embedded S may be followed by any number of S's, each preceded by *and*. We need another rule specifying the NOM:

$$NOM \rightarrow (DET) + N + \begin{Bmatrix} SG \\ PL \end{Bmatrix}$$

The term *nominal* now includes what the term *noun phrase* used to include. Thus when we say that a potential adjectivalization must have a nominal identical to the matrix nominal that is to be modified, we mean that the two nouns must be the same and that they must have the same determiner and the same indication of number.

Let us once again generate (in an informal way) *the huge, ugly, dirty, old, dilapidated, deserted, yellow house*, this time using the transformational approach. First, we rewrite NP as

$$NOM + S + and + S + and + S + and + S + and$$
$$+ S + and + S + and + S$$

---

[2] *According to transformational theory, an article precedes every noun which is not functioning as a proper noun and which is not a pronoun. For many transformationalists, the article words are* the, a(n), some, any, no, this, these, that, those. *If no actual article word precedes the noun, then it is said to be preceded by a zero article. We will not attempt to justify the concept of the zero article here but will assume that all common nouns are preceded by an article.*

Then we rewrite NOM as DET + N + SG:

DET + N + SG + S + and + S + and + S + and
+ S + and + S + and + S + and + S

Proceeding informally, we have

       the house    [the house is huge]
                     [and the house is ugly]
                     [and the house is dirty]
                     [and the house is old]
                     [and the house is dilapidated]
                     [and the house is deserted]
                     [and the house is yellow]

The first step in the adjectivalization process is to replace the "shared" insert nominals with the nonhuman relative pronoun *which*, to give

       the house    [which is huge]
                     [and which is ugly]
                     [and which is dirty]
                     [and which is old]
                     [and which is dilapidated]
                     [and which is deserted]
                     [and which is yellow]

The WH-word transformation applies vacuously once again, since *which* already occurs at the front of the insert sentences. In order to generate prenoun adjectivals, we must apply the optional transformation that deletes the relative pronoun and the BE verb:

       the house    [huge]
                     [and ugly]
                     [and dirty]
                     [and old]
                     [and dilapidated]
                     [and deserted]
                     [and yellow]

The insert sentences have been reduced to single-word adjectivals, which usually must be moved to a position between the determiner and the noun. All the adjectivals except the first are preceded by *and*, which moves with them to prenoun position:

the    [huge]    [and ugly]    [and dirty]    [and old]
[and dilapidated]    [and deserted]    [and yellow]    house

The *and's* can be either retained or converted into commas,
to give

the huge, ugly, dirty, old, dilapidated, deserted, yellow house

## SELF-EMBEDDED RELATIVE CLAUSES

In Part II we mentioned that there is a distinction between
grammaticality and acceptability: a sentence can be grammatical but not acceptable. We are now in a position to clarify the
distinction between **grammatical** and **acceptable.** As a minimum condition for a sentence to be grammatical, it must be
constructed in accordance with rules which are necessary in
an adequate grammar of the language. But sentences which
are grammatical according to this definition do not always
sound well-formed to the native speaker, and hence they may
be unacceptable. This difference is perhaps best illustrated
by what linguists call self-embedded relative clauses:

this is the house that the woman that the man that the
judge that we admire sentenced killed lived in

An adequate grammar of English must certainly allow for one
or more adjectivalizations (relative clauses or their reductions)
to occur with every noun, but this necessary provision may result in such unacceptable sentences as the one above. The
essential structure of this sentence is as follows:

this is the house + S
the woman + S + lived in the house
the man + S + killed the woman
the judge + S + sentenced the man
we admire the judge

As this series suggests, *we admire the judge* is made into a
relative clause modifying *the judge* in *the judge sentenced the
man;* the resulting sentence, *the judge that we admire sentenced the man,* is made into a relative clause modifying *the
man* in *the man killed the woman;* the resulting sentence *the
man that the judge that we admire sentenced killed the woman,*
is made into a relative clause modifying *the woman* in *the
woman lived in the house;* the resulting sentence, *the woman
that the man that the judge that we admire sentenced killed*

*lived in the house,* is made into a relative clause modifying the house in *this is the house.* The final result is *this is the house that the woman that the man that the judge that we admire sentenced killed lived in.* This sentence consists of one relative clause, which is embedded into another relative clause, which is embedded into a third relative clause, which is embedded into a fourth relative clause, which modifies *the house* in *this is the house.* This successive embedding of one kind of construction into another kind of construction of the same type is called **self-embedding.** Obviously, sentences with self-embedded constructions are difficult to understand. They may be grammatical, but often they are not acceptable.

The following sentence is composed of the same underlying sentences, but three of the four inserts have been passivized:

> this is the house that was lived in by the woman that was killed
> by the man that was sentenced by the judge that we admire

This sentence is much easier to understand than the self-embedded version. Notice that each relative S occurs at the end of a sentence rather than in the middle:

> this is the house + S
> the house was lived in by the woman + S
> the woman was killed by the man + S
> the man was sentenced by the judge + S
> we admire the judge

As illustrated, this sentence has a series of **right-branchings:** one clause (*this is the house*) ends in a nominal that is modified by a relative clause that ends in a nominal that is modified by a second relative clause that ends in a nominal that is modified by a third relative clause that ends in a nominal that is modified by a fourth relative clause. (The sentence you have just read contains seven right-branching relative clauses.)

As these examples suggest, sentences with multiple self-embeddings are so awkward that most people consider them unacceptable. A series of self-embeddings is much more difficult to understand than a series of right-branchings or left-branchings, the series being of the same length. (An example of a sentence containing a left-branching is *I ran over Mary's friend's husband's cousin's dog,* where every possessive modifies the word to its right.)

Early in the development of transformational theory, successive self-embeddings were considered entirely *grammatical* because they are generated by rules which are needed in any adequate grammar of English. More recently, however, transformationalists have rejected successive self-embeddings as ungrammatical. Transformationalists are coming closer to explaining the native speaker's intuition about the well-formedness of sentences. *Grammatical* and *acceptable* are becoming increasingly synonymous, as transformational theory becomes more sophisticated.

## RESTRICTIVE RELATIVE CLAUSES NOT CONTAINING A *BE* FORM[1]

We are now ready to discuss in detail the derivation of restrictive relative clauses that do not contain a BE form.
Let us look first at the following informal derivations:

Matrix:      **the woman** + S + is intelligent
Insert:      **the woman** loves him
                              who
Process:     the woman [~~the woman~~ loves him] is intelligent
Results:     the woman who loves him is intelligent
             the woman that loves him is intelligent


Matrix:      **the barn** + S + was old
Insert:      **the barn** burned
                        which
Process:     the barn [the barn burned] was old
Results:     the barn which burned was old
             the barn that burned was old


Matrix:      **the woman** + S + is intelligent
Insert:      he loves **the woman**
                                  whom
Process:     the woman [ he loves ~~the woman~~] is intelligent
Results:     the woman whom he loves is intelligent
             the woman that he loves is intelligent
             the woman he loves is intelligent


Matrix:      **the pancakes** + S + were delicious
Insert:      she made **the pancakes**
                                  which
Process:     the pancakes [ she made ~~the pancakes~~] were delicious
Results:     the pancakes which she made were delicious
             the pancakes that she made were delicious
             the pancakes she made were delicious

Judging from these typical examples, is there any restriction as to when *that* can replace *who* or *which* in restrictive relative clauses? Under what conditions can the relative pronoun be deleted altogether? In the last two examples, which result sentences seem most natural: the sentences with *who* or *which* as the relative pronoun; the sentences with *that* as the relative pronoun; or the sentences with no relative pronoun?

## RESTRICTIVE RELATIVE CLAUSES CONTAINING A *BE* FORM

As the last two examples above show, restrictive relative clauses that do not contain a BE form can be reduced by deleting the relative pronoun when it has replaced the object of a verb. Restrictive relative clauses that do contain a BE form can generally be reduced by deleting the WH word and the BE form, as the following examples indicate:

| | |
|---|---|
| Matrix: | the barn + S + is on the hill |
| Insert: | the barn is old |
| | which |
| Process: | the barn [~~the barn~~ is old] is on the hill |
| Results: | the barn which is old is on the hill |
| | the barn that is old is on the hill |
| | the **old** barn is on the hill |

| | |
|---|---|
| Matrix: | the barn + S + is old |
| Insert: | the barn is on the hill |
| | which |
| Process: | the barn [~~the barn~~ is on the hill] is old |
| Results: | the barn which is on the hill is old |
| | the barn that is on the hill is old |
| | the barn **on the hill** is old |

| | |
|---|---|
| Matrix: | the dog + S + is cute |
| Insert: | the dog is performing over there |
| | which |
| Process: | the dog [~~the dog~~ is performing over there] is cute |
| Results: | the dog which is performing over there is cute |
| | the dog that is performing over there is cute |
| | the dog **performing over there** is cute |

| | |
|---|---|
| Matrix; | the jewels + S + were in Mason's car |
| Insert: | the jewels were stolen by Higgins |

| | |
|---|---|
| | which |
| Process: | the jewels [~~the jewels~~ were stolen by Higgins] were in Mason's car |
| Results: | the jewels which were stolen by Higgins were in Mason's car |
| | the jewels that were stolen by Higgins were in Mason's car |
| | the jewels **stolen by Higgins** were in Mason's car |

In the first set of sentences, the BE form of the insert is followed by an adjective, *old,* and the relative clause *which is old* is clearly reducible; indeed, from a stylistic point of view it seems almost obligatory to reduce *the barn which is old is on the hill* to *the old barn is on the hill.* All the other relative clauses above can also be reduced by deleting the WH word plus the BE form. In each case the BE form is originally followed by a different kind of construction: in the second instance it is followed by an adverbially-functioning prepositional phrase (*the barn is* ***on the hill***); in the third case it is followed by a present participle which is functioning as the main verb of the sentence (*the dog is* ***performing*** *over there*); and in the last case it is followed by a past participle functioning as the main verb after passivization has taken place (*the jewels were* ***stolen*** *by Higgins*).

From these examples, it might seem as if a restrictive relative clause can always be reduced by deleting the WH word plus the BE form. There is, in fact, only one kind of restrictive relative clause from which the WH word and BE form cannot be deleted. Consider the following examples:

| | |
|---|---|
| Matrix: | the militant + S + accepted the challenge |
| Insert: | the militant was the leader |
| | who |
| Process: | the militant [~~the militant~~ was the leader] accepted the challenge |
| Result: | the militant who was the leader accepted the challenge |
| | but not ***the militant the leader accepted the challenge** |

| | |
|---|---|
| Matrix: | our friend + S + saved her |
| Insert: | our friend is a lifeguard |
| | who |
| Process: | our friend [~~our friend~~ is a lifeguard] saved her |
| Result: | our friend who is a lifeguard saved her |
| | but not ***our friend a lifeguard saved her** |

The BE form in both of the insert sentences is followed by a nominal phrase and, in each case, deletion of the WH word plus the BE verb produces an unacceptable result.[3] (The sentences would be acceptable if the nominal phrases *the leader* and *a lifeguard* were set off by commas, but transformationalists believe that appositives such as these have a different source than reduced restrictive clauses.) Thus if an insert containing a main verb BE followed by a nominal is made into a *restrictive* clause, the WH word and BE verb usually cannot be deleted. But in all other cases, deletion of a WH word plus BE verb is possible; indeed, from a stylistic viewpoint, such reduction is often desirable.

## SINGLE-WORD ADJECTIVALIZATIONS

We mentioned in Chapter 1 that single-word adjectivals usually precede the noun they modify. One exception is found in a small group of stereotyped expressions, including *mother dear* and *time immemorial;* these presumably should not be generated by the transformations regularly involved in adjectivalization. The following sets of sentences illustrate five other kinds of exceptions:

| | |
|---|---|
| Matrix: | something + S + happened |
| Insert: | something was wonderful |
| |             which |
| Process: | something [~~something~~ was wonderful] happened |
| Results: | something which was wonderful happened |
| | something that was wonderful happened |
| | **something wonderful** happened |

| | |
|---|---|
| Matrix: | the party + S + was a success |
| Insert: | the party was yesterday |
| |             which |
| Process: | the party [~~the party~~ was yesterday] was a success |
| Results: | the party which was yesterday was a success |
| | the party that was yesterday was a success |
| | **the party yesterday** was a success |

| | |
|---|---|
| Matrix: | the dog + S + is cute |
| Insert: | the dog is performing |

---

[3] *But note that* our friend **the** lifeguard saved her *would be grammatical. Why do you suppose that this is so?*

|  | which |
|---|---|
| Process: | the dog [~~the dog~~ is performing] is cute |
| Results: | the dog which is performing is cute |
|  | the dog that is performing is cute |
|  | **the dog performing** is cute |

| Matrix: | they liked the fence + S |
|---|---|
| Insert: | the fence was outside |
|  | which |
| Process: | they liked the fence [~~the fence~~ was outside] |
| Results: | they liked the fence which was outside |
|  | they liked the fence that was outside |
|  | they liked **the fence outside** |

| Matrix: | the jewels + S + were in Mason's car |
|---|---|
| Insert: | the jewels were stolen |
|  | which |
| Process: | the jewels [~~the jewels~~ were stolen] were in Mason's car |
| Results: | the jewels which were stolen were in Mason's car |
|  | the jewels that were stolen were in Mason's car |
|  | **the jewels stolen** were in Mason's car |

In the first of these examples, the single-word adjectival modifies an indefinite pronoun, *something;* single-word modifiers of indefinite pronouns normally occur after them rather than before. In the second example, the insert verb *was* is not functioning as a BE verb; the fact that this *was* seems synonymous with *occurred* and the fact that it is followed by just an adverbial of *time* indicates that it is functioning intransitively. When the main verb of a relative clause is a form of *to be* that is functioning intransitively, the WH word and the form of *to be* can be deleted, but the resulting adjectival apparently must remain in a postnominal position even if the adjectival consists of only a single word; it would not sound right to say, for example, *the **yesterday** party was a success.* In the third example, *was* in the insert is functioning as a BE verb followed by an adverbial of location, *outside.* This adverbial becomes a single-word modifier of *fence;* again, the modifier can remain in a postnominal position, but in this case the adjectivally functioning adverbial can also occur in prenoun position (*they liked the **outside** fence*). The insert sentences of the last two derivations have participles functioning as main verbs. The clauses derived from these inserts can be reduced to single-word participial modifiers, which can remain—somewhat awkwardly—in postnominal position (*the dog **performing** is cute, the* *jewels **stolen** were in Mason's car)*; the participles can also occur in prenoun positions (*the **performing** dog is cute, the **stolen** jewels were in Mason's car*). These four examples suggest: 1) that single-word modifiers of indefinite pronouns and single-word modifiers derived from adverbials of time *must* occur in postnominal position; 2) that single-word modifiers derived from adverbials of place and some single-word participial modifiers *may* occur in postnominal position.

The last three examples above bring up the question of whether it is always possible to move a single-word adjectival from a postnominal position to a prenoun position without changing the essential meaning of the sentence. In your opinion, does *they liked the fence outside* mean the same as *they liked the outside fence*? Does *the dog performing is cute* mean the same as *the performing dog is cute*? And does *the jewels stolen were in Mason's car* mean the same as *the stolen jewels were in Mason's car*? How about the following pairs of sentences? Do you sense any consistent difference in meaning between the first and second sentences of these sets?

> he is the man responsible
> he is the responsible man

> the only stars visible are Aldebaran and Sirius
> the only visible stars are Aldebaran and Sirius

> the only river navigable is to the north
> the only navigable river is to the north

In each case, we think the postnominal adjectival suggests a temporary state or characteristic, whereas the prenoun adjectival suggests a basic attribute of the noun modified.[4]

It seems to us that this difference can be accounted for by stipulating that each word which could occur as both a postnominal and a prenoun adjectival must be marked ⟨+ temporary⟩ or ⟨− temporary⟩. A word marked ⟨+ temporary⟩ must remain in postnominal position when it occurs there as the reduction of a relative clause:

---

[4] *These examples are adapted from Dwight Bolinger, "Adjectives in English: Attribution and Predication," Lingua, 18 (1967), 3–4. Bolinger states that all attributive adjectivals (adjectivals occurring before the noun they modify) specify a basic characteristic of the noun they modify; all postpositional (postnominal) adjectivals specify a relatively temporary or occasional characteristic; and all adjectivals in predicate adjective position (the river is **navigable**) are ambiguous: they may indicate either a basic characteristic or a temporary characteristic or state. Bolinger suggests that a grammar should not derive prenoun and postnominal adjectivals from predicate adjectivals because of the fact that adjectivals occurring in predicate position have a wider range of meanings than either prenoun or postnominal adjectivals.*

Matrix:     he is the man $+$ S
Insert:     the man is **responsible**
$$\begin{bmatrix} \langle + \text{ VB} \rangle \\ \langle - \text{ V} \rangle \\ \langle + \text{ temporary} \rangle \end{bmatrix}$$
Results:    he is the man responsible
but not       *he is the responsible man

Conversely, single-word adjectivals marked $\langle -$ temporary$\rangle$ *must* be moved into prenoun position:

Matrix:     he is the man $+$ S
Insert:     the man is **responsible**
$$\begin{bmatrix} \langle + \text{ VB} \rangle \\ \langle - \text{ V} \rangle \\ \langle - \text{ temporary} \rangle \end{bmatrix}$$
Result:     he is the responsible man
but not *he is the man responsible

It seems that all words should be marked $+$ or $-$ with respect to some feature such as $\langle$temporary$\rangle$ if they have the potential for occurring as both a single-word postnominal adjectival and a single-word prenoun adjectival. Apparently adjectives ending in *-ible* and *-able* (words such as *responsible, visible,* and *navigable*) must be so marked. It also seems necessary to mark as $\langle +$ temporary$\rangle$ or $\langle -$temporary$\rangle$ all single-word adverbials of location that occur after a BE verb, since such words seem to have a different meaning in prenoun position than in postnominal position. For example, *you can sleep in the bedroom* **downstairs** does not mean precisely the same as *you can sleep in the* **downstairs** *bedroom. The bedroom downstairs* suggests merely the location of the bedroom, whereas *the downstairs bedroom* suggests its classification; it is a downstairs bedroom rather than an upstairs bedroom. *They liked the fence* **outside** *and they liked the* **outside** *fence* seem to have a similar relationship: *outside* in *the fence outside* seems to be giving nondistinguishing information about the fence, whereas *outside* in *the outside fence* seems to be distinguishing this fence from an inside fence.

Participles functioning as the sole constituent of the verbal phrase of a sentence also need to be marked $\langle +$ temporary$\rangle$ or $\langle -$ temporary$\rangle$. For example, many people think *the jewels stolen were in Mason's car* suggests that someone stole jewels from Mason's car, whereas *the stolen jewels were in Mason's car* suggests that the jewels which had been stolen were put in Mason's car. In *the jewels were stolen,* the participle *stolen* calls attention to the act of stealing, whereas *stolen* in *the stolen jewels* describes a characteristic of the jewels. Many people find a similar difference between *number 7 was the elevator broken* and *number 7 was the broken elevator.*

The same contrast between a temporary characteristic and a basic characteristic seems to be illustrated by *the dog performing is cute* and *the performing dog is cute,* sentences in which the single-word adjectival is a present participle. The following examples are similar:

> the nun singing is popular
> the singing nun is popular

> the baby crying is sick
> the crying baby is sick

*The nun singing* seems to refer to a nun who just happens to be singing at a particular time, whereas *the singing nun* (with no special emphasis on *singing*) refers to a nun who has a reputation as a singer; the nun who is singing is not necessarily "the singing nun." There is a similar contrast between *the baby crying* and *the crying baby.*

One way to account for the difference in meaning between present participles occurring as postnominal modifiers and the same participles occurring as prenoun modifiers would be to derive the former from BE + ING constructions (*the nun is singing*) but to derive the latter from strings containing a present tense marker as the only auxiliary element (*the nun sings*); this method would adequately account for the fact that *the nun singing* suggests a temporary action whereas *the singing nun* suggests the forte of the nun. To account for the meaning differences between prenoun and postnominal present participles in this way would, however, obscure the fact that there are other words that show essentially the same meaning difference. Adjectives ending in *-able* and *-ible,* single-word adjectivals derived from adverbials of place, and present and past participles all seem to indicate a basic characteristic or profession in prenoun position but a temporary characteristic or state in postnominal position. We tentatively adopt a very general method of accounting for these phenomena: we suggest that all verbal phrases should be assigned the feature ⟨+ temporary⟩ or the feature ⟨− temporary⟩. The ⟨+ temporary⟩ marking would keep single-word adjectivals from being moved into prenoun position, and the ⟨− temporary⟩ marking would make such movement obligatory.

Some of the examples in this section may seem unacceptable, and hence the reader may question the value of showing that the position of an adjectival can partially determine the meaning of the sentence. We are aware of this possibility but consider the discussion an interesting indication of the kinds of concerns that intrigue linguists today, as they attempt to specify relationships between sentence structure and meaning.


## POSSESSIVES


Many possessives can apparently be accounted for as being derived from relative clauses containing HAVE as the main verb. The following example indicates the process of derivation:

| | |
|---|---|
| Matrix: | I like the new picture + S |
| Insert: | Jill has the new picture |

Process:   I like the new picture [ Jill has ~~the new picture~~]   (which)

Results:
I like the new picture which Jill has
I like the new picture that Jill has
I like the new picture Jill has
I like **the new picture of Jill's**
I like **Jill's new picture**

The last two results contain possessives. The noun phrase *Jill's new picture* is ambiguous; it can be derived from either *Jill has the new picture,* as explained, or from *the new picture is of Jill.* In the former case Jill is the possessor of the picture, while in the latter case Jill is the subject of the picture.

Notice that when a possessive nominal (*Jill's,* in the above case) moves into prenoun position, it replaces the article of the matrix nominal that is modified. This is illustrated in the following examples also:

| | |
|---|---|
| Matrix: | Mary borrowed the book + S |
| Insert: | he has the book |

Process:   Mary borrowed the book [ he has ~~the book~~]   (which)

Results:
Mary borrowed the book which he has
Mary borrowed the book that he has
Mary borrowed the book he has
Mary borrowed **the book of his**
Mary borrowed **his book**

| | |
|---|---|
| Matrix: | she rides the motorcycle + S |
| Insert: | the neighbor has the motorcycle |

Process:     she rides the motorcycle

[ the neighbor has ~~the motorcycle~~ (which)]

Results:     she rides the motorcycle which the neighbor has
she rides the motorcycle that the neighbor has
she rides the motorcycle the neighbor has
she rides **the motorcycle of the neighbor's**
she rides **the neighbor's motorcycle**

Note that possessive pronouns which function as noun modifiers are derived in the same way as possessive nouns.

One interesting question concerning possessives is whether
postnominal possessives (such as *of his* in *the book of his*)
and their corresponding prenoun possessives (such as *his* in
*his book*) are equally acceptable. How do you react to the two
kinds of possessives in the examples given above?

Possessives can be replaced by *whose* to form relative
clauses, as the following example indicates:

Matrix:      she liked the professor + S
Insert:      she borrowed the professor's book
Process:     she liked the professor

[ she borrowed ~~the professor's~~ book (whose)]

Result:      she liked the professor whose book she borrowed

Note that in this case the matrix nominal *the professor* is
matched by a possessive determiner in the insert: *the professor's*. Judging by this example, in what other ways does the
derivation of relative clauses introduced by *whose* differ from
the derivation of relative clauses introduced by *who(m)* or
*which*?

Which of the two sentences in each of the following sets would
you be most likely to use: the sentence with the postnominal
possessive or the sentence with the prenoun possessive?

our baby hid the collar **of the dog**
our baby hid the **dog's** collar

the leaves **of the tree** were eaten by bugs
the **tree's** leaves were eaten by bugs

the nest **of the bird** was destroyed
the **bird's** nest was destroyed

the farmer shut the door **of the barn**
the farmer shut the **barn's** door

When the possessor is nonanimate, as in the last example, people often prefer a postnominal possessive to a prenoun possessive.[5]

These possessives are derived by the process illustrated above; the only difference is that the *'s* does not occur in the postnominal possessives. For some speakers, however, the "double genitive" might be possible in at least the first of these examples: *the collar of the dog's.*

Since there is considerable disagreement among transformationalists as to how possessives should be accounted for, we will not discuss them further but will simply ask some exploratory questions about them in the next section.


## WORKING WITH RESTRICTIVE ADJECTIVALIZATIONS


**1.** Pairs of matrix sentences and insert sentences are given below. Make each insert sentence into an adjectivalization modifying the shared noun in the matrix. First give the *full relative clause* which is derived from the insert sentence, and then give the possible reduction(s) of the relative clause.

    a.  Matrix: the girl + S + bought the skunk
          Insert: the girl was little
    b.  Matrix: the little girl was wearing a dress + S
          Insert: her sister had a dress
    c.  Matrix: the little girl was wearing her sister's dress + S
          Insert: the dress was starched
    d.  Matrix: the little girl + S + bought the skunk
          Insert: the girl was wearing her sister's starched dress
    e.  Matrix: the little girl wearing her sister's starched dress
             bought the skunk + S
          Insert: the skunk was purple
    f.  Matrix: the little girl wearing her sister's starched dress
             bought the purple skunk + S
          Insert: the girl had stared at the skunk every day for weeks

**2.** Try to determine a process whereby the matrix and insert sentences below could be combined to give the result sentences indicated:

    a.  Matrix: the doctor + S + is friendly
          Insert: we go to the doctor
          Result: the doctor to whom we go is friendly

[5] *Edward Sapir,* Language: An Introduction to the Study of Speech *(New York: Harcourt Brace Jovanovich, Inc., 1921), p. 165.*

    b.   Matrix: I didn't need the pills + S
       Insert: I was given a prescription for the pills
       Result: I didn't need the pills for which I was given a
       prescription

Would you be likely to use these result sentences? If not, what variants would you be more likely to use?

**3.** How could the process you established in the above exercise be extended to produce the result sentences below? Determine what the original matrix and insert would be in each case, and show each step of the embedding process.

    a.   the town where he lived is now famous
    b.   I remember the time when you got hurt
    c.   the reasons why he quit his job were understandable

**4.** How are the adjectivals in the following sentences related to each other? That is, are they left- or right-branchings, self-embeddings, and/or something else?

> This is the preacher all shaven and shorn that
> married the man all tattered and torn that kissed
> the maiden all forlorn that milked the cow with
> the crumpled horn that tossed the dog that
> worried the cat that killed the rat that ate
> the malt that lay in the house that Jack built.

**5.** The following excerpt from William Faulkner's "The Bear" contains an adjectival self-embedding. What is the main clause? Try to disentangle the clauses so that the meaning becomes more readily apparent.

>     and, his father and Uncle Buddy both gone
> now, one day without reason or any warning the
> almost completely empty house in which his uncle
> and Tennie's ancient and quarrelsome great-
> 5    grandfather (who claimed to have seen Lafayette
> and McCaslin said in another ten years would be
> remembering God) lived, cooked and slept in
> one single room, burst into peaceful conflagration,
> a tranquil instantaneous sourceless unanimity
> 10   of combustion, walls floors and roof: [6]

[6] *William Faulkner, "The Bear," The Portable Faulkner (New York, The Viking Press, Inc., 1946), p. 337.*

**6.** The first sentence in each of the sets below contains a possessive nominal; the second sentence contains a corresponding noun adjunct. Should such noun adjuncts be derived from the corresponding possessives? Why or why not?

> our baby hid the **dog's** collar
> our baby hid the **dog** collar
>
> the **tree's** leaves were eaten by bugs
> the **tree** leaves were eaten by bugs
>
> the **bird's** nest was destroyed
> the **bird** nest was destroyed
>
> the farmer shut the **barn's** door
> the farmer shut the **barn** door

**7.** Try to think of an insert sentence which could logically account for each of the bold-faced words in the sentences below. All or most of the bold-faced words in a given set can be accounted for in essentially the same way.

a.  he has a **nine o'clock** class
the new **Ohio** senator made his first speech yesterday
we stopped at the **corner** drugstore

b.  it's a **brick** house
it's a **stone** wall
it's a **rubber** ball

c.  he has some **snow** boots
he has some **shoe** polish
he has a **wastepaper** basket
he has a **rain** coat
he has a **wishing** well
he has a **swimming** pool
he has a **wading** pool
he has a **sleeping** bag
he has a **waiting** room
he has a **hearing** aid

d.  he's a **part-time** policeman
he's a **regular** policeman

e.  he's a **criminal** lawyer
he's a **corporate** lawyer
he's a **divorce** lawyer

   f.   our baby hid the **dog** collar
       the **bird** nest was destroyed
       the **tree** leaves were being eaten
       the farmer shut the **barn** door

   g.   he got the **main** idea
       he knew the **chief** reason
       he is a **total** stranger
       he is a **mere** kid
       he is a **distant** cousin
       he is a **personal** friend

**8.** Do all of the bold-faced words below indicate possession? Try to think of an insert sentence which could logically account for each of the bold-faced words.

   a.   the **girl's** father is mean
   b.   the **horse's** hoof was sore
   c.   I drink **Nestle's** chocolate
   d.   **women's** clothing is sometimes sexy
   e.   **Chicago's** weather is abominable
   f.   the **room's** temperature is unbearable
   g.   it's only an **hour's** work
   h.   **yesterday's** paper was late
   i.   the **man's** rudeness annoyed her
   j.   she got the **doctor's** permission
   k.   the **man's** murderer was ruthless

**9.** Nouns of direct address, called "vocatives," often precede or follow imperatives. Discuss whether or not such nouns of address can be logically explained as reduced adjectivalizations. Here are some examples:

> **Sally,** feed the dog
> answer me, **Bobby**
> **Raffles,** leave her alone
> cut out the blarney, **Sullivan**

**10 a.** Does the location of the italicized words in either or both of the quotations below seem odd to you? Discuss.

> "Often people display a curious respect for a man *drunk,* rather like the respect of simple races for the insane"

>       —F. Scott Fitzgerald, *Tender is the Night*
>       (italics added)

"The two *next-door* girls had arranged some
Hallow Eve games and soon everything was
merry again"

—James Joyce, "Clay," in *Dubliners*
(italics added)

b.   Do either or both of these examples support the idea
that prenoun adjectivals indicate basic characteristics whereas
postnominal adjectivals indicate temporary characteristics or
states? Discuss.

**11** a.   Should the source for *starched* in *the girl was wearing
her sister's starched dress* be *the dress **was** starched* or *the
dress **had been** starched*? Discuss.

b.   Should *big* in *that big elephant trampled its owner five
years ago, when it was a baby* be derived from *that elephant
**was** big*, or from *that elephant **is** big*?

**12.**   Since transformations are not supposed to change the
basic meaning of a sentence, the meaning of a derived sentence should be the sum of the meanings of the matrix and
insert(s). This being the case, what is wrong with deriving
*a lion that doesn't have enough to eat is a dangerous animal*
from *a lion is a dangerous animal* and *a lion doesn't have
enough to eat*? Similarly, what is wrong with deriving the result
sentences below from the matrix and insert sentences given?

Some linguists have proposed deriving sentences like *a lion
that doesn't have enough to eat is a dangerous animal* from a
conditional proposition: *if a lion doesn't have enough to eat, it
is a dangerous animal.* [7] Try to devise a conditional proposition
that will account for the result sentences below. Is the conditional proposition possible in all cases? If not, why not?

a.   Matrix:   people are lucky
     Insert:   people need people
     Result:   people who need people are lucky

b.   Matrix:   any student will pass the course
     Insert:   any student can spell acceptably
     Result:   any student who can spell acceptably will pass
               the course

---

[7] *For the idea behind this exercise, and for some of the examples, we are indebted
to Robert P. Stockwell, Paul Schachter, and Barbara Hall Partee,* Integration of Transformational Theories on English Syntax *(Los Angeles, Calif.: University of California
at Los Angeles, 1968), Vol. 1, pp. 454–466.*

c.  Matrix:   few students will fail the course
    Insert:   few students study hard
    Result:   few students who study hard will fail the course

d.  Matrix:   each student should pass the course
    Insert:   each student studies hard
    Result:   each student who studies hard should pass
              the course

e.  Matrix:   all students should do well
    Insert:   all students study hard
    Result:   all students who study hard should do well

f.  Matrix:   all the students did well
    Insert:   all the students studied hard
    Result:   all the students who studied hard did well

g.  Matrix:   every student should do well
    Insert:   every student studies hard
    Result:   every student who studies hard should do well

h.  Matrix:   every student did well
    Insert:   every student studied hard
    Result:   every student who studied hard did well

i.  Matrix:   no student should pass the course
    Insert:   no student cheats
    Result:   no student who cheats should pass the course

j.  Matrix:   no student passed the course
    Insert:   no student cheated
    Result:   no student who cheated passed the course

## NONRESTRICTIVE ADJECTIVALIZATIONS

In this section we will first discuss some of the distinctions between nonrestrictive and restrictive clauses, then explain some similarities between coordinated clauses and nonrestrictive clauses. Finally, we will discuss various kinds of nonrestrictive adjectivalizations.

## SOME DISTINCTIONS BETWEEN
## NONRESTRICTIVES AND RESTRICTIVES

Early in the section on restrictive relative clauses, we asked you to look at the following sets of sentences and decide whether the second sentence is closer to the first in meaning, or closer to the third:

our grocer sells melons which are mouldy
our grocer sells mouldy melons
our grocer sells melons, which are mouldy

the policeman who was drowsy was on the corner
the drowsy policeman was on the corner
the policeman, who was drowsy, was on the corner

they ate all the candy which was half-melted
they ate all the half-melted candy
they ate all the candy, which was half-melted

As we have explained, transformationalists generally agree that a prenoun adjectival, such as *drowsy* in *the drowsy policeman,* means essentially the same as a postnominal restrictive relative clause containing that same adjectival as the verbal phrase: *who was drowsy* in the noun phrase *the policeman who was drowsy.* Transformationalists generally assume that nonrestrictive relative clauses have a somewhat different meaning and that, in fact, a sentence containing a nonrestrictive relative clause is equivalent to two sentences conjoined by *and.* The process of conjoining sentences is called **conjunction.** For example,

the policeman, who was drowsy, was on the corner

is equivalent to

the policeman was on the corner, and he was drowsy

(We have replaced *the policeman* with *he* in the second clause.) Similarly, *our grocer sells melons, which are mouldy* is equivalent to *our grocer sells melons, and they are mouldy.* Likewise, *they ate all the candy, which was half-melted* is equivalent to *they ate all the candy, and it was half-melted.*

By deriving nonrestrictive relative clauses from conjoined sentences, transformationalists are in effect supporting the convention that such clauses give information which is not essential in identifying the person, place, thing, or idea referred to by the noun that is modified. On the other hand, a restrictive relative clause is said to give information which *is* needed to identify the referent of the noun it modifies. For example, the fact that the relative clause is nonrestrictive in *the policeman, who was drowsy, was on the corner* implies that the listener or reader knows what policeman is being designated. On the other hand, *the policeman who was drowsy was on the corner* identifies the policeman being referred to: it was the *drowsy* policeman who was on the corner, not the other(s).

The following example should help clarify the distinction between restrictive and nonrestrictive clauses:

> those people, who cannot read, are unfortunate
> those people who cannot read are unfortunate

In the first sentence, *those people* apparently refers to people that have been identified in previous discourse. *Those* people cannot read, and they are unfortunate. In the second sentence, the relative clause tells which people are unfortunate: the non-readers, the illiterates. The first sentence consists, in effect, of one subject with two predicates:

$$\text{those people} \quad \left\langle \begin{array}{l} \text{and} \end{array} \right. \begin{array}{l} \text{cannot read} \\ \text{are unfortunate} \end{array}$$

The second sentence, on the other hand, logically has only one subject with one predicate:

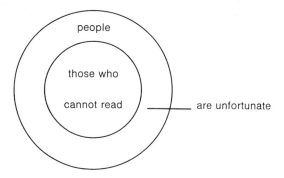

A similar example is provided by the following sentences:

> those people, who drink, should be warned about the dangers
>    of drinking

> those people who drink should be warned about the dangers
>    of drinking

The second sentence is equivalent to *drinkers should be warned about the dangers of drinking.*

The most obvious surface distinction between restrictive and nonrestrictive clauses is that in speech, nonrestrictive clauses and their reductions are preceded by primary stress and by a noticeable pause that is itself preceded by a slight rise in pitch; in contrast, restrictive relative clauses and their reductions are never immediately preceded by such a pause. Nonrestrictive relative clauses are also followed by this kind of pause, except when they occur at the end of a sentence, where they are most frequently located in informal conversation. In writing, a comma corresponds to the pause that occurs before a nonrestrictive clause. A comma also follows a nonrestrictive clause, unless the clause occurs at the end of a sentence. The following sentences are illustrative:

> the boy, ‖ who suddenly appeared in the doorway, ‖ was
>     screaming unintelligibly
> the boy who suddenly appeared in the doorway | was
>     screaming unintelligibly

The symbols here are structural rather than transformational. The / | / corresponds to a short pause, the kind of pause that often (as here) separates a subject from its predicate; such pauses do not involve a rise in pitch level and are not represented by any punctuation mark. The / ‖ / symbol corresponds to a longer pause; when associated with a nonrestrictive relative clause, such pauses are represented in writing by a comma.

A restrictive relative clause is not preceded by a comma. Or, to put it another way, any clause (or reduction of a clause) that is immediately preceded by a comma is, by definition, nonrestrictive.


## PROVIDING FOR COORDINATE CLAUSES
## AND NONRESTRICTIVES


One way to provide for coordinate clauses within a sentence would be to add a new phrase structure rule which would precede all the others and which might be formulated as follows:

$$S' \rightarrow S + (and + S)^*$$

This rule says that the master sentence, S′ (read as "S-prime") consists of a sentence plus, optionally, an unlimited number of additional sentences, each preceded by *and*. Every nonrestrictive clause will be generated from an optional *and* + *S* provided by this first phrase structure rule.

Although the sources of restrictive and nonrestrictive relative clauses are different, reflecting the fact that they are interpreted differently, the process of transforming insert sentences into relative clauses is the same for both types.


NONRESTRICTIVE RELATIVE CLAUSES

NOT CONTAINING A *BE* FORM


In order to generate a nonrestrictive clause, one must rewrite S′ as

S + and + S

If the second S is to be made into a nonrestrictive clause modifying a noun in the first S, the second S must have a nominal which is identical to the nominal to be modified. The following string meets this condition:

**the woman** is intelligent [and **the woman** loves him]

Since both S's contain *the woman,* the second sentence can be made into a nonrestrictive clause modifying *the woman* in the first sentence:

the woman, **who loves him,** is intelligent

We are assuming that there is an optional transformation to move the second S to a position after the shared noun in the first S, and that there is later an optional transformation to delete the *and* before the second S. Then the first S will be a matrix sentence and the second S will become a nonrestrictive clause, as indicated in the following example:

```
Matrix (first S):    the barn + S + was old
Insert (second S):   the barn burned
                         which
      Process:    the barn [the barn burned] was old
      Result:     the barn, which burned, was old
```

In formal standard English, the *who* or *which* introducing a nonrestrictive clause is not often replaced by *that*. Formally, we write

the woman that loves him is intelligent
the barn that burned was old

rather than

the woman, that loves him, is intelligent
the barn, that burned, was old

The next four examples are parallel to the last two examples of restrictive clauses presented on page 183.

Matrix:     the woman + S + is intelligent
Insert:     he loves the woman

Process:    the woman [ he loves ~~the woman~~ (whom)] is intelligent
Result:     the woman, whom he loves, is intelligent

Matrix:     the pancakes + S + were delicious
Insert:     she made the pancakes

Process:    the pancakes [ she made ~~the pancakes~~ (which)]
            were delicious
Result:     the pancakes, which she made, were delicious

Compare the result sentences given here with the result sentences given for the corresponding restrictive clauses. What variants are possible with restrictives but not with nonrestrictives? What generalizations can be made, at this point, about the differences between restrictives and nonrestrictives?

NONRESTRICTIVE RELATIVE CLAUSES

CONTAINING A *BE* FORM

Nonrestrictive relative clauses containing a BE form can often be reduced by deleting the WH word and the BE form, as the following examples indicate:

Matrix:     the man + S + was staring at the boy
Insert:     the man was upset
Results:    the man, who was upset, was staring at the boy
            the man, **upset,** was staring at the boy

Matrix:     the woman + S + was yelling at us
Insert:     the woman was some distance away

Results:    the woman, who was some distance away, was
        yelling at us
       the woman, **some distance away,** was yelling at us

Matrix:    our friend + S + saved her
Insert:    our friend is a lifeguard
Results:    our friend, who is a lifeguard, saved her
       our friend, **a lifeguard,** saved her

Matrix:    the woman + S + was some distance away
Insert:    the woman was yelling at us
Results:    the woman, who was yelling at us, was some
       distance away
       the woman, **yelling at us,** was some distance away

Matrix:    the letters + S + contained several misspellings
Insert:    the letters were typed by Miss Lemon
Results:    the letters, which were typed by Miss Lemon,
       contained several misspellings
       the letters, **typed by Miss Lemon,** contained
       several misspellings

Notice that although *restrictive* relative clauses containing a BE form followed by a predicate nominal cannot be ordinarily reduced by deleting the WH word and the BE form, *nonrestrictives* can; the reduction is an **appositive.** We can reduce, for example,

    our friend, who is a lifeguard, saved her

to

    our friend, a lifeguard, saved her

even though we cannot reduce

    our friend who is a lifeguard saved her

to

    *our friend a lifeguard saved her

We noted above that nonrestrictive clauses can often be reduced by deleting the WH word plus the BE form. Examine the sentences below, plus any others you wish, to determine which kind or kinds of nonrestrictive inserts seem least acceptable when reduced: inserts with BE + ADJ, BE + ADVP $_{+ \text{ loc}}$,

BE + NP, BE + ING (BE followed by a present participle), or BE + EN (BE followed by a past participle). The following sentences with reduced nonrestrictives correspond to the examples with restrictive clauses that were given on pages 184–185:

the barn, old, is on the hill
the barn, on the hill, is old
the militant, the leader, accepted the challenge
our friend, a lifeguard, saved her
the dog, performing over there, is cute
the jewels, stolen by Higgins, were in Mason's car

## MOVABILITY OF REDUCED NONRESTRICTIVES

Again, generally speaking, a reduced medial nonrestrictive can often be moved to the front of its sentence and/or to the end without a change of basic meaning. (Very frequently, of course, a nonrestrictive is originally located at the end of its sentence, as in *I felt sorry for the boy, an orphan.*) Consider the following examples:

the man, **upset**, was staring at the boy
**upset**, the man was staring at the boy
the man was staring at the boy, **upset**

the woman, **some distance away**, was yelling at us
**some distance away**, the woman was yelling at us
the woman was yelling at us, **some distance away**

our friend, **a lifeguard**, saved her
**a lifeguard**, our friend saved her
our friend saved her, **a lifeguard**

the woman, **yelling at us**, was some distance away
**yelling at us**, the woman was some distance away
the woman was some distance away, **yelling at us**

the letters, **typed by Miss Lemon**, contained several misspellings
**typed by Miss Lemon**, the letters contained several misspellings
the letters contained several misspellings, **typed by Miss Lemon**

In which sets of sentences does the second sentence and/or the third seem to be unacceptable as a paraphrase of the first? What are your reasons for considering these particular variants unacceptable? Do all three of the variants seem acceptable in one or more of these sets? If so, which of the three variants do you prefer, in each case?


## SUMMARY OF DIFFERENCES BETWEEN
## RESTRICTIVES AND NONRESTRICTIVES


We have noted several differences between restrictives and nonrestrictives:

**1.** Nonrestrictives are immediately preceded by a comma in writing, or by a pause signaling a comma, in speech; restrictives are never immediately preceded by a comma or by such a pause.

**2.** The relative pronoun *that* can replace *who* or *which* in restrictive clauses, but not usually in nonrestrictives.

**3.** If the relative pronoun replaces a direct object in the insert, the pronoun can be deleted from restrictive clauses but not from nonrestrictives.

**4.** Nonrestrictive clauses containing a predicate nominative can be reduced by deleting the WH word plus the BE form, but restrictive clauses containing a predicate nominative usually cannot be reduced.

**5.** Reductions of nonrestrictive. clauses are often movable. Reductions of restrictive clauses are not movable except when they are single words; in such cases they may, and usually must, be moved to a position immediately before the noun they modify.

Can you think of any other consistent differences between restrictives and nonrestrictives? Consider, for example, the following pairs of sentences:

> any man who drives while drunk is living dangerously
> *any man, who drives while drunk, is living dangerously

> *I just found out that he won which pleased me very much
> I just found out that he won, which pleased me very much

Why is only the restrictive relative clause acceptable in the first set? And why is only the nonrestrictive clause acceptable in the second set?

## ABSOLUTES

As we saw in the introduction to this chapter, there are two kinds of absolute constructions. One kind resembles a reduced nonrestrictive clause (*the boy suddenly appeared in the doorway, **his lips moving unintelligibly***); the other kind resembles an adverbialization (*she could not see very well, **the light being out***). We will discuss each of these kinds in turn.

### ABSOLUTES THAT ARE RELATED TO NONRESTRICTIVES

Examine the structure of the bold-faced phrases in the following passage from D. H. Lawrence's *Women in Love:*

> Gudrun, **with her arms outspread** and **her face uplifted,** went in a strange palpitating dance towards the cattle, lifting her body towards them as if in a spell, **her feet pulsing as if in some little frenzy of unconscious sensation, her arms, her wrists, her hands stretching and heaving and falling and reaching and reaching and falling, her breasts lifted and shaken towards the cattle, her throat exposed as in some voluptuous ecstasy towards them,** whilst she drifted imperceptibly nearer, an uncanny white figure, towards them, carried away in its own rapt trance, ebbing in strange fluctuations upon the cattle, that waited, and ducked their heads a little in sudden contraction from her, watching all the time as if hypnotized, **their bare horns branching in the clear light,** as the white figure of the woman ebbed upon them, in the slow, hypnotizing convulsion of the dance.[8]

In each case, the underlined phrase would be a sentence if an appropriate BE form were added:

[8] *D. H. Lawrence,* Women in Love *(New York: The Viking Press, 1950), p. 159.*

her arms **were** outspread
her face **was** uplifted
her feet **were** pulsing . . .
her arms, her wrists, her hands, **were** stretching . . .
her breasts **were** lifted . . .
her throat **was** exposed . . .
their bare horns **were** branching in the clear light

Constructions of this sort, which can be made into sentences by the addition of a BE form, are called **absolutes.** Absolutes often begin with a noun modified by a possessive pronoun, as in these examples. Sometimes an absolute is introduced by *with: with her arms outspread.*

Like nonrestrictives, absolutes are both preceded and followed by a comma—unless, of course, the absolute occurs at the beginning or end of a sentence. In fact, the kind of absolute illustrated above is so much like a nonrestrictive that both kinds of constructions can be provided for in the same way. Thus our new initial phrase structure rule

$$S' \rightarrow S + (\text{and} + S)^*$$

provides for conjoined clauses, nonrestrictives, and one type of absolute.

Before deriving an absolute construction, let us derive the nonrestrictive clause that corresponds to it:

| | |
|---|---|
| Matrix: | the boy + S + suddenly appeared in the doorway |
| Insert: | the boy's lips were moving unintelligibly |
| | whose |
| Process: | the boy [the boy's lips were moving unintelligibly] |
| | suddenly appeared in the doorway |
| Result: | the boy, whose lips were moving unintelligibly, |
| | suddenly appeared in the doorway |

As explained earlier, we are assuming that the first step in deriving a nonrestrictive clause is to move the second S to a position following the shared nominal in the first sentence, then delete the *and* that originally precedes the second S. Here, as in the generation of all relative clauses that begin with *whose,* a nominal phrase of the matrix (*the boy*) matches up with a possessive determiner phrase (*the boy's*) of the insert, the two phrases being identical except for the possessive marker (*'s*) in the insert phrase. An absolute phrase can be derived from the same matrix and insert:

| | |
|---|---|
| Matrix: | the boy + S + suddenly appeared in the doorway |
| Insert: | the boy's lips were moving unintelligibly |

|  |  |
|---|---|
| | his |
| Process: | the boy [~~the boy's~~ lips ~~were~~ moving unintelligibly] suddenly appeared in the doorway |
| Basic result: | the boy, his lips moving unintelligibly, suddenly appeared in the doorway |

There are two obvious differences here between the nonrestrictive clause and the absolute: 1) the nonrestrictive clause begins with *whose lips* whereas the absolute begins with *his lips;* and 2) the absolute has had its underlying BE form deleted.

A nonrestrictive clause beginning with *whose* cannot be reduced and must therefore remain immediately after the word it modifies. Absolutes, however, are like reduced nonrestrictives in that they usually can be moved to the beginning of the sentence or to the end. (Of course either an absolute or a relative clause may originally occur at the end of a sentence.) The following sentences illustrate the freedom of movement of absolutes:

> the boy, *his lips moving unintelligibly,* suddenly
> appeared in the doorway
> *his lips moving unintelligibly,* the boy suddenly
> appeared in the doorway
> the boy suddenly appeared in the doorway, *his lips
> moving unintelligibly*

Which of these variants do you like least? Which do you like best?

We noted earlier that the derivation of this type of absolute involves the deletion of a BE form. The following derivations are typical:

|  |  |
|---|---|
| Matrix: | the cat + S + fearfully awaited his approach |
| Insert: | the cat's body was taut |
| Transforming | its |
| the insert: | ~~the cat's~~ body ~~was~~ taut |
| Results: | the cat, **its body taut,** fearfully awaited his approach |
| | **its body taut,** the cat fearfully awaited his approach |
| | the cat fearfully awaited his approach, **its body taut** |

|  |  |
|---|---|
| Matrix: | the duchess + S + swept past haughtily |
| Insert: | the duchess' nose was in the air |
| Transforming | her |
| the insert: | ~~the duchess'~~ nose ~~was~~ in the air |

| | |
|---|---|
| Results: | the duchess, **her nose in the air**, swept past haughtily |
| | **her nose in the air**, the duchess swept past haughtily |
| | the duchess swept past haughtily, **her nose in the air** |

| | |
|---|---|
| Matrix: | Grandfather + S + walked slowly |
| Insert: | Grandfather's back was a gnarled bole |
| Transforming the insert: | his |
| | Grandfather's back was a gnarled bole |
| Results: | Grandfather, **his back a gnarled bole**, walked slowly |
| | **his back a gnarled bole**, Grandfather walked slowly |
| | Grandfather walked slowly, **his back a gnarled bole** |

| | |
|---|---|
| Matrix: | two evergreens + S + stood by the creekside |
| Insert: | two evergreens' branches were cradling snow |
| Transforming the insert: | their |
| | two evergreens' branches were cradling snow |
| Results: | two evergreens, **their branches cradling snow**, stood by the creekside |
| | **their branches cradling snow**, two evergreens stood by the creekside |
| | two evergreens stood by the creekside, **their branches cradling snow** |

| | |
|---|---|
| Matrix: | the hills + S + rose majestically |
| Insert: | the hills' tops were drenched by the sun |
| Transforming the insert: | their |
| | the hills' tops were drenched by the sun |
| Results: | the hills, **their tops drenched by the sun**, rose majestically |
| | **their tops drenched by the sun**, the hills rose majestically |
| | the hills rose majestically, **their tops drenched by the sun** |

Each insert sentence above illustrates a different kind of internal construction: BE + ADJ, BE + ADVP$_{\langle + \text{ loc}\rangle}$, BE + NP, BE + ING (present participle verb), and BE + EN (past participle verb). No matter what follows the BE form, the sentence can be made into an absolute.

Notice that there is a nonrestrictive clause corresponding to each of these absolutes:

the cat, **whose body was taut,** fearfully awaited his approach
the duchess, **whose nose was in the air,** walked past haughtily
Grandfather, **whose back was a gnarled bole,** walked slowly
two evergreens, **whose branches were cradling snow,** stood
    by the creekside
the hills, **whose tops were drenched by the sun,** rose
    majestically

Stylistically, what advantage does the absolute construction have over the nonrestrictive clause? In which position do these absolutes generally sound best: in medial position immediately after the noun they refer to; in initial position; or in final position?

In the following sentences, the structure of the matrix is somewhat different than in the sentences above:

**the cat's** body was taut, **its** legs stiff
**the boy's** jeans were bloodstained, **his** shirt torn

Here, the possessive pronoun in the insert refers to a possessive determiner phrase in the matrix. In such cases the absolute usually occurs in final position, though it may also occur, more awkwardly, in initial position. Also, the insert sentence cannot be transformed into a nonrestrictive clause in such cases: we do not say *the boy's jeans, whose shirt was torn, were bloodstained.* These last two examples of absolutes clearly reveal a relationship to sentences with coordinate clauses: *the cat's body was taut, its legs stiff* is simply a more economical way of saying *the cat's body was taut and its legs were stiff.*


## ABSOLUTES THAT ARE RELATED TO
## ADVERBIALIZATIONS


Some absolutes, though, seem more like adverbial clauses that are introduced by *since* or *because*:

he decided to play golf, **since the day was sunny**
    (adverbial clause)
he decided to play golf, **the day being sunny** (absolute)

This absolute is different from our previous examples in two ways: 1) it does not begin with a possessive pronoun; and 2) the underlying past tense BE form *was* (*the day **was** sunny*) has been transformed into the present participle form *being.*

Speaking in transformational terms, the tense marker is re-placed by the present participle affix ING, which is later moved by the affix transformation to a position following BE:

the day + PAST + BE + sunny
the day + ING + BE + sunny

the day + BE + ING # sunny
the day being sunny

Similar absolutes can be derived from strings containing BE as an auxiliary verb, from strings containing HAVE as a main verb, and from strings containing HAVE as an auxiliary. In each case there must be no auxiliary preceding the HAVE or BE which turns out as *having* or *being*. The following are some examples:

|  |  |
|---|---|
| Matrix: | we have to eat hamburgers + S |
| Insert: | the steak + PAST + BE + EN + eat + already |
| Transforming | ING |
| the insert: | the steak + ~~PAST~~ + BE + EN + eat + already |
|  | the steak + BE + ING # eat + EN # already |
|  | the steak being eaten already |
| Results: | we have to eat hamburgers, **the steak being eaten already** |
|  | **the steak being eaten already,** we have to eat hamburgers |

|  |  |
|---|---|
| Matrix: | she couldn't go to college + S |
| Insert: | her father + PAST + HAVE + little money |
| Transforming | ING |
| the insert: | her father + ~~PAST~~ + HAVE + little money |
|  | her father + HAVE + ING # little money |
|  | her father having little money |
| Results: | she couldn't go to college, **her father having little money** |
|  | **her father having little money,** she couldn't go to college |

|  |  |
|---|---|
| Matrix: | she was forced to go barefoot + S |
| Insert: | the boy + PAST + HAVE + EN + steal + her shoes |
| Transforming | ING |
| the insert: | the boy + ~~PAST~~ + HAVE + EN + steal + her shoes |
|  | the boy + HAVE + ING # steal + EN # her shoes |
|  | the boy having stolen her shoes |

Results:     she was forced to go barefoot, **the boy having stolen her shoes**
**the boy having stolen her shoes,** she was forced to go barefoot

Notice that in these examples, the S representing the insert sentence is located at the end of the matrix sentence rather than after some specific noun: *we have to eat hamburgers + S, she couldn't go to college + S.* We are assuming that absolutes derived by replacing the tense marker with ING are sentence adverbials of reason, and sentence adverbials always occur at the end of a sentence in the deep structure. (See Chapter 4, pages 149-152, for a fuller discussion of sentence adverbials and of adverbials of reason in particular.)

The last two examples above have a possessive pronoun which refers to a noun in the matrix:

**she** couldn't go to college, **her** father having little money
**she** was forced to go barefoot, the boy having stolen **her** shoes

However, absolutes with *being* and *having* do not necessarily contain a possessive that refers to a matrix noun, as the following examples show:

she could not see very well, **the light being out**
we have to eat hamburgers, **the steak being eaten already**
she had to walk, **everyone else having left already**

## WORKING WITH ADJECTIVALIZATIONS AND ABSOLUTES

1. Which of the following sentences have formal internal punctuation? Explain.

    a. I like Hemingway's book, *A Farewell to Arms*
    b. I like Hemingway's book *A Farewell to Arms*
    c. in his book, *A Farewell to Arms,* Hemingway describes a wartime love affair
    d. in his book *A Farewell to Arms,* Hemingway describes a wartime love affair

2. Examine the following three versions of Kay Boyle's description of Hilary in "The Ballet of Central Park." Each succeeding version grows shorter—from seventy-one words in four

sentences, to sixty-one words in two sentences, to fifty-eight words in two sentences. Count the number of adjectivalizations in each version to see to what extent the declining number of words is due to a decrease in the number of adjectivalizations. Which version seems better to you? Does the number or nature of the adjectivalizations affect your choice?

### Draft #1

Over her leotard, she wore a short blue dress, and her ballet slippers, their pink cotton laces knotted together, were carried across her shoulder. Her hair was wrenched back into a glossy pony-tail, and her brow was round and smooth as a doll's. But it was her eyebrows that startled one in disbelief. They were as delicate and jet black as the markings on a butterfly's wing, and seemingly as perishable.

### Draft #3

Over her black leotard, she wore a short dress of gentiane blue, and her ballet slippers were strung across her shoulder by their knotted strings. Her hair, as light as cornsilk, was wrenched back from her brow into a glossy pony-tail, and her eyebrows were jet-black in contrast, and seemingly as perishable as the markings on the wing of a butterfly.

### Published version

She wore a short blue dress over the black legs of her leotard, and her pink satin toe shoes were slung across her shoulder by their knotted strings. Her light hair was wrenched away from her scalp into a glossy ponytail, and her eyebrows were jet black and seemingly as perishable as the markings on a night-flying moth.[9]

**3.** In the poem below, underline the present participle words and phrases that are functioning adjectivally. Notice that the nonrestrictive phrases (those preceded by a comma) do not immediately follow the noun they modify. Is the placement of these adjectivals effective? Discuss.

[9] As quoted in John Kuehl, ed., Creative Writing and Rewriting: Contemporary American Novelists at Work (New York: Appleton-Century-Crofts, 1967), pp. 22–23.

### Between the World and Me

And one morning while in the woods I stumbled
    suddenly upon the thing,
Stumbled upon it in a grassy clearing guarded by
    scaly oaks and elms.
And the sooty details of the scene rose, thrusting
    themselves between the world and me . . . .

There was a design of white bones slumbering
    forgottenly upon a cushion of ashes.
There was a charred stump of a sapling pointing
5        a blunt finger accusingly at the sky.
There were torn tree limbs, tiny veins of burnt
    leaves, and a scorched coil of greasy hemp;
A vacant shoe, an empty tie, a ripped shirt, a
    lonely hat, and a pair of trousers stiff with black
    blood.
And upon the trampled grass were buttons, dead
    matches, butt-ends of cigars and cigarettes,
    peanut shells, a drained gin-flask, and a whore's
    lipstick;
Scattered traces of tar, restless arrays of feathers,
    and the lingering smell of gasoline.
And through the morning air the sun poured yellow
10      surprise into the eye sockets of a stony skull . . . .
And while I stood my mind was frozen with a cold
    pity for the life that was gone.
The ground gripped my feet and my heart was
    circled by icy walls of fear—
The sun died in the sky; a night wind muttered
    in the grass and fumbled the leaves in the trees;
    the woods poured forth the hungry yelping
    of hounds; the darkness screamed with thirsty
    voices; and the witnesses rose and lived:
The dry bones stirred, rattled, lifted, melting
    themselves into my bones.
The gray ashes formed flesh firm and black,
15      entering into my flesh.
The gin-flask passed from mouth to mouth; cigars
    and cigarettes glowed, the whore smeared
    the lipstick red upon her lips,
And a thousand faces swirled around me,
    clamoring that my life be burned . . . .

And then they had me, stripped me, battering my
    teeth into my throat till I swallowed my own
    blood.

My voice was drowned in the roar of their voices,
    and my black wet body slipped and rolled
    in their hands as they bound me to the sapling.
And my skin clung to the bubbling hot tar, falling
20          from me in limp patches.
And the down and quills of the white feathers sank
    into my raw flesh, and I moaned in my agony.
Then my blood was cooled mercifully, cooled
    by a baptism of gasoline.
And in a blaze of red I leaped to the sky as pain
    rose like water, boiling my limbs.
Panting, begging I clutched childlike, clutched to
    the hot sides of death.
Now I am dry bones and my face a stony skull
25          staring in yellow surprise at the sun . . . .[10]

—Richard Wright

**4.** It has been suggested that both restrictive and nonrestrictive relative clauses are derived from coordinate clauses, with a restrictive clause corresponding to the first coordinate clause in a sentence and a nonrestrictive clause corresponding to the second coordinate clause, as illustrated below.[11] Does this method of accounting for restrictive clauses seem more sensible than that explained in the text? Discuss.

the man **who lives next door** is a hermit
**the man lives next door** and the man is a hermit

the man, **who lives next door,** is a hermit
the man is a hermit and **the man lives next door**

**5.** Make the insert sentences below into absolutes modifying the matrix, thus creating one sentence from each set of two or more sentences. The possessive **pronoun** introducing the absolute may be deleted. *With* may be added to introduce the absolute, whether or not the possessive pronoun is retained.

Some inserts can be transformed into either kind of absolute: the kind with a BE form deleted, and the kind with *being* or *having*.

[10] *Arnold Adoff, ed., I Am the Darker Brother (New York: The Macmillan Company, Collier Books, 1968), pp. 70–71.*
[11] *Bernhard Drubig, "Some Remarks on Relative Clauses in English,"* Journal of English as a Second Language, 3 *(Fall 1968), 23–40.*

a.   Matrix:   she looked funny
     Insert:   her hat was askew

b.   Matrix:   he stood there precariously
     Insert:   his left foot was on the very edge of the cliff

c.   Matrix:   she kissed him softly
     Insert:   her lips were a delicate caress

d.   Matrix:   he pulled on his coat and stalked out the door
     Insert:   his eyes were glancing neither right nor left

e.   Matrix:   the girl stared listlessly at nothing
     Insert:   the girl's heart was broken by the death of her
               dog

f.   Matrix:   I need both kinds
     Insert:   each kind is useful in its own way

g.   Matrix:   she bought all her clothes at Saks
     Insert:   her parents had lots of money

h.   Matrix:   they laughed at him helplessly
     Insert:   his bathing trunks had come off when he dived

i.   Matrix:   the little dog finally got some food
     Insert:   the big dog had eaten his fill

j.   Matrix:   they made friends with the girl
     Insert:   the girl's mother had bought her a new jump
               rope

k.   Matrix:   she bought a new purse
     Insert:   her old purse had been stolen

l.   Matrix:    the dog leaped toward the man
     Insert 1: the dog's hackles were up
     Insert 2: the dog's teeth were bared
     Insert 3: the dog's eyes were registering fierce deter-
               mination

m.   Matrix:    the cyclist sped down the street
     Insert 1: the cyclist's hands were gripping the handle-
               bars
     Insert 2: the cyclist's head was lowered
     Insert 3: the cyclist's eyes were nearly closed

n.   Matrix:    the youth staggered forward
     Insert 1: the youth's arms were jerking convulsively
     Insert 2: the youth's eyes were glazed with shock

**6.** In the following excerpts from Ralph Ellison's *Invisible Man*,[12] locate all the absolute phrases, and all the present participle phrases derived from nonrestrictive clauses. Put square brackets around the absolutes and parentheses around the participial phrases, or distinguish them in some other consistent way.

a. I watched the flashing past of cotton fields and cabins, feeling that I was moving into the unknown.

b. The audience was mixed, their claims broader than race.

c. I saw the giant bend and clutch the posts at the top of the stairs with both hands, bracing himself, his body gleaming bare in his white shorts.

d. Up ahead I saw the one who thought he was a drum major strutting in front, giving orders as he moved energetically in long, hip-swinging strides, a cane held above his head, rising and falling as though in time to music.

e. Suddenly I saw a boy lifted into the air, glistening with sweat like a circus seal, and dropped, his wet back landing flush upon the charged rug, heard him yell and saw him literally dance upon his back, his elbows beating a frenzied tattoo upon the floor, his muscles twitching like the flesh of a horse stung by many flies.

f. Before me, in the panel where a mirror is usually placed, I could see a scene from a bullfight, the bull charging close to the man and the man swinging the red cape in sculptured folds so close to his body that man and bull seemed to blend in one swirl of calm, pure motion.

g. A new Ras of a haughty, vulgar dignity, dressed in the costume of an Abyssinian chieftain; a fur cap upon his head, his arm bearing a shield, a cape made of the skin of some wild animal around his shoulders.

h. And then it is suddenly winter, with the moon high above and the chimes in the steeple ringing and a sonorous choir of trombones rendering a Christmas carol; and over all is a quietness and an ache as though all the world were loneliness.

[12] *Ralph Ellison*, Invisible Man *(New York: The New American Library, Inc., 1952).*

**7.** Underline all of the absolute phrases in the following two passages from Ernest Hemingway's *The Sun Also Rises.* Discuss the stylistic differences between the two passages. What kind of construction is primarily responsible for advancing the action, in each case?

I

The bull charged as Romero charged.
Romero's left hand dropped the muleta
over the bull's muzzle to blind him, his
left shoulder went forward between the
5    horns as the sword went in, and for just
an instant he and the bull were one,
Romero way out over the bull, the
right arm extended high up to where
the hilt of the sword had gone in
10   between the bull's shoulders. Then
the figure was broken. There was a
little jolt as Romero came clear, and
then he was standing, one hand up,
facing the bull, his shirt ripped out
15   from under his sleeve, the white
blowing in the wind, and the bull,
the red sword hilt tight between his
shoulders, his head going down and
his legs settling.

II

The bull charged and Romero waited for
the charge, the muleta held low, sighting
along the blade, his feet firm. Then
without taking a step forward, he became
5    one with the bull, the sword was in high
between the shoulders, the bull had
followed the low-swung flannel, that
disappeared as Romero lurched clear to
the left, and it was over. The bull tried
10   to go forward, his legs commenced to settle,
he swung from side to side, hesitated, then
went down on his knees, and Romero's older
brother leaned forward behind him and drove
a short knife into the bull's neck at the base
15   of the horns.[13]

[13] *Ernest Hemingway,* The Sun Also Rises *(New York: Charles Scribner's Sons, 1962). The first passage is from pp. 218–219, the second from p. 220.*

**8.**   Below is W.B. Yeats' final version of "Leda and the Swan" (1928), followed by his first version (Sept. 18, 1923). Compare the syntactic structures of the first four lines. In which case is the syntactic structure more effective? Why? [14]

### Final Version

A sudden blow: the great wings beating still
Above the staggering girl, her thighs caressed
By the dark webs, her nape caught in his bill,
He holds her helpless breast upon his breast.
5   How can those terrified vague fingers push
The feathered glory from her loosening thighs?
And how can body, laid in that white rush,
But feel the strange heart beating where it lies?
A shudder in the lions engenders there
10   The broken wall, the burning roof and tower
And Agamemnon dead.
                                    Being so caught up,
So mastered by the brute blood of the air,
Did she put on his knowledge with his power
15   Before the indifferent beak could let her drop?

### First Version

Now can the swooping godhead have his will
Yet hovers, though her helpless thighs are pressed
By the webbed toes; and that all powerful bill
Has suddenly bowed her face upon his breast.
5   How can those terrified vague fingers push
The feathered glory from her loosening thighs?
All the stretched body's laid in that white rush
And feels the strange heart beating where it lies.
A shudder in the loins engenders there

[14] *For the idea behind this comparison, we are indebted to Stanley B. Greenfield, "Grammar and Meaning in Poetry," PMLA, 82 (October 1967), 383–384. The first draft of "Leda" comes originally from Richard Ellmann, The Identity of Yeats (New York: Oxford University Press, 1954), pp. 176–177. The final version was taken from p. 178 of this same book.*
    *Leda was the wife of King Tyndareus of Sparta. Two of her children, Pollux and Helen (the Helen who was responsible for the Trojan war), were offspring of the god Zeus, who in the form of a swan seduced the mortal Leda. According to myth, when Paris took Menelaus' wife Helen with him to Troy, Menelaus organized the Greek army under the command of his brother, Agamemnon. In the* Odyssey *we are told that Agamemnon was killed by Aegisthus, who had become the lover of Agamemnon's wife, Clytemnestra, while Agamemnon was fighting in Troy. But a later version of Agamemnon's death, described by Aeschylus about 450 B.C., says that Clytemnestra killed Agamemnon upon his return from Troy because he had sacrificed their daughter Iphigenia in order to calm the winds so the Greeks could sail to Troy. Edith Hamilton,* Mythology *(New York: The New American Library, Inc., 1942), pp. 41, 240–243.*

10          The broken wall, the burning roof and Tower
               And Agamemnon dead . . . .
                           Being so caught up
               Did nothing pass before her in the air?
               Did she put on his knowledge with his power
15          Before the indifferent beak could let her drop?

**9.** What makes the absolutes below awkward? Are they properly formed, in grammatical terms?

    a. we got to the table late, **everyone else being eating already**

    b. the children are no longer poorly clothed, **their father having been working for some time**

**10.** From each of the following sets of sentences, create *one* sentence (the sentence may contain two or more coordinate clauses, if this seems stylistically desirable). You may omit or add words, provided these words do not subtract from or add to the meaning embodied in the sentences given.

Make note of the major processes (transformations) you use in combining each set of sentences. You will probably use at least the following: adjectivalization, absolutization, conjunction, and adverb placement.

    a.   the horses came late in the evening
          the horses were strange

    b.   a warship passed us on the third day
          the warship was heading north
          bodies were piled on the deck
          the bodies were dead

    c.   the rain came at the start of the winter
          the rain was permanent
          the cholera came with the rain

    d.   we lived in a house in the late summer of that year
          the house was in a village
          the village looked across the river
          the village looked across the plain
          the village looked to the mountains

    e.   Nadalee rode her horse to a lake in the afternoon when
            it was hot
          the lake was small
          the lake was surrounded by pine trees
          Nadalee tossed off her shirt

Nadalee tossed off her bra
Nadalee stepped out of her levis
Nadalee stepped out of her underpants
Nadalee dived into the water
the water was cold
the water was blue


f.   the trunks of the trees too were dusty
     the leaves fell early that year
     we saw the troops
     the troops were marching along the road
     we saw the dust
     the dust was rising
     we saw leaves
     leaves were stirred by the breeze
     leaves were falling
     we saw the soldiers
     the soldiers were marching


g.   the teenage girl walked gracefully across the "quad"
     her hips rotated from side to side with each step
     they undulated
     the undulating movement was like waves of soft jello
     her arms were swinging
     they swung slowly
     the calves of her legs reflected the heel-toe weight of
         her stride
     the calves lengthened as her heel struck the asphalt
     the calves tightened as her body rose on her toes
     the tightened muscles bunched
     the bunched muscles showed separation like those of an
         over-trained dancer [15]


## ADVERBIALIZATIONS


In this section we first discuss similes, which always function
as adverbials. We then discuss the major kinds of sentence
adverbials: adverbials of time, place, reason, contrast, and
condition.


[15] These sentences come from Philip H. Cook, "Putting Grammar to Work: The
Generative Grammar in the Generative Rhetoric," English Journal, 57 (November
1968), 1173. One of Cook's former students made a list of these sentences and
then combined them into a single sentence as a writing exercise.

## THE STRUCTURE OF SIMILES

Observe the following similes, all from Ralph Ellison's *Invisible Man*:

The words struck **like bullets fired close range,** blasting
my satisfaction to earth.

Now I was tired, too tired; my mind retreating, the image of the
two glass eyes running together **like blobs of melted lead.**

And just then a paper bag sailed from a window to my left
and burst **like a silent grenade,** scattering garbage into the
trees and pancaking to earth with a soggy, exhausted plop!

I rolled away **as a fumbled football rolls off the receiver's
fingertips,** back into the coals.

The last of these similes consists of a subordinator, *as,* plus
a sentence: *a fumbled football rolls off the receiver's fingertips.*
The other similes are prepositional phrases on the surface, but
in the deep structure they too consist of a subordinator plus
a sentence:

| *Subordinator* | *Sentence* |
|---|---|
| like | bullets fired close range **strike** |
| like | blobs of melted lead **run together** |
| like | a silent grenade **bursts** |

Notice that in restoring the simile to a full sentence, we have in
each case added a verb (a two-word verb, in the case of *run
together*). This main verb could be deleted from the deep structure because it was identical to the main verb in the main
clause:

the words **struck** [like bullets fired close range **strike**]
the image of the two glass eyes (was) **running together**
   [like blobs of melted lead **run together**]
a paper bag . . . **burst** [like a silent grenade **bursts**]

The affixes on the main verbs are different here, but the two
main verbs themselves are the same in each sentence. Since
the second verb is recoverable, it can be deleted with no loss
of meaning. The following diagram illustrates the relevant structure of the last example above:

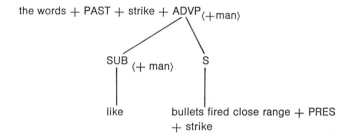

Since the two main verbs are identical, the second one (plus the affix to be attached to it, in this case PRES) can be deleted to give

the words struck like bullets fired close range

Such similes seem to be one possible expansion of the ADVP $_{\langle+man\rangle}$ introduced in the phrase structure rule that expands S.

The following similes modify adverbs rather than verbs:

the words struck **as** forcefully **as bullets fired close range**
the paper bag burst **as** unexpectedly **as a silent grenade**

The other internal difference between these similes and the previous ones is that here the subordinator consists of two words, *as . . . as*; the two words are separated in the surface structure by the adverb of the matrix.

In what ways are the similes bold-faced below similar to the ones just discussed? In what ways are they different?

she's **as** blind **as a bat**
she's **as** slow **as a turtle**
she's **as** dumb **as an ox**
she's **as** stubborn **as a mule**
she looks **as** happy **as a lark**
she looks **as** cool **as a cucumber**

In these similes, which are clichés, the adverbial modifies an adjective: how blind is she? as blind as a bat (is blind). There is one other major difference between these similes and the previous set: here a verb and a predicate adjective have been deleted from the embedded adverbial, whereas in the previous similes just a main verb was deleted, and that main verb was neither a BE verb nor a linking verb.

The following diagram illustrates the essential structure of these adjectival-modifying similes:

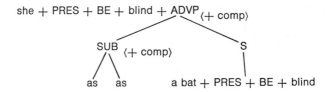

The first part of the subordinator is moved to a position before the predicate adjective in the matrix, to give

> she is as blind as a bat

The feature ⟨+ comp⟩ on the ADVP indicates that it is an adverbial of comparison; the subordinator derived from the ADVP is likewise marked ⟨+ comp⟩, specifying a comparison subordinator.

There are three basic pairs of comparison subordinators: *as . . . as, less . . . than,* and *more . . . than.* The latter pair is illustrated below:

> she is **more** blind **than** a bat
> she is **more** slow **than** a turtle
> she is **more** dumb **than** an ox
> she is **more** stubborn **than** a mule
> she is **more** happy **than** a lark
> she is **more** cool **than** a cucumber

The first part of the subordinator, *more,* often shows up in the surface structure as the suffix *-er,* added to the adjective:

> she is blind**er** than a bat
> she is slow**er** than a turtle
> she is dumb**er** than an ox
> she is stubborn**er** than a mule
> she is happi**er** than a lark
> she is cool**er** than a cucumber

In which instances do you prefer the version with *more*? Which sentences with the *-er* variant sound better?

If the first four pairs of matrix and insert sentences above are joined by the *less . . . than* subordinator, the results are likely to sound sarcastic:

> she is **less** blind **than** a bat (but not much)
> she is **less** slow **than** a turtle (but not much)
> she is **less** dumb **than** an ox (but not much)
> she is **less** stubborn **than** a mule (but not much)

Up to this point, our phrase structure rule rewriting the verbal phrase has allowed for just single-word adjectives, symbolized as ADJ. To account for the adverbial clauses of comparison that can modify adjectives, we can change this rule to provide for adjectival phrases in general rather than just adjectives, then add a new rule specifying ADJP as ADJ + (SUB $_{\langle+\text{comp}\rangle}$ + S):

$$\text{VBP} \to \begin{Bmatrix} \text{VP} \\ \text{ADJP} \end{Bmatrix} + \left( \begin{Bmatrix} \text{NP} \\ \text{ADJP} \end{Bmatrix} \right)$$

$$\text{ADJP} \to \text{ADJ} + (\text{SUB}_{\langle+\text{comp}\rangle} + \text{S})$$

The rule rewriting ADVP must be similarly expanded to allow for comparison clauses that modify adverbials:

$$\text{ADVP} \to \text{ADV} + (\text{SUB}_{\langle+\text{comp}\rangle} + \text{S})$$

The subordinators *as . . . as, more . . . than* (or *-er than*), and *less . . . than* can all introduce similes that modify adverbs as well as similes that modify adjectives. We have given two examples with *as . . . as: the words struck as forcefully as bullets fired close range,* and *the paper bag burst as unexpectedly as a silent grenade.* Can you think of examples with *more . . . than* and *less . . . than?*

One further question: can a reduced comparison clause be moved to the front of its sentence? Do some clauses or types of clauses seem more easily movable than others?

## SENTENCE ADVERBIALS

There are a number of other subordinators, all of which are used to introduce sentence adverbials, adverbials that modify an NP + VP construction:

*Time*

|  |  |
|---|---|
| *point in time* | before, after, since, until, till, when |
| *duration of time* | when, while, as |

|  |  |
|---|---|
| *Place* | where |
| *Reason* | because, since, as, so (that) |
| *Contrast* | though, although, even though |
| *Condition* | if, unless, whether (or not) |

The ADVP rewrite rule will now have to be expanded to include SUB + S as a basic alternative to ADV:

$$\text{ADVP} \rightarrow \begin{cases} \text{ADV} + (\text{SUB}_{\langle + \text{comp} \rangle} + \text{S}) \\ \text{SUB} + \text{S} \end{cases}$$

We are assuming than an adverbial phrase of time, ADVP $_{\langle + \text{tm} \rangle}$, will entail a subordinator of time, SUB $_{\langle + \text{tm} \rangle}$; an adverbial phrase of place (location, direction) will entail a subordinator of place, and so forth. Thus the essential structure for *he paid his bill when the electric company threatened to cut off the power* would be:

he paid his bill + ADVP $_{\langle + \text{tm} \rangle}$

SUB $_{\langle + \text{tm} \rangle}$                    S

when                    the electric company threatened
                        to cut off the power

The ADVP and SUB might also have a feature marking such as $\langle - \text{duration} \rangle$, to guarantee that the adverbial phrase indicates a point in time rather than the duration of time. This contrast is illustrated in the following sentences:

*Point in time*

the host got drunk **before half his guests had arrived**
you'll have to do dishes **after your friend has left**
things haven't been the same **since he left**
we can't leave $\begin{cases} \textbf{until} \\ \textbf{till} \end{cases}$ **they move their car**
he slammed the door **when he left**

*Duration of time*

don't bother him **when he's studying**
he watched T.V. **while I did the dishes**
I'll say goodbye to him **as he leaves**

If the S following the subordinator *when* contains BE + ING in the auxiliary, the clause indicates duration of time; otherwise, a *when* + *S* adverbial will indicate a point in time. The time subordinators *while* and *as* are often followed by a clause with BE + ING in the auxiliary, but even when they are not, they signal the duration of time rather than a point in time, as in *he watched T.V. while I did the dishes* and *I'll say goodbye to him as he leaves.*

In present-day English, *where* is the only subordinator signaling place, but *whither* also existed in earlier English. For example, in the King James Bible, Ruth says to Naomi, "*whither* thou goest, I will go; and *where* thou lodgest, I will lodge." *Whither* indicated direction, and *where* indicated location. Today, *where* performs both functions:

*Direction*

he hit the ball **where it could never be found**
she drove the car **where she had been told to drive it**

*Location*

he paid his bill **where he had been told to pay his bills**
he lives **where the hogs used to live**

Do the two types of place adverbials seem equally movable to the front of the sentence? If not, which kind can be moved more readily?

Our present discussion is based upon the assumption that all adverbial clauses consist of a subordinator plus a sentence; these clauses are provided for in the rule which allows ADVP to be specified as SUB + S. According to this assumption, the essential structure of *he lives where the hogs used to live* must be:

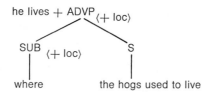

Can you think of any better way or ways to account for adverbial clauses beginning with *where* (and also *when*)?

Adverbial clauses beginning with *where* and *when* are sometimes confused with relative clauses and nominals that begin with these words. The following sentences illustrate these three functions:

he lives **where the hogs used to live** (adverbial clause of place)
she knew about the place **where the hogs used to live**
(adjectival clause modifying **the place**)
we didn't remember **where the hogs used to live**
(nominal clause, direct object of **remember**)

*Where the hogs used to live* performs a different function in each of these three sentences. The following examples with *when* are similar:

> he slammed the door **when he left** (adverbial clause of time)
> the day **when he left** was miserable (adjectival clause modifying **the day**)
> I knew **when he left** (nominal clause, direct object of **knew**)

Once again, the clause performs three surface-structure functions. Our presentation assumes three somewhat different deep structures for these *where* and *when* clauses, but it is possible that the adverbial clauses should be accounted for in the same way as the nominal clauses (see the next section, on nominalizations).

The following sentences illustrate adverbial clauses of reason, contrast, and condition:

> *Reason*
>
> he couldn't play in the concert **because his trombone had been stolen**
> he's been cutting grass all summer **so (that) he can go to camp**
>
> *Contrast*
>
> he wouldn't eat his supper, **even though he was very hungry**
> we can't afford to buy a car now, **though it might be a possibility next year**
>
> *Condition*
>
> I won't go **if he can't go**
> we'll play golf **unless it rains**
> we'll play golf **whether or not it rains**

In the last sentence, all three words of the subordinator occur together. However, the included sentence could separate *whether* from *or not: we'll play golf **whether** it rains **or not.***

## WORKING WITH ADVERBIALIZATIONS

**1.** Examine the similes in the sentences below. Can they all be accounted for by the processes discussed in this chapter? If not, try to account for them.

a.   she's like a witch

b.   . . . . the Cambridge ladies do not care, above
     Cambridge if sometimes in its box of
     sky lavender and cornerless, the
     moon rattles like a fragment of angry candy

               —E. E. Cummings, "the Cambridge ladies"

c.   You are beautiful and faded
     Like an old opera tune
     Played upon a harpsichord;
     Or like the sun-flooded silks
     Of an eighteenth-century boudoir.

               —Amy Lowell, "A Lady"

d.   His head bounced against the steps making a sound
     like a series of gunshots as they ran dragging him
     by his ankles, like volunteer firemen running with a hose.

               —Ralph Ellison, *Invisible Man*

**2.** In each of the following sentences, what kind of word is being modified by the adverbial clause introduced by *so . . . that*?

> he ran *so* fast *that he quickly became exhausted*
> he was *so* tired *that he had to rest for a while*

**3 a.** What kind of word is being modified by the adverbial clause italicized in the following sentence?

> she looks *as if she ought to go on a diet*

**b.** In the sentence immediately above, what subordinator(s) could replace *as if*?

**c.** In the sentence below, how is the italicized construction functioning?

> it looks *as if she ought to go on a diet*

## NOMINALIZATIONS

The process of nominalization transforms an insert sentence into a construction that can function in most of the positions normally occupied by nouns.

### WH-WORD NOMINALIZATIONS

WH-word nominalizations are the easiest type to describe. The following sentences illustrate the various syntactic functions of WH-word nominalizations ("nominals" for short, since all nominalizations are nominals too):

> **how the janitor smoked a cigar** amused me (subject of sentence)
> **when the janitor will smoke a cigar** is a mystery (subject of sentence)
> what I want to know is **where the janitor will smoke a cigar** (predicate nominative, after WHAT-cleft transformation has been performed on the sentence)
> the question is **why the janitor will smoke a cigar** (predicate nominative)
> I wonder **what the janitor will smoke** (direct object)
> he knows **who the janitor will smoke a cigar with** (direct object)
> he wonders **who will smoke a cigar** (direct object)
> he is concerned about **whose cigar the janitor will smoke** (object of preposition)

Nominalization of the insert sentence is taken care of by the WH-word transformation, which moves a WH word to the front of the sentence of which the WH word is immediately a part:

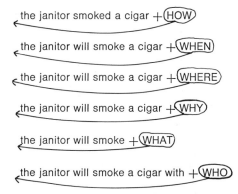

the janitor smoked a cigar + HOW

the janitor will smoke a cigar + WHEN

the janitor will smoke a cigar + WHERE

the janitor will smoke a cigar + WHY

the janitor will smoke + WHAT

the janitor will smoke a cigar with + WHO

WHO + will smoke a cigar

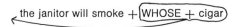

the janitor will smoke + WHOSE + cigar

In the last sentence, the noun modified by *whose* must also be moved to the front of the sentence.

The sentences with the WH-word nominal in subject position may read more easily if the IT-inversion transformation (to be discussed later in this chapter) changes them into

> it amused me how the janitor smoked a cigar
> it is a mystery when the janitor will smoke a cigar

In the last example above, the WH-word nominal functions as the object of the preposition *about: he is concerned about whose cigar the janitor will smoke.* The preposition plus the nominal together function as an adverbial modifier of the adjective *concerned.* Three other adjectives which can be modified by a prepositional phrase containing a WH-word nominal are *curious, afraid,* and *aware:*

> she's curious about **where he's going**
> she's afraid of **what he might do**
> they're aware of **why he's been going out every evening**

Sometimes an adjective is immediately followed by a WH word, as in *they are uncertain what he's going to do.* In such sentences we assume that there is an underlying preposition (*about,* in this case) and that the adverbially functioning modifier is derived from a prepositional phrase with a WH-word nominal as the object of the preposition.


FACTIVITY


The following sentences illustrate what appears to be a basic correlation between the meaning of certain verbs and the kinds of nominalizations they can take as object: [16]

> I **regret** the fact that he stayed so late
> I **regret** his staying so late
> *I **regret** for him to stay so late

---

[16] *This discussion of factives and nonfactives is based on Paul Kiparsky and Carol Kiparsky, "Fact." In* Progress in Linguistics, *ed. Manfred Bierwisch and Karl Erich Heidolph (The Hague: Mouton & Company, N.V. Publishers, 1970), pp. 143–173.*

he didn't **mind** the fact that she wanted to shop
he didn't **mind** her wanting to shop
*he didn't **mind** for her to want to shop

*I **assume** the fact that she is pretty
*I **assume** her being pretty
I **assume** her to be pretty

*we **suppose** the fact that she is guilty
*we **suppose** her being guilty
we **suppose** her to be guilty

The verbs *regret* and *mind* can be followed by nominalizations introduced by *the fact: I regret **the fact** that he stayed so late; he didn't mind **the fact** that she wanted to shop.* These verbs can be followed not only by "factive" nominalizations but also by **gerundive** nominalizations, nominalizations in which the present participle form of a verb (the *-ing* form) functions as the head noun:

I regret his **staying** so late
he didn't mind her **wanting** to shop

On the other hand, *regret* and *mind* cannot be followed by **infinitival** nominalizations, nominalizations characterized by *to* plus the base form of a verb:

*I regret for him **to stay** so late
*he didn't mind for her **to want** to shop

In contrast to *regret* and *mind,* the verbs *assume* and *suppose* cannot be followed by nominalizations beginning with *the fact,* nor can they be followed by gerundive nominalizations; they can however, be followed by infinitival nominalizations.

It seems rather obvious why *assume* and *suppose* cannot be followed by factive nominalizations: one does not assume or suppose anything which one knows to be a fact. On the other hand, one may regret or mind a fact, so it seems logical that *regret* and *mind* can be followed by factive nominalizations.

Certain adjectives and certain verbs can occur in predicate position with a factive nominalization as subject:

**the fact** that he capitulated is **significant**
**the fact** that he choked on the hot peppers **amused** us

Once again, the factive nominalization can be replaced by a gerundive, but, for many speakers, not by an infinitival. A question mark indicates that the grammaticality of a sentence is questionable:

> **his capitulating** is significant
> ?**for him to capitulate** is significant
>
> **his choking** on the hot peppers amused us
> ?**for him to choke** on the hot peppers amused us

Gerundive nominalizations seem to imply the *prior* occurrence of the action designated; for example, *his capitulating* implies that he has already capitulated, and *his choking* implies that he has already choked. In contrast, infinitive nominalizations seem to imply the *future* occurrence of the action named; the above questionably grammatical sentences containing infinitival subjects could be made more grammatical by adding *would* (i.e., by replacing the present tense marker with *PAST + will*):

> for him to capitulate **would** be significant
> for him to choke on the hot peppers **would** amuse us

We use *would* rather than *will* because *would* appropriately implies that there is some doubt about whether or not the action expressed in the infinitival will actually occur. Infinitival constructions usually imply doubt about the action or state expressed, which is why they generally correlate with *that*-clause nominalizations that cannot be preceded by *the fact*. In contrast, gerundives usually imply certainty and therefore generally correlate with factive nominalizations. The following sentences should help clarify this distinction:

> I remembered **his being intelligent,** and so I was not surprised
>     when he solved the problems
> I remembered **him to be intelligent,** and so I was surprised
>     when he answered so stupidly

The fact that *remember* can be followed by both gerundives and infinitivals indicates that it is neutral with respect to factivity.

To introduce the insert sentences that are transformed into nominalizations, we will provide for another option in the NP rewrite rule:

$$NP \rightarrow \left\{ \begin{array}{l} NOM + (S + (and + S)^*) \\ (the\ fact) + S \end{array} \right\}$$

If we choose the top line, we will get a nominal which is optionally modified by an unlimited number of restrictive relative clauses or their reductions; if we choose the bottom line, we will get a nominalization. If *the fact* is chosen, the verb or predicate adjective of the *matrix* sentence must be marked

⟨+ fact⟩, to indicate that it is factive, or ⟨± fact⟩, to indicate that it is neutral with respect to factivity. If *the fact* is not chosen, the verb or predicate adjective of the matrix must be ⟨— fact⟩ or ⟨± fact⟩, unless the insert contains a WH word; in the latter case the insert will become a WH-word nominalization. Of course if the WH-word nominalization is also to be an infinitival (such as *what to do,* in *he knows **what to do***), the verb or predicate adjective of the matrix must be ⟨— fact⟩ or ⟨± fact⟩.

With this discussion of factivity as a foundation, we will describe the processes involved in generating the three major types of nominalizations: gerundives, infinitivals, and *that-*clauses.

## GERUNDIVE NOMINALIZATIONS

As explained above, almost all gerundive nominalizations are derived from a noun phrase consisting of

the fact + S

The basic gerundive transformation does three things:

**1.** it replaces the tense marker of the insert with ING
**2.** it usually makes the subject of the insert into a possessive, in formal written English
**3.** it adds *of* after *the fact* or, alternatively, it deletes *the fact*

This process can be illustrated as follows:

|  |  |
|---|---|
| Matrix: | I regret the fact + S |
| Insert: | he + PAST + stay + so late |
| Transforming | his ING |
| the insert: | ~~he + PAST~~ + stay + so late |

The affix transformation will move ING to a position after *stay,* thus resulting in

his + stay + ING # so late
his staying so late

|  |  |
|---|---|
| intermediate |  |
| result: | I regret the fact his staying so late |

Now *of* must be added after *the fact,* or else *the fact* must be deleted, to give either of the following:

Final
results:        I regret the fact of his staying so late
                I regret his staying so late

Usually the shorter variant is stylistically preferable.

The following examples are similar:

Matrix:         I regret the fact + S
Insert:         my husband + PAST + HAVE + EN + stay +
                so late
Transforming        husband's   ING
the insert:     my husband + PAST + HAVE + EN + stay +
                so late
                my husband's + HAVE + ING # stay + EN #
                so late
                my husband's having stayed so late
Intermediate
result:         I regret the fact my husband's having stayed
                so late
Final results:  I regret the fact of my husband's having stayed
                so late
                I regret my husband's having stayed so late


Matrix:         the fact + S + bothered me
Insert:         she + PAST + BE + so stubborn
Transforming    her     ING
the insert:     she + PAST + BE + so stubborn
                her + BE + ING + so stubborn
                her being so stubborn
Intermediate
result:         the fact her being so stubborn bothered me
Final results:  the fact of her being so stubborn bothered me
                her being so stubborn bothered me


The following sentences illustrate the positions in which
gerundive nominals can function:

**his capitulating** is significant (subject)
what I regret is **his staying so late** (predicate nominative,
    after WHAT-cleft transformation has been performed)
his justification was **her needing help** (predicate nominative)
I regret **his staying so late** (direct object)
her parents are sorry about **her having to work** (object
    of preposition)

Sometimes the possessive that precedes the *-ing* form is deleted from the insert sentence:

he warned her about ~~her~~ driving too fast
he didn't remember ~~his~~ having done it himself
he insisted on ~~his~~ doing the job himself

Does deletion seem obligatory in all of these instances? Judging from these examples and any others you can think of, what condition(s) seem to require deletion of the possessive that precedes the *-ing* form?

## INFINITIVE NOMINALIZATIONS

Essentially an infinitive construction consists of *to* plus the base form of a verb. The following sentences illustrate various sorts of infinitives:

we prefer **for him to go to college**
he prefers **for him to go to college**
he prefers **to go to college**

**to feed bears** is dangerous (this sentence is more acceptable
    if it undergoes IT-inversion: **it is dangerous to feed bears**)

he supposed **her to have done it**
he believes **himself to be competent**

INFINITIVES WITH *FOR . . . TO.* The sentence *we prefer for him to go to college* can be paraphrased as *we prefer that he go to college*. Note that in this paraphrase, *go* does not agree with its subject, *he*; rather, *he* is followed by the base form of the verb. The base form may be used to indicate the subjunctive mood, which is used in *that*-clauses when a preceding verb indicates a recommendation, resolution, request, demand, preference, and the like. Since the *that*-clause contains a subjunctive, the insert sentence for the infinitive construction must likewise be subjunctive. The insert will thus have SBJ for subjunctive, instead of a tense marker:

he + SBJ + go to college

To generate *for him to go to college* from *he + SBJ + go to college,* *for* is added before the subject, *he;* next, the symbol SBJ is replaced by *to;* and finally, the subject of the insert is changed from ⟨− accusative⟩ to ⟨+ accusative⟩:

Matrix:              we prefer + S
Insert:              he + SBJ + go + to college
Transforming
the insert:          for he + SBJ + go to college
                     for he to go to college
                     for him to go to college
Result:              we prefer for him to go to college

Similar derivations account for our second and third examples of infinitivals:

he prefers for him to go to college
he prefers to go to college

In the first of these sentences, it is assumed that the *he* of the insert does not refer to the same individual as the *he* of the matrix. In this case the insert will be transformed exactly as illustrated above. If the sentence *he prefers to go to college* is to be generated, it is assumed that the *he* of the insert refers to the same individual as the *he* of the matrix. We can illustrate the transformational process as follows:

Matrix:              he prefers + S
Insert:              he + SBJ + go to college
Transforming
the insert:          for he + SBJ + go to college
                     for he to go to college
                     for to go to college
                     to go to college
Result:              he prefers to go to college

Instead of changing *he* to *him,* we delete *he* altogether; the *for* must then be deleted also, in most dialects, though the *for to* infinitives occur in all parts of the U.S. along with the *to* infinitives, in the speech of the uneducated. In New England (where it is clearly an older form) and in the Middle and South Atlantic States, the *for to* infinitive is occasionally used colloquially by educated speakers as well.

INFINITIVES THAT CAN BE TRANSFORMED INTO GERUNDS. The insert *to feed bears* in *to feed bears is dangerous* must have the indefinite ⟨+ human⟩ pronoun *someone* (or the pronoun *one*) as its subject; the vagueness of the subject allows it to be deleted, just as the vague agent phrases *by someone* and *by something* can be deleted from passives. From *to feed bears is dangerous,* we can derive *feeding bears is dangerous;* we simply replace the *to* with ING, which the affix transformation will later move to a position after *feed.* It seems to us that all subjectless gerundives that function as subjects of other sentences are derived in this way, from reduced *for . . . to* constructions that have *someone* as the subject.[17] Here are two more examples:

~~for someone~~ to climb mountains is fun
climbing mountains is fun

~~for someone~~ to drive in heavy traffic is difficult
driving in heavy traffic is difficult

When the reduced infinitive (*to feed, to climb, to drive*) is not further transformed into a gerundive, the IT-inversion transformation can be applied:

it is dangerous to feed bears
it is fun to climb mountains
it is difficult to drive in heavy traffic

In at least some speakers' dialects, the gerundives can also optionally undergo IT-inversion:

it is dangerous feeding bears
it is fun climbing mountains
it is difficult driving in heavy traffic

INFINITIVES WITH *TO.*  Our last two examples at the beginning of the section on infinitivals were

he supposed **her to have done it**
he believes **himself to be competent**

These examples differ from the preceding ones in that *for* cannot occur before the subject of the infinitive:[18]

*he supposed **for** her to have done it
*he believes **for** himself to be competent

The derivation of the latter sentence differs from all previous derivations in that the subject of the insert sentence is made into a reflexive instead of being deleted:

---

[17] *For this idea we are indebted to Stockwell et al., Vol. 2, pp. 591–592.*
[18] *The Kiparskys say that an infinitival will take* for . . . to *rather than just to when-ever the predicate expresses "the subjective value of a proposition rather than knowledge about it or its truth value" ("Fact," p. 169).*

Matrix:          he believes + S
Insert:          he + PRES + BE competent
Transforming          to
the insert:          he + ~~PRES~~ + BE competent
                 he to be competent
                 **himself** to be competent

Result:          he believes himself to be competent

Note that in this particular case, *to* plus *be* can be deleted from the infinitival, giving *he believes himself competent. To be* is optionally deletable from infinitival direct objects after verbs like *consider, believe,* and *think.*

THE PROCESS OF INFINITIVALIZATION.   There seems to be a strong correlation between infinitival constructions and non-factive *that*-clauses, as we have explained. Therefore most infinitivals are derived from an NP rewritten simply as S. The basic infinitivalization process can be summarized as follows:

   **1.**   *for* is added before the subject of the insert when the predicate of the matrix expresses "the subjective value of a proposition rather than knowledge about it or its truth value" (see footnote 18)
   **2.**   *to* replaces PRES, PAST, or SBJ
   **3.**   if *for* has been inserted:
     a.   the subject of the insert is deleted if the subject is the indefinite pronoun *someone,* or if it is strongly identical to (has the same referent as) a preceding direct object or, there being no direct object, if it is strongly identical to a preceding subject in the matrix; when the subject has been deleted, *for* is usually deleted also
     b.   if the subject of the insert has not been deleted by step 3a, the subject is changed from ⟨— accusative⟩ to ⟨+ accusative⟩, when the subject is a pronoun
     c.   *for* can optionally be deleted from any infinitival functioning as direct object (unless of course *for* has already been deleted by step 3a)
   **4.**   if *for* has not been inserted, the subject of the insert is transformed into its corresponding reflexive if it is strongly identical to (has the same referent as) the subject of the matrix.

All of these steps except 3c have already been illustrated. *I wanted her to do well* shows the application of this step; it is derived from *I wanted **for** her to do well.*
   The following sentences illustrate the positions in which infinitivals can occur:

**for you to leave now** would be a mistake (subject)
**to feed bears** is dangerous (subject)
his solution was **for us to stop spending money** (predicate
  nominative)
his plan is **to leave at dawn** (predicate nominative)
I wanted **(for) them to leave** (direct object)
he hoped **to play the saxophone** (direct object)
there is no alternative except **for him to answer the challenge**
  (object of preposition)
he has no alternative except **to answer the challenge**
  (object of preposition)
he spent lots of money in order **to win the election** (object
  of preposition **in order**)

WH-WORD INFINITIVES.   One other kind of infinitive nominalization remains to be discussed: the WH-word infinitival. The
following examples are typical:

**how to do it** puzzled us (subject)
our question is **where to go** (predicate nominative)
we wonder **when to leave** (direct object)
they know **what to buy** (direct object)
she wonders **who(m) to invite** (direct object)
she wonders **which dress to buy** (direct object)

The following example indicates the process of deriving typical
WH-word infinitivals:

|  |  |
|---|---|
| Matrix: | our question is + S |
| Insert: | we + PRES + go + WHERE |
| Transforming | |
| the insert: | for we + PRES + go + WHERE |
|  | for we + to + go + WHERE |
|  | for to go + WHERE |
|  | to go + WHERE |
|  | where to go |

The subject of the insert was deleted because it was assumed
to be strongly identical to the subject of the matrix. (Note that in
*how to do it puzzled us,* it is the matrix *object* that is identical to
the subject of the insert.) In your opinion, should the insert
sentence contain a modal? Which modal or modals would seem
appropriate in the insert? Would a modal be appropriate in the
other WH-word inserts above?

If we were to generate

> **the** question is where to go

instead of

> **our** question is where to go

the insert sentence would have to have *someone* as the subject:

> someone + PRES + go + WHERE

Most WH-word infinitives are like these examples in that the WH word is immediately followed by *to;* the subject of the insert and the preceding *for* are usually not present in the surface structure.

DISTINGUISHING *FOR . . . TO* NOMINALIZATIONS FROM *FOR . . . TO* ADVERBIALS OF PURPOSE. Infinitives can function not only as nominals but also as adverbials of purpose. Compare the following:

> he wanted **(for) her to wear the dress** (nominal, direct object
>     of **wanted**)
> he wanted the dress **for her to wear** (adverbial, modifier
>     of **wanted the dress**)

In both cases, the deep structure insert seems to be *she + PRES + wear the dress* (unless the nominal insert has SBJ instead of PRES). The following pair of sentences similarly illustrates the contrast between infinitive nominal and infinitive adverbial:

> Jon wanted **to eat the hamburger** (nominal)
> Jon wanted the hamburger **to eat** (adverbial)

The insert for both these sentences seems to be *Jon + PRES + eat the hamburger* (unless, again, the nominal has SBJ rather than PRES).

In the adverbials of purpose, there is a shared noun which is deleted from the insert. Thus *he wanted the dress [for her to wear the dress]* becomes *he wanted the dress for her to wear,* and *Jon wanted the hamburger [for Jon to eat the hamburger]* becomes *Jon wanted the hamburger for Jon to eat,* which is further reduced to *Jon wanted the hamburger to eat.*

## *THAT*-CLAUSE NOMINALIZATIONS

There are two basic sources for *that*-clause nominalizations:

the fact + S

S

If a noun phrase consisting of *the fact + S* is not made into a gerundive nominalization, a *that*-insertion transformation normally adds *that* before the insert S to give a factive *that*-clause. Similarly, if a noun phrase consisting of just S is not made into an infinitive nominalization and/or a WH-word nominalization, the same *that*-insertion transformation normally adds *that* before the insert S to give a nonfactive *that*-clause.

The following sentences illustrate the syntactic functions of *that*-clause nominalizations, both factive and nonfactive:

> **the fact that he capitulated** is significant (subject; factive)
> **that he choked on the hot peppers** is not true (subject; nonfactive, since **the fact** cannot occur before **that**)
> what I regret is **the fact that he stayed so late** (predicate nominative, after WHAT-cleft transformation; factive)
> what I assume is **that she is pretty** (predicate nominative after WHAT-cleft; nonfactive)
> his justification was **the fact that she needed help** (predicate nominative; apparently factive)
> his theory was **that she needed help** (predicate nominative; nonfactive)
> I regret **the fact that he stayed so late** (direct object; factive)
> I assume **that she is pretty** (direct object; nonfactive)
> her parents are sorry about **the fact that she has to work** (object of preposition; factive)
> he spent lots of money, **in order that he might win the election** (object of preposition **in order**; nonfactive)

Let us try deleting *the fact* from all the factive *that*-clauses:

> ~~the fact~~ that he capitulated is significant
> what I regret is ~~the fact~~ that he stayed so late
> his justification was ~~the fact~~ that she needed help
> I regret ~~the fact~~ that he stayed so late
> *her parents are sorry about ~~the fact~~ that she has to work

One can either delete *the fact* from the next to last sentence, or replace *the fact* with *it: I regret it that he stayed so late.* In the last example above, the preposition *about* must be deleted also if *the fact* is deleted. As the following examples illustrate, there are a number of adjectives that can be modified by *about* + *the fact* + *S* and/or *of* + *the fact* + *S*; in each case, the prepositional phrase can be reduced to just the *that*-clause:

> her parents are **glad** ~~about the fact~~ that she has to work
> her parents are **ashamed** ~~about the fact~~ that she has to work
> her parents are **certain** ~~about the fact~~ that she has to work
> her parents are **sure** ~~about the fact~~ that she has to work
> her parents are **aware** ~~of the fact~~ that she has to work
> her parents aren't **proud** ~~of the fact~~ that she has to work
> her parents are **convinced** ~~of the fact~~ that she has to work

Once *the fact* has been deleted from a nominalization which functions in subject position, the sentence containing this subject nominal can undergo IT-inversion:

> **that he capitulated** is significant
> it is significant **that he capitulated**

Of course, a sentence containing a nonfactive *that*-clause as subject can also undergo IT-inversion:

> **that he choked on the hot peppers** is not true
> it is not true **that he choked on the hot peppers**

In each set, which variant seems stylistically preferable? What do you suppose accounts for your preference?

Sometimes the includer word *that* can be deleted from nonfactive *that*-clauses and from factives which no longer contain *the fact*. Try deleting *that* from the following sentences to determine for yourself what conditions permit and what conditions prevent *that*-deletion:

### Factives

> **that he capitulated** is significant
> it is significant **that he capitulated**
> what I regret is **that he stayed so late**
> his justification was **that she needed help**
> I regret **that he stayed so late**
> her parents are sorry **that she has to work**

*Nonfactives*

**that he choked on the hot peppers** is not true
what I assume is **that she is pretty**
his theory was **that she needed help**
I assume **that she is pretty**
he spent lots of money in order **that he might win the election**


# IT-INVERSION


We have referred a number of times to the **IT-inversion** transformation, which linguists often call the **extraposition** transformation.[19] When a nominalization occurs as the subject of a sentence, the sentence can usually undergo IT-inversion: the nominal is moved to the end of the sentence, and *it* is inserted in subject position. Here are some examples, all taken from the previous discussion:

**how the janitor smoked a cigar** amused me ⇒)
it amused me **how the janitor smoked a cigar**

**when the janitor will smoke a cigar** is a mystery ⇒)
it is a mystery **when the janitor will smoke a cigar**

**for you to leave now** would be a mistake ⇒)
it would be a mistake **for you to leave now**

**to feed bears** is dangerous ⇒)
it is dangerous **to feed bears**

~~the fact~~ **that he capitulated** is significant ⇒)
it is significant **that he capitulated**
(**the fact** must be deleted from factive *that*-clauses before
   they can undergo IT-inversion)

~~the fact~~ **that he choked on the hot peppers** amused us ⇒)
it amused us **that he choked on the hot peppers**

**that he choked on the hot peppers** is not true ⇒)
it is not true **that he choked on the hot peppers**

---

[19] *For a different view of nominalization and of extraposition, see Roderick A. Jacobs and Peter S. Rosenbaum,* English Transformational Grammar *(Waltham, Mass.: Blaisdell Publishing Company, 1968), pp. 163–178.*

You may have noticed that none of the subject nominalizations above are gerundives. In your dialect, can *his capitulating
is significant* be transformed into *it is significant his capitulating?* Does it seem more acceptable to transform *climbing
mountains is fun* into *it is fun climbing mountains?* If so, what
seems to account for the difference in acceptability?

Sometimes IT-inversion is obligatory. Compare the sentences in the following sets:

> that she will win seems likely
> *that she will win seems

> that he will stay overnight appears probable
> *that he will stay overnight appears

IT-inversion is optional with the first sentence of each set but
obligatory with the second, in which the linking verb has no
following adjective. Similarly, *that I haven't enough money
happens* must be transformed into *it happens that I haven't
enough money,* and *that he's rich turns out* must be transformed into *it turns out that he's rich.*


## WORKING WITH NOMINALIZATIONS
## AND OTHER EMBEDDINGS


1.   Here are three matrix sentences:

> Susan noticed (the fact) + S
> S + would be unlikely
> (the fact) + S + bothered Susan

Which of the nominalizations below can be inserted into the
first matrix? into the second? the third? Try to account for the
fact that certain of these nominalizations cannot be inserted
into certain of these matrices.

> that Nancy ate three banana splits
> for Nancy to eat three banana splits
> Nancy's eating three banana splits
> how many banana splits Nancy ate

2.   Pairs of matrix sentences and insert sentences are given
below. Transform the insert 1) into a *that*-clause nominaliza-

tion, and 2) into a gerundive and/or infinitival nominalization, whatever seems appropriate. If it seems to you that an insert *can* appropriately be made into a kind of nominalization that it is not "supposed" to be, do it anyway, and compare your results with other people's. If you prefer an objective pronoun to a possessive in the gerundive nominalizations, use the objective, and again compare your results with other people's.

a. Matrix: the fact + S + was tragic
Insert: he + PAST + die so young

b. Matrix: the fact + S + mattered a lot to them
Insert: they + PAST + HAVE + EN + win the award

c. Matrix: I appreciated the fact + S
Insert: he + PAST + do his assignment

d. Matrix: S + wasn't possible
Insert: he + PAST + HAVE + EN + lose

e. Matrix: he claimed + S
Insert: she + PAST + BE + an impostor

f. Matrix: we know + S
Insert: he + PRES + BE + innocent

**3.** In the following sentences, the "subject" of the gerund (the nominal preceding the ING form) is not in the possessive case. In your opinion, should the possessive be used in any or all of these instances? Discuss.

a. he doesn't approve of **women smoking**
b. we don't approve of **them drinking**
c. I couldn't imagine **fear getting the better of him**
d. we couldn't believe **the roof falling in**
e. in spite of **the plan of the governor being rejected,** no one could offer a better solution
f. have you heard about **John quitting school?**
g. we are disturbed by **so many being killed**

**4.** Underline all the nominalizations in the following passage. Identify each of the nominalizations as to type: gerundive, infinitival, *that*-clause.

We got used to standing in line at 7 o'clock in the morning, at 12 noon and again at

seven o'clock in the evening. We stood in a long
queue with a plate in our hand, into which
5       they ladled a little warmed-up water with a salty
or a coffee flavor. Or else they gave us a few
potatoes. We got used to sleeping without a bed,
to saluting every uniform, not to walk on the
sidewalks and then again to walk on the sidewalks.
10      We got used to undeserved slaps, blows and
executions. We got accustomed to seeing people
die in their own excrement, to seeing piled-up
coffins full of corpses, to seeing the sick amidst
dirt and filth and to seeing the helpless
15      doctors. We got used to it that from time to time,
one thousand unhappy souls would come here
and that, from time to time, another thousand
unhappy souls would go away.[20]

**5.** The Kiparskys' list of factive and nonfactive predicates is
given below.[21] Try to prove, for each verb and adjective, the
accuracy of the classification. Do any of the verbs or adjectives
seem to be incorrectly classified? Can you add any other words
to either classification?

| *With factive subjects* | *With nonfactive subjects* |
| --- | --- |
| significant | likely |
| odd | sure |
| tragic | possible |
| exciting | true |
| relevant | false |
| matters | seems |
| counts | appears |
| makes sense | happens |
| suffices | chances |
| amuses | turns out |
| bothers | |

---

[20] *This is from the prose of 15-year-old Petr Fischl, who perished in the Oswiecim extermination center in 1944. The passage has been taken from . . .* I Never Saw Another Butterfly . . .: Children's Drawings and Poems from Terezin Concentration Camp 1942–1944 *(New York: McGraw Hill Book Company, n.d.), p. 14.*
[21] *Paul and Carol Kiparsky, "Fact," pp. 143, 145.*

| *With factive objects* | *With nonfactive objects* |
|---|---|
| regret | suppose |
| be aware (of) | assert |
| grasp | allege |
| comprehend | assume |
| take into consideration | claim |
| take into account | charge |
| bear in mind | maintain |
| ignore | believe |
| make clear | conclude |
| mind | conjecture |
| forget (about) | intimate |
| deplore | deem |
| resent | fancy |
| care (about) | figure |

**6** a.  Try to determine how the second sentence in each of the following sets has been derived from the first sentence:

it seems **likely** that she will win
she seems **likely** to win

it **happens** that I haven't enough money
I **happen** not to have enough money

it **turns out** that he's rich
he **turns out** to be rich

b.   In each of the above sentences, the underlying predicate of the matrix (bold-faced) is nonfactive. Can the same kind of operation be performed on all nonfactives? To find out, try performing this operation on the following sentences:

it **seems** that she will win
it **appears** that he will stay overnight

c.   Can the same kind of operation be performed on factives? Try it with the following sentences, plus any others you might think of:

it is **significant** that he capitulated
it **amused** us that he choked on the hot peppers
it is **odd** that there has been no rain lately

**7.** What seems to account for the fact that *it* can occur before *that* in the first set of sentences below, but not in the second?

> I resent **it** that he stayed so late
> I regret **it** that you have to leave
> I'll bear **it** in mind that you have had problems at home

> *I assume **it** that she is pretty
> *I conclude **it** that he ought to go
> *I suppose **it** that I ought to work harder

**8.** How might we account for the bold-faced constructions in the sentences below? (Not all sentences in a given set will necessarily be accounted for in the same way.)

> a.   I like **to sing**
>      I like **singing**
>      I like my **singing**

> b.   she is eager **to help her parents**
>      I am ready **to go**
>      we're anxious **to know what happened**

> c.   they elected **him president**
>      Mary saw **him slip on the ice**
>      Mary felt **herself slip on the ice**

> d.   the baby would do nothing except **cry**
>      we wished he would do something more useful, like **wash the car**

**9.** What insert sentence seems to underlie each of the in-finitivals in the following sentences?

> a.   he wanted **her to leave**
>      he expected **her to leave**
>      he asked **her to leave**
>      he promised **her to leave**

> b.   he expected **her to have done it**
>      he ordered **her to do it**
>      he believed **her to be working on it**

**10.** For each of the following verbs, construct a sentence in which the verb is followed by a *that*-clause. What kind of auxiliary must the *that*-clause have, in each case?

a. anticipate
b. expect
c. foresee
d. predict

e. promise
f. prophesy
g. stipulate

**11.** Are the following sentences grammatical? Discuss.

> I wonder what will the janitor smoke
> I don't know when will he go
> I haven't any idea why did he do it
> I don't know how did I do it [22]
> where did she get the coat from I don't know
> "Then she thought what else would she buy; she wanted to buy
>    something really nice"—James Joyce, "Clay," in *Dubliners*
> " 'I wonder where did they dig her up,' said Kathleen"—
>    James Joyce, "A Mother," in *Dubliners*

**12.** How would you account for the clauses in the following sentences?

> I wonder **whether he went to town**
> **whether or not he will go** remains to be seen
> I wonder **if he has gone to town**
> I don't know **if he has left or not**

**13.** Compare the two sentences in each of the following sets. If a sentence with a nominalization as subject is to be transformed into a yes/no question, what transformation must it apparently undergo?

> *did that he stayed so late bother you?
> did it bother you that he stayed so late?

> *is that she will win likely?
> is it likely that she will win?

> *has that she will win appeared likely?
> has it appeared likely that she will win?

**14.** Each of the following sentences contains a bracketed adjectivalization, adverbialization, or nominalization. Put ADJ in the blank if the bracketed embedding is an adjectivalization, ADVB if it is an adverbialization, or NOM if it is a nominalization.

[22] *This example and the next one are from William Labov, Paul Cohen, Clarence Robins, and John Lewis,* A Study of the Non-Standard English of Negro and Puerto Rican Speakers in New York City, 1968. Vol. 1 *(available from the Educational Resources Information Center: ED 028 423), p. 299.*

_____ a. [that he didn't object to the plan] surprised her

_____ b. she quickly began to carry out the plan [that he didn't object to]

_____ c. she made very modest demands [so that he wouldn't object to the plan]

_____ d. it was obvious [that he didn't object to the plan]

_____ e. the house [where she was staying] was old and run-down

_____ f. he wondered [where she was staying]

_____ g. no one could find her [where she was staying]

_____ h. [to get to Aurora,] you go south on I-69

_____ i. the place [to go to] is Hawaii

_____ j. her dream is [to go to Hawaii]

**15.** In the following sentences, identify all the words, phrases, and clauses that have been derived from an embedded sentence. In each case, what process is involved: adjectivalization, absolutization, adverbialization, or nominalization?

    a. we spotted a bird flying through the downstairs window

    b. she dreamed that every enemy she'd ever made was lurking in that haunted house

    c. the question is, what can we do about it?

    d. she is happy about having learned to knit

    e. behind them were boxes filled with evaporated milk

    f. we told her what a good deal she had gotten

    g. my brother, who lives in Cincinnati, works for the telephone company

    h. Mark gets better grades than I do because he studies harder

    i. they were huddled in little groups, staring blankly at nothing

    j. they finally climbed out of the pool, their hair dripping

    k. his eyes glazed, he stared straight ahead

## LOOKING BACKWARDS AND FORWARDS

The first two parts of this book have described two approaches to the study of modern English grammar—structural and transformational. We have given greater attention to transformational grammar because it has had more influence on linguistic thinking in recent years, and more influence on other disciplines. Its impact has been felt in anthropology, biology, education, philosophy, psychology, and sociology.

We have formulated and discussed phrase structure and transformational rules that express some of the basic regularities of the grammatical system of English. Yet always there are exceptions to these rules, or related phenomena that are not accounted for by the rules; we have pointed out many of these limitations specifically and have highlighted others in discovery exercises. Sometimes our generalizations—our rules—are not as all-encompassing as we could have made them, because simplicity was a prime consideration. Linguists have formulated similar but more complicated rules which do account for a greater range of phenomena.

Whenever linguists find exceptions to their rules, they reexamine the structure of the language to see what underlying regularity they may have missed; they then expand or modify their rules to cover the newly perceived regularity. We can hope, but only hope, that someday all the basic regularities of the language will be perceived. We know that such regularities must exist, or we could not have learned our language in the first five or six years of our life, as does every normal child everywhere in the world, no matter what his language. Perhaps someday we will also be able to perceive the regularities common to all languages, the language universals.

Our discussions so far have not covered the most recent developments in transformational theory. Since 1965, when Chomsky's *Aspects of the Theory of Syntax* was published, linguists have been asking new questions, particularly about the role of semantics in transformational theory. Indeed, Chomsky pointed out the need for asking such questions in his *Aspects* chapter, "Some Residual Problems." He noted that sentences like *John strikes me as pompous* and *I regard John as pompous* seem to be related "in some unclear sense" that could not be explained by current transformational theory; specifically, the theory could not explain the semantic connection between the *me* of *John strikes me as pompous* and the *I* of *I regard John as pompous.* Chomsky concluded, "Consequently, it seems that beyond the notions of surface structure . . . and deep structure . . . there is some still more abstract notion of 'semantic function' still unexplained." [23]

Problems like this have concerned transformationalists in recent years. The next chapter discusses some of their explorations and proposals in the late 1960s and early 1970s.

[23] *Noam Chomsky,* Aspects of the Theory of Syntax *(Cambridge, Mass.: M.I.T. Press, 1965), pp. 162–163.*

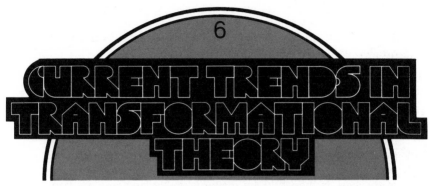

# 6

# CURRENT TRENDS IN TRANSFORMATIONAL THEORY

"A discourse is a set of grammatical structures with meanings," Richard Ohmann writes.[1] To the layman, the phrase "with meanings" may seem unnecessary, because to him language (the vehicle of discourse) and meaning are inseparable. Yet we know from our survey of structural linguistics that some analysts of language avoid involvement with meaning. And the word *meaning* has itself been used in many different ways—by philosophers, psychologists, literary critics, information theorists, and so on. Chomsky summarized the situation in *Syntactic Stuctures* in 1957:

> . . . "meaning" tends to be used as a catch-all term to include every aspect of language that we know very little about.[2]

This chapter concentrates on how linguists have used the word *meaning* and how they have moved from the study of language structure to the investigation of the relationship between language structure and the meanings of words. The chapter ends with a discussion of the promise of transformational grammar, a suggestion of the kinds of insights it may provide concerning the character of human mental processes.

[1] *Richard Ohmann, "Speech, Action, and Style." In* Literary Style: A Symposium, *ed. and (in part) trans. Seymour Chatman (New York: Oxford University Press, 1971), p. 248.*
[2] *Noam Chomsky,* Syntactic Structures *(The Hague: Mouton & Company, N.V. Publishers, 1957), Footnote 10, pp. 103–104.*

# TRANSFORMATIONAL SEMANTICS

In 1933 the structural linguist Leonard Bloomfield defined semantics as "the study of meaning"[3] and (as we saw in Chapter 1) concluded that "The statement of meanings is . . . the weak point in language study, and will remain so until human knowledge advances very far beyond its present state."[4] Therefore in their linguistic analyses, the structuralists tended to ignore meaning. This tendency was partly a reaction against the practices of schoolroom grammarians who mixed statements about form with statements about meaning. Structural linguists decided to avoid such unclear definitions by confining themselves to statements about form and function. They admitted meaning into their study of language only to determine whether two forms or constructions had the same meaning or a different meaning. The study of meaning itself was taboo.

As we saw in Chapter 3, it was largely Chomsky's interest in the relationship between sentence structure and meaning that led him to postulate a deep level of language structure, related to the surface structure by means of transformations. But while admitting in *Syntactic Structures* that "undeniable, though imperfect correspondences hold between formal and semantic features in language,"[5] he believed that "the correspondences are so inexact . . . that meaning will be relatively useless as a basis for grammatical description."[6] Largely because of such negative attitudes toward the study of meanings, linguists continued to pay little attention to semantics until well into the 1960s.

## KATZ AND FODOR'S SEMANTICS

In 1963, the transformationalists Jerrold J. Katz and Jerry Fodor constructed a semantic theory to explain how a speaker of any language assigns semantic interpretations to sentences.[7]

---

[3] *Leonard Bloomfield,* Language *(New York: Holt, Rinehart and Winston, Inc., 1933), p. 513.*
[4] *Bloomfield,* Language, *p. 140.*
[5] *Chomsky,* Syntactic Structures, *p. 101.*
[6] *Chomsky,* Syntactic Structures, *Footnote 9, p. 101.*
[7] *Jerrold J. Katz and Jerry Fodor, "The Structure of a Semantic Theory,"* Language, *39 (April–June 1963), 170–210.*

They pointed out that some sentences are ambiguous (*biting dogs can cause trouble*) and some sentences are anomalous (*the paint is silent*). Moreover, some sentences are paraphrases of each other and some are not. For example, *I expected John to be examined by a doctor* paraphrases *I expected a doctor to examine John,* but a sentence with a very similar surface structure, *I persuaded a doctor to examine John,* is not paraphrased by *I persuaded John to be examined by a doctor.* Other kinds of sentences are paraphrases too:

> John looked up the number:   John looked the number up
> Washington and New York are cities:   New York and
>     Washington are cities
> John plays tennis better than Joe plays tennis:   John plays
>     tennis better than Joe does

According to Katz and Fodor, the semantic component of a grammar would include a dictionary with entries like the following for the noun *bachelor:* [8]

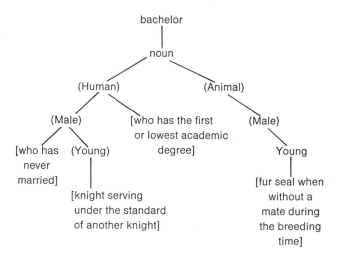

This dictionary entry analyzes the meaning of *bachelor* into its most elementary parts and states the semantic relations among them. The form of the dictionary entry shows every piece of semantic information we need in order to assign the correct semantic interpretation to the word in context. In the graph, the words enclosed in parentheses are **semantic markers;** they indicate broad classes of semantic information. Here the semantic classes are *human, animal, male,* and *young.* All of these are very broad semantic categories; we find these properties in many other entries in the dictionary.

The words enclosed in square brackets are **distinguishers.** They convey quite specific information about the word in the entry. They tell precisely how each meaning is different from every other meaning of the word.

The dictionary entry for *bachelor* shows that *bachelor* has four meanings, or readings: 1) a male human being who, though of marriageable age, has not married; 2) a young male human being who is a knight serving under the standard of another knight (this is an archaic meaning because we no longer have knights in our society); 3) a human being, not specified by sex, who has received the first or lowest academic degree, the bachelor's degree; 4) a young male fur seal that has no mate during the breeding time.

Each of these four meanings is represented by a distinct path, and each path is a reading or meaning of that word. If a word has only one reading, it is unambiguous. If it has more than one reading, it is ambiguous. The word *bachelor,* with its four paths, is four ways ambiguous.

In the theory of Katz and Fodor, the meanings of individual words are combined in sentences by projection rules. The projection rules select only those semantic markers and distinguishers of a word which are appropriate in the context of the given sentence. Thus in the sentence *Mary is a bachelor of arts,* the noun *Mary* rules out the semantic markers *male* and *animal* and all the distinguishers except "who has the first or lowest academic degree." The projection rules then show how the meanings of the individual words in the sentence combine to provide the meaning of the whole sentence.

The Katz-Fodor theory has been criticized [9] because it fails to explain logically contradictory and/or metaphorical uses of words which we all recognize and understand, such as *married bachelor* or *bachelor girl.* The semantic base of an adequate theory would account for such uses also, these critics assert. Nor does the theory account for relational concepts like *Betty is prettier than Mary,* which presupposes that Betty is pretty. Nor does it explain what we understand as the differences among the sentences in the following sets:

she understands Korean
she even understands Korean
she doesn't even understand Korean

[9] Dwight Bolinger, "The Atomization of Meaning," Language, 41 (October–December 1965), 555–573, and Uriel Weinreich, "Explorations in Semantic Theory," Current Trends in Linguistics, Vol. III, ed. Thomas A. Sebeok (The Hague: Mouton & Company, N.V. Publishers, 1966), 395–477.

he doesn't swim either
**he** doesn't swim, either

John thinks that he is a genius
John realizes that he is a genius

In other words the Katz-Fodor theory cannot explain all that we know about the meanings of sentences. One of the limitations is that their lexicon contains a separate entry for each part of speech that the word can function as. For example, the word *fast* would have several entries, one entry corresponding to the sense illustrated in *the fast lasted a week,* where *fast* functions as a noun; another entry corresponding to its use in *he fasted for a week,* where *fast* functions as a verb; and two more entries corresponding to its adjectival and adverbial uses in sentences like *his car is fast* (adjective) and *he drives fast* (adverbial). Chomsky, in particular, has criticized this aspect of the Katz-Fodor theory. He believes not only that there should be a single lexical entry for a word like *fast,* which can function as several parts of speech without adding derivational endings, but also that there should be a single lexical entry for groups of words like *create* (verb), *creation* (noun), *creative* (adjective), *creatively* (adverb); *beauty* (noun), *beautify* (verb), *beautiful* (adjective), *beautifully (*adverb); and so forth. The single lexical entry for the first group would be *creat-* and for the second group, *beaut-.* The form and meaning of the surface-structure words would be provided by lexical transformations that combine these bases with one or more derivational suffixes. This is known as Chomsky's **lexicalist hypothesis:** the idea that the lexicon has word-forming transformations. [10]

## FILLMORE'S CASE GRAMMAR

In 1966 and 1967, in his search for linguistic universals, Charles Fillmore proposed that "the grammatical notion of **case** deserves a place in the base component of every language." [11] Traditionally, the term *case* refers to the inflectional form indicating the grammatical function of the noun or pronoun. In English, nouns have only two cases, a common case (*the* **boy** *is here, I see the* **boy**) and a possessive case (*the*

[10] Noam Chomsky, *"Remarks on Nominalization." In* Readings in English Transformational Grammar, *ed. Roderick A. Jacobs and Peter S. Rosenbaum (Waltham, Mass.: Ginn and Company, 1970), pp. 184–221.*
[11] *Charles Fillmore, "The Case for Case." In* Universals in Linguistic Theory, *ed. Emmon Bach and Robert T. Harms (New York: Holt, Rinehart and Winston, Inc., 1968), p. 2.*

*boy's* *dog is here, the* *boys'* *dog is here*); the common case has no inflectional ending. Pronouns have a nominative case (*he* is here), an accusative case (*I see* *him*), and a possessive case (*it's* *his* *dog, the dog is* *his*).

To Fillmore, *case* means the underlying semantic relationship between a nominal and its verbal, or **predicator.** The predicator may be a verb, adjective, or noun: *the lion* **growls,** *the lion is* **dangerous,** *the lion is* **a mammal.** In Fillmore's **case grammar,** the underlying semantic structure of a sentence consists of a predicator with one or more noun phrases, each associated with the predicator in a particular case relationship. For example, the predicator *smashed* in *Bill smashed the bottle with a rock* has three nominals associated with it: *Bill* is the agent of the action, *the bottle* is the object of the action, and *a rock* is the instrument. Thus these three nominals are in the agent, object, and instrument cases, respectively. Each case occurs only once in a simple sentence, although coordinate nouns may be joined to form a compound which fills a single case role. In addition, embedded constructions may fill a case role.

According to Fillmore, we need the cases listed below. In the following list, each case is immediately preceded by the symbol that will be used to identify it in this chapter.

*Agent* (A):   the case of the animate instigator of the action or state identified by the predicator

> **Bill** smashed the bottle
> the bottle was smashed by **Bill**
> **Bill** was the bottle smasher
> the bottle smasher was **Bill**

*Experiencer* (E):   the case of the animate being affected by the action or state identified by the predicator

> Frank taught **Mary** the answer
> **the children** are warm
> they handed **Joe** the money
> they handed the money to **Joe**
> **Joe** believed she would laugh
> we persuaded **Joe** that she would laugh
> it was clear to **Joe** that she would laugh
> it amuses **me**

*Instrument* (I):   the case of the inanimate force, object, or cause involved in the action or state identified by the predicator

Bill smashed the bottle with **a rock**
the bottle was smashed by Bill with **a rock**
the bottle was smashed by **a rock**
**a rock** smashed the bottle
**this sweater** is warm

*Object* (O):   the case limited essentially to things which are contained, which move or undergo change, or which are affected by the action or state identified by the predicator (not to be confused with the syntactic notion "direct object" or "accusative" —Fillmore says he uses this case as "a wastebasket")

Joe opened **the door**
**the door** opened
**Joe** died
they filled the bowl with **soup**
**soup** filled the bowl
Bill smashed **the bottle** with a rock

*Source* (So):   the case of the origin or starting point of the action or state identified by the predicator

he traveled from **Chicago** to Detroit
he traveled from **dawn** till dusk
**an argument** began the discussion
**his motion** initiated the idea

*Goal* (G):   the case of the end point or objective of the action or state of the action identified by the predicator

he traveled from Chicago to **Detroit**
he traveled from dawn till **dusk**
he wrote **a novel**
the engineers built **a bridge**
he went to **the theater**
Paul dreamed **a dream** about Mary
the group sang **a song** in the park

*Location* (L):   the case of the spatial orientation of the action or state identified by the predicator

it is rainy in **Cleveland**
**Cleveland** is rainy
they filled **the bowl** with soup
**the bowl** was filled with soup
soup filled **the bowl**
**the room** is warm

*Time* (T):   the case that specifies the time of the state or action identified by the predicator

> they sang a song after **dark**
> on **Thursday** they took the plane
> they graduated in **June**
> **summer** is warm [12]

Every English sentence requires a surface-structure subject, and the subject position can be filled by a variety of cases:

> **Bill** smashed the bottle with a rock
> (Agent)

> **Joe** believed she would laugh
> (Experiencer)

> **a rock** smashed the bottle
> (Instrument)

> **the bottle** was smashed with a rock
> (Object)

> **his motion** initiated the idea
> (Source)

> **Chicago** was his destination
> (Goal)

> **Cleveland** is rainy
> (Location)

> **autumn** is rainy
> (Time)

Fillmore assumes that in its deep semantic structure, every sentence consists of a predicator and a series of deep structure cases. Thus the first rule of Fillmore's case grammar reads:

> Sentence $\longrightarrow$ Predicator + Case$_1$ + Case$_2$, etc.

and the second rule reads

> Case$_1$ $\longrightarrow$ NP$_1$; Case$_2$ $\longrightarrow$ NP$_2$, etc.

---

[12] *Charles Fillmore, "Some Problems for Case Grammar." In* Report of the Twenty-second Annual Round Table Meeting on Linguistics and Language Studies, *ed. Richard J. O'Brien, S.J., Georgetown Monograph Series on Language and Linguistics, No. 24 (Washington, D.C.: Georgetown University Press, 1971), pp. 35–36.*

The NP may be a word, a phrase, or a nominalized sentence. When the predicator takes only one NP, that NP will be the subject of the surface sentence. Such predicators will have the following lexical feature, a **case frame** in which the underline indicates the predicator. (Fillmore uses square brackets to indicate lexical features, including case frames):

$$+ \text{[_____ A] we} \left\{ \begin{matrix} \text{go} \\ \text{went} \end{matrix} \right\}$$
$$\phantom{+ \text{[_____ A] we}} \text{A}$$

$$+ \text{[_____ E] Hank} \left\{ \begin{matrix} \text{is} \\ \text{was} \end{matrix} \right\} \text{sad}$$
$$\phantom{+ \text{[_____ E] Han}} \text{E}$$

Often predicators have two cases of NP's specified. Examples are verbs like *remove* or *open* and verbs like *terrorize* or *murder:*

$$+ \text{[_____ A + O] the movers} \left\{ \begin{matrix} \text{open} \\ \text{opened} \end{matrix} \right\} \text{the trunk}$$
$$\phantom{+ \text{[_____ A + O] the mo}} \text{A} \phantom{\left\{ \begin{matrix} \text{open} \\ \text{opened} \end{matrix} \right\}} \text{O}$$

$$+ \text{[_____ A + E] the ghoul} \left\{ \begin{matrix} \text{terrorizes} \\ \text{terrorized} \end{matrix} \right\} \text{the children}$$
$$\phantom{+ \text{[_____ A + E] the gho}} \text{A} \phantom{\left\{ \begin{matrix} \text{terrorizes} \\ \text{terrorized} \end{matrix} \right\}} \text{E}$$

A predicator can even have three cases, as indicated in a frame like the following:

$$+ \text{[_____ A + E + O] Henry} \left\{ \begin{matrix} \text{sends} \\ \text{sent} \end{matrix} \right\} \text{Joe the money}$$
$$\phantom{+ \text{[_____ A + E + O] Hen}} \text{A} \phantom{\left\{ \begin{matrix} \text{sends} \\ \text{sent} \end{matrix} \right\} \text{Joe}} \text{E} \phantom{ma} \text{O}$$

Verbs like *turn* can appear in a number of case frames, depending on their intended meaning:

$$+ \text{[_____ O] the key turned}$$
$$\phantom{+ \text{[_____ O] t}} \text{O}$$

$$+ \text{[_____ A + O] Nancy turned the key}$$
$$\phantom{+ \text{[_____ A + O] Nan}} \text{A} \phantom{turned t} \text{O}$$

$$+ \text{[_____ I + O] the pliers turned the key}$$
$$\phantom{+ \text{[_____ I + O] the pl}} \text{I} \phantom{turned t} \text{O}$$

$$+ \text{[_____ A + I + O] Nancy turned the key with the pliers}$$
$$\phantom{+ \text{[_____ A + I + O] Nan}} \text{A} \phantom{turned th} \text{O} \phantom{with the pl} \text{I}$$

The most economical way to summarize these possibilities is to use parentheses to indicate optional elements. Obligatory elements are always given first:

$$+ [\underline{\hspace{2cm}} O\ (A)\ (I)].$$

Such abbreviated statements, called **frame features,** classify the predicators of the language. Other predicators with the same case frame as *turn* are *open, move, rotate,* and *bend.*

To characterize a verb like *kill,* we need another notation. Consider the meanings of the following sentences:

> Bill killed the bear
> a rock killed the bear
> Bill killed the bear with a rock

We need a case frame to state that, to use the verb *kill,* we must specify either an agent (*Bill*) or an instrument (*rock*), or both. Fillmore uses linked parentheses to indicate that at least one of the linked elements must appear:

$$+ [\underline{\hspace{2cm}} E\ (I \widehat{\phantom{x}} A)]$$

Now examine the frame feature for the verb *murder* in the following sentences:

> Bill murdered Jack
> Bill murdered Jack with a rock
> *a rock murdered Jack

With *murder,* the agent must appear; that is, *murder* requires an animate NP as agent, and may also use an inanimate instrument. The case frame can state these facts thus:

$$+ [\underline{\hspace{2cm}} E\ A\ (I)]$$

However, to subclassify predicators thoroughly we need more than case specifications. The label *S* is used in a case frame to specify that the predicator's *O* element is an embedded nominalization, a deep-structure sentence that has been nominalized. Thus the case frame

$$+ [\underline{\hspace{2cm}} S]$$

characterizes predicators like *true* and *interesting:*

**that he is old** is true  *or*
          S

it is true **that he is old**
                    S

**to know you** is interesting  *or*
          S

it is interesting **to know you**
                          S

The case frame

$$+ [\underline{\hspace{2cm}} S + E]$$

characterizes such predicators as *want* and *expect:*

**Sallie** wants **John to stay home**
     E                    S

**we** expect **them to win the argument**
     E                    S

The case frame

$$+ [\underline{\hspace{2cm}} S + A]$$

characterizes such predicators as *say, predict,* and *cause:*

**Ernest said that Bill would be there**
     A                    S

**Al** predicted **that the concert would end at eleven**
     A                              S

Predicators like *force* and *persuade* are characterized by the following case frame:

$$+ [\underline{\hspace{2cm}} S + E + A]$$

**Bill** forced **Joe to go**
     A          E
                ⎵⎵⎵
                S
**the cops** will persuade **the addicts to confess**
        A                       E
                          ⎵⎵⎵⎵⎵
                                S

We turn now to the conversion of semantic deep structures into surface structures. Every English sentence has a surface subject, and the following general rule apparently applies:

If there is an A, it becomes the subject;
otherwise, if there is an E, it becomes the
subject; otherwise, if there is an I, it becomes
the subject; otherwise, the subject is the O.[13]

In other words, the cases seem to exist in the following hierarchy: Agent, Experiencer, Instrument, Object, Source, Goal, Location, Time.

We can draw semantic representations, or meaning-trees, of sentences. These meaning-trees resemble syntactic tree diagrams in their branching form but differ from them by being much farther from the surface structure of actual sentences. Below are some semantic representations of sentences, according to Fillmore's case grammar. (The symbol P stands for *predicator*.) Note that tense and number are not represented in these meaning trees, since tense and number are considered syntactic rather than semantic notions.

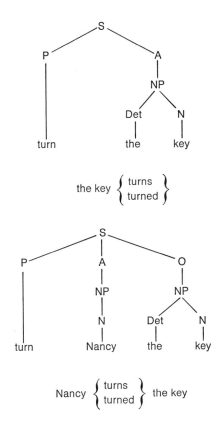

[13] Fillmore, "Some Problems for Case Grammar," pp. 42–43.

or, if passivized,

$$\text{the key} \begin{Bmatrix} \text{is} \\ \text{was} \end{Bmatrix} \text{turned by Nancy}$$

$$\text{the pliers} \begin{Bmatrix} \text{turn} \\ \text{turned} \end{Bmatrix} \text{the key}$$

or, if passivized,

$$\text{the key} \begin{Bmatrix} \text{is} \\ \text{was} \end{Bmatrix} \text{turned by the pliers}$$

$$\text{Nancy} \begin{Bmatrix} \text{turns} \\ \text{turned} \end{Bmatrix} \text{the key with the pliers}$$

Jessie $\left\{ \begin{array}{l} \text{sends} \\ \text{sent} \end{array} \right\}$ my mother the money

or

Jessie $\left\{ \begin{array}{l} \text{sends} \\ \text{send} \end{array} \right\}$ the money to my mother

or, if passivized,

the money $\left\{ \begin{array}{l} \text{is} \\ \text{was} \end{array} \right\}$ sent (to) my mother by Jessie

or

my mother $\left\{ \begin{array}{l} \text{is} \\ \text{was} \end{array} \right\}$ sent the money by Jessie

In 1968 Fillmore's studies in case grammar led him to the following conclusions:

> The question arises whether there is a "level" of syntactic description that is discoverable one language at a time on the basis of purely syntactic criteria. If it is possible to discover a semantically justified universal syntactic theory along the lines I have been suggesting, if it is possible by rules . . . to make these "semantic deep structures" into surface forms of sentences, then it is likely that the syntactic deep structure of the type that has been made familiar from the work of Chomsky and his students is going to go the way of the phoneme. It is an artificial level between the empirically discoverable "semantic deep structure" and the observationally observable surface structure, a level the properties of which have more to do with the methodological commitments of grammarians than with the nature of human languages.[14]

---

[14] Fillmore, "The Case for Case," p. 88.

## WORKING WITH CASE GRAMMAR

**1.** From the following meaning tree produce as many synonymous surface sentences as you can.

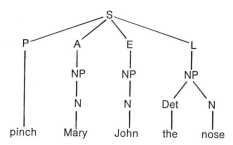

**2.** Explain the similarities among the members of the following sets, using the insights you have gained from case grammar. Add to these sets any other pairs that fit:
- a.  buy:sell/ get:give/ learn:teach/ bring:take
- b.  see:show/ die:kill
- c.  hear:listen/ see:know/ look:learn

**3.** Illustrate by surface sentences the statement on page 263 that *open, move, rotate,* and *bend* have the same case frame as *turn.*

**4.** Draw deep-structure meaning trees for the following sentences.
- a.  Frank will handle the books
- b.  Ralph is carving his career
- c.  this chaos reminds me of a traffic jam
- d.  Bloch refuses to answer
- e.  the clouds blackened the sky
- f.  Sheila must be ready
- g.  the picture was painted by a new student
- h.  the picture was painted by a new method
- i.  the recipe was devised by a new chef
- j.  Jon wanted the guest to eat
- k.  Jon wanted the baby to eat
- l.  Jon wanted the hamburger to eat

**5.** Draw meaning trees to reveal the ambiguities of the sentence *I threw the man in the ring.*

**6.** Whereas English uses characteristic prepositions to express cases, many languages use inflections. If you are acquainted with Latin, German, Greek, or any other more highly inflected language, compare its case system with that of English. Would the meaning tree diagrams be different for a highly inflected language?

## GENERATIVE SEMANTICS

Like Fillmore, and at approximately the same time, James D. McCawley and a number of other transformationalists concluded that Chomsky's deep syntactic level, as discussed here in Chapters 3–5, was an artificial level between the semantic deep structure and the surface structure. In rejecting Chomsky's idea of deep structure, McCawley and the other **neo-transformationalists,** as they call themselves, proposed instead that a single set of transformations connects a *semantic* representation of a sentence with its surface structures.

This position contrasts with Chomsky's in *Aspects of the Theory of Syntax.* There, Chomsky holds that the generative power of the language resides in its *syntactic* system; his semantic rules merely interpret the syntax. This theory is called **interpretive semantics.** McCawley and the neo-transformationalists hold that the generative power of the language resides in its semantic system. This theory is called **generative semantics.**

McCawley graphs a model of grammar as follows:

This generative semantic model lacks a deep syntactic level: the base component gives a semantic interpretation that is transformed by both lexical and syntactic transformations. The surface structure is the result of output constraints which block any output that is not grammatical in English. For example, the passive sentence:

not many of the boys weren't examined by the doctor

is grammatical in English, but its active counterpart is not:

*the doctor didn't examine not many of the boys

Therefore the ungrammatical active will be blocked by surface structure constraints which permit only the passive sentence.[15]

---

[15] *The preceding discussion of McCawley's position leans heavily on John C. Mc-Laughlin,* Aspects of the History of English *(New York: Holt, Rinehart and Winston, Inc., 1970), pp. 282–287. He quotes McCawley's "Meaning and the Description of Languages,"* Kotoba no uchu, *Nos. 9, 10, 11 (Tokyo, 1967), 1–27, and a paper McCawley delivered at the University of Iowa* Language Colloquium, *December 1968.*

Thus generative semanticists hold that the generative power of the theory lies not in the syntax but in the deep semantic level. There is some question, however, as to whether all the semantic information is contained in the semantic base or whether some of it resides in the surface structure. Having modified his *Aspects* theory of interpretive semantics, Chomsky more recently has held that the surface structure does indeed contribute to meaning. Phonological rules assign an intonation pattern to surface sentences, and the meaning of a sentence differs depending on the location of its primary stress—its **intonation center,** in Chomsky's terminology. That is, it makes a difference in focus whether we say

does Bill go to school in **Chicago?**
does **Bill** go to school in Chicago?
does Bill go to **school** in Chicago?

These different focuses imply different presuppositions on the part of the speaker about the meaning of the sentence. The sentences will be reacted to differently by the hearer. For example, in reply to the first question, the answer might be

no, he goes to school in New York

To the second, the answer might be

no, but Joe does

And to the third, the answer might be

no, he works in Chicago

These three answers reveal the three different presuppositions about the meaning of the sentence, given the three different intonation centers.[16]

Generative semanticists agree that an adequate grammatical theory must account for **presupposition,** for the fact that some sentences presuppose the truth of certain underlying propositions. For example, factive nominalizations include a presupposition by the speaker about the real-world truth of what he is saying, whereas nonfactive nominalizations include no such presupposition:

Factive:     I regret (the fact) that he stayed late
Nonfactive:  I suppose that he stayed late

---

[16] *Chomsky explains his post-*Aspects *semantic theory in "Deep Structure, Surface Structure, and Semantic Interpretation." In* Semantics, An Interdisciplinary Reader in Philosophy, Linguistics and Psychology, *ed. D.D. Steinberg and L.A. Jakobovits (Cambridge: Cambridge University Press, 1971), pp. 183–216.*

In the first sentence, the real-world truth is that he stayed late. The speaker takes it for granted; the sentence carries with it the presupposition "he stayed late." In the second sentence, the speaker makes no such presupposition about his staying late. As we would expect, the verb *remember* is ambiguous, or neutral, with respect to presupposition as well as to factivity:

I remember that he stayed late

One's memory could be accurate or faulty about his staying late. Only a larger context will remove this ambiguity.

Presuppositions contrast with assertions. In the latter, the speaker asserts the truth of his proposition; in the former he presupposes his proposition to be true.

A semantic mapping of the sentence *Larry cleaned the car* shows the deep meaning of the sentence rephrased into *Larry caused the car to become clean.* The underlying semantic propositions are as follows (the examples and notation system are taken from the Kiparskys [17]):

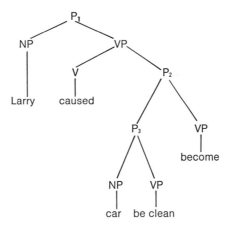

The assertions are *Larry caused the car to become clean* and *the car became clean.* In addition, there is a presupposition that the car was dirty before Larry cleaned it. This presupposition can be treed as follows:

---

[17] Paul Kiparsky and Carol Kiparsky, "Fact." In Progress in Linguistics, ed. Manfred Bierwisch and Karl Erich Heidolph (The Hague: Mouton & Company, N.V. Publishers, 1970), pp. 149–150.

This tree says that until Larry caused the car to become clean, it was not clean.

In the sentence *he didn't mind (the fact) that she wanted to shop,* the speaker presupposes the truth of the embedded clause *she wanted to shop* and makes the assertion *he didn't mind* about that presupposition. Other relevant examples from Chapter 5 are

> the fact that he capitulated is significant
> the fact that he choked on the hot peppers amused us

In these sentences the speakers presuppose the truth of the embedded clauses *he capitulated* and *he choked on the hot peppers,* and assert that the first is *significant* and that the second *amused us.*

Presuppositions contrast with assertions in that the meaning of presuppositions is stable under negation and Yes/No questioning, whereas the meaning of assertions is not. Note that when we make the sentences above into either negatives or questions, their presuppositions retain the same truth value.

> the fact that he capitulated is not significant
> is the fact that he capitulated significant?

> the fact that he choked on the hot peppers did not amuse us
> did the fact that he choked on the hot peppers amuse us?

By contrast, consider the assertions

> it is true that Betty is a beauty
> I supposed that Frank fell down
> we believe the world will end tomorrow
> the attorney charged that the defendant was guilty

If these assertions are negated or Yes/No questioned, the meaning of their embedded clauses changes:

> it isn't true that Betty is a beauty
> is it true that Betty is a beauty?

> I didn't suppose Frank fell down
> didn't I suppose that Frank fell down?

> we don't believe the world will end tomorrow
> do we believe that the world will end tomorrow?

> the attorney did not charge that the defendant was guilty
> did the attorney charge that the defendant was guilty?

In *it is true that Betty is a beauty,* the truth of Betty's beauty is asserted, but in *it isn't true that Betty is a beauty,* the truth of Betty's beauty is denied, and in *is it true that Betty is a beauty* the truth of Betty's beauty is called into question. The other sets of sentences have similar relationships.

The semantic complexity of sentences can be further illustrated by observing the ambiguities of *Larry cleaned the car* under negation: *Larry didn't clean the car.* It can mean any of the following paraphrases:

> someone may have cleaned the car, but not Larry
> Larry may have cleaned something, but not the car
> Larry may have done something, but not clean the car
> Larry may have done something to the car, but not clean it

Since the syntactic deep structure is

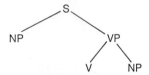

any one of the major constituents—*Larry, the car, clean the car, clean*—may be negated. Moreover, another reading is possible, too: Larry may have been cleaning the car, but it didn't get clean. In other words, the entire sentence may be negated.

Such study reveals the complexity of the semantic structure of sentences. Most attention is now being given to the semantic analysis of specific surface structures. This is essential detail work that must be done to undergird generalizations. The state of semantic study is chaotic but highly encouraging.

## WORKING WITH PRESUPPOSITION
## AND ASSERTION

1.   In the light of this section, how could you explain the differences among the sentences in the sets cited on page 257? Examine the presuppositions of each.

> she understands Korean
> she even understands Korean
> she doesn't even understand Korean

he doesn't swim either
**he** doesn't swim, either

John thinks that he is a genius
John realizes that he is a genius

**2.** Chomsky's explanation of the auxiliary, as we have described it in this book, has been challenged by the generative semanticists. They propose that at the deep semantic level, the auxiliary is actually the verb, and the balance of the predicate is an embedded sentence. This analysis, they contend, coincides more accurately with the native speaker's intuitive presuppositions about the meaning of sentences. For example, the sentence

they must study linguistics

means that the speaker believes that "they" have a duty of some sort with reference to the study of linguistics. The speaker also is aware that "they" are the ones who will do the studying. That is, at the semantic deep level, *they* is the subject of both *must* and *study.* Therefore the sentence has a deep-level structure that can be paraphrased as:

they must do something; namely, they study linguistics

This structure can be treed as follows: [18]

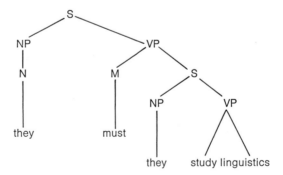

Before the structure surfaces as an actual sentence, the second *they* deletes by the Identical Noun Phrase Deletion rule. This rule applies when a subject NP in an embedded sentence is identical with one in its matrix sentence. Here this rule produces *they must study linguistics.* The form *must* is seman-

---

[18] *This discussion and diagram are based on Roderick A. Jacobs and Peter S. Rosenbaum,* Transformations, Style, and Meaning *(Waltham, Mass.: Xerox College Publishing, 1971), pp. 73–82.*

tically synonymous with *has to,* differing from it only in not needing *to* before the verb of the embedded sentence (*study*). This fact reveals the similarity between *they must study linguistics* and such sentences as *he permitted them to study linguistics,* and suggests that both exemplify the same underlying semantic structural type.

In the light of the preceding discussion, explain how the meanings of the modals change the meanings of the following sentence. Again, examine the presuppositions.

$$
\text{the package} \left\{ \begin{array}{l} \text{may} \\ \text{might} \\ \text{should} \\ \text{ought to} \\ \text{could} \end{array} \right\} \text{be full of ice cream}
$$

**3.** It has been remarked that a violated presupposition produces unhappiness which we feel as an uneasy sensation in the pit of the stomach. In the light of your knowledge of presuppositions and how to analyze them, explain why we might experience this feeling if we remarked

only Maurice voted for Isabel

and someone replied with one of the two following answers:

he didn't
the election never took place

In the same vein explain the uneasy feeling produced by the old joke *have you stopped beating your wife?* [19]

## FOR FURTHER EXPLORATION

Roderick A. Jacobs and Peter S. Rosenbaum, *Transformations, Style, and Meaning.* Waltham, Mass.: Xerox College Publishing, 1971. This book discusses some relationships of syntax and semantics within the framework of transformational-generative grammar and some implications these relationships have for style.

[19] *This exercise was suggested by Laurence R. Horn's "A Presuppositional Analysis of Only and Even." In* Papers from the Fifth Regional Meeting of the Chicago Linguistic Society *(Chicago: Department of Linguistics, University of Chicago, 1969), pp. 98–107.*

Roderick A. Jacobs and Peter S. Rosenbaum, eds., *Readings in English Transformational Grammar.* Waltham, Mass.: Ginn and Company, 1970. The essays in this collection, written between 1964 and 1968, overview developments at that time in transformational grammar and generative semantics. The essays are of varying degrees of difficulty.

Emmon Bach and Robert T. Harms, eds., *Universals in Linguistic Theory.* New York: Holt, Rinehart and Winston, Inc., 1968. Gives further information about recent developments in generative semantics, including Fillmore's seminal "The Case for Case." Again, the essays are of varying degrees of difficulty but are basic to understanding generative semantics.

Charles J. Fillmore and D. Terence Langendoen, eds., *Studies in Linguistic Semantics.* New York: Holt, Rinehart and Winston, Inc., 1971. This book shows how generative semanticists examine particular problems in semantics in order to arrive at generalizations about linguistic universals. Of varying degrees of difficulty, the essays reflect recent developments in semantic research.

Adrienne Lehrer, "Semantics: An Overview," *The Linguistic Reporter,* Supplement 27 (Fall 1971), 13–23. This overview of semantics discusses background, semantic universals, and current controversies. The article ends with a fairly comprehensive bibliography. A useful summary, although somewhat technical.

Wallace L. Chafe, *Meaning and the Structure of Language.* Chicago: The University of Chicago Press, 1970. Chafe presents an approach to semantics that he has developed independently. Although not a transformationalist, he uses several ideas compatible with transformationalist thought.

# THE PROMISE OF TRANSFORMATIONAL GRAMMAR

Underlying all the linguistic thinking of the transformationalists and neo-transformationalists is the basic transformationalist assumption that human language is organized very differently than the communication systems of other animals. Man is qualitatively different in this respect. Chomsky says:

> Every animal communication system that is known
> (if we disregard some science fiction about
> dolphins) uses one of two basic principles: Either
> it consists of a fixed, finite number of signals,
> each associated with a specific range of behavior
> or emotional state, as is illustrated in the extensive
> primate studies that have been carried out by
> Japanese scientists for the past several years; or it
> makes use of a fixed, finite number of linguistic
> dimensons, each of which is associated with
> a particular nonlinguistic dimension in such a way
> that selection of a point along the linguistic
> dimension determines and signals a certain point
> along the associated nonlinguistic dimension.[20]

The latter type of communication system is the more complex. Chomsky cites as an example the song of the European
robin, "in which the rate of alternation of high and low pitch
signals the intention of the bird to defend its territory; the higher
the rate of alternation, the greater the intention to defend the
territory." [21] He argues that human language has an entirely
different principle of organization:

> When I make some arbitrary statement in a human
> language, say that "the rise of supranational
> corporations poses new dangers for human
> freedom," I am not selecting a point along some
> linguistic dimension that signals a corresponding
> point along an associated nonlinguistic dimension,
> nor am I selecting a signal from a finite behavioral
> repertoire, innate or learned.[22]

Because human language seems to be organized differently
than animal communication systems, transformationalists assume that man has a unique language-learning ability. They
hypothesize that the form of a language is largely determined

[20] Noam Chomsky, Language and Mind (New York: Harcourt Brace Jovanovich, Inc.,
1968), p. 61.
[21] Language and Mind, p. 61. Chomsky has taken his example from W.H. Thorpe,
"Animal Vocalization and Communication." In Brain Mechanisms Underlying Speech
and Language, ed. F.L. Darley (New York: Grune and Stratton, 1967), pp. 2–10 and
the discussions on pp. 19 and 84–85. Thorpe uses this example in arguing that the
characteristic properties of human language can be found in animal communication
systems.
[22] Chomsky, Language and Mind, p. 61.

by the structure of the human mind and assume that various language universals are also determined by that unique structure. Transformationalists hope to determine these language universals by studying the organizing principles and elements common to all human languages. From this study, they expect to discover certain **formal universals,** the constraints the human mind imposes on the kinds of rules a grammar must have if it is to adequately describe a native speaker's grammatical competence, his basic ability to form and understand sentences. For example, it may be that a grammar adequate to describe man's innate language competence must contain rules to map deep structures into surface structures, rules which operate essentially like the transformational rules postulated by Chomsky and others. It may also turn out that there are **substantive** language **universals,** that all human languages have certain elements in common. For example, it seems possible that the sounds of all languages can be described in terms of a rather limited number of distinctive features.

In order to determine the contribution the mind makes to the learning of a language, transformationalists must compare the output of the mind, the grammatical system actually learned, with the input—the data fed into the system. A study of the output suggests that a child does not merely learn to place lexical items in grammatical frames. This concept is inadequate because sentences with the same kind of surface structure may have a very different kind of deep structure, as we have demonstrated with such pairs of sentences as *the picture was painted by a new student* and *the picture was painted by a new method.* The logical relationship among the elements of a sentence is not necessarily reflected by the grammatical relationship among the surface-structure elements; in *Jon wanted the hamburger to eat,* for instance, *hamburger* is logically the object of *eat,* but *baby* in *Jon wanted the baby to eat* is logically the subject of *eat.* Thus it seems clear that in learning a language, a child does not simply learn to put words into grammatical frames.

Neither does a child simply learn to repeat the sentences he has heard. Statisticians have determined that it would take more years than the number of seconds in the estimated lifetime of the universe for one person to recite to another all of the possible English sentences of twenty words or less. Clearly, then, learning a language does not depend upon hearing and memorizing the sentences of the language; we are constantly creating new sentences never before spoken or written.

The languages of man make infinite use of finite means; that is, although human languages have a finite number of elements (such as distinctive phonological features), these elements can combine and recombine to form a potentially infinite number of sentences. In English, for example, we might say *I like that old house, I like that old, old house, I like that old, old, old house,* and so forth. Theoretically there is no limit to the number of repetitions of *old* in any given sentence. This is one of the ways in which English is **recursive:** there is no theoretical limit to the number of times an adjective can occur before a given noun in a sentence. Each person learning a language must consciously or unconsciously learn how the principle of recursiveness applies in that particular language; this principle seems to be one of the innate organizing principles of the human mind.

Normally, a child first begins to learn a specific language when he hears it spoken by those around him. Much of the data he collects is degenerate, though; that is, he hears many ungrammatical phrases and sentences. (Listen to your own casual speech, and you will quickly be convinced that this is so.) Some of the ungrammatical sentences a child hears will probably be sentences with a simplified grammatical structure —*Johnny go bye-bye? Johnny want cereal?*—and the first sentences a child speaks will normally have a simplified grammatical structure, whether or not people have spoken to him in this way. But eventually he will learn to use the full syntactic forms, the full syntactic potential of the language. He may never actually hear the sentences *does Johnny want to go bye-bye?* and *does Johnny want some cereal?* but he will be able to produce them. He will know, subconsciously, that *the picture was painted by a new student* has a different underlying structure than *the picture was painted by a new method.* And he will know that *the picture was painted by a new student* means the same as *a new student painted the picture,* even though the surface structures of the sentence are different. He will know these things because he will somehow have become aware of the principles and processes of sentence production, even though this awareness lies below the level of consciousness. It is this "somehow" that intrigues transformationalists. They want to find out what the child himself contributes to the process of language learning, how his mind can make infinite use of a finite number of language elements.

Chomsky has criticized the structural linguists for not adequately explaining man's language-learning ability. Their lack of interest in language acquisition led to inadequate analytical procedures, he says: "knowledge of grammatical structure cannot arise by application of step-by-step inductive operations (segmentation, classification, substitution procedures, filling of slots in frames, association, etc.) of any sort that have yet been developed within linguistics, psychology, or philosophy." [23] It

[23] *Noam Chomsky,* Aspects of the Theory of Syntax *(Cambridge, Mass.: M.I.T. Press, 1965), p .57.*

is time, then, to assume that we do not know how the mind is organized or how it operates; time to study the structure of the mind's output; time, specifically, to study the structure of language and to determine the universal properties common to all human languages, in order to learn about the essential and distinctive properties of human intelligence.

 FOR FURTHER EXPLORATION

Jerrold J. Katz, "Mentalism in Linguistics," *Language,* 40 (April–June, 1964), 124–137. Discusses structuralists' and transformationalists' basic assumptions and procedures. Of medium difficulty.

Noam Chomsky, "Language and the Mind," *Psychology Today,* 1 (February 1968), 48, 50–51, 66–68. Discusses empiricism versus rationalism; competence versus performance; language acquisition; language universals; and related matters. Of medium difficulty.

Noam Chomsky, *Aspects of the Theory of Syntax.* Cambridge, Mass.: M.I.T. Press, 1965, pp. 3–9, 47–59, 204–207. Discusses essentially the same matters as those discussed in the "Language and Mind" article. Rather difficult.

Noam Chomsky, *Language and Mind.* New York: Harcourt Brace Jovanovich, Inc., 1968. Discusses essentially the same matters as the two Chomsky references immediately above. Most of the second chapter is quite difficult, but the first and third chapters are not more difficult than the two preceding references.

A knowledge of the structure of English as described by structuralists and transformationalists can be used in studying such other language phenomena as style in writing and dialects in speech.

We cannot fully appreciate a literary work until we understand its unique uses of language, its style. Similarly, we cannot thoroughly understand the nature of a dialect until we understand its phonological and syntactic patterns and how these differ from the patterns of other dialects of the same language. Thus Part IV of this book puts structure to work in examining style and dialects.

PART IV

grammatical theory:
practical applications

# 7

## THE STRUCTURE OF STYLE

One significant aspect of a literary work is its style. The style of a work includes that work's unique groupings of word structures and meanings, sounds, and sentence patterns. Thus we need a knowledge of the structure of the language in order to study styles of nonfictional and fictional writing. The ultimate aim of stylistic analysis should be critical evaluation, but here we are primarily concerned with the prior task of describing styles by looking at word and sentence patterns.

## SYNTACTIC MATURITY

## AND SYNTACTIC APPROPRIATENESS

Behind every piece of writing we can assume a narrator or persona, a mind reporting and/or commenting on an event or telling a story. In literary analysis, it is common to assume that the author of the work is never to be equated with the narrator of the work, regardless of apparent resemblances. For example, the first-person narrator of Ernest Hemingway's *A Farewell to Arms* resembles Hemingway in a number of ways, but it would be an oversimplification to say that he *is* Hemingway. He is a literary character, and the style of his narration—the style of the novel—is *his* style, not merely Hemingway's. Even in third-person narrations there is a distinction between author and narrator, since most authors are stylistically versatile, not limited to the style they use in any given work.

A narrator is characterized in part by his unique patterns of word structures and meanings and by his characteristic sentence patterns. In analyzing and comparing sentence patterns, we will make use of several criteria of **"syntactic maturity,"** criteria that are particularly useful in describing and comparing first-person narratives and narrators. First, then, we will discuss two men's widely accepted measures—definitions, really—of syntactic maturity.

In 1965 Kellogg Hunt examined seventy-two 1000-word samples of writing from eighteen writers in each of four groups: fourth graders, eighth graders, twelfth graders, and adult professional writers for *The Atlantic* and *Harper's.* Hunt defined syntactic maturity simply as "the observed characteristics of writers in an older grade." [1] Statistical analysis of Hunt's data revealed that the best measure of syntactic maturity was the length of what Hunt called the "minimum terminable unit," or "T-unit" for short.[2]

A T-unit consists of one main clause plus whatever full or reduced clauses are embedded within it.[3] A sentence cannot be divided into two T-units if only one of the parts can stand alone as a grammatical sentence, with independent subject and predicate. For example, we cannot cut *I drove downtown and bought some art supplies* after the word *downtown,* because the latter part of the sentence has no surface subject. Although we might sometimes punctuate *and bought some art supplies* as a sentence, it is not a T-unit. Therefore the original sentence cannot be divided; it is one T-unit, with a compound predicate. The following sentences give further illustrations of how sentences, clauses, and T-units are related:

| | |
|---|---|
| 1 independent clause; 1 T-unit | I drove downtown |
| 1 independent clause, with compound predicate; 1 T-unit | I drove downtown and bought some art supplies |
| 2 clauses, 1 independent and 1 subordinate; 1 T-unit | I drove downtown and bought some art supplies after I ate my breakfast |
| 2 independent clauses; 2 T-units | I drove downtown and I bought some art supplies |

According to Hunt's research, clause length is the second-best measure of syntactic maturity, the number of clauses per T-unit is the third-best measure, and sentence length is the fourth-best. Hunt's statistics on these four measures of syntactic maturity are as follows: [4]

---

[1] *Kellogg Hunt,* Grammatical Structures Written at Three Grade Levels *(Urbana, Ill.: National Council of Teachers of English, 1965), p. 5.*

[2] *Hunt,* Grammatical Structures, *pp. 21, 23.*

[3] *Embedded clauses (adjectival, adverbial, and nominal) are traditionally called* subordinate *or* dependent *clauses. Hunt himself uses the term "subordinate."*

[4] *Hunt,* Grammatical Structures, *p. 56.*

|                              | 4th   | 8th   | 12th  | Adult |
|------------------------------|-------|-------|-------|-------|
| No. of words per T-unit      | 8.60  | 11.50 | 14.40 | 20.30 |
| No. of words per clause      | 6.60  | 8.10  | 8.60  | 11.50 |
| No. of clauses per T-unit    | 1.30  | 1.42  | 1.68  | 1.78  |
| No. of words per sentence    | 13.50 | 15.90 | 16.90 | 24.70 |

Another useful measure of syntactic maturity is the percentage of words in what Francis Christensen calls **free modifiers.** Christensen explains that all words and constructions that stand before the subject nominal are free modifiers, with the exception of coordinate conjunctions like *and* and *but.* Every medial or final word or construction that is set off by commas or dashes or parentheses is a free modifier. Grammatically speaking, there are three types of free modifiers: 1) movable adverbials; 2) absolutes; and 3) nonrestrictive adjectivalizations, either in their full relative clause form or, more often, reduced to appositives, participles, or other adjectival phrases or words. The following sentences illustrate these various categories:

> **yesterday** we went to shop at the new mall (movable adverbial)
> she fixed the rattlesnake meat for dinner, **because there was nothing else in the house** (movable adverbial)
> the boy suddenly appeared in the doorway, **his lips moving unintelligibly** (absolute)
> she could not see very well, **the light being out** (absolute)
> his best friend, **who was a lifeguard,** saved her (nonrestrictive adjectival clause)
> his best friend, **a lifeguard,** saved her (appositive)
> the woman, **yelling at us,** was some distance away (participial phrase)
> **upset by recent events,** the man stared uncomprehendingly at his son (adjectival phrase)
> the woman, **behind us now,** was still yelling (prepositional phrase functioning adjectivally)

Christensen analyzed fifty T-units in the essays of six writers for *Harper's.* On the average, thirty-two per cent of their total number of words occurred in free modifiers.[5] The two professional writers had a higher percentage of words in free modifiers than the two semiprofessionals, and the two semiprofessionals had a higher percentage than the two nonprofessionals.

Obviously Hunt's and Christensen's criteria for measuring syntactic maturity are interrelated, since the number and length of free modifiers affects the number of words per T-unit, clause, and sentence.

---

[5] *Francis Christensen, "The Problem of Defining a Mature Style,"* English Journal, *57 (April 1968), 577.*

But it is important to realize that syntactically mature sentences as defined by these measures are not always as appropriate in context as sentences that are syntactically less mature. As an example, let us compare the two paragraphs below. The first is the original;[6] the second is a rewriting by a student, who was asked to change the style of the original without changing the basic meaning of the sentences. The contrasting parts are bold-faced:

## I
## Original Version

Pollo's father, Felipe Calderón, ran a good business. **He was clever with his hands and made a decent living fixing broken toasters, lawnmowers, and other small mechanical objects, and**
5 **sharpening all kinds of tools, from scissors to power saws. The people of Santa Margarita brought their small mysteries of mechanical failure to Felipe for two reasons: he was a good mechanic, and he charged less for his work than**
10 **did Santa Margarita Feed & Hardware. Goose Fortner, owner of the hardware, did not envy Felipe's business. There was little money in fix-it jobs anyway.** Goose always spoke of Felipe as "a good, honest Mex that does good work."
15 Then, winking a cheerless hound-dog's eye, he might add: "Just so long's he don't start selling feed. Them chiles'd ruin your stock!"

## II
## Rewritten Version

Pollo's father, Felipe Calderón, ran a good business. **Being clever with his hands, he made a decent living fixing broken toasters and lawnmowers and other small mechanical objects. He**
5 **also worked with sharpening all kinds of tools, from scissors to power saws. Because Felipe was a good mechanic and charged less for his work than did Santa Margarita Feed and Hardware, the people of Santa Margarita brought**

[6] Robert La Rue, "Mercy Killing," Sage (Spring 1967), 181–200.

10          their small mysteries of mechanical failure to
            him. Goose Fortner, the owner of the hardware,
            didn't envy Felipe's business since there was
            little money in fix-it jobs anyway. Goose always
            spoke of Felipe as "a good, honest Mex that does
15          good work." Then, winking a cheerless hound-
            dog's eye, he might add: "Just so long's he don't
            start selling feed. Them chiles'd ruin your stock!"

The bold-faced part of the student version has 21.8 words per T-unit, on the average; this is slightly above the average number of words per T-unit for the adult professional writers in Hunt's study. Also the bold-faced part of the student version has 49.4 per cent of its words in free modifiers, much more than the average for the *Harper's* essays Christensen analyzed. Thus by these criteria the student version is syntactically mature.

The bold-faced part of the original version has only 14.3 words per T-unit, about the same as Hunt's twelfth graders. And it has only 10.4 per cent of its words in free modifiers.

The main syntactic difference affecting these statistics involves adverbial clauses of reason. The student version has two such clauses: *Because Felipe was a good mechanic* . . . , and *since there was little money in fix-it jobs anyway.* Where the student version has a subordinate adverbial clause, the original version has two independent clauses:

            The people of Santa Margarita brought their
            small mysteries of mechanical failure to Felipe for
            two reasons: he was a good mechanic, and he
            charged less for his work than did Santa
            Margarita Feed & Hardware. [boldface ours]

In the other instance, the causal relation is again made explicit in the student version with the subordinator *since*. But in the original the causal relationship is merely implied, through the juxtaposition of independent clauses. The first independent clause states a fact, and the second gives the cause:

            Goose Fortner, owner of the hardware, did not
            envy Felipe's business. There was little money
            in fix-it jobs anyway.

Since the original passage has independent clauses corresponding to the subordinate clauses of the rewritten version, the original version has shorter T-units and a much lower percentage of words in free modifiers. But this does not mean that the rewritten version is stylistically *better.* The original author created an omniscient narrator who apparently was not meant to be of interest in himself. The avoidance of adverbial clauses of reason in the original version helps to keep the narrator much less obtrusive than in the rewritten version, which does use adverbial clauses of reason.

This is one indication, then, that syntactically mature sentences are not always stylistically appropriate sentences. Neither are syntactically mature sentences necessarily syntactically clear; that is, the syntax of a syntactically mature sentence may be difficult to unravel. Let us look, for example, at one T-unit from William Faulkner's "The Bear." The free modifiers are bold-faced below:

and, **his father and Uncle Buddy both gone now,
one day without reason or any warning** the almost
completely empty house in which his uncle and
Tennie's ancient and quarrelsome great-grand-
5     father **(who claimed to have seen Lafayette and
McCaslin said in another ten years would be
remembering God)** lived, cooked and slept in
one single room, burst into peaceful conflagration,
**a tranquil instantaneous sourceless unanimity
10    of combustion, walls floors and root:** [7]

This T-unit is seventy-two words long, three and a half times as long as the average for the adult professional writers in Hunt's study. The free modifiers constitute almost sixty per cent of the total number of words. This is nearly twice as high as the average for the *Harper's* essays that Christensen analyzed. Thus according to these criteria, the T-unit is very mature syntactically. But on a first reading it is far from clear.

One explanation for the lack of clarity is that most of the free modifiers occur in the middle of the sentence. This admittedly is an extreme example, but it does suggest why today's readers might find clearest the kind of syntactically mature sentence that Christensen advocates, the **cumulative sentence,** in which most of the free modifiers occur in final position. In examining a thousand sentences of fiction, Christensen found that over

---

[7] *William Faulkner, "The Bear." In* The Portable Faulkner *(New York: The Viking Press, Inc., 1946), p. 337.*

half the free modifiers were in final position.[8] And in analyzing the *Harper's* essays referred to above, he found the same pattern: over half the free modifiers occurred in final position for the two semiprofessional and the two professional writers.[9]

Thus, according to Christensen, syntactically mature writing is clear writing, and clear modern American prose seems to have a high percentage of its free modifiers in final position.

But a further caution is needed: in fiction, at least, clear writing is not necessarily good writing. Good writing suits the style to the narrator, to the subject and purpose, to the audience. Thus a *good* style is an *appropriate* style. As an example, let us consider once again the lengthy T-unit above, from "The Bear." This T-unit is hard to read because a high percentage of its words occur in medial modifiers, and because these medial modifiers are self-embedded adjectival clauses, one within another. The deepest embedding is the parenthetical adjectivalization *(who claimed to have seen Lafayette and McCaslin said in another ten years would be remembering God).* This adjectivalization modifies *great-grandfather,* which is the subject of another adjectivalization: *in which his uncle and Tennie's ancient and quarrelsome* **great-grandfather** *lived, cooked and slept in one single room.* And this latter adjectivalization modifies *house,* the main subject of the T-unit. T-units are difficult to read if, like this one, they contain one adjectival clause embedded into another.

But in context, this kind of construction is appropriate. Faulkner has used an interior monologue technique; the sentence structure suggests the way the protagonist's mind operates, not completing one thought before moving on to another but holding one memory in suspension while recalling something else, and holding *that* in suspension while recalling yet another detail from the past.

Thus stylistically appropriate sentence structures are not necessarily clear or syntactically mature. It is important to keep these facts in mind as we make use of Hunt's and Christensen's criteria (among others) in analyzing and comparing styles.


WORKING WITH SYNTACTIC MATURITY

AND SYNTACTIC APPROPRIATENESS


1.   Compare the two following speeches by Eliza in Shaw's *Pygmalion.* The first is from Act II, near the beginning of Pro-

---

[8] *Francis Christensen, "A Generative Rhetoric of the Sentence." In* Notes Toward a New Rhetoric *(New York: Harper and Row, Inc., 1967), p. 18.*
[9] *Christensen, "The Problem of Defining a Mature Style," p. 577.*

fessor Higgins' training of Eliza to change her from Cockney flower girl to fine lady; the second is from Act V, six months later, after Eliza has successfully performed as a lady at an Embassy ball. In both passages Eliza is speaking to Professor Higgins. Judging by the average length of the T-units in each passage, how do Eliza the flower girl and Eliza the lady compare in syntactic maturity?

## I

Youre a great bully, you are. I wont stay here if
I dont like. I wont let nobody wallop me. I never
asked to go to Bucknam Palace, I didn't. I
was never in trouble with the police, not me.
5     I'm a good girl— . . . Well, what I say is right.
I wont go near the King, not if I'm going to have
my head cut off. If I'd known what I was
letting myself in for, I wouldnt have come here.
I always been a good girl; and I never offered to say
10    a word to him; and I don't owe him nothing;
and I dont care; and I wont be put upon; and I
have my feelings the same as anyone else— [10]

## II

Oh, you are a cruel tyrant. I cant talk to you;
you turn everything against me: I'm always in the
wrong. But you know very well all the time that
youre nothing but a bully. You know I cant go back
5     to the gutter, as you call it, and that I have no
real friends in the world but you and the Colonel.
You know well I couldnt bear to live with a
low common man after you two; and it's wicked
and cruel of you to insult me by pretending I
10    could. You think I must go back to Wimpole Street
because I have nowhere else to go but father's.
But don't you be too sure that you have me under
your feet to be trampled on and talked down.
I'll marry Freddy, I will, as soon as he's able to
15    support me.[11]

[10] *George Bernard Shaw*, Pygmalion. *In* Selected Plays *(New York: Dodd, Mead and Company, 1948), p. 221.*
[11] *Shaw*, Pygmalion, *p. 279.*

**2.** The passages below are from *Flowers for Algernon,* by Daniel Keyes. The novel consists of a series of "progress reports" purportedly written by the main character, Charlie Gordon. At the beginning of the book, Charlie has an intelligence quotient of sixty-eight. After brain surgery in March, he becomes a genius. But this result is only temporary, and by November, at the end of the book, his intelligence has deteriorated almost to its initial level. To see to what extent Keyes has varied Charlie's level of syntactic maturity to depict his progress from moron to genius and back again, compare the average T-unit length and the average percentage of words in free modifiers for the three passages below. The first passage is dated March 4, preceding his brain surgery. The second passage is from July 28, when Charlie is at the peak of his intellectual development. The third is from November 21, at the end of the book, when Charlie's intelligence has been reduced almost to its original level.[12]

I

progris riport 2—martch 4
    I had a test today. I think I faled it and I think
mabye now they wont use me. What happind
is I went to Prof Nemurs office on my lunch time
5    like they said and his secertery took me to a
place that said psych dept on the door with a long
hall and alot of littel rooms with onley a desk
and chares. And a nice man was in one of the
rooms and he had some wite cards with ink
10    spilld all over them. He sed sit down Charlie and
make yourself cunfortible and rilax. He had a
wite coat like a docter but I dont think he was no
docter because he dint tell me to opin my
mouth and say ah. All he had was those wite
15    cards. His name is Burt. I fergot his last name
because I dont remembir so good.

II

July 28
    When he [the mouse, Algernon] found himself
moving along the unfamiliar path, he slowed

[12] *Daniel Keyes,* Flowers for Algernon *(New York: Harcourt Brace Jovanovich, Inc., 1966). The passages appear on pp. 1–2, 166–167, and 216, respectively.*

down, and his actions became erratic: start, pause,
5    double back, turn around and then forward
again, until finally he was in the cul-de-sac that
informed him with a mild shock that he had made
a mistake. At this point, instead of turning back to
find an alternate route, he began to move in
10   circles, squeaking like a phonograph needle
scratched across the grooves. He threw himself
against the walls of the maze, again and
again, leaping up, twisting over backwards and
falling, and throwing himself again. Twice he caught
15   his claws in the overhead wire mesh, screeching
wildly, letting go, and trying hopelessly again.
Then he stopped and curled himself up into
a small, tight ball.
    When I picked him up, he made no attempt to
20   uncurl, but remained in that state much like
a catatonic stupor.

III

nov 21
    I dont no why im dumb agen or what I did rong.
Maybe its because I dint try hard enuf or just
some body put the evel eye on me. But if I try and
5    practis very hard mabye Ill get a littel smarter
and no what all the words are. I remembir a littel
bit how nice I had a feeling with the blue book
that I red with the toren cover. And when I close
my eyes I think about the man who tored the book
10   and he looks like me only he looks different and
he talks different but I don't think its me because its
like I see him from the window.
    Anyway thats why Im gone to keep trying to get
smart so I can have that feeling agen. Its good to
15   no things and be smart and I wish I new
evrything in the hole world.

**3.** Here are three comparable descriptions of the Boston Tea
Party, taken from three different fifth-grade history textbooks.[13]

[13] *The passages are from the following books, respectively: Edna McGuire and Catherine M. Broderick,* The Story of American Freedom *(New York: The Macmillan Company, 1961), pp. 108–109; Clarence L. Ver Steeg,* The Story of Our Country *(New York: Harper and Row, Inc., 1965), p. 154; Jerome R. Reich and Edward L. Biller,* Building the American Nation *(New York: Harcourt Brace Jovanovich, Inc., 1968), pp. 165–166.*

For each of the passages, determine the average T-unit length, the average clause length, and the average number of clauses per T-unit. Then compare these statistics with Hunt's statistics for fourth-grade writing. Assuming that a textbook should not be much more syntactically mature than the writing of the students for whom it is intended, which passage seems most syntactically appropriate for fifth graders?

I

The tea ships lay in Boston harbor. They could not return to England without a pass from the governor. Meetings were held. People talked of little else as they went about their business. Samuel
5    Adams moved among the people. He spoke a word here, gave a nod there.

The day came when the captain went to ask the governor for the pass. Several thousand people gathered to wait for his return. They filled Old
10   South Meeting House and the streets outside. It was five o'clock and nearly dark when the captain returned. The governor had not given him a pass. The crowd grew quiet when the captain had reported. What would happen next? Samuel
15   Adams declared, "This meeting can do no more to save the country."

From outside came a shout. A group of men dressed as Indians started toward the harbor. The people left the church and followed. There they saw
20   the men in Indian clothes dash onto the tea ships and break open the tea boxes. The crowd watched the men pour three hundred forty-two boxes of tea into Boston Bay.

The British government held that Boston must
25   be punished for this act, so it passed several laws. One closed Boston harbor to all trading ships until the city paid for the tea. This was a hard blow, for Boston people lived by trade. Quickly the other colonies sent help. Wheat, corn, fish and
30   other supplies arrived by wagon.

II

It was in Boston that trouble started. There, on the night of December 16, 1773, some colonists

painted their faces and dressed themselves
like Indians and slipped quietly down to the harbor.
5    Waving their tomahawks and shouting an Indian
war whoop, they went on board the tea ships and
dumped the tea into the harbor. That was the end of
the tea; but it was not the end of the trouble.

The king and Parliament became angry when
10   they learned what had happened in Boston. They
made up their minds to punish the people of
Boston and show all of the colonists that the laws
of Parliament had to be obeyed.

British soldiers were sent to Boston, and
15   warships were ordered to enter the harbor to stop
all of the city's trade. Parliament also passed a
law to take away the right of Massachusetts people
to govern themselves. These actions were taken
because the British believed that they could govern
20   the colonies as they pleased, without paying any
attention to the wishes of the colonists.

## III

Colonial tea sellers quickly asked the Sons of
Liberty for help. In Boston, the Sons of Liberty
boarded the East India Company's ships and
dumped the tea into the harbor. This famous event
5    was called the "Boston Tea Party." Other "tea
parties" took place in other colonial seaports.

The British government was very angry and
decided to punish the people of Boston. General
Gage, the leader of the British army in America,
10   was given full power to govern Massachusetts.
At the same time, the powers of the Massachusetts
legislature and the powers of the town meetings
were cut down.

General Gage closed the port of Boston until the
15   colonists agreed to pay for the tea that was
destroyed. No ship was allowed to enter or leave
the port. Thousands of people in Boston were
thrown out of work. Food became hard to get.

The Committee of Correspondence quickly took
20   action. Before long, the other colonies sent
help to Boston. Jobs were found for many Boston
workers in nearby towns. Food and money were
sent to Boston from as far south as the Carolinas.
Boston did not give in to the British government.

4.   Locate and underline all the free modifiers in the following passage and determine the percentage of words in free modifiers. Is the passage syntactically mature, compared with the *Harper's* excerpts Christensen analyzed? (They had an average of thirty-two per cent of their words in free modifiers.) What percentage of the free modifiers are in final position? Is the placement of free modifiers stylistically clear?

### New York Times, May 5, 1970

The crackle of the rifle volley cut the suddenly still air. It appeared to go on, as a solid volley, for perhaps a full minute or a little longer.

Some of the students dived to the ground, crawl-
5   ing on the grass in terror. Others stood shocked or half crouched, apparently believing the troops were firing into the air. Some of the rifle barrels were pointed upward.

Near the top of the hill at the corner of Taylor
10   Hall, a student crumpled over, spun sideways and fell to the ground, shot in the head.

When the firing stopped, a slim girl, wearing a cowboy shirt and faded jeans, was lying face down on the road at the edge of the parking lot, blood
15   pouring out onto the macadam, about 10 feet from this reporter.

The youths stood stunned, many of them clustered in small groups staring at the bodies. A young man cradled one of the bleeding forms
20   in his arms. Several girls began to cry. But many of the students who rushed to the scene seemed almost too shocked to react. Several gathered around an abstract steel structure in front of the building and looked at a 30-caliber bullet hole
25   drilled through one of the plates.

5.   Determine the percentage of words in free modifiers for the passage below. Is the passage stylistically mature, by this criterion? Second, determine what percentage of the free modifiers occurs in final position. Is the placement of the free modifiers stylistically effective?

### Europe Trip Slated by Professor

Busily preparing for his coming trip to France is Dr. Henry Makeweather, professor of French.

Granted a sabbatical leave next semester,
Professor Makeweather plans a tour of France,
for further work on his dissertation, "A Dictionary
of French Proverbs."

Having written the dictionary for his Ph.D.,
Professor Makeweather will expand the work on
this trip, adding proverbs that he hopes to find
still in use by French peasants.

"It will be very interesting to see the changes
made since the war," he said, although admitting
that transportation might prove a little difficult
at first.

This is not the first trip to France for the
professor. He did graduate work for a year at
the Sorbonne in 1932-33 and took a summer course
in 1936.

An alumnus of this university, Professor
Makeweather graduated in 1928, having been
president of the French club. A French major with
a minor in political science, he was a charter
member of the International Relations Club.

Just a few of his affiliations are Phi Beta Kappa
and Modern Language Association.

Newly elected president of the Southern
California branch of the Teachers of Modern
Languages, he is also a member of the Men's
Faculty Club.

His M.A. was awarded in 1930 at Stanford.
Before that time he taught in the San Francisco
schools. In 1931 he began teaching at this
university.

Although born in Colorado, Professor Makeweather graduated from high school in San
Francisco.

"If I were starting over again, I would probably
become a scholar," he said. "Proverbs have been
very interesting to work with." [14]

**6.** The first passage below consists of the opening two paragraphs of William Faulkner's "The Bear"; the second passage
is the first paragraph of Henry James' *The Ambassadors.* In
each case, is the passage syntactically mature, judging by the
length of the T-units and the percentage of words in free modifiers? Is the syntax appropriate and functional *in the context*

---

[14] *Christensen,* Notes Toward a New Rhetoric, *pp. 47–48. Christensen took this*
*article from a university student newspaper.*

*of the story?* For more ideas concerning the style of "The Bear," you might consult Yakira H. Frank, "Correlating Languages and Literature," *English Journal,* 61 (February 1972), 239–245 and William Van O'Connor, "Rhetoric in Southern Writing: Faulkner," *Georgia Review,* 12 (Spring 1958), 83–86, reprinted in F. L. Utley, ed. *Bear, Man and God: Eight Approaches to Faulkner's "The Bear"* (New York: Random House, Inc., 1971), 293–296. Also informative is F. C. Riedel's "Faulkner as Stylist," *South Atlantic Quarterly,* 56 (1957), 462–479. And you might wish to compare your conclusions about the opening paragraph of *The Ambassadors* with the conclusions of Ian Watt in "The First Paragraph of *The Ambassadors:* An Explication," *Essays in Criticism,* 10 (July 1960), 250–274; the essay is reprinted in the Norton critical edition of the novel and elsewhere.

## I
## The Bear

There was a man and a dog too this time. Two beasts, counting Old Ben, the bear, and two men, counting Boon Hogganbeck, in whom some of the same blood ran which ran in Sam Fathers, even
5    though Boon's was a plebeian strain of it and only Sam and Old Ben and the mongrel Lion were taintless and incorruptible.

Isaac McCaslin was sixteen. For six years now he had been a man's hunter. For six years now
10   he had heard the best of all talking. It was of the wilderness, the big woods, bigger and older than any recorded document—of white man fatuous enough to believe he had bought any fragment of it, of Indian ruthless enough to pretend that any
15   fragment of it had been his to convey; bigger than Major de Spain and the scrap he pretended to, knowing better; older than old Thomas Sutpen of whom Major de Spain had had it and who knew better; older even than old Ikkemotubbe, the
20   Chickasaw chief, of whom old Sutpen had had it and who knew better in his turn. It was of the men, not white nor black nor red, but men, hunters, with the will and hardihood to endure and the humility and skill to survive, and the dogs and the
25   bear and deer juxtaposed and reliefed against it, ordered and compelled by and within the wilderness in the ancient and unremitting contest according to the ancient and immitigable rules which voided all regrets and brooked no quarter;—the best game

30 of all, the best of all breathing and forever the
best of all listening, the voices quiet and
weighty and deliberate for retrospection and
recollection and exactitude among the concrete
trophies—the racked guns and the heads and
35 skins—in the libraries of town houses or the offices
of plantation houses or (and best of all) in the
camps themselves where the intact and still-warm
meat yet hung, the men who had slain it sitting
before the burning logs on hearths, when there were
40 houses and hearths, or about the smoky blazing
of piled wood in front of stretched tarpaulins when
there were not. There was always a bottle
present, so that it would seem to him that those
fine fierce instants of heart and brain and courage
45 and wiliness and speed were concentrated
and distilled into that brown liquor which not
women, not boys and children, but only hunters
drank, drinking not of the blood they spilled
but some condensation of the wild immortal spirit,
50 drinking it moderately, humbly even, not with
the pagan's base and baseless hope of acquiring
thereby the virtues of cunning and strength and
speed but in salute to them. Thus it seemed to
him on this December morning not only natural but
55 actually fitting that this should have begun with
whisky.[15]

## II
## The Ambassadors

Strether's first question, when he reached
the hotel, was about his friend; yet on his learning
that Waymarsh was apparently not to arrive till
evening he was not wholly disconcerted. A
5 telegram from him bespeaking a room "only if not
noisy," reply paid, was produced for the enquirer at
the office, so that the understanding they should
meet at Chester rather than at Liverpool remained
to that extent sound. The same secret principle,
10 however, that had prompted Strether not absolutely
to desire Waymarsh's presence at the dock, that
had led him thus to postpone for a few hours
his enjoyment of it, now operated to make him
feel he could still wait without disappointment. They

[15] *Faulkner*, The Portable Faulkner, *pp. 227–228.*

15      would dine together at the worst, and, with all
        respect to dear old Waymarsh—if not even, for that
        matter, to himself—there was little fear that in
        the sequel they shouldn't see enough of each other.
        The principle I have just mentioned as operating
20      had been, with the most newly disembarked of
        the two men, wholly instinctive—the fruit of a sharp
        sense that, delightful as it would be to find
        himself looking, after so much separation, into his
        comrade's face, his business would be a trifle
25      bungled should he simply arrange for this coun-
        tenance to present itself to the nearing steamer as
        the first "note," of Europe. Mixed with everything
        was the apprehension, already, on Strether's part,
        that it would, at best, throughout, prove the note of
30      Europe in quite a sufficient degree.[16]

 FOR FURTHER EXPLORATION

Kellogg W. Hunt, "A Synopsis of Clause-to-Sentence
Length Factors," *English Journal,* 54 (April 1965), 300–
309. Summarizes the major conclusions of Hunt's seminal study, *Grammatical Structures Written at Three Grade
Levels* (see below).

Kellogg W. Hunt, *Grammatical Structures Written at Three
Grade Levels.* Urbana, Ill.: National Council of Teachers
of English, 1965. This research report gives the details of
Hunt's work on syntactic maturity and the T-unit. Useful
for its reference tables.

John C. Mellon, *Transformational Sentence-Combining:
A Method for Enhancing the Development of Syntactic
Fluency in English Composition.* Urbana, Ill.: National
Council of Teachers of English, 1969. This report of
Mellon's work extends Hunt's to establish some practical
applications using transformational concepts and termi-
nology. Mellon presents interesting sentence-combining
exercises.

Francis Christensen, "The Problem of Defining a Mature
Style," *English Journal,* 57 (April 1968), 572–579. Challenging Hunt's conclusion that the average length of a
writer's T-units indicates his writing maturity, Christensen
here argues that writing maturity is revealed through
one's use of "free modifiers."

[16] *Henry James,* The Ambassadors *(New York: W.W. Norton and Company, Inc., 1964),*
*p. 17.*

Francis Christensen, *Notes Toward a New Rhetoric*. New York: Harper and Row, Inc., 1967. An in-depth explanation of his analysis of sentences, with particular emphasis on the cumulative sentence. Contains interesting examples from many authors.

## COMPARING STYLES IN NONFICTION

The remainder of this chapter compares passages that contrast in style. Usually the comparisons are based on T-unit length and the percentage of words in free modifiers, plus whatever other aspects seem relevant in highlighting the significant differences between the passages.

### TWO NEWS REPORTS

There are often significant stylistic contrasts between two newspaper reports of the same event. As an example, we will compare two accounts of evictions in 'Chicago, reported in news stories by the *Chicago Daily Defender* (p. 3) and the *Chicago Sun-Times* (p. 16) on May 5, 1970.

I
*Chicago Daily Defender*
Evictions Mount in CBL Struggle

—Sheryl Butler

Yesterday afternoon had all the appearances of
a balmy, lazy spring day. But on the Southside
of Chicago the laziness of the spell was broken
by the Pied Piper procession of Cook County
5     sheriff Joseph I. Woods' deputies as they went
about an almost methodical eviction of eight
families from their homes.
The orderly caravan included a white bus, filled
with helmeted, billy club-equipped deputy sheriffs,
10    a small van with emergency enclosures to board up
windows, a larger truck and several carloads of
policemen and sheriffs.
Going down Vincennes, King drive, 87th st,

Emerald South Lowe, and Wentworth, the caravan
quickly halted. Sheriff's deputies quickly poured out
of the vehicles, running down the street and
standing spread-eagled as a human barricade in
front of the houses marked for eviction.

Blue-overall clad workers went into the houses
and brought out the furnishings while carpenters
whipped out wooden boards and nailed them
on the picture windows.

"Lord! They've got the whole block," said one
startled woman as she gazed from her front
door. "It is a crying shame," she added.

As the sheriff's moving men were carrying
out his mattresses, Robert Durham, of 9438 S.
Lowe, whose home was slated to be evicted
several months ago but was postponed, spoke
with a quiet anger. "At least I wasn't an oreo
cookie . . . I went down swinging, like a black
man. I didn't do what a lot of them did, I refused
to submit," he added.

Among those evicted was Mrs. Juanita Menzies
of 9012 Emerald Avenue. As she watched from
the streets, the movers emptied her house
of its contents. She said bitterly, "We never even
received a writ from the court ordering us to move.
There are major repairs to be done on that
house, so they can have it."

Mrs. Menzies said the toilet was tiled in the
bathroom and that tiles surrounding it had started
popping up. Also reported there was extensive
damage in the basement from last week's heavy
rains.

"I bought the house for $26,500, and $14,000 has
gone for interest, insurance and taxes. Only $6,000
has gone for the principal. I still owe nearly
$19,000."

Next door, Mrs. Menzies' sister, Mrs. Johnnie
Ramsey, at 9208 Emerald, was also being
evicted.

Where will Mrs. Menzies, her disabled husband
and two children go now? "I think we will probably
set up a tent in a park, because we have no
place to go."

"But we are not defeated by a long shot," she
said proudly. "Universal's Builders good
niggers paid them and gave in. If we could have
gotten them to join us, we would have won six
months ago," she said.

15

20

25

30

35

40

45

50

55

60

## II
### *Chicago Sun-Times*
### 14 CBL Families Evicted on S. Side

Sheriff's deputies Monday evicted at least 14 more Contract Buyers League families living on the South Side.

Chief Deputy Sheriff Richard N. Anderson reported there was no trouble at any of the sites.

Some 70 deputies blocked off streets as 25 movers emptied the houses one by one. The residents stood behind police lines and watched.

"I'm frightened of what is happening to this world," said Mrs. Doris Humphries, 43, who stood outside her vacant home at 8547 S. King Dr. "You'd think we were living in the time of Nazism [sic] or Caesar."

In addition to the Henrick Humphries family, deputies evicted the families of: Dee Bellanfant, of 216 E. 87th; Richard Bell, of 7951 S. Stewart; Sammie Fillmore, of 8900 S. Halsted; Florence Smith, of 9431 S. Emerald; Robert Anderson, of 9063 S. Parnell; Johnnie Ramsey, of 9208 S. Emerald; James Menzies, of 9212 S. Emerald; Lawrence Hughes, of 9440 S. Lowe; Robert Durham, of 9438 S. Lowe; Pink Harrison, of 603 W. 95th; Arthur Green, of 557 W. 95th; Jade Allen, of 615 W. 95th, and Leonard Perry, of 9219 S. Emerald.

CBL members have been withholding payments on their homes since July, contending that contract holders overcharge and that because of racial discrimination they were unable to get mortgages.

Evictions began last December.

The *Defender* article has 441 words, more than one-fourth appearing in direct quotations; the *Sun-Times* article has 193 words with less than ten per cent in direct quotations. Excluding the *Sun-Times'* long list of evicted families, the *Defender* article has a somewhat higher number of words per T-unit: nineteen, compared with just under fifteen for the *Sun-Times* article. (In both cases, sentences with direct quotations were also excluded from the count, as not representing the style of the reporting persona.) The major syntactic difference is in the percentage of words in free modifiers. The *Defender* article has forty-five per cent of its words in free modifiers, while the *Sun-Times* article has only thirty per cent.

All these statistics merely provide objective evidence for what should be apparent on a first reading: that the *Defender* article describes the evictions in greater and more emotional detail. This is evident, too, from a comparison of their respective uses of adjectives and adverbials. The narrative portion (quotations excluded) of the *Sun-Times* article uses just one adjective, *racial,* a **factual adjective.** Factual adjectives involve no subjective judgment by the persona but merely state physically observable facts. The *Defender* includes not only factual adjectives like *white, small,* and *larger,* but also some adjectives that seem **evaluative,** that reflect a subjective opinion: *balmy, lazy, methodical, startled.* Another difference is that none of the *Sun-Times'* verbs are modified by adverbials, but the *Defender's* verbs frequently have adverbial modifiers: *quickly halted, quickly poured out, said bitterly, spoke with quiet anger, said proudly.*

These contrasts result from the differing perspectives and purposes. The *Defender* reporter, identified by name, describes the evictions by quoting several of those who are being evicted and by describing the action of the deputy sheriffs in considerable detail. Through his use of direct quotations and narrative details, he recreates the scene for the reader and enlists the reader's sympathy for those being evicted. The *Sun-Times* is more objective, quoting only one of the residents evicted and giving few details concerning the action of the deputies. This reporter arouses less emotion in the reader because he confines himself almost exclusively to the bare *who, what, when, where,* and *why.*


## TWO EDITORIALS


Sometimes two editorials expressing similar views on a topic are very different stylistically. As an example, let us compare the following two editorials, both published about two weeks after the event: [17]


I
*New York Times,* March 28, 1964
"What Kind of People Are We?"

Seldom has The Times published a more horrifying story than its account of how 38 respectable,

---

[17] *We first discovered these editorials in Thomas F. Van Laan and Robert B. Lyons,* Language and the Newsstand, *2nd ed. (New York: Charles Scribner's Sons, 1972), p 99.*

law-abiding, middle-class Queens citizens watched
a killer stalk his young woman victim in a parking
5      lot in Kew Gardens over a half-hour period, without
one of them making a call to the Police Department
that might have saved her life. They would not
have been exposed to any danger themselves: a
simple telephone call in the privacy of their own
10    homes was all that was needed. How incredible it
is that such motivations as "I didn't want to get
involved" deterred them from this act of simple
humanity. Does residence in a great city destroy
all sense of personal responsibility for one's
15    neighbors? Who can explain such shocking indifference on the part of a cross section of our fellow
New Yorkers? We regretfully admit that we do
not know the answers.

II
*Newark Evening News,* March 30, 1964
"Civic Duty"

Fighting crime is essentially a police job. But it
is the responsibility of decent citizens not only
to obey the law, but also to help authorities
enforce it.
5     A shocking demonstration of public default
occurred recently in a Long Island community. A
thug, in three separate attacks within half an hour,
stabbed a woman to death. A number of neighbors
watched the ghastly street scene from their win-
10    dows. None called police. Finally, after the attacker
had fled, the police were notified. The neighbors'
excuse? They didn't want to "get involved!"
The police do not suggest that any witness
should have engaged the armed thug. But
15    it is cowardly and callous when anyone in a
position to summon help fails to do so. In a moral,
if not legal sense, that is abetting the crime
and aiding the criminal. Citizens have an obligation
to the law as well as a right to its protection.

The *New York Times* editorial has on the average a higher
number of words per T-unit, twenty-one compared to 12.7 for
the *Newark Evening News* editorial. But the first sentence of
the *Times* article accounts for most of this difference: it is fifty-

six words long, and contains the only free modifier in the entire editorial. The sentence begins with inverted word order (*Seldom has The Times . . . .*), which calls attention to the significance of what is being said. This sentence recounts the murder of Kitty Genovese. But she is not mentioned by name; the editorial writer is not interested so much in her personal death as in the behavior of those who witnessed her murder. They are numbered, classified socially, and located geographically: they are *38 respectable, law-abiding, middle-class Queens citizens.* "It could have been you," the editorial writer is saying. He is calling to task the conscience of New Yorkers, asking whether they have lost all sense of humanity, and leaving his questions to be answered by his readers.

The second editorial is more concerned with exhortation than with castigation. It therefore plays down the specific murder of Kitty Genovese even more than the *Times* editorial. The murderer is classified simply as a *thug,* not as a *killer.* There are no adjectives describing the onlookers, and their failure to call the police is generalized as a demonstration of *public* default, not merely indifference on the part of a cross section of New Yorkers. The adjectives *cowardly* and *callous* refer not only to the neighbors who watched Kitty's murder but to *anyone* who might fail to summon help in a similar situation. The reader is implicitly appealed to as a *decent* citizen who has an *obligation,* a *responsibility* to help enforce the law.

The title of the first editorial is a WH question, "What Kind of People Are We?" The reader is asked to search his own moral conscience for the answer. The title of the second editorial, "Civic Duty," has the force of an imperative (do your civic duty!), telling the reader of his social responsibility.

## A NEWS REPORT AND A NEWS ANALYSIS

A news report and a news analysis of the same event often have contrasting styles, because their purposes are different. As an example, we will compare two articles on the death of singer Janis Joplin. The first is a news report, published three days after her death; it is from the *St. Cloud Daily Times,* October 5, 1970. The second passage consists of the first four paragraphs of a news analysis taken from *Life* magazine, October 16, 1970.[18]

---

[18] *We first encountered these articles in Frances Voelker and Ludmilla Voelker,* Mass Media: Forces in Our Society *(New York: Harcourt Brace Jovanovich, Inc., 1972), pp. 141 and 144–145, respectively.*

I

## "Top Pop Singer Janis Joplin Is Found Dead"

HOLLYWOOD (UPI)———Singer Janis Joplin, whose husky, near-shouting vocal style propelled her to the top of the pop charts, was found dead at her apartment late Sunday.

Her body was found wedged between a bed and nightstand by one of the members of her group, "Janis Joplin Full Tilt Boogie Band." She was clad in a short nightgown.

Sgt. Ed Sanchez of the Hollywood Police Department said the singer had "numerous hypodermic needle marks on her left forearm." Some appeared to be covered over by makeup but were from 2 to 14 days old, he said. No drugs or narcotic paraphernalia was found in the room.

Sanchez said an autopsy would be performed to determine the cause of death.

Miss Joplin, 27, shot to the top of the recording world shortly after her appearance at the 1967 Monterey Pop Festival. At the time she was with "Big Brother and the Holding Company," a San Francisco rock group which had a large Western following. She left Big Brother in 1968 to form her own group.

Miss Joplin drank "Southern Comfort" by the quart while on stage and her fans would bring her scores of bottles of the liquor.

Her two biggest hits, "Piece of My Heart" and "Ball and Chain" came while she was with Big Brother on their "Cheap Thrills" album.

The oldest child of a refinery executive in Port Arthur, Tex., she ran away from home at the age of 17. She began singing professionally in clubs near the University of Texas at Austin and it was there she started her "white" blues style, which she called "cosmic."

Heavily influenced by negro singers Otis Redding and Bessie Smith, nearly all her songs were of rural blues origin.

She had been in the Los Angeles area since Aug. 24 recording a new album. Her body was discovered by guitarist John Cooke who said she failed to show up for a date.

It was the second death in the pop singing world in two weeks. Singer-guitarist Jimi Hendrix died of an overdose of drugs in London Sept. 18.

## II

### "Drugs and Death in the Run-Down World of Rock Music"

—Albert Goldman

First, it was Jimi Hendrix, rock's flamboyant superstar, snuffed out last month at 27, dead on arrival at a London hospital. The cause? Suffocation from vomiting while unconscious from sleeping pills. Accidental overdose? Suicide? The coroner could not say.

Then it was Janis Joplin, rock's greatest soul belter, also 27, found dead on the floor of a Los Angeles motel room last week, fresh needle marks on her left arm, a red balloon filled with a white powder stashed in her trash can. Coroner's finding: overdose of drugs.

Why should a young man and woman of such energy and talent, endorsed with immense success, imperil their lives with dope? If you were drawn even for a moment into Jimi Hendrix's breathless quest for life, his urgent headlong pursuit not simply of pleasure but of the most elusive and exotic states of mind and soul, you would know that his death was an inevitable product of his life. Hendrix once sent someone a bag of cocaine with a high-flown note inscribed in flowery script: "Within I grace thee with wings. O lovely and true Birds of Heavenly Snow and Crystals. Fly my love as you have before. Pleasures are only steps and this . . . just one more." That was the rhetoric of his life and it swept him along heedless of dangers that made his mere existence a daily miracle. It sent him flickering among the candles and bottles and fuming incense of his nocturnal day, it moved him to sniff cocaine and drop acid and drink wine all in a row, like the chord changes in a tune on which he was improvising.

Janis Joplin was possessed by a very different demon. She doted on the image of the hard-drinking, hard-living, hard-loving red-hot mama. She gloried in self-destruction, tearing out her throat with every song, brandishing a bottle of Southern Comfort on the stage, turning rock-solid blues like *Ball and Chain* into screaming, wailing nightmares. "Sure I could take better care of my health," she once said. "It might add a few years—but what the hell!"

The news report refers to the singer formally as "Miss Joplin." This formality suggests that the article is written for an audience that does not necessarily know of her, and the impression is reinforced by the nature of the free modifiers. Most of these are appositives; one appositive gives the title of her musical group (*"The Janis Joplin Full Tilt Boogie Band"*), one gives explanatory details about a group she had been with earlier in her career (*a San Francisco rock group which had a large Western following*), one gives the names of her two biggest hits (*"Piece of My Heart" and "Ball and Chain"*), and one gives details about her family background (*The oldest child of a refinery executive in Port Arthur, Tex.*). Such use of background-providing appositives is typical of news reports addressed to a general audience. These details would not be necessary for an audience well acquainted with Janis Joplin.

The frequent use of passives is also common in a news report, to avoid having to specify the doer of an action. Thus we find *Singer Janis Joplin . . . was found dead, Her body was found wedged between a bed and a nightstand, No drugs or narcotic paraphernalia was found in the room, Sanchez said an autopsy would be performed.* All these passives occur in the first four paragraphs. Near the end of the article is the only passive with a specific agent: *Her body was discovered by guitarist John Cooke.*

Another feature typical of a news report is the lack of evaluative adjectives. The only adjective that might possibly be considered evaluative is *husky,* describing Janis Joplin's vocal style.

The news analysis compares the lives and deaths of Jimi Hendrix and Janis Joplin, referring to the singers by their full names or by the last name only. In contrast to the news report, the *Life* article makes considerable use of evaluative adjectives: *flamboyant, greatest, immense, urgent, elusive, exotic, inevitable, high-flown, flowery, heedless.*

The article begins *First it was Jimi Hendrix.* This is a truncated IT-cleft, and the reader is immediately intrigued. It was Jimi Hendrix who *what?* the reader asks himself, and continues reading to find the answer. The question is answered only partially, if at all, by two free modifiers in the same sentence: *snuffed out last month at 27, dead on arrival at a London hospital.* The reader moves along quickly by way of sentence fragments to the beginning of the second paragraph: *Then it was Janis Joplin.* The structure of this paragraph is closely parallel to that of the preceding one, reinforcing the parallelism between Jimi and Janis, but some variety is introduced into the structure by the absolutes which tell about the needle marks on her arm and the drugs in her room. The sentence structures here suggest the hard-hitting Joplin singing style.

The writing suits syntax to sense. In explaining how Hendrix was swept along by the "rhetoric of his life," the writer uses two compound sentences. In the first sentence the T-units are joined with *and;* in the second they are connected only by a comma:

> That was the rhetoric of his life and it swept him
> along heedless of dangers that made his mere exis-
> tence a daily miracle. It sent him flickering among
> the candles and bottles and fuming incense of
> his nocturnal day, it moved him to sniff cocaine
> and drop acid and drink wine all in a row, like the
> chord changes in a tune on which he was
> improvising.

There is also coordination within these last two T-units (*candles and bottles and fuming incense, sniff cocaine and drop acid and drink wine*). This heavy use of coordination propels the reader through the sentences, suggesting the way Hendrix was swept through life.

The following paragraph, on Janis Joplin, describes her as doting on the image of the *hard-drinking, hard-living, hard-loving red-hot mama.* The hyphenated adjectives strike the reader like a series of punches. Then, in the next sentence, the four present-participle phrases suggest Janis' rush to self-destruction.

To what use is this style put? The title gives us a clue: "Drugs and Death in the Run-Down World of Rock Music." The question is whether there is an implied causal connection between rock music, drugs, and an early death. Janis is depicted as *possessed* by the urge to destory herself, and Jimi's death is described as *an inevitable product* of his *breathless quest for life.* Thus far in the article, the writer seems to ascribe their deaths more to tragic personal flaws than to the music-and-drug culture.

The persona of the first article is objective, reporting the facts about Janis' death and the more important facts about her career. Directing his article to a general audience, the reporter explains the *who, what, when, where,* but not the *why.*

In contrast, it is the *why* that concerns the involved persona of the *Life* article. The question he attempts to answer is "Why should a young man and woman of such energy and talent, endorsed with immense success, imperil their lives with dope?" His article is directed toward readers who have asked themselves this question, readers interested in learning enough about the personal lives of Hendrix and Joplin to understand the reasons for their deaths.

# FROM NONFICTION TO FICTION:
# A NEWS REPORT AND A SHORT STORY

Our next stylistic analysis contrasts a newspaper report with a use of the same event by the same writer in a short story. The event is the death of a man named Billy Higgins, who died in the sinking of the *Commodore.* Stephen Crane is the author of both passages. The first passage below is the news report he wrote for the *New York Press:* the second is from his short story "The Open Boat."

## I
### *New York Press* (1897)

John Kitchell of Daytona came running down
the beach, and as he ran the air was filled
with clothes. If he had pulled a single lever and
undressed, even as the fire horses harness,
5    he could not seem to me to have stripped with
more speed. He dashed into the water and grabbed
the cook. Then he went after the captain, but the
captain sent him to me, and then it was that he
saw Billy Higgins lying with his forehead on sand
10   that was clear of the water, and he was dead.[19]

## II
### "The Open Boat" (1898)

Presently he saw a man running along the
shore. He was undressing with most remarkable
speed. Coat, trousers, shirt, everything flew
magically off him . . . .
5    Then he [the correspondent] saw the man who
had been running and undressing, and undressing
and running, come bounding into the water. He
dragged ashore the cook, and then waded toward
the captain; but the captain waved him away and
10   sent him to the correspondent. He was naked
—naked as a tree in winter; but a halo was about
his head, and he shone like a saint. He gave a

---

[19] *Stephen Crane, "Stephen Crane's Own Story." In* The Red Badge of Courage and Other Writing *(Boston: Houghton-Mifflin Company, 1960), p. 323.*

15

strong pull, and a long drag, and a bully heave at
the correspondent's hand. The correspondent
schooled in the minor formulae, said, "Thanks, old
man." But suddenly the man cried, "What's
that?" He pointed a swift finger. The correspondent
said, "Go."

20

In the shallows, face downward, lay the oiler. His
forehead touched sand that was periodically,
between each wave, clear of the sea.[20]

The reporter refers to himself as *me,* and he gives the name
of the rescuer and the dead oiler. In contrast, the short story is
told in the third person, and people are identified only by
occupation, not by name. Thus the short story is less personal.

The news report has eight T-units in four sentences; the
T-units are 11.6 words long, on the average, and about 19
per cent of the words occur in free modifiers. "The Open
Boat" has sixteen T-units in thirteen sentences. The T-units are
an average of 9.7 words long, and nearly 12 per cent of the
words occur in free modifiers. Thus the short story's T-units are
only slightly shorter than the news report's, but the decidedly
lower percentage of free modifiers in "The Open Boat" make
this description less leisurely than the news report, more
staccato.

There are other significant differences, too. First, the news
report contains no direct quotes, but in the short story there are
three. Second, the news report has only one adjective, *clear*
(a factual adjective), while in the short story there are nine
adjectives: *remarkable, naked, strong, long, bully, minor, old,
swift* and *clear.* Seven of these in context are factual adjectives,
but *remarkable* and *bully* ("excellent") are evaluative adjectives, offering value judgments on the runner's speed and on
the quality of his heave on the correspondent's hand. A third
difference is in the use of figurative language. In the news
report there is just one figure of speech, an extended simile
which compares the speed of Kitchell's undressing to the speed
of harnessing the horses used in Crane's day for pulling fire
engines. But the short story has two similes (*naked as a tree
in winter* and *he shone like a saint*), a metaphor (*a halo was
about his head*), and an instance of metonymy (*He pointed a
swift finger*).

Thus the narrator of the short story is more removed from
events. Also, the story is more staccato and forceful in sentence
structure than the news report. And, as the preceding three

[20] Crane, The Red Badge, *pp. 312–313.*

comparisons have shown, the short story is more dramatic, through its use of direct quotations, and more descriptive, through its greater use of adjectives and figures of speech.

## COMPARING STYLES IN FICTION

The Crane comparison of the preceding section contrasted nonfictional and fictional writings. The following section is devoted to contrasts in fiction. The stylistic analyses illuminate differences between two first-person narrators, between a first-person and a third-person narrator describing a similar scene, and between a first-person and a third-person narrator describing the same event.

### TWO FIRST-PERSON NARRATORS

Herman Melville's *Moby Dick* (1851) and Saul Bellow's *Henderson the Rain King* (1959) are both quest novels in which the protagonist goes on a physical journey in order to find himself. Both are told in the first person. Doubtless some of the stylistic differences can be attributed to the predominant styles of the periods in which the novels were written, but it is fruitful to compare the passages as if the differences were attributable merely to the narrators.

I

**Herman Melville, *Moby Dick* (1851)**

Call me Ishmael. Some years ago—never mind
how long precisely—having little or no money
in my purse, and nothing particular to interest me
on shore, I thought I would sail about a little
5      and see the watery part of the world. It is a way I
have of driving off the spleen, and regulating
the circulation. Whenever I find myself growing
grim about the mouth; whenever it is damp, drizzly
November in my soul; whenever I find myself
10     involuntarily pausing before coffin warehouses, and
bringing up the rear of every funeral I meet; and
especially whenever my hypos get such an upper
hand of me, that it requires a strong moral principle
to prevent me from deliberately stepping into the

15   street, and methodically knocking people's hats off
     —then, I account it high time to get to sea as
     soon as I can. This is my substitute for pistol and
     ball. With a philosophical flourish Cato throws
     himself upon his sword; I quietly take to the ship.
20   There is nothing surprising in this. If they but knew
     it, almost all men in their degree, some time or
     other, cherish very nearly the same feelings towards
     the ocean with me.[21]


     II
     Saul Bellow, *Henderson the Rain King* (1959)


     What made me take this trip to Africa? There is no
     quick explanation. Things got worse and worse
     and worse and pretty soon they were too com-
     plicated.
5    When I think of my condition at the age of
     fifty-five when I bought the ticket, all is grief. The
     facts begin to crowd me and soon I get a pressure
     in the chest. A disorderly rush begins — my
     parents, my wives, my girls, my children, my farm,
10   my animals, my habits, my money, my music les-
     sons, my drunkenness, my prejudices, my brutality,
     my teeth, my face, my soul! I have to cry, "No, no,
     get back, curse you, let me alone!" But how can
     they let me alone? They belong to me. They are
15   mine. And they pile into me from all sides. It
     turns into chaos.
     However, the world which I thought so mighty
     an oppressor has removed its wrath from me. But
     if I am to make sense to you people and explain
20   why I went to Africa I must face up to the facts. I
     might as well start with the money. I am rich. From
     my old man I inherited three million dollars after
     taxes, but I thought myself a bum and had my
     reasons, the main reason being that I behaved
25   like a bum.[22]


Probably the only word that clearly identifies Henderson as a
modern man is the slang word *bum*. Ishmael is definitely of an

---

[21] Herman Melville, *Moby Dick (New York: The Macmillan Company, 1966), p. 1.*
[22] *Saul Bellow,* Henderson the Rain King *(New York: The Viking Press, Inc., 1959),*
p. 3.

earlier time, with his talk about *driving off the spleen,* his *hypos* (feelings of hypochondria), and his substitute for *pistol and ball* (suicide?). Word choice suggests little about the narrators as individuals, but a comparison of the percentage of polysyllabic words is more revealing. Approximately ten per cent of Ishmael's words consist of three or more syllables; only five per cent of Henderson's words are three or more syllables long. This suggests that Henderson is a less educated man, perhaps, or that, unlike Ishmael, he is too hurried or upset to be concerned with using an educated style.

There is considerable syntactic evidence in the opening paragraphs to bear out the latter assumption. First, Ishmael has longer T-units; 22.3 words on the average, compared with Henderson's average of 10.7. Also, Ishmael has a higher percentage of free modifiers: 52.2 per cent, compared with Henderson's 41.2 per cent. These statistics suggest that Ishmael is more syntactically mature than Henderson, but they only begin to suggest differences in personalities.

Henderson's longest sentence (T-unit) is more a list than a sentence:

> A disorderly rush begins — my parents, my wives,
> my girls, my children, my farm, my animals,
> my habits, my money, my music lessons, my
> drunkenness, my prejudices, my brutality,
> my teeth, my face, my soul!

Instead of *explaining* why he went to Africa, he at first is able only to list the things which had been bothering him. He gets "a pressure in the chest," and this pressure results not only in this long list of problems, but in short, very short, sentences. Nine of them (almost half) consist of ten words or fewer, and five of them (just under thirty per cent) consist of five words or fewer.

Ishmael is much more in control of himself and his syntax. Henderson begins only four of his twenty T-units (twenty per cent) with a free modifier, and two of these free modifiers are under five words long. Ishmael, however, begins almost half of his T-units (four out of nine) with free modifiers; one of these is twenty-four words long, and one stretches to seventy-two words. This use of lengthy initial modifiers marks Ishmael's style as more formal than Henderson's. The longest free modifier is a carefully-constructed series of clauses beginning with *whenever:*

> **Whenever** I find myself growing grim about the mouth; **whenever** it is damp, drizzly November in my soul; **whenever** I find myself involuntarily pausing before coffin warehouses, and bringing up the rear of every funeral I meet; and especially **whenever** my hypos get such an upper hand of me, that it requires a strong moral principle to prevent me from deliberately stepping into the street, and methodically knocking people's hats off . . . .

The main clause follows these four *whenever* clauses. The first two clauses set the mood with alliteration: *growing grim,* and *damp, drizzly.* These two clauses are short, nine and ten words long respectively; the third clause is much longer, nineteen words; and the last clause is thirty-four words long. By the time the reader finishes the last of these *whenever* clauses, their effect is almost overwhelming — Ishmael certainly had better get to the sea as soon as he can!

The stylistic differences between the two passages suggest, then, that Ishmael is much more in control of himself than Henderson the Rain King.

## A FIRST-PERSON AND A THIRD-PERSON
## NARRATOR, DIFFERENT AUTHORS

The two passages below both describe a village on a plain, in summer, with a view of mountains and a river. Each of these passages is the opening of the novel. The second passage has a first-person narrator, Frederic Henry, in Ernest Hemingway's *A Farewell to Arms.* The first passage, from William Dean Howell's *A Modern Instance,* is in the third person, yet it too can be said to have a narrator, or persona. A stylistic comparison can be thought of as illuminating primarily not the differences between Howells as a writer and Hemingway as a writer, but the differences between the Howells narrator and the Hemingway narrator. For our present purposes, it is only incidental that these passages happen to typify what we think of as the two men's characteristic styles, and to a certain extent the styles characteristic of their times.[23]

---

[23] *The ideas for this discussion were largely stimulated by Walker Gibson's* Tough, Sweet and Stuffy: An Essay on Modern American Prose Styles *(Bloomington, Ind.: Indiana University Press, 1966), pp. 28–42.*

## I
## W. D. Howells, *A Modern Instance* (1888)

The village stood on a wide plain, and around it
rose the mountains. They were green to their tops
in summer, and in the winter white through their
serried pines and drifting mists, but at every season
serious and beautiful, furrowed with hollow
shadows, and taking the light on masses and
stretches of iron-grey crag. The river swam through
the plain in long curves, and slipped away at last
through an unseen pass to the southward, tracing a
score of miles in its course over a space that
measured but three or four. The plain was very
fertile, and its features, if few and of purely
utilitarian beauty, had a rich luxuriance, and there
was a tropical riot of vegetation when the sun of
July beat on those northern fields. They waved
with corn and oats to the feet of the mountains, and
the potatoes covered a vast acreage with the lines
of their intense, coarse green; the meadows were
deep with English grass to the banks of the river,
that, doubling and returning upon itself, still
marked its way with a dense fringe of alders and
white birches.[24]

## II
## Ernest Hemingway, *A Farewell to Arms* (1929)

In the late summer of that year we lived in a house
in a village that looked across the river and the
plain to the mountains. In the bed of the river there
were pebbles and boulders, dry and white in the
sun, and the water was clear and swiftly moving and
blue in the channels. Troops went by the house and
down the road and the dust they raised powdered
the leaves of the trees. The trunks of the trees
too were dusty and the leaves fell early that year
and we saw the troops marching along the road
and the dust rising and leaves, stirred by the
breeze, falling and the soldiers marching and
afterward the road bare and white except for
the leaves.

[24] *William Dean Howells*, A Modern Instance *(Boston: Houghton-Mifflin Company, 1957), p. 1.*

15          The plain was rich with crops; there were many
            orchards of fruit trees and beyond the plain the
            mountains were brown and bare. There was
            fighting in the mountains and at night we could
            see the flashes from the artillery. In the dark it
20          was like summer lightning, but the nights were cool
            and there was not the feeling of a storm coming.[25]

The number of words in the two passages is the same, but the passages differ syntactically in several significant respects:

|                                      | Howells Narrator | Hemingway Narrator |
| ------------------------------------ | ---------------- | ------------------ |
| No. of words per T-unit              | 18.9             | 11.8               |
| No. of words per clause              | 14.5             | 10.5               |
| No. of words per sentence            | 37.8             | 27.0               |
| Per cent of words in free modifiers  | 32.8             | 18.2               |

The Howells narrator has decidedly more words per T-unit, words per clause, and words per sentence; he also has a much higher percentage of words in free modifiers. There is a difference in the nature of the free modifiers, too. Five of the Hemingway narrator's seven free modifiers are initial adverbials; only two are adjectival. In contrast, five of the Howells narrator's nine free modifiers are adjectival. Thus the Howells narrator seems more concerned with describing the countryside in detail.

Another difference appears in the use of coordinating conjunctions to join T-units. The Howells narrator uses four *and*'s to join T-units, while the Hemingway narrator uses seven. This difference and the statistical differences above characterize the Howells narrator as more syntactically mature than the Hemingway narrator, according to Hunt's and Christensen's measures.

The use of nouns differs too. The two passages have nearly the same number of nouns: between forty-five and fifty in each case. But there is much more repetition of nouns in the Hemingway passage:

---

[25] *Ernest Hemingway,* A Farewell to Arms *(New York: Charles Scribner's Sons, 1929), p. 3.*

| Howells Passage | Hemingway Passage |
|---|---|
| plain—3 times | leaves—4 times |
| mountains—2 times | road—3 times |
| river—2 times | trees—3 times |
| | plain(s)—3 times |
| | mountains—3 times |
| | river—2 times |
| | year—2 times |
| | troops—2 times |
| | dust—2 times |
| | night(s)—2 times |

Obviously the Howells narrator has varied his nouns much more than the Hemingway narrator.

There is a difference also in the use of adjectives. In the Howells passage there are several adjectives of more than one syllable: *serried, hollow, fertile, tropical, northern,* and so forth; in the Hemingway passage there is only one: *dusty.* Also, the Howells passage contains several adjectives which are evaluative in context: *serious, beautiful, intense, utilitarian,* and perhaps some others. In contrast, the Hemingway adjectives all seem to be factual.

What, then, can we tell about the two narrators from this analysis? The narrator of the third-person Howells passage is the leisurely, gentlemanly writer of the nineteenth century. His sentences, T-units, and clauses are relatively long by modern American standards, longer than those of the Hemingway narrator. He has fewer T-units per sentence because he does not join T-units with *and* so often as does the Hemingway narrator. The Howells narrator shows syntactic maturity. Also, his word choice is careful, with few repetitions; he displays a large and varied vocabulary, and an interest in descriptive detail. He uses evaluative adjectives, giving his personal interpretation of the scene as he describes it.

In contrast, the Hemingway narrator, Frederic Henry, uses a deliberately unfancy, unliterary, unemotional style. His adjectives are factual rather than evaluative. His sentences, T-units, and clauses are not particularly long; he often uses *and* to join T-units; and he does not make much effort to vary his words or to use big words. He seems to be saying, "This is just the way it was."

## A FIRST-PERSON AND A THIRD-PERSON
## NARRATOR, SAME AUTHOR

The following two passages again show a contrast in narrative viewpoint. But this time the author of both passages is the same, William Faulkner. He is describing the antics of a wild horse belonging to the Snopes family. The first version is from "The Spotted Horses," which appeared in *Scribner's Magazine* in June 1931. The second version is from "The Peasants," which is the last of the four parts of *The Hamlet* (1940), a novel about the Snopes family. The short story is narrated by an unnamed sewing machine agent; he is identified as Ratliff in the second version.

### I
### "The Spotted Horses" (1931)

"There goes ourn, paw!" Eck says his boy said. "There it goes, into Mrs. Littlejohn's house." Eck says it run right up the steps and into the house like a boarder late for supper. I reckon so. Any-
5 way, I was in my room, in my underclothes, with one sock on and one sock in my hand, leaning out the window when the commotion busted out, when I heard something run into the melodeon in the hall; it sounded like a railroad engine. Then
10 the door to my room come sailing in like when you throw a tin bucket top into the wind and I looked over my shoulder and see something that looked like a fourteen-foot pinwheel a-blaring its eyes at me. It had to blare them fast, because I was
15 already done jumped out the window.
I reckon it was anxious too, I reckon it hadn't never seen barbed wire or shell corn before, but I know it hadn't never seen underclothes before, or maybe it was a sewing-machine agent it hadn't
20 never seen..Anyway, it whirled and turned to run back and up the hall and outen the house, when it met Eck Snopes and that boy just coming in, carrying a rope. It swirled again and run down the hall and out the back door just in time to meet
25 Mrs. Littlejohn. She had just gathered up the clothes she had washed, and she was coming onto the back porch with a armful of washing in one hand and a scrubbing-board in the other, when

30

35

40

45

50

55

the horse skidded up to her, trying to stop and
swirl again. It never taken Mrs. Littlejohn
no time a-tall.

"Git outen here, you son," she says. She hit it
across the face with the scrubbing-board; that
ere scrubbing-board split as neat as ere a axe
could have done it, and when the horse swirled to
run back up the hall, she hit it again with what
was left of the scrubbing-board, not on the head
this time. "And stay out," she says.

Eck and that boy was half-way down the hall by
this time. I reckon that horse looked like a pinwheel
to Eck too. "Get to hell outen here, Ad!" Eck says.
Only there wasn't time. Eck dropped flat on his
face, but the boy never moved. The boy was about
a yard tall maybe, in overalls just like Eck's; that
horse swoared over his head without touching a
hair. I saw that, because I was just coming back
up the front steps, still carrying that ere sock and
still in my underclothes, when the horse come
onto the porch again. It taken one look at me and
swirled again and run to the end of the porch
and jumped the banisters and the lot fence like a
hen-hawk and lit in the lot running and went out
the gate again and jumped eight or ten upside-
down wagons and went on down the road. It was
a full moon then. Mrs. Armstid was still setting in
the wagon like she had done been carved outen
wood and left there and forgot.[26]

## II
## "The Peasants" (1940)

5

10

"Look out, paw!" the boy chattered out of the
violent shaking. "There's ourn! There he goes!" It
was the horse the Texan had given them again.
It was as if they owned no other, the other one did
not exist; as if by some absolute and instantaneous
rapport of blood they had relegated to oblivion
the one for which they had paid money. They ran
to the gate and down the lane where the other men
had disappeared. They saw the horse the Texan
had given them whirl and dash back and rush

[26] *William Faulkner, "The Spotted Horses." In* The Literature of the United States,
*ed. Walter Blair, Theodore Hornberger, and Randall Stewart, rev. ed. (Chicago:
Scott, Foresman and Company, 1953), Vol. 2, p. 1120.*

through the gate into Mrs. Littlejohn's yard and run
up the front steps and crash once on the wooden
veranda and vanish through the front door. Eck
and the boy ran up onto the veranda. A lamp sat on
15 a table just inside the door. In its mellow light they
saw the horse fill the long hallway like a pinwheel,
gaudy, furious and thunderous. A little further down
the hall there was a varnished yellow melodeon.
The horse crashed into it; it produced a single note,
20 almost a chord, in bass, resonant and grave, of
deep and sober astonishment; the horse with its
monstrous and antic shadow whirled again and
vanished through another door. It was a bedroom;
Ratliff, in his underclothes and one sock and with
25 the other sock in his hand and his back to the door,
was leaning out the open window facing the lane,
the lot. He looked back over his shoulder. For an
instant he and the horse glared at one another.
Then he sprang through the window as the horse
30 backed out of the room and into the hall again and
whirled and saw Eck and the little boy just entering
the front door, Eck still carrying his rope. It
whirled again and rushed on down the hall and
onto the back porch just as Mrs. Littlejohn, carrying
35 an armful of clothes from the line and the washboard, mounted the steps.
    "Get out of here, you son of a bitch," she said.
She struck with the washboard; it divided neatly
on the long mad face and the horse whirled and
40 rushed back up the hall, where Eck and the
boy now stood.
    "Get to hell out of here, Wall!" Eck roared. He
dropped to the floor, covering his head with his
arms. The boy did not move, and for the third time
45 the horse soared above the unwinking eyes and
the unbowed and untouched head and onto the
veranda again just as Ratliff, still carrying the sock
ran around the corner of the house and up the
steps. The horse whirled without breaking or
50 pausing. It galloped to the end of the veranda and
took the railing and soared outward, hobgoblin and
floating, in the moon. It landed in the lot still running and crossed the lot and galloped through the
wrecked gate and among the overturned wagons
55 and the still intact one in which Henry's wife still
sat, and on down the lane and into the road.[27]

[27] William Faulkner, "The Peasants." In The Hamlet (New York: Random House, 1940), pp. 307–308.

The change from the first person of "Spotted Horses" to the third person of "The Peasants" results in certain other changes. The speaker in the latter is omniscient and can therefore describe much that the first-person narrator could not know about or see. Moreover, the change in speaker dictates a change in dialect. The sewing machine agent uses nonstandard English: double negatives like *it hadn't never seen,* three times in one sentence; nonstandard verb forms like *busted* for *burst, run* for *ran, taken* for *took, come* for *came, swoared* for *soared, setting* for *sitting, had done been carved* for *had been carved;* and a miscellany of other nonstandard usages like *a axe* for *an axe, ere* for *here* twice, *outen* for *out of* four times, and *ourn* for *ours.* Nonstandard English appears in "The Peasants" only in the direct quotations from the participants in the story; in fact, *ourn* is the only nonstandard form. Note that Mrs. Littlejohn and Eck both say *out of* in "The Peasants," but *outen* in "The Spotted Horses."

This difference in viewpoint results in a difference in the kinds of comparisons, too. The similes of the short story are homespun, whereas those of the novel are poetical. Also, two similes in the short story become more subtle comparisons in the novel:

"The Spotted Horses"   (short story)

like a boarder late for supper
like a fourteen-foot pinwheel a-blaring its eyes at me
it sounded like a railroad engine
the door . . . come sailing in like when you throw a tin
    bucket top into the wind
jumped the banister and the lot fence like a hen-hawk

"The Peasants"   (novel)

like a pinwheel, gaudy, furious, and thunderous
it [the melodeon] produced a single note, almost a chord, in
    bass, resonant and grave, of deep and sober astonishment
took the railing and soared outward, hobgoblin and floating,
    in the moon

There is little difference between the two passages in the average number of words per T-unit and the percentage of words in free modifiers, but the first version has a type of free modifier that is not found in the second version. There are four T-units having the structure "X did (was doing, or had just done) Y, when Z occurred." One example is

> Anyway, it whirled and turned to run back and up
> the hall and outen the house, when it met Eck
> Snopes and that boy just coming in, carrying
> a rope.

The *when* clause is one of the free modifiers in the sentence. This colloquial kind of sentence structure is appropriate to the first-person narrator. The third-person narrator, more formal, avoids this kind of construction in various ways. For example, compare the following sentence with the one just quoted:

> Then he [Ratliff] sprang through the window as the
> horse backed out of the room and into the hall
> again and whirled and saw Eck and the little boy
> just entering the front door, Eck still carrying
> his rope.

Another difference is that certain sentences in the first-person narration are syntactically ambiguous or misleading, while the corresponding sentences in the third-person narration are not. Consider, for instance, the sentence *Anyway, I was in my room . . . when I heard something run into the melodeon in the hall; it sounded like a railroad engine.* Here it is not entirely clear whether *it* refers to the melodeon, or to the something which ran into the melodeon. In the second version, it is definitely the melodeon which makes the noise. Also, the first version contains a misplaced participle which creates misunderstanding or, at best, ambiguity:

> it met Eck Snopes and that boy just coming in, *carrying a rope.*

The phrase *carrying a rope* seems to modify *boy,* though it can possibly be interpreted as modifying *Eck Snopes* as well as *boy.* The second version has an unambiguous absolute:

> the horse . . . saw Eck and the little boy just entering the
> front door, *Eck still carrying his rope.*

Once again the contrast is between a colloquial style and a more formal style. The first-person narrator is telling his story all in a rush, and he can't be bothered by the niceties of pronoun reference and properly located participles. The third-person narrator is much more careful.

The first-person narrator is depicted as an uneducated man, down to earth, excitedly describing the events that happened.

The third-person narrator is educated, even poetical, and more restrained and careful of syntax in his description of events. In each case Faulkner has characterized his narrator through the use of appropriate dialect, figures of speech, and sentence structures.

## WORKING WITH STYLISTIC CONTRASTS

**1.** Compare the following two accounts of the Kent State University shootings on May 4, 1970. One excerpt, which we saw before on p. 296, is from the *New York Times* newspaper, May 5, 1970, and the other from *Time* magazine, May 18, 1970. Contrast the style of the newspaper report with the style of the news analysis. What is the significance of the stylistic differences you find?

I
*New York Times,* May 5, 1970

The crackle of the rifle volley cut the suddenly still air. It appeared to go on, as a solid volley, for perhaps a full minute or a little longer.

5     Some of the students dived to the ground, crawling on the grass in terror. Others stood shocked or half crouched, apparently believing the troops were firing into the air. Some of the rifle barrels were pointed upward.

    Near the top of the hill at the corner of Taylor
10    Hall, a student crumpled over, spun sideways and fell to the ground, shot in the head.

    When the firing stopped, a slim girl, wearing a cowboy shirt and faded jeans, was lying face down on the road at the edge of the parking lot, blood
15    pouring out onto the macadam, about 10 feet from this reporter.

    The youths stood stunned, many of them clustered in small groups staring at the bodies. A young man cradled one of the bleeding forms in his arms.
20    Several girls began to cry. But many of the students who rushed to the scene seemed almost too shocked to react. Several gathered around an abstract steel structure in front of the building and looked at a 30-caliber bullet hole drilled through
25    one of the plates.

## II
*Time*, May 18, 1970

Within seconds, a sickening staccato of rifle fire signaled the transformation of a once-placid campus into the site of an historic American tragedy.

5      "They are shooting blanks — they are shooting blanks," thought Kent State Journalism Professor Charles Brill, who nevertheless crouched behind a pillar. "Then I heard a chipping sound and a ping, and I thought, 'My God, this is for real.'" An Army

10    veteran who saw action in Korea, Brill was certain that the Guardsmen had not fired randomly out of individual panic. "They were organized," he said. "It was not scattered. They all waited and they all pointed their rifles at the same time. It looked

15    like a firing squad." . . .

The campus was suddenly still. Horrified students flung themselves to the ground, ran for cover behind buildings and parked cars, or just stood stunned. Then screams broke out. "My God,

20    they're killing us!" one girl cried. They were. A river of blood ran from the head of one boy, saturating his school books. One youth held a cloth against the abdomen of another, futilely trying to check the bleeding. Guardsmen made no move to

25    help the victims. The troops were still both frightened and threatening. After ambulances had taken away the dead and wounded, more students gathered. Geology Professor Glenn Frank, an ex-Marine, ran up to talk to officers. He came back

30    sobbing. "If we don't get out of here right now," he reported, "the Guard is going to clear us out any way they can — they mean *any* way."

2.   Write an essay in which you compare and contrast the styles of two or more of the passages below, excerpts from articles about the death of Janis Joplin.[28] Each article says different things about her death. What is the thesis of each article? What details of style help make the thesis clear? Each article also reveals a unique narrator, a mind reporting the death of Janis Joplin or commenting on it. In each case, what

[28] *The first of these articles is found in* Mass Media, *pp. 146–147; the others are found in* Language and the Newsstand, *pp. 212–215, 225–227, and 233–234, respectively. Both books contain other articles concerning the death of Janis Joplin.*

is this narrator like, and what stylistic details serve to create this narrator? Third, who is the assumed audience? What is the assumed audience like? And what stylistic details serve to characterize this audience?

I

*Rolling Stone,* October 29, 1970
"Janis Joplin"

When Janis Joplin failed to show up at Sunset Sound Studios by 6 PM Paul Rothschild, her producer, gave in to the strange "flashing" he had been feeling all day and sent John Cooke, a road
5    manager for the Full Tilt Boogie Band, over to the Landmark Motor Hotel to see why she wasn't answering her phone. "I'd never worried about her before," Rothschild said, "although she'd been late lots of times. It was usually that she stopped to
10   buy a pair of pants or some chick thing like that." October 4th was a Sunday however, and there were few places to go, even in Hollywood. Even for Janis.

The Landmark is a big stucco building on
15   Franklin Avenue. It is convenient to the sound studios on Sunset Blvd. and near the offices of the record companies and music publishers. It is painted a garish "sunburst orange" and "bear brown" (according to the man at the desk), and
20   it is the favorite motel for visiting performers. The lobby has large plastic plants and some vaguely psychedelic designs on its walls, but the motel's attraction is its tolerance. The guy behind the desk remembered, laughing, the time a guest called to
25   complain about the noise from a series of rooms where members of the Jefferson Airplane were having a party. "The guy who complained was thrown out," he said. It was Janis' kind of place.

When John Cooke got there it was almost 7 PM.
30   He noticed Janis' car in the lot, and that the drapes in her first floor room were drawn. She didn't answer her door when he knocked, or even when he banged and yelled. He spoke to the manager, Jack Hagy, who agreed that they should
35   go into the room. Janis was lying wedged between the bed and a nightstand, wearing a short nightgown. Her lips were bloody when they turned

her over, and her nose was broken. She had $4.50
clutched in one hand.

40        Cooke called a doctor, then phoned Janis'
attorney, Robert Gordon. Gordon claims he went
over the room carefully but found no narcotics or
drug paraphernalia. The police were called. When
they arrived at around 9 PM, they found no drugs or

45        "works." But they told reporters Janis had "fresh
needle marks on her arm, 10 to 14 of them,
on her left arm."


II
*Rolling Stone,* October 29, 1970
"Perspectives: Another Candle Blown Out"

—Ralph J. Gleason

*My candle burns at both ends;*
*It will not last the night;*
*But, ah, my foes, and, oh, my friends*
*It gives a lovely light.*

—Edna St. Vincent Millay

God knows, that blazing candle did cast a lovely
light, even though from time to time when it flick-
ered and the light dimmed, the looming face of
tragedy appeared.

5        For Janis, gamin-faced, husky voiced little girl
lost, seemed to me from the moment I first saw her
to have that fatal streak of tragedy present. And
what's more, to know it.
Laughin' just to keep from crying.

10        It was just paralyzing to hear the radio bulletin
that she was dead. Inevitable but paralyzing still
when it happened. How could it be? Why?
And it makes no difference, really, what any
inquest finds. She's dead and that's it and the

15        truth, which is sometimes much more difficult to
see than the facts, ma'am, just the facts, is that she
was driven to self-destruction by some demon
deep within her from the moment she left that
Texas high school where they had laughed at her.

20        She showed them, all right, she showed them
plenty and the dues she paid to show them proved
too much in the end.
Janis' effect on the San Francisco scene was like
a time bomb or a depth charge. There was a long

25  lag before it went off. She came up from Texas,
a beatnik folk singer, and sang in the Coffee
Gallery and the other crummy joints that were
available at the end of the Beat era and just
before the Haight blossomed so briefly only, like
30  Janis, to self-destruct.

.   .   .   .   .

Little girl blue, with the floppy hats and the brave
attempt to be one of the guys. She took a little
piece of all of us with her when she went. She was
35  beautiful. That's not corny. It's true.

III
*The New York Times,* October 27, 1970
"Overdosing on Life"

—Jacob Brackman

Most likely, neither Jimi Hendrix nor Janis Joplin
meant much of anything to you. Jimi died on
September 18, Janis on October 4, both, it was
said, in connection with drugs. They were young
5  rock stars. A little over three years ago, only the
most ardent music buffs had heard of either
of them.
Perhaps you generally keep abreast, yet never
heard of Jimi alive — nor of Janis for that matter.
10  Perhaps you read of them for the first time in this
newspaper — struck, fleetingly, tsk, at the coinci-
dence: "Second this month, isn't it?" perhaps right
where you're reading this now: an office, a coffee
shop, a commuter train. Forgive me, I am trying
15  to get a picture of you. Asked to comment on their
deaths for this page, I feel like a kind of foreign
correspondent.
You see, millions of Americans were untellably
stirred by these deaths. Maybe — if you have
20  kids, or know any — you felt surprise at how much
feverish talk they inspired. Or maybe you over-
heard no post-mortems. They went on, I know, only
in certain neighborhoods, among street people,
hill people, students, fellow travelers of the New
25  Consciousness, many of whom, having just lately
grown old enough for mourning, lack proportion.
Lack, you might say, an adult sense of who is
worthy of being mourned.

IV
*The Christian Century,* November 4, 1970
"Of Apollo and Dionysus"

30    To those who don't feel connected with, thankful
for, sustained by statesmen, Hendrix and Joplin
were a more grievous loss than any statesmen
could be.

The same October week that saw the death at
age 27 of rock singer Janis Joplin also witnessed
the spectacle of the United States Congress
finally shedding its lethargy, only to indulge in an
5     orgy of excessive and constitutionally dubious
anticrime legislation. The juxtaposition of the two
events is a symbolic reminder that the current
struggle over the future of American society is
deeply rooted in an age-old, classic conflict. On
10    the one hand, "Apollo": order, stability, statis. On
the other, "Dionysus": disorder, creative
energy, kenesis. [sic]
At their best, both forces meet real needs.
Without order there can be neither society nor
15    individual creativity; crimes do cause suffering,
and individuals often do need protection afforded
by laws and police. At the same time, total order
means banality or repression. A totally ordered
society destroys vibrancy, creativity, life. Rollo May
20    warns that order's issue may be apathy rather than
stability. He acknowledges the *daimonic* as the
power both of destructiveness and of creativity.
Janis Joplin (or Jimi Hendrix, who died of a drug
overdose three weeks earlier) embodied both poles
25    of the *daimonic*. Treading the razor edge between
creation and destruction, Janis' music was the
extension of her life. Challenging the power of
chaos by making herself vulnerable to it, she
granted her fans and followers a vision of life in
30    the face of the stultified, ordered, repressed and
repressive culture they perceived about them.
Though order and energy are both necessary, in
their extremes order is the rock Scylla, disorder
the whirlpool Charybdis. Both kill. Janis and
35    Hendrix challenged the chaotic and were swept
under by it. The peace, love and flowers of three
summers past has, for many, degenerated into a
horror of hard drugs, destructiveness and paranoia.

40

But preoccupation with order is also self-destructive. The anticrime deluge, which the *New Republic's* T.R.B. calls "hysterical," mocks the Constitution and invites anarchy by its own disrespect for law and due process. Expedience fosters sloppy legislation, the antithesis of order.

**3.** In the first of the passages below, James Baldwin is discussing André Gide; in the second, Norman Mailer is discussing Henry Miller. Although both passages concern the effects of sex for its own sake, the styles are different. Compare the styles and discuss their differing effects.

I

5

10

15

20

It is possible, as it were, to have one's pleasure without paying for it. But to have one's pleasure without paying for it is precisely the way to find oneself reduced to a search for pleasure which grows steadily more desperate and more grotesque. It does not take long, after all, to discover that sex is only sex, that there are few things on earth more futile or more deadening than a meaningless round of conquests. The really horrible thing about the phenomenon of present-day homosexuality, the horrible thing which lies curled like a worm at the heart of Gide's trouble and his work and the reason that he so clung to Madeleine, is that today's unlucky deviate can only save himself by the most tremendous exertion of all his forces from falling into an underworld in which he never meets either men or women, where it is impossible to have either a lover or a friend, where the possibility of genuine human involvement has altogether ceased. When this possibility has ceased, so has the possibility of growth.[29]

II

Poor Henry. He has spent his literary life exploring the watershed of sex from that uncharted side which goes by the name of lust and it is an

[29] *James Baldwin,* Nobody Knows My Name *(New York: Dell Publishing Company, Inc., 1961), p. 131.*

5
epic work for any man; over the centuries, most of
the poets of the world have spent their years on
the other side; they wrote of love. But lust is a
world of bewildering dimensions, for it is that
power to take over the ability to create and convert
it to a force. Curious force. Lust exhibits all the

10
attributes of junk. It dominates the mind and other
habits, it appropriates loyalties, generalizes
character, leaches character out, rides on the fuel
of almost any emotional gas — whether hatred,
affection, curiosity, even the pressures of boredom

15
— yet it is never definable because it can alter
to love or be as suddenly sealed from love, indeed
the more intense lust becomes, the more it is
indefinable, the line of the ridge between lust and
love is where the light is first luminous, then blind-

20
ing, and the ground remains unknown.[30]

**4.** Following are two versions of "The Three Bears." [31] The first is written in the style of *The Catcher in the Rye,* by J. D. Salinger, and the second in the style of *A Farewell to Arms,* by Ernest Hemingway. In the light of your own perceptions of these two styles, how well does the writer of the parody succeed in selecting markers that will identify the style of the writer being imitated?

I
## "Catch Her in the Oatmeal"

If you actually want to hear about it, what I'd
better do is I'd better warn you right now that you
aren't going to believe it. I mean it's a true *story*
and all, but it still sounds sort of phony.

5
Anyway, my name is Goldie Lox. It's sort of a
boring name, but my parents said that when I was
born I had this very blonde hair and all. Actually
I was born bald. I mean how many babies get born
with blonde hair? None. I mean I've *seen* them and

10
they're all wrinkled and red and slimy and
everything. And bald. And then all the phonies
have to come around and tell you he's as cute as
a bug's ear. A bug's ear, boy, that really kills
me. You ever *seen* a bug's ear? What's cute

15
about a bug's *ear,* for Chrissake! Nothing,
that's what.

[30] *Norman Mailer,* The Prisoner of Sex *(New York: New American Library Signet Book, 1971), pp. 81–82.*
[31] *Dan Greenberg, "Three Bears in Search of an Author,"* Esquire, *February 1958, pp. 46–47.*

So, like I was saying, I always seem to be
getting into these very stupid situations. Like this
time I was telling you about. Anyway, I was
20   walking through the forest and all when I see this
very interesting house. A *house.* You wouldn't think
anybody would be living way the hell out in the
goddam *forest,* but they were. No one was home
or anything and the door was open, so I walked in.
25   I figured what I'd do is I'd probably horse around
until the guys that lived there came home and
maybe asked me to stay for dinner or something.
Some people think they *have* to ask you to stay
for dinner even if they *hate* you. Also I didn't
30   exactly feel like going home and getting asked
a lot of lousy questions. I mean that's *all* I ever
seem to do.

Anyway, while I was waiting I sort of sampled
some of this stuff they had on the table that tasted
35   like oatmeal. *Oatmeal.* It would have made you puke,
I mean it. Then something very spooky started
happening. I started getting dizzier than hell. I
figured I'd feel better if I could just rest for a while.
Sometimes if you eat something like lousy oatmeal
40   you can feel better if you just rest for awhile, so
I sat down. That's when the goddam *chair* breaks
in half. No kidding, you start feeling lousy and
some stupid *chair* is going to break on you every
time. I'm not kidding. Anyway I finally found the
45   crummy bedroom and I lay down on this very
tiny bed. I was really depressed.

I don't know how long I was asleep or anything
but all of a sudden I hear this very strange voice
say, "Someone's been sleeping in *my* sack, for
50   Chris-sake, and there she is!" So I open my eyes
and here at the foot of the bed are these three
crummy *bears. Bears!* I swear to God. By that time
I was *really* feeling depressed. There's nothing
more depressing than waking up and finding
55   three *bears* talking about you, I mean.

So I didn't stay around and shoot the breeze
with them or anything. If you want to know the
truth, I sort of ran out of there like a madman or
something. I do that quite a little when I'm
60   depressed like that.

On the way home, though, I got to figuring. What
probably happened is these bears wandered in
when they smelled this oatmeal and all. Probably
bears *like* oatmeal, I don't know. And the voice I

65 heard when I woke up was probably something I
dreamt.

So that's the story.

I wrote it all up once as a theme in school, but
my crummy teacher said it was too *whimsical.*
70 Whimsical. That killed me. You got to meet her
sometime, boy. She's a real queen.


II

## "A Farewell to Porridge"

In the late autumn of that year we lived in a
house in the forest that looked across the river to
the mountains, but we always thought we lived
on the plain because we couldn't see the forest
5 for the trees.

Sometimes people would come to the door and
ask if we would like to subscribe to *The Saturday
Evening Post* or buy Fuller brushes, but when
we would answer the bell they would see we were
10 only bears and go away.

Sometimes we would go for long walks along
the river and you could almost forget for a little
while that you were a bear and not people.

Once when we were out strolling for a very long
15 time we came home and you could see that
someone had broken in and the door was open.

*"La porte est ouverte!"* said Mama Bear. "The
door should not be open." Mama Bear had French
blood on her father's side.

20 "It is all right," I said. "We will close it."

"It should not have been left open," she said.

"It is all right," I said. "We will close it. Then
it will be good like in the old days."

*"Bien,"* she said. "It is well."

25 We walked in and closed the door. There were
dishes and bowls and all manner of eating utensils
on the table and you could tell that someone had
been eating porridge. We did not say anything
for a long while.

30 "It is lovely here," I said finally. "But someone
has been eating my porridge."

"Mine as well," said Mama Bear.

"It is all right," I said. "It is nothing."

"Darling," said Mama Bear, "do you love me?"

35 "Yes I love you."

"You really love me?"

"I really love you. I'm crazy in love with you."

"And the porridge? How about the porridge?"
"That too. I really love the porridge too."
40    "It was supposed to be a surprise. I made it
as a surprise for you, but someone has eaten it all
up."
"You sweet. You made it as a surprise. Oh,
you're lovely," I said.
45    "But it is gone."
"It is all right," I said. "It will be all right."
Then I looked at my chair and you could see
someone had been sitting in it and Mama Bear
looked at her chair and someone had been sitting
50    in that too and Baby Bear's chair is broken.
"We will go upstairs," I said and we went
upstairs to the bedroom but you could see that
someone had been sleeping in my bed and in
Mama Bear's too although that was the same bed
55    but you have to mention it that way because that
is the story. Truly. And then we looked in Baby
Bear's bed and there she was.
"I ate your porridge and sat in your chairs and
I broke one of them," she said.
60    "It is all right," I said. "It will be all right."
"And now I am lying in Baby Bear's bed."
"Baby Bear can take care of himself."
"I mean that I am sorry. I have behaved badly
and I am sorry for all of this."
65    "Ça ne fait rien," said Mama Bear. "It is
nothing." Outside it had started to rain again.
"I will go now," she said. "I am sorry." She
walked slowly down the stairs.
I tried to think of something to tell her but
70    it wasn't any good. "Good-by," she said.
Then she opened the door and went outside and
walked all the way back to her hotel in the rain.

5.    In studying the data from Kellogg Hunt's research, John
Mellon concluded that another significant measure of syntactic
maturity is the number of embedded constructions per T-unit,
in particular the number of nominalizations and the number of
full and reduced adjectival clauses. Using the data from Hunt's
study, Mellon computed the following statistics on nominal and
adjectival embeddings: [32]

---

[32] *John Mellon,* Transformational Sentence-Combining: A Method for Enhancing the
Development of Syntactic Fluency in English Composition *(Urbana, Ill.: National
Council of Teachers of English, 1969), p. 19.*

Frequencies of Constructions per 100 T-units

| Construction type | 4th | 8th | 12th | Adult |
|---|---|---|---|---|
| Factive and WH-word nominals | 9 | 12 | 27 | 21 |
| Gerundive and infinitive | | | | not |
| nominals | 6 | 10 | 23 | available |
| Adjectival clauses | 5 | 9 | 16 | 25 |
| Adjectival phrases | 13 | 28 | 46 | 92 |
| Adjectival words | 33 | 68 | 81 | 152 |

Select for comparison 100 consecutive T-units from *Moby Dick* and 100 consecutive T-units from *Henderson the Rain King,* making sure that the two passages are comparable in content. Compare the number of nominalizations and adjectivalizations in the two passages. By this criterion, which passage is more syntactically mature? Do your conclusions reinforce or contradict what was said earlier about the two narrators?

**6.** The following novels are narrated in the first person. From two or more, select passages which are similar in content. Then compare the narrators, using whatever criteria seem appropriate.

John Barth, *Giles Goat-Boy*
Ralph Ellison, *Invisible Man*
F. Scott Fitzgerald, *The Great Gatsby*
Robert Gover, *One Hundred Dollar Misunderstanding*
Mark Harris, *The Southpaw*
Ernest Hemingway, *A Farewell to Arms*
Warren Miller, *The Cool World*
J. D. Salinger, *The Catcher in the Rye*
Mark Twain, *The Adventures of Huckleberry Finn*
Mark Twain, *A Connecticut Yankee in King Arthur's Court*

 FOR FURTHER EXPLORATION

Walker Gibson, *Tough, Sweet and Stuffy: An Essay on Modern American Prose Styles.* Bloomington, Indiana: Indiana University Press, 1966. Gibson is pleasingly independent and witty in his analysis of the writing characteristics of our culture.

Glen A. Love and Michael Payne, eds., *Contemporary Essays on Style: Rhetoric, Linguistics, and Criticism.* Glenview, Ill.: Scott, Foresman and Company, Inc., 1969. An excellent collection of articles.

Stoddard Malarkey, ed., *Style: Diagnoses and Prescriptions.* New York: Harcourt Brace Jovanovich, Inc., 1972. Contains a number of interesting essays on style, including some essays which analyze the style of specific works.

John Kuehl, *Creative Writing and Rewriting: Contemporary American Novelists at Work.* New York: Appleton-Century-Crofts, 1967. A collection of one or more early versions of passages from published novels, followed in each case by the published version.

Thomas F. Van Laan and Robert B. Lyons, eds., *Language and the Newsstand: A Critical Reader.* 2nd ed. New York: Charles Scribner's Sons, 1972. A collection of materials useful for stylistic comparisons.

Walker Gibson, *Persona: A Style Study for Writers and Readers.* New York: Random House, 1969. Makes several interesting suggestions for stylistic analysis.

Sallie Isaacs, "From Language to Linguistic Criticism," *English Journal,* 57 (January 1968), 47–51. Presents an in-depth analysis of two excerpts from D. H. Lawrence's "The Blind Man."

Yakira H. Frank, "Stylistics in the Classroom," *English Journal,* 55 (November 1966), 1051–1055, 1075. Presents an illuminating comparison of a sentence from Washington Irving's "The Legend of Sleepy Hollow" with a sentence from Hemingway's "A Way You'll Never Be."

Milton A. Kaslan, "Style Is Content," *English Journal,* 57 (December 1968), 1330–1334. Discusses excerpts from several literary works.

Roderick A. Jacobs, "Focus and Presupposition: Transformations and Meaning," *College Composition and Communication,* 20 (October 1969), 187–190, and "Transformations, Style and the Writing Experience," *English Journal,* 60 (April 1971), 481–484, 490. Both articles discuss some stylistic differences which can be accounted for in transformational terms.

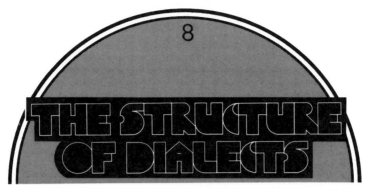

# 8

# THE STRUCTURE OF DIALECTS

All dialects are structured subsystems of a language, with definite phonological and syntactic patterns. In this chapter we will put our knowledge of phonology and syntax to work in discussing the nature of dialect variation and describing the distinctive structural patterns of the two major nonstandard dialects within the United States today, Spanish-influenced English and Afro-American English.

## THE NATURE OF DIALECT VARIATION

In speech as in fingerprints, every human being differs from every other human being. Each person has his own individual set of speech patterns, his **idiolect,** which differs in infinitesimal ways from the idiolects of other persons around him. Sound spectrograms produced in physics laboratories make visible records of these minuscule differences, showing that in fact it is impossible for anyone to reproduce even a single sound identically.

These idiolectal differences are usually too small to be linguistically significant. However, idiolects group into *dialects,* linguistically significant subvarieties of a language. When a linguist speaks of someone's "dialect," he does not mean that the person has a quaint rural manner of speaking, or that the person speaks a nonstandard variety of the language. To the linguist, the term **dialect** simply refers to a recognizable subvariety of a language, a subvariety used by an identifiable speech community, a group of people united not only by their speechways but by various extralinguistic factors, such as geographic location and/or social status.

Dialects are of two major kinds, *geographic* or *regional,* and *social.* In each case there are lexical, syntactic, and phonological differences among the dialects. Most people are aware, for example, that there are lexical differences from one area of the country to another. Many of these lexical differences were uncovered by investigations made in order to compile a linguistic atlas of the United States. In the 1930s and 1940s linguistic field interviewers called *dialectologists* conducted extended interviews with informants of three types in New England, the Middle Atlantic States, and the South Atlantic States. The informants were classified essentially in terms of education, economic status, and social position. Using a questionnaire of some three hundred items, the dialectologists established three main dialect areas: Northern, Midland, and Southern, marked by dialect differences in vocabulary, phonology, and syntax. On the basis of the vocabulary alone, Hans Kurath documented the existence of these three areas in *A Word Geography of the Eastern United States,* published in 1949.[1] The accompanying map shows the clear separations on the eastern coast, as well as the blending and fusing that resulted from westward migrations. Wherever men move, they take their dialects with them.

The impact of travel and the mass media has eroded many regional differences, to a certain extent creating a consensus dialect, or "network English," the kind of English most frequently heard on the national television networks. Nevertheless, local terms for locally made items, special services, foods, pastimes, and characteristic geographical features still persist. For example, *cottage cheese* is also *dutch cheese* or *pot cheese* in certain areas of the North, *smear-case* in certain Midland areas, and *clabber cheese* or *curds* in much of the South; *cornbread* is also *johnny cake* in the North and *corn pone* in the South.

In addition to regional differences in vocabulary there are a few—but only a few—syntactic differences from one area to another. Most of these differences involve nonstandard verb forms. For example, the nonstandard past participle of *see* is usually *see* in the North, *seen* in the Midland, *seed* in North Carolina.[2]

The major differences among regional dialects are phonological. For example, most of the country is "*r*-pronouncing," but the Northeast, New York City, the Upper South (Virginia and the adjoining counties of Maryland and North Carolina)

[1] *Hans Kurath,* A Word Geography of the Eastern United States *(Ann Arbor: University of Michigan Press, Studies in American English, 1).*
[2] *William Labov, "Variation in Language." In* The Learning of Language, *Carroll E. Reed, ed. (New York: Appleton-Century-Crofts, 1971), p. 195.*

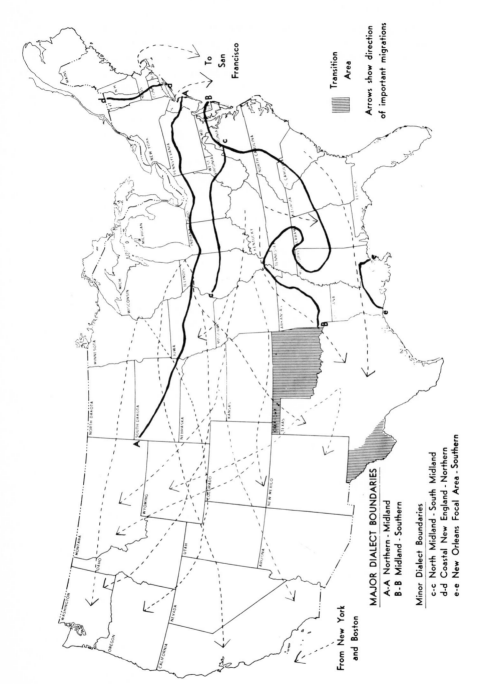

To
San
Francisco

Transition
Area

Arrows show direction
of important migrations

MAJOR DIALECT BOUNDARIES
A-A  Northern - Midland
B-B  Midland - Southern

Minor Dialect Boundaries
c-c  North Midland - South Midland
d-d  Coastal New England - Northern
e-e  New Orleans Focal Area - Southern

From New York
and Boston

Figure 8-1

and the Lower South (South Carolina and Georgia) have traditionally been considered "*r*-less" regions: that is, speakers in these regions frequently pronounce *r* as a schwa-like sound before a consonant within the same word (*card*) or at the end of a word when the next word begins with a consonant (*car crash*). Another regional phonological distinction is reflected by the term "Southern drawl," which refers mainly to two things: 1) the weakening or absence of the semivowel glide in /ay/, /aw/, and /ɔy/, "so that southern *ride* can be quite similar to northern *rod*, *proud* to northern *prod*, *oil* to northern *all*";[3] 2) the addition of a front or back glide plus an in-gliding schwa after a short vowel, giving /siyət/ for *sit*, /leyəs/ for *less*, /klæyəs/ for *class*, /dɔwəg/ for *dog*, /puwət/ for *put*, and so forth. Such differences are differences in phonological *systems*.

Each major dialect region, however defined, contains dialect subregions, and each subregion has a collection of structurally similar local dialects. Within every local dialect community, there are social contrasts among groups, based primarily on education and economic status. These contrasts usually correlate with dialectal variations considered *social*. Such social differences give rise to the terms "standard" and "nonstandard." That is, the terms "standard English" and "nonstandard English" refer to the social acceptability of various dialects and, more broadly, to the social status of the people who habitually speak these dialects. Thus "standard English" is commonly used to designate the habitual speech of most college-educated persons, who are considered members of the middle class. The term "nonstandard English" is commonly used to designate the speech of the less well-educated classes, when that speech is structurally different from standard English. Thus the terms "standard" and "nonstandard" have as much basis in social reality as in linguistic reality, if not more.

The less well-educated typically are aware of this designation of their speech patterns as nonstandard and socially inferior. This awareness was shown quite clearly in a Detroit study, where respondents were asked to rate speech samples on a seven-point semantic differential scale using polar adjectives:

| awkward | ___:___:___:___:___:___:___ | graceful |
|---------|------------------------------|----------|
| relaxed | ___:___:___:___:___:___:___ | tense |
| formal  | ___:___:___:___:___:___:___ | informal |
| thin    | ___:___:___:___:___:___:___ | thick |
| correct | ___:___:___:___:___:___:___ | incorrect |

---

[3] Labov, "Variation," p. 194. Labov further says that "these pairs can coincide in the certain southern dialects as well, but not necessarily."

The responses indicate that many members of the lower socio-economic classes recognize the stigma generally attached to lower class speech.[4] A somewhat comparable study in New York City produced similar results.[5]

There are not only social contrasts within each local dialect area but also stylistic contrasts within each individual's speech. A person's speech will be closer to standard norms when he is talking to someone who has power or authority over him than when talking with friends or family. Thus *all* dialects (regional or social, standard or nonstandard) have varying degrees of formality. We will call the extremes *casual speech* and *careful speech.* Our *reading style,* the style we use in reading aloud, is even more formal than our careful speech.

The structural differences between careful and casual standard English are mainly phonological. For instance, the spoken sentence *that's not a cat* is relatively careful if the final /t/ and /s/ of *that's* are both pronounced. In everyone's casual speech, final consonant clusters are often reduced if both consonants are voiced or both are unvoiced, and if the following word begins with a consonant. Thus the casual standard equivalent of the above sentence would be *thass not a cat,* with the /t/ omitted and the /s/ lengthened.

Between standard and nonstandard English, there are both phonological differences and syntactic differences. In nonstandard English, *that,* for example, would commonly be *dat,* with /d/ rather than /ð/ as the initial consonant. Syntactically, *ain't* would replace *isn't,* so that in nonstandard dialects one might say *dat ain't a cat,* or more likely, *dat ain't no cat.* The use of the double negative (*ain't no*) is another syntactic difference between nonstandard and standard English.

Since the mid-1960s, dialect study in the United States has been dominated by **sociolinguists,** who investigate the relationship between social factors and dialect structures. William Labov was the first to use rigorous population-sampling procedures in selecting the individuals whose speech would be studied, and he was the first to thoroughly investigate urban speech differences as they correlate with the extralinguistic factors of socioeconomic status, ethnic background, speech context (casual versus formal situation), age, and sex.

Labov's first major sociolinguistic investigation, reported in *The Social Stratification of English in New York City,* indicates that the same linguistic features register both social stratifica-

---

[4] *Roger W. Shuy, "Subjective Judgments in Sociolinguistic Analysis." In* Report of the Twentieth Annual Round Table Meeting on Linguistics and Language Studies, ed. James E. Alatis, Georgetown Monograph Series on Languages and Languistics, *No. 22 (Washington, D.C.: Georgetown University Press, 1970), pp. 175–188.*
[5] *William Labov,* The Social Stratification of English in New York City *(Washington, D.C.: Center for Applied Linguistics, 1966), pp. 405–454.*

tion and style shifting. One example is the percentage of formal /iŋ/ rather than /in/ in the -ing suffix used to form present participles and gerunds (*working, living,* etc). Figure 8-2 graphs Labov's data for white New York City adults: [6]

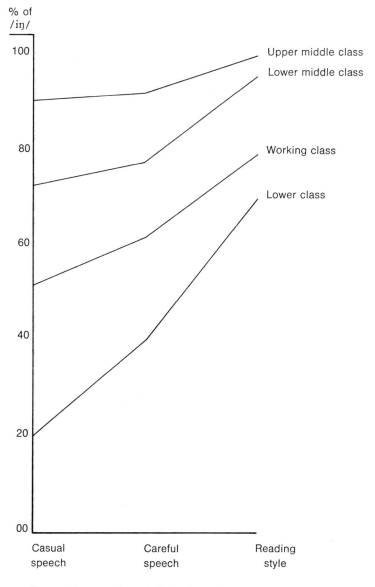

% of
/iŋ/

**Figure 8-2**    Class & Style Stratification of /iŋ/

[6] *Adapted from William Labov,* The Study of Nonstandard English *(Urbana, Ill.: National Council of Teachers of English, 1970), p. 24.*

All the socioeconomic classes use the /in/ pronunciation at least part of the time. For each contextual style (casual speech, careful speech, reading style) there is a regular pattern of stratification: in each style, each socioeconomic class has a higher percentage of /iŋ/ than the next lowest class. There is a regular pattern of style stratification, too: the percentage of /iŋ/ increases as the context becomes more formal. Thus the same feature shows both class stratification and style stratification.

A similar example is the degree of *r*-lessness in New York City. Figure 8-3 shows the precentage of /r/ occurring preconsonantally (*card, car crash*) in the speech of native New York City adults (those who were born in New York City or who moved there before the age of eight): [7]

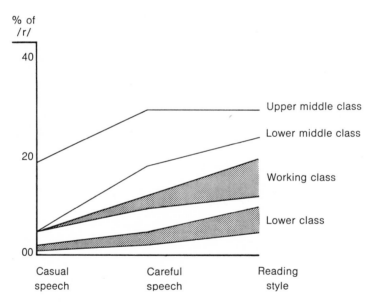

**Figure 8-3**     Class & Style Stratification of /r/

Again the graph shows a highly regular pattern of both class *and* style stratification. The regular pattern of style stratification shows that the pronunciation of preconsonantal *r* as the sound /r/ is becoming a prestige marker in New York City.

[7] *Labov*, The Study of Nonstandard English, *p. 27.*

These pronunciation patterns for -*ing* and for preconsonantal *r* in New York City are typical: the same linguistic features normally register both social stratification and style stratification.

Since the pronunciation of preconsonantal *r* varies with social class and style, preconsonantal *r* can be termed a **linguistic variable.** Linguistically, we would say that the *r* in words like *card* and *car* has an underlying phonological entity, R. This underlying R usually becomes an /r/ or a schwa-like sound in actual speech; thus /r/ and /ə/ are the two primary **variants** of the R variable. CARD on the underlying phonological level will become /kard/ or /kaəd/, CAR will become /kar/ or /kaə/, and so forth.

Transformational theorists are primarily concerned with specifying underlying linguistic structures (linguistic competence) rather than with describing or accounting for actual speech (performance). They hypothesize that all the dialects of a language have essentially the same deep structure, and they are trying to specify the underlying semantic, syntactic, and phonological structures presumably common to the dialects of English. However, they have not attempted to explain how real-world factors affect the choice of one linguistic variant over another, as for example the choice of /r/ or /ə/ as the surface manifestation of underlying preconsonantal R.

The sociolinguist William Labov has been a pioneer in attempting to account for actual speech performance. He says that to account for speech variation, a grammar must have rules of the following sort:

> Category A is realized as Subcategory B (and not B') in environment C with a frequency F, where F is a function of other linguistic or extralinguistic variable (sex, age, class, style, ethnic group).[8]

For example, one might write a rule such as

> Underlying R is realized as /r/ (and not /ə/) in preconsonantal position 0 to 1 per cent of the time in the casual speech of working-class black adolescent males living in New York City.

Such a rule must be based on detailed empirical investigation, as this one is; it is based on data from Labov's study of non-

[8] Labov, "Variation," p. 218.

standard English in New York City.[9] A rule of this sort is both a description and a prediction of actual speech.

As the above rule suggests, the extralinguistic factors affecting the use of a particular variant can be quite complex. So can the linguistic factors. Let us take, as an example, the pronunciation of the final consonant in words like the following:

| Type I | Type II |
|--------|---------|
| mist   | missed  |
| past   | passed  |
| find   | fined   |
| band   | banned  |

According to formal standard English norms, the words in the left column are pronounced exactly the same as the corresponding words in the right column (*mist* and *missed* are pronounced /mist/, *find* and *fined* are pronounced /faynd/, and so forth. There is a tendency to reduce final consonant clusters by not pronouncing the final consonant, provided both consonants are unvoiced or both are voiced. Two major linguistic factors affect this tendency: the following phonological environment, and the grammatical status of the final consonant. The pattern emerges from Labov's data on the casual speech of male black and white preadolescent and adolescent gangs in Harlem: [10]

Omission of Final /t/ and /d/

|       | Type I Words | | Type II Words | |
|-------|---------------------|------------------|---------------------|------------------|
|       | Before a consonant | Before a vowel | Before a consonant | Before a vowel |
| White | 67%                 | 9%               | 14%                 | 4%               |
| Black | 95%                 | 50%              | 85%                 | 13%              |

---

[9] *We have based this rule on data from William Labov et al.*, A Study of the Non-Standard English of Negro and Puerto Rican Speakers in New York City, *Vol. 1 (Washington, D.C.: Educational Resources Information Center: ED 028 423, 1968), p. 102.*
[10] *These statistics are our averages of Labov's data from* A Study of the Non-Standard English of Negro and Puerto Rican Speakers in New York City, *Vol. 1, pp. 128, 149.*

Despite the quantitative differences, both groups show the same pattern of variation: they omit final /t/'s and /d/'s less often before a word beginning with a vowel than before a word beginning with a consonant, and they omit final /t/'s and /d/'s less often when the /t/ or /d/ represents past tense or past participle than when it has no grammatical significance. Thus there are two interrelated linguistic constraints affecting the pronunciation of final /t/'s and /d/'s, one phonological and the other syntactic.

In Detroit, Walter Wolfram found exactly the same pattern among upper middle-class whites (the only whites he studied) and among blacks of all socioeconomic classes. Even the upper middle class showed a high percentage of /t/ and /d/ omission in preconsonantal position when the consonant did not represent a grammatical signal: Wolfram's study showed 66.4 per cent omission for the upper middle-class whites, and 78.9 per cent omission for the upper middle-class blacks.[11]

Through such detailed investigation and description of actual speech, sociolinguists can determine the structural norms for a particular dialect, a particular speech community. These norms will take listeners' subjective reactions into account, along with other extralinguistic and linguistic factors. If speakers use a linguistic variant beyond a certain frequency, they are heard as "always" using that variant. Sociolinguists have not yet determined the critical point beyond which a speaker is heard as always using a given variant. But in determining the norms for a given dialect, this subjective factor must be combined with the types of objective factors already discussed.

In the next section we will describe the "features" of two nonstandard dialects. Technically these features are the variants that function as norms for the given dialect. But nobody's speech reflects all of these norms all of the time, because everyone's speech patterns fluctuate according to the formality of the social context, plus other factors. The norms of a dialect are only tendencies; "standard" speech always reveals some nonstandard variants, and "nonstandard" speech always reveals some standard variants.

We are finally in a position to define the term "dialect" sociolinguistically. A **dialect** is a structured language subsystem defined by the sum total of the phonological and syntactic norms abstracted from the patterned speech variation of a given speech community.

The New York speech often labeled "Brooklynese" is one such sociolinguistically defined dialect. This dialect is marked

[11] *Walter Wolfram*, A Sociolinguistic Description of Detroit Negro Speech *(Washington, D.C.: Center for Applied Linguistics, 1969), pp. 62, 68; the statistics are from p. 62.*

by the frequent use of /in/ instead of /iŋ/ in words like *work-ing* and *living;* by *r*-lessness; by the use of /e/ instead of /æ/ in words like *bad;* by the use of [ɑ] instead of /ɔ/ in words like *office;* and by the use of /t/ for /θ/ and /d/ for /ð/ in words like *thin* and *then* respectively. Some of these items occur at least occasionally in the speech of every New Yorker, but a preponderance of the low prestige forms characterizes a person's speech as "Brooklynese." Thus, the dialect is characterized by a distinctive set of phonological norms.

 FOR FURTHER EXPLORATION

David L. Shores, ed. *Contemporary English: Change and Variation.* New York: J.B. Lippincott Company, 1972. An interesting collection of articles concerned with temporal, regional, and social variations in American dialects. The article by De Camp is an especially good treatment of dialect variation.

Jean Malmstrom and Annabel Ashley, *Dialects—U.S.A.* Urbana, Ill.: National Council of Teachers of English, 1963. An introduction to the study of regional dialects, containing a map of the main dialect areas of the United States and a chapter on dialect in literature.

Roger W. Shuy, *Discovering American Dialects.* Urbana, Ill.: National Council of Teachers of English, 1967. An introduction to the study of regional dialects, with a brief chapter on social dialects and much information on techniques of field interviewing.

Carroll E. Reed, *Dialects of American English.* Cleveland, Ohio: World Publishing Company, 1967. In addition to providing information on eastern U.S. regional dialects, Reed describes the main dialect studies in the middle and far western United States.

William Labov, *The Study of Nonstandard English.* Urbana, Ill.: National Council of Teachers of English, 1970. A coherent discussion of linguistic stratification, with particular reference to Afro-American English.

William Labov, "Variation in Language." In *The Learning of Language,* ed. Carroll E. Reed. New York: Appleton-Century-Crofts, 1971, pp. 187–221. A clear, comprehensive overview of regional and social dialect study, surveying findings and implications of both in the light of recent research in transformational grammar and sociolinguistics.

Walter A. Wolfram, *A Sociolinguistic Description of Detroit Negro Speech*. Washington, D.C.: Center for Applied Linguistics, 1969. Describes a detailed investigation of sociolinguistic stratification among the blacks in Detroit. Fairly difficult to read.

# THE STRUCTURE OF DIALECTS: TWO STUDIES

In this section we will discuss the structure of two nonstandard American social dialects, Spanish-influenced English and West African-influenced English; the latter we call "Afro-American English." The two dialects are similar in that they reflect a foreign-language influence upon their phonological and syntactic structures. Spanish-influenced English (SIE) reflects the structure of present-day Spanish, the native language of many citizens of the United States. Afro-American English (AAE) reflects a West African influence dating from the sixteenth century through plantation days, an influence that still persists due to the cultural isolation of blacks from whites.

There are two main reasons for using Spanish-influenced English and Afro-American English to illustrate the fact that all dialects are structured language subsystems. One reason is simply that in recent years these dialects have been described in considerable detail, thanks partly to an upsurge of interest in our largest ethnic minorities. The second reason is to combat the popular notion that nonstandard dialects are a result of lazy, sloppy speech. A nonstandard dialect may arise when older forms of the language are preserved in a given area because the speakers are geographically and hence culturally isolated from the surrounding society; such is largely the case with the Mountain Speech of the Appalachians and the Ozarks. Second, a nonstandard dialect may arise from a conflict of language systems. Thus a nonstandard dialect arises from a cultural and/or linguistic conflict, not from lazy or sloppy speech.

In this section, we will discuss the cultural and linguistic history of Spanish-influenced English and Afro-American English and will describe the outstanding phonological and syntactic features of the dialects. Our methods of approach will differ, reflecting the fact that Spanish exerts an ongoing influence on English, whereas the West African influence is primarily historical. We will approach the structure of Spanish-influenced English by discussing the points of conflict between Spanish and standard English, but in treating Afro-American English we will simply describe the outstanding features of the dialect, mentioning whatever West African origins are known.

It must be remembered that the patterns and features we describe are structural norms, abstracted from actual speech; no one uses all of these nonstandard features all of the time.

When we refer to the *speakers* of these dialects, we mean those whose casual speech reflects the nonstandard structural patterns characteristic of the dialect. It is possible for the speaker of a nonstandard dialect to speak standard English as well; a person may learn to use standard English in formal situations while using a nonstandard dialect with family and friends. Thus a speaker of a nonstandard dialect ordinarily has a range of nonstandard styles, from casual to careful, and he may also have one or more distinctive styles in the standard range.

## SPANISH-INFLUENCED ENGLISH [12]

A historical perspective throws light on the structure of the Spanish-influenced English spoken by most of the six and one-half million native speakers of Spanish who are citizens of the United States. Spanish settlement in Florida and the Southwest began in the sixteenth century. The westward movement brought the United States pioneers into contact with a rich Spanish culture, especially in present-day California and Texas. Texas was annexed in 1845, and California and the rest of the Southwest became part of the United States in 1848. Since

---

[12] *This section draws heavily on Daniel N. Cadenas, "Dominant Spanish Dialects Spoken in the United States" (available from Educational Resources Information Center ED 042 137); A. L. Davis, "English Problems of Spanish Speakers." In* Contemporary English: Change and Variation, *ed. David L. Shores (New York: J. B. Lippincott Company, 1972); Rudolph C. Troike, "English and the Bilingual Child," pp. 306–318 of the Shores book just cited; Muriel R. Saville and Rudolph C. Troike,* A Handbook of Bilingual Education *(Washington, D.C.: Teachers of English to Speakers of Other Languages, 1971); Ralph F. Robinett and Richard C. Benjamin,* Developing Language Curricula: Programed Exercises for Teachers, American Council on the Teaching of Foreign Languages *edition (Ann Arbor, Mich.: Michigan Migrant Primary Interdisciplinary Project, 1970); Robert P. Stockwell, J. Donald Bowen, and John W. Martin,* The Grammatical Structures of English and Spanish *(Chicago: The University of Chicago Press, 1965).*

then thousands of Mexicans have migrated to the United States for economic reasons. Today the southwestern United States still has the largest concentration of people with Spanish surnames.

Other Spanish speakers have come from the Commonwealth of Puerto Rico, ceded to the United States by Spain in 1898 after the Spanish-American War. The Puerto Ricans have settled mostly in New York City, although there are large groups in Chicago and Philadelphia also. Since Castro's rise to power in 1959, it is estimated that about 500,000 Cubans have come to this country. Relatively few immigrants come from Spain, speaking the dialect we shall call **Peninsular Spanish.**

As we would expect, because of these various geographic origins, dialectal differences exist among our native speakers of Spanish. However, many generalizations can be made about the structure of Spanish-influenced English.

PHONOLOGICAL FEATURES.   There are a number of phonological contrasts between Spanish and English, giving rise to distinctive SIE (Spanish-influenced English) pronunciation patterns. These contrasts exist in consonant and vowel patterns, and in intonation.

*Consonants.* Spanish words never begin with /s/ followed by another consonant, but many English words do. To such words SIE prefixes /e/ before the initial consonant cluster. Thus *spin* becomes /espin/, *skin* becomes /eskin/, *stick* becomes /estik/, and so forth.

The only consonants that can end Spanish words are /d, n, l, r, s, θ/; no Spanish words end in consonant clusters, as many in English do. Therefore, Spanish-influenced English shows the simplification of final consonant clusters. For example, an SIE speaker tends to say *car* for *card, cart, Carl, carp,* and *cars.* Because of this tendency to simplify final consonant clusters, noun and verb endings are often absent in SIE. We may hear, for example, *cat* for *cats, cat's* or *cats',* *dog* for *dogs, dog's,* or *dogs',* *pack* for *packs* and *packed, plug* for *plugs* and *plugged.*

Moreover, certain sounds that are distinctive in English are not distinctive in Spanish; the SIE speaker hears them as the same, and has great difficulty pronouncing them distinctively and avoiding false English homonyms. The following chart shows how the consonant sounds overlap.[13]

---

[13] *The charts comparing Spanish and English consonants and vowels are adapted from Saville and Troike,* A Handbook of Bilingual Education, *pp. 38–39.*

Spanish                                    English

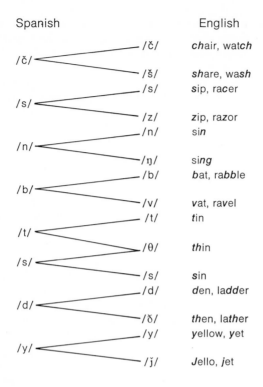

The overlapping between /č/ and /š/ explains why SIE may substitute /č/ for /š/ in, for example, *she's, brush, shape, shoes, share.* Conversely, the SIE speaker who has partially learned the use of English /š/ may substitute /š/ for /č/ in, for example, *chair* and *teacher.*

The SIE speaker's tendency to hear English /s/ and /z/ as the same explains his characteristic unvoicing of the final sibilant in such words as *size, triangles, circles,* and *squares.* These words end with English /z/, but the SIE speaker tends to say /s/ instead. His difficulty in hearing the English contrast between /n/ and /ŋ/ affects his pronunciation of English present participles, causing him to substitute /n/ for /ŋ/. He also has problems with /m/, which in syllable-final position he often confuses with /n/ or /ŋ/. Thus the following triplets are hard for SIE speakers to distinguish:

| whim | win | wing |
| simmer | sinner | singer |

Standard English /ð/ at the beginning of a word or syllable commonly appears as /d/ in SIE, as for example in *the, this, these, that, those, they,* and *there.* Standard English /θ/ commonly becomes either /t/ or /s/, as in *wit* or *wis* for *with.* Syllable-final /d/ can be unvoiced to /t/, as in *beat* for *bead, ret* for *red, site* for *side.*

SIE speakers rarely use either /b/ or /v/ but substitute for both a bilabial fricative /β/. To native speakers of English, they often seem to be saying *Habana* for *Havana* or *Cordoba* for *Cordova,* but in truth the sound is somewhere in between. Similarly, SIE speakers often do not have a clearly separate /y/ and /ĭ/. Therefore it is difficult to be sure, out of context, whether they are saying *yet* or *jet, yellow* or *Jello, you* or *Jew.*

Spanish has certain consonant sounds that English lacks: a voiceless velar fricative /x/; a prepalatal voiced nasal /ñ/; and a trilled /ř/. These occasionally appear for standard English, /h/, /n/, and /r/, respectively.

*Vowels.* Spanish has a much simpler vowel system than English. It consists of only five simple vowels. Four of these vowels are similar to our /iy/, /ey/, /uw/, and /ow/, except that they are shorter; they differ from the English vowels in not ending in a /y/ or /w/ glide. Since there are five Spanish vowels corresponding to eleven vowels in English, each Spanish vowel covers the range of two or three English vowels. Therefore, for example, the SIE speaker will tend to hear *beet* and *bit* as if they were both pronounced with the short counterpart of our /iy/, and in saying the words he may use this one vowel for both.

The contrasts between the Spanish and English vowel systems can be illustrated by using a combination of Trager-Smith symbols (enclosed between slash marks) and IPA symbols (enclosed in square brackets), as in the following chart and diagram:

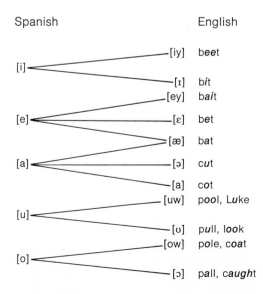

| Spanish | English | |
|---|---|---|
| | [iy] | beet |
| [i] | [ɪ] | bit |
| | [ey] | bait |
| [e] | [ɛ] | bet |
| | [æ] | bat |
| [a] | [ə] | cut |
| | [a] | cot |
| | [uw] | pool, Luke |
| [u] | [ʊ] | pull, look |
| | [ow] | pole, coat |
| [o] | [ɔ] | pall, caught |

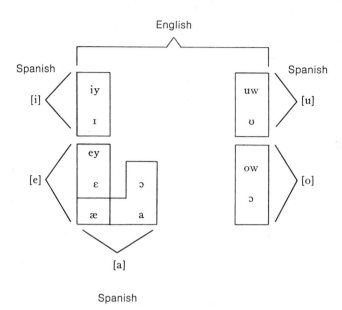

*Intonation.* In its intonation also, Spanish contrasts with English. In addition to different rhythm and stress patterns, Spanish has one degree of stress fewer than English. Differences in the stress patterns of the two languages are reflected in the SIE speaker's tendencies to shorten stressed syllables, giving each syllable approximately the same pronunciation time; to stress English words on the wrong syllable; and not to reduce vowels in unstressed syllables, as standard English speakers normally do. In pitch, apparently three levels are adequate for describing any dialect of Spanish. Generally, Spanish pitch stays within levels /1/ and /2/ in normal conversation and uses level /3/ for emphasis, contrast, and questions; Spanish does not use English pitch level /4/. In Spanish the pitch level consistently rises to /2/ (or /3/) on stressed syllables and falls to level /1/ on unstressed syllables. This regular fluctuation tends to give Spanish and SIE a sing-song rhythm. The following table summarizes the contrast among the most common English and Spanish sentence intonation patterns. The ~ means "alternates with":

| | English | Peninsular Spanish | Mexican, Puerto Rican and Cuban Spanish |
|---|---|---|---|
| Declarative Statement | /231#/ | /211#/ | /121#/ |
| Emphatic Statement, or Contrast | /241#/ | /231#/ | /232\|/ |
| Yes/No Question | /233\|\|/ | /233\|\|/ | /222\|\|/ |
| WH Question | /231#/ | /311#/~/311\|\|/ | /211#/~/211\|\|/~ /222\|\|/ |

English makes greater use of the high pitch levels than Mexican, Puerto Rican, and Cuban Spanish. Therefore English influenced by these Spanish dialects sometimes shows overcorrections: pitch level /4/ for standard English /3/, and a rising intonation for standard English falling intonation.

SYNTACTIC FEATURES. In syntax also, Spanish contrasts with English. The two languages show differences in their use of verbs and verbal structures, nouns, pronouns and determiners, and prepositions. These structural contrasts are reflected in SIE.

*Verbs and Verbal Constructions.* SIE speakers tend to omit standard English third singular and past tense endings, conveying time by adverbs alone or by the larger speech context. Thus *he play ball* could be equivalent to either *he plays ball* or *he played ball.* Since Spanish has fewer verb auxiliaries than English, the SIE speaker tends to omit the standard English auxiliaries and also the inflections associated with them. Thus, *he play ball* might be equivalent to all of the following standard English sentences:

> he plays ball
> he is playing ball
> he played ball
> he was playing ball
> he has played ball
> he had played ball
> he will play ball
> he does play ball

Since Spanish verbs have endings with pronominal functions, a subject pronoun is redundant in Spanish. Thus SIE may contain statements like *is a man* for *he is a man,* questions like *is round?* for *is it round?* and negatives like *no, is not* for *no, it is not.*

Spanish negatives are formed by placing *no* before the verb; when a negative word follows the verb, the word *no* is required before the verb, creating a "double negative." Because such double negatives are a regular feature of Spanish, the SIE speaker may produce double negatives such as *Sarah no talk to no one, we no have nothing, they no went nowhere.*

The lack of a Spanish auxiliary equivalent to *do* also affects negatives in SIE (*I no have* for *I don't have*) and questions (*what you want?* for *what do you want?*). If *do* is used, it may appear with an inflected form instead of the base form of the English verb: *he doesn't needs* or *did he needed?* (Another complicating factor may be that in Spanish one verb, *hacer,* may mean both *do* and *make.* Thus these two English verbs may be easily confused by the SIE speaker.) Other typical Spanish-type questions are *this is round?* or *is round this?* for *is this round?*

Another area of contrast is contractions, which are frequent in English but very rare in Spanish. For example, *am, is,* and *are* often contract to /m/, /z/ or /s/, and /r/ respectively, and therefore the SIE speaker may not be fully aware of these verb forms, even when they function as main verbs rather than auxiliaries. At any rate, he often omits them entirely or contracts them in structures where English does not permit contraction, saying, for example, *yes, I'm* for *Yes, I am.*

*Nouns.* Spanish and English have contrasts in the area of noun endings, too. As we have mentioned, Spanish has no final consonant clusters, and SIE speakers may therefore omit /s/ or /z/ signaling plural or possessive when the base word ends in a consonant (*cat* for *cats, cat's,* or *cats'; dog* for *dogs, dog's,* or *dogs'*). The possessive marker (/s/, /z/, or /ɨz/) is especially likely to be absent because Spanish does not inflect nouns to indicate possession, using instead the equivalent of the English *of*-possessive: *the hat of the boy, the bark of the dog.* Even when the inflectional ending is present, it may contrast with standard English pronunciation, since SIE tends to use /s/ for English /z/ in word final positions.

There are also differences in noun categorization between English and Spanish. Spanish classifies some English noncount nouns as count nouns. Therefore SIE speakers may say *a chalk* for *a piece of chalk, a merchandise* for *an item of merchandise* or *a lightning* for *a flash of lightning.*

*Pronouns and Determiners.* Spanish and standard English contrast also in the use of personal pronouns and possessive determiners. Since Spanish nouns have grammatical gender—that is, all nouns are either masculine or feminine—each noun is referred to by a matching masculine or feminine pronoun or possessive determiner (somewhat comparable to English *he, him, his* or *she, her, hers*). Thus, since in Spanish *table* (mesa) is feminine and *book* (*libro*) is masculine, the SIE speaker may refer to tables as *she* and to books as *he.* Moreover, in Spanish, possessive determiners agree in gender with the noun they modify; in English they agree in gender with the noun to which they refer (the "possessor"). Therefore, the SIE speaker may say *his husband* and *her wife,* in each case matching the possessive determiner, *his* or *her,* to the gender of the following noun rather than to the referent, the "possessor," as is done in standard English: *she saw **her** husband; he saw **his** wife.*

The situation is further complicated for the Spanish learner of English because one of the Spanish possessive pronouns, *su,* can refer to the second and third persons singular and plural. Thus *his, her, its, your,* and *their* tend to fall together in SIE. In some cases, when the possessor is clear from the context, the definite article *the* will replace the possessive, as in *take the shirt off, he stuck out the tongue,* and *she washed the hands.*

Spanish has other contrasts with English articles. For example, a definite article is required in Spanish before modified place or person names. Thus the SIE speaker will say:

> the Mr. Smith is here
> I saw him on the Market Street
> the courthouse is on the Grand Avenue

English *a* and *an* contrast with the Spanish indefinite articles, *un* and *una.* The indefinite article category in Spanish distinguishes *un* and *una* on the basis of syntactic gender, whereas the English distinction is determined by whether the following word begins with a vowel or a consonant. Therefore constructions like *a eraser* for *an eraser* and *a orange* for *an orange* may occur in SIE.

*Prepositions.* The area of prepositions presents contrasts. English uses a variety of prepositions corresponding to the Spanish preposition *en.* For example, the Spanish equivalent of the bold-faced preposition in the following sentences would, in each case, be *en:*

> the book is **on** the table
> the man is **in** the room
> he was **at** home
> they put it **into** the box

it will change **to** ice
he bought it **for** five cents
I am thinking **about** leaving

As this example shows, many English prepositions do not exist in Spanish.

Another contrast involves the Spanish requirement that all transitive verbs (except *tener* meaning 'to have') have a preposition *a* (meaning 'to') before direct objects referring to a definite person or persons, before the indefinite pronouns *someone* or *anyone,* and before unmodified geographical names. Thus SIE speakers may say *Bill saw to Mary* for *Bill saw Mary, the hijacker killed to someone* for *the hijacker killed someone, we love to Cuba* for *we love Cuba.*

## WORKING WITH SPANISH-INFLUENCED ENGLISH

The following story illustrates some of the features of Spanish-influenced oral English, approximated in nonstandard spelling. Identify as many of these features as you can.

### Afraid of the Dark
(Juan Castaniegos—a young Mexican)

Help me to leave from thees place.
But, Señor Capitan, me—I 'av do notheeng.
Notheeng, Señor Capitan . . . To them I am say
I know not of what they speak.
5      They are currse me an' say a foreigner ees keel
a white lady. They whip me until my eyes cannot
see, and my legs they cannot stand.
And me—I 'av done notheeng to anybody.
I am no sure. I 'ave expect to die, surely—but
10    no so soon.
That ees it, Señor Capitan. That ees it . . . thee
darkness on thee other side of life.
Eef I die like thees—thee death of a criminal—
will I go to . . . thee hell?
15    Please, Padre, I 'ave no words to say.
Padre mio, ees eet that I am to be forgiven for
something I 'ave not do?
No, no, Padre. Eet ees not me who should 'ave
thee forgiveness. Eet ees thee men who say I am to
20    die. Thee men who send me to thees place . . .

thee men who take me to thees chair . . . those men
keel me . . . . You pray for those men, no, Padre?
    I am crazy because I speak thee truth?
    Padre mio, thee heart of me is full of theengs to
25      say, but only of one theeng would I speak to you.
    The lady they say I 'ave keeled, I 'ave never seen
her . . . when she is alive . . . or when she ees
dead.
    Thee good God weel understand.
30      I 'ave pray all thee night long.
    I go to meet heem.
    Eet ees permitted me that I speak weeth my
friends? [14]

—William E. Callahan

 FOR FURTHER EXPLORATION

Claude Merton Wise, *Applied Phonetics.* Englewood Cliffs,
N.J.: Prentice-Hall, Inc., 1957. Antedating the current sociolinguistic study of dialects, this book is a humanistic,
practical, broadly focused introduction to the use of IPA
and the main American and British dialects. It also discusses the characteristics of the English dialects of native speakers of other Indo-European languages, including Spanish. Fairly technical on phonology, but a
storehouse of useful information on dialects.

A. L. Davis, "English Problems of Spanish Speakers." In
David L. Shores, ed., *Contemporary English: Change and
Variation.* New York: J. B. Lippincott Company, 1972,
pp. 123–133. An excellent article contrasting the major
phonological and syntactic features of Spanish and English and showing some of the resulting features of SIE.

Rudolph C. Troike, "English and the Bilingual Child." In
David L. Shores, ed., *Contemporary English: Change and
Variation.* New York: J. B. Lippincott Company, 1972, pp.
306–318. This article contrasts the phonological features of Spanish and English and shows how the structural conflict affects the Spanish speaker who is learning
English.

Muriel R. Saville and Rudolph C. Troike, *A Handbook of
Bilingual Education,* rev. ed. Washington, D.C.: Teachers
of English to Speakers of Other Languages, 1971. A use-

[14] *Claude Merton Wise,* Applied Phonetics *(Englewood Cliffs, N.J.: Prentice-Hall,
Inc., 1957), pp. 471–472.*

ful overview of bilingual education programs in the United States, including selected relevant information from linguistics, psychology, and sociology. Good discussion of contrasts between Spanish and English and of the problems Spanish speakers have in learning English.

Robert P. Stockwell, J. Donald Bowen, and John W. Martin, *The Grammatical Structures of English and Spanish.* Chicago: The University of Chicago Press, 1965. A contrastive analysis of Spanish and English syntax, highlighting differences and similarities between them.

## AFRO-AMERICAN ENGLISH

The nonstandard English spoken by many blacks in the U.S. today shows the influence of a trade language originally established through black-white contact on the western coastal bulge of Africa; it is for this reason that we refer to black nonstandard English as West African-influenced English. We use the term Afro-American English to designate the West African-influenced English widely spoken in the United States today. (The Gullah dialect is discussed below as a distinctive variety of West African-influenced English, not included in the term "Afro-American English.") We will first discuss the history of Afro-American English and then its structural features.

THE HISTORY OF AFRO-AMERICAN ENGLISH. English traders began to visit the coastal areas of Africa around the middle of the sixteenth century, thus bringing into contact speakers of mutually unintelligible and structurally very different languages. In such circumstances, when minimal communication must take place, a **pidgin language** normally develops. The linguist Orlando Taylor describes the process of pidginization as follows:

Pidginization is usually carried out by speakers of nondominant cultural groups who are in direct contact with a dominant group which speaks another language. At the outset of its development a pidgin is usually very informal, consisting of single-word utterances (mainly nouns) and many gestures. Over time, it becomes more formal in that the vocabulary of the dominant language is embedded into the phonological (sound) and

syntactic (grammatical) system of the nondominant
language.[15]

Probably, it is an oversimplification to say that the vocabulary
of the dominant language is simply "embedded into" the phonological and syntactic system of the nondominant language,
but certainly the structure of the pidgin strongly reflects the
structure of the nondominant language(s).

Another structural characteristic of pidgins is that they avoid
redundant grammatical features, such as the third singular verb
ending of standard English (*he walks, the man runs, it fizzes*).
This ending is redundant because the notion "third singular"
is already conveyed by the subject. Pidgin languages charac-
teristically omit such redundant endings, and therefore a pidgin
is almost always less complex syntactically than the languages
from which it is derived.

When a pidgin language becomes the native language of a
speech community, the language used among family members
and close friends, the language is said to be a **creole language.** A creole has a much larger stock of lexical items than
the pidgin from which it arises, since the creole is used in
more spheres of life. A creole is also more grammatically complex, especially when there is continuing influence from a long-
established language. This has been the case with West African-influenced English in the United States; since blacks were
first brought here as slaves, their language has had ongoing
contact with nonpidginized, noncreolized English.

The first Europeans to trade with the West Africans were the
Portuguese, in the latter half of the fifteenth century. This trade
relationship gave rise to a pidgin with a Portuguese vocabulary
and an essentially West African structure. With the coming of
the Dutch and later the French, a Dutch pidgin and a French
pidgin were established. The rise of West African Pidgin English probably began about 1557 when three African interpret-
ers returned to the Gold Coast from England, where William
Towerson had taken them in 1554 for training in English.

Around 1630 an English port was established on the Gold
Coast, and West African Pidgin English began to flourish as a
trade language. Its vocabulary was basically English, but its
structure in many respects reflected the structure of the West
African languages (Twi, Hausa, Yoruba, Ibo, etc.), which had
a number of phonological and syntactic features in common.
For example, West African Pidgin English did not have the
standard English inflections on nouns, verbs, and pronouns,
reflecting the fact that the West African languages did not have

[15] Orlando Taylor, "An Introduction to the Historical Development of Black English:
Some Implications for American Education" (Washington, D.C.: Educational Resources Information Center: ED 035 863, 1969), pp. 3–4. Footnote 1.

such inflections. Structurally this English pidgin was similar to the Portuguese, Dutch, and French pidgins, since each pidgin reflected the structure of the West African languages. These pidgins were used for intertribal communication among Africans as well as for communication with Europeans and men from the New World. Such pidgins still exist today, with West African Pidgin English being spoken in several areas of West Africa: in Gambia, in Sierra Leone, and in eastern Nigeria and the western area of the Cameroon Republic.[16]

When they were brought to the United States as slaves, many blacks already spoke this West African Pidgin English; the others learned it in this country. It was during plantation days that this pidgin became their native language, a creole language.

One full-fledged Afro-American creole still exists in the United States today. This is Gullah, the language of the blacks in the Carolina Sea Islands and the coastal regions of South Carolina, Georgia, and northeast Florida. Structurally, it has creole markers in both phonology and syntax. For example, Gullah speakers often substitute /t/ or /f/ for /θ/, and /d/ for /ð/, as speakers of related West African languages do. These languages also lack /v/, for which Gullah speakers substitute a bilabial fricative [β] which we lack in standard English but which we hear in Gullah as /b/. Final consonant clusters are often modified by inserting a vowel between the consonants or by dropping one of the consonants. Gullah creole syntax reflects its African sources mainly in the absence of inflections on nouns, verbs, and pronouns and by the omission of BE as a linking verb.[17]

These features are all reflected in the following literary representation of Gullah, from Ambrose E. Gonzales' *With Aesop Along the Black Border:*

### The Hare and the Tortoise

One time Buh Rabbit meet up wid Buh Tarrypin, en', soon ez 'e shum, 'e tek'um fuh mek fun. 'E laugh at de Cootuh dat hebby, 'tel all de t'odduh annimel wuh yeddy'um, haffuh come close fuh see
5     how de news stan'!

W'en Buh Rabbit look 'puntop all dem creetuh, en' shum duh grin, 'e t'ink him *done* fuh smaa't! 'E tu'n 'pun Buh Tarrypin en' try fuh cheap'um befo' de cump'ny. "Eh, eh!", 'e say. "Weh dish-yuh t'ing'

[16] David Dalby, "Black Through White: Patterns of Communication in Africa and the New World." In Black-White Speech Relationships, ed. Walt Wolfram and Nona H. Clarke (Washington, D.C.: Center for Applied Linguistics, 1971), pp. 99–138.
[17] These markers and many more are explained by Lorenzo D. Turner in Africanisms in the Gullah Dialect (1949; reprint, New York: Arno Press, 1969).

10          foot? 'E mus' be got foot, 'cause him kin moobe!
                W'en Uh shum, fus', Uh bin tek' um fuh light'ood
                junk—one deseyuh pineknot wuh de fire bu'n obuh
                en' chaar'um 'tel 'e black—but, w'en Uh watch'um
                close, Uh shum duh moobe, but Uh t'aw't 'e bin
15          crawl 'pun 'e belly lukkuh snake."
                 W'en 'e say dat, Buh Tarrypin rise high 'pun all
                fo' 'e foot, 'e 'tretch' out 'e neck, 'e onkibbuh 'e
                yeye, en' 'e grin!
                 Buh Rabbit look lukkuh 'e 'stonish! 'E jump up
20          en' crack 'e foot togedduh en' 'e holluh: " 'E *yiz*
                gott'um! 'E *yiz* gott'um! *Shum! Shum!*" lukkuh him
                nebbuh bin look 'puntop cootuh' foot befo'!
                 Buh Tarrypin nebbuh crack 'e teet'. Him know
                suh Buh Rabbit ent wu't'. 'E schemy, but 'e yent got
25          nutt'n' een 'e c'arricktuh fuh 'pen' 'pun, so, 'e
                le'm 'lone 'tel 'e laugh run' out. Him know suh w'en
                man hab 'e mout' full'uh talk, 'e head berry aps fuh
                empty! Attuhw'ile, w'en Buh Rabbit see suh nobody
                else duh laugh 'cep' him, one, 'e biggin fuh
30          shame, en' de laugh all dry' up 'pun 'e face.[18]

The widespread creole language of early plantation days was similar to early twentieth-century Gullah, as represented in the above excerpt from Gonzales. The following poem is a literary representation of a later stage in the development of modern Afro-American English. The dialect represented is much closer to standard English than Gullah is, but it nevertheless shows several features no longer common in AAE adult dialects. One such feature is the use of one pronoun form where standard English has three (for example, *him* for *he, him, his*); today such undifferentiated pronouns usually appear only in the speech of very young children.

What other creole features do you find represented in the poem?

### De Cunjah Man

O chillen run, de Cunjah man,
Him mouf ez beeg ez fryin' pan,
Him yurs am small, him eyes am raid,
Him hab no toof een him ol' haid,
5      Him hab him roots, him wu'k him trick,

[18] Ambrose E. Gonzales, With Aesop Along the Black Border (New York: Negro Universities Press, 1924), pp. 75–76.

Him roll him eye, him mek you sick—
    De Cunjah man, de Cunjah man,
    O chillen run, de Cunjah man!

Him hab ur ball ob raid, raid ha'r,
10   Him hide it un' de kitchen sta'r,
Mam Jude huh pars urlong dat way,
An' now huh hab ur snaik, dey say.
Him wrop ur roun' huh buddy tight,
Huh eyes pop out, ur orful sight—
15     De Cunjah man, de Cunjah man,
    O chillen run, de Cunjah man!

Miss Jane, huh dribe him f'un huh do',
An' now huh hens woan' lay no mo';
De Jussey cow huh done fall sick,
20   Hit all done by de cunjah trick.
Him put ur root un' 'Lijah's baid,
An' now de man he sho' am daid—
    De Cunjah man, de Cunjah man,
    O chillen run, de Cunjah man!

25   Me see him stand' de yudder night
Right een de road een white moon-light;
Him toss him arms, him whirl him 'roun;
Him stamp him foot urpon de groun';
De snaiks come crawlin', one by one,
30   Me hyuh um hiss, me break an' run.
    De Cunjah man, de Cunjah man,
    O chillen run, de Cunjah man! [19]

                  —James Edwin Campbell

**AFRO-AMERICAN ENGLISH TODAY.** For years the claim has often been made, by linguist and nonlinguist alike, that the non-standard speech of blacks and whites is essentially the same, particularly in the South. Certainly there are far more similarities than differences,[20] for black nonstandard and white non-

[19] *James Edwin Campbell, "De Cunjah Man." In* Early Black American Poets, *ed. William H. Robinson, Jr. (Dubuque, Iowa: Wm. C. Brown Company, 1969), pp. 234–235.*
[20] *Where there are similarities in the nonstandard speech of blacks and whites, they may sometimes be due to black influence upon white speech. This certainly is the case in the Charleston area, where even today Gullah characteristics are found in the speech of the white community as a whole (Labov, "Variation," p. 205).*

standard Southern dialects share various nonstandard features, along with all the features typical of Southern dialects generally. But recently specialists in creole languages have claimed that there *are* significant black/white speech differences, even in the South, since the phonological and syntactic structure of black nonstandard dialect shows the partial survival of the structure of the creole language that blacks spoke during plantation days.[21]

Obviously the question of black/white speech differences is open to empirical investigation. The most promising investigation to date has been undertaken in the rural area around Lexington, Mississippi, where the speech of lower socioeconomic-class black children is being compared with the speech of lower socioeconomic-class white children.[22] For the most part, the investigation supports the transformationalists' hypothesis that all dialects of a language (in this case English) have the same deep structure.[23] However, the investigators did find some systematic differences. One is in the use of the third-person singular verb inflection (*he walks, he runs, it fizzes*). In spontaneous conversation, the white children pronounced this ending eighty-five per cent of the time, whereas the black children pronounced it only thirteen per cent of the time. Also, all the white children pronounced the third-person singular ending at least part of the time, whereas six of the twenty-five black children showed no use of the third-person inflection at all. From these differences, the investigators concluded that the third-person inflection is an inherent part of the white children's dialect system but not of the black children's system; the black children's occasional use of the third-person singular is taken to be "dialect importation," borrowing from another dialect.[24]

Three other features that were found to show significant black/white differences are: the absence of the possessive inflection (*the cat tail, the dog tail, the horse tails*); the absence of *are* and especially *is* (*we running home, he running home*); and the use of *be* to indicate a repeated action or state (*he be fighting, she be busy*). The possessive inflection appears to be

---

[21] For an excellent summary of the linguistic controversy concerning black/white speech differences, consult Wolfram's Sociolinguistic Description of Detroit Negro Speech, pp. 9–14.

[22] Walt Wolfram, "Black-White Speech Differences Revisited." In Social and Educational Insights into Teaching Standard English to Speakers of Other Dialects, Maurice L. Imhoof, ed. Viewpoints: Bulletin of the School of Education, Indiana University, 47 (March 1971), p. 32.

[23] Wolfram, "Black-White Speech Differences Revisited," p. 46.

[24] Wolfram, "Black-White Speech Differences Revisited," pp. 34–35. The children in the study were all between the ages of six and eight. According to Wolfram, "The specific age range was chosen to represent a period when the children would be past the developmental stage, but at an age when the awareness of the social consequences of speech would be minimal" (p. 33).

an inherent part of the white dialect but not of the black; the omission of *are* is much greater for the black dialect, and the omission of *is* occurs almost exclusively in the black dialect (27.6 per cent of the time for the black children, 1.7 per cent for the white children); and *be* to indicate a repeated occurrence is used exclusively in the black dialect.[25] These differences can be traced to an early West African influence on the black dialect, since West African languages have no verb or noun inflections and no verb comparable to our BE verb, though they use more auxiliaries to indicate concepts like repeated occurrence. Apparently cultural isolation of blacks from whites has served to maintain structural features that reflect the West African origin of the dialect.

For the most part, sociolinguists have studied Afro-American English in the urban areas of the North rather than in the South. In these urban areas they have found that the most radically nonstandard black speech is the casual speech of male adolescent and preadolescent gang members in black ghettos. Naturally the speech of these youths shows some structural differences from one area to another. For example, the degree of *r*-lessness is greater in New York than in Detroit, because New York has long been an *r*-less region and Detroit an *r*-pronouncing region. Similarly, the absence of the possessive inflection is greater in New York than in Detroit. The families of the majority of New York City blacks come from the eastern coastal area of the South, where blacks seldom use the possessive inflection. In contrast, the families of most Detroit blacks come from the central inland area of the South, where blacks make much greater use of the possessive endings.[26] A number of regional differences would probably be found if the speech of Northern blacks were rigorously compared with the speech of Southern blacks.[27] However, Labov says his own work in New York City and work in Detroit, Philadelphia, Chicago, Cleveland, and Los Angeles suggest that, in structure, the dialect of black male adolescent and preadolescent gang members in Northern ghettos is essentially the same in structure.[28]

These youths speak the most radically nonstandard black

---

[25] Wolfram, "Black-White Speech Differences Revisited," pp. 36, 38, 42.

[26] Wolfram, Sociolinguistic Description of Detroit Negro Speech, p. 141. This explanation for the New York-Detroit difference in use of the possessive inflection was suggested to Wolfram by William Stewart.

[27] William A. Stewart mentions four regional differences (including the difference in use of the possessive) in "On the Use of Negro Dialect in the Teaching of Reading." In Teaching Black Children to Read, ed. Joan C. Baratz and Roger W. Shuy (Washington, D.C.: Center for Applied Linguistics, 1969), p. 199.

[28] Labov, "Variation," p. 205.

dialect, which we label pure AAE.[29] Other blacks speak AAE in varying degrees, with even middle-class standard-speaking adults using a sprinkling of AAE features in their most casual speech. There are also nonblacks who speak AAE; in particular, there are a number of Puerto Rican youths in New York City who have acquired AAE as a prestige dialect. In many cases, their speech shows a vestigial Spanish influence along with distinctive AAE features.[30]

PHONOLOGICAL FEATURES.[31] Perhaps the most striking markers of Afro-American English are the unique intonation patterns (pitch, stress, and rhythm) apparent to even the casual listener. These distinctively black intonation patterns probably derive from the West African languages spoken by the ancestors of present-day AAE speakers. But since linguists have not yet described these AAE intonation patterns thoroughly, we will discuss mainly those phonological features that concern the consonant and vowel sounds.

*Consonants.* Five of the most characteristic consonant features of AAE are the absence of *r* and *l,* the absence of final /t/ and /d/, substitutions for voiced and unvoiced *th,* the devoicing and omission of /d/, and the use of nasals.

Absence of r and l. In the standard speech of *r*-less areas, postvocalic *r* (*r* occurring after a vowel) is almost always pronounced as a schwa-like sound when the *r* occurs before a consonant (*card, car crash*). AAE extends this pattern by often pronouncing *r* as a schwa-like sound before a vowel sound as well as before a consonant (*car accident, merry*). Also, postvocalic *l* often reduces to a schwa-like sound in AAE (*cold,*

---

[29] As one might expect, casual speech is not easy to elicit from adolescents and preadolescents when they know their speech is being tape recorded. The procedures developed by Labov's research staff (and particularly by his black co-worker John Lewis) have provided a model for later researchers. Over a two-year period (July 1965 to September 1967), Labov's staff became well acquainted with four black gangs, two adolescent and two preadolescent. The staff members took these boys on outings, recording their spontaneous conversation in the staff's minibus, and taped their jive talk in group sessions held in a basement (Labov, A Study of the Non-Standard English of Negro and Puerto Rican Speakers in New York City, Vol. 1, pp. ii–iii, 57–64.

[30] See, for example, Walt Wolfram, "Linguistic Assimilation in the Children of Immigrants," The Linguistic Reporter, 14 (February 1972), 1–3.

[31] The information on AAE phonological and grammatical features is drawn from Ralph W. Fasold and Walt Wolfram, "Some Linguistic Features of Negro Dialect." In Teaching Standard English in the Inner City, ed. Ralph W. Fasold and Roger W. Shuy (Washington, D.C.: Center for Applied Linguistics, 1970), pp. 41–86; Labov, A Study of the Non-Standard English of Negro and Puerto Rican Speakers in New York City; Wolfram, "Black-White Speech Differences Revisited"; Lorenzo D. Turner, "Problems Confronting the Investigator of Gullah." In Black-White Speech Relationships, ed. Walt Wolfram and Nona H. Clarke (Washington, D.C.: Center for Applied Linguistics, 1971), pp. 1–15; David Dalby, "Black through White: Patterns of Communication in Africa and the New World"; J.L. Dillard, Black English: Its History and Usage in the United States (New York: Random House, 1972).

*coal bin, coal oil, cola).* The reduction is more frequent before a following consonant than before a following vowel.

The fact that postvocalic *r* often becomes a schwa-like sound may make near-homonyms of such pairs as the following:

| | |
|---|---|
| Carol/Cal | guard/god |
| court/caught | nor/gnaw |
| fort/fought | Paris/pass |

These pairs would be near-homonyms for most speakers in *r*-less regions; it is only in the *r*-pronouncing areas that the absence of preconsonantal *r* is perceived as a marker of AAE speech.

Since postvocalic *l* often becomes a schwa-like sound in AAE, such pairs as the following are near-homonyms in Afro-American English:

| | |
|---|---|
| all/awe | Saul/saw |
| fault/fought | toll/toe |
| help/hep | tool/too |

These phonological facts correlate with syntax in complicated ways. The loss of *r* affects the possessives *your* and *their,* making them near-homonyms of *you* and *they* respectively. The loss of *l* affects the future-time forms: for example, *you'll* and *you* become nearly identical, as do *he'll* and *he.*

Absence of Final /t/ and /d/. When English words end in a cluster of two consonants, both voiced or both unvoiced, the last consonant is sometimes unpronounced. In standard English the second consonant may be absent when the cluster is followed by a word beginning with a consonant, as in *test program.* AAE extends this pattern by showing the same lack when the consonant cluster is followed by a word beginning with a vowel, as in *test analysis.* In such cases, standard English speakers usually pronounce the final consonant.

Most final consonant clusters end in /t/ or /d/, in formal standard English. When the /t/ or /d/ does not represent a grammatical signal (as in *mist* and *find*) it is more likely to be absent than when it represents past tense or past participle (as in *missed* and *fined*). Omission of /t/ and /d/ occurs more often before a following consonant than before a following vowel. The following table gives examples of words in which /t/ or /d/ does not represent a grammatical signal (Type I) and examples in which the /t/ or /d/ represents past tense or past participle (Type II).

Consonant Clusters in Which the Final Member
of the Cluster May Be Absent

| Phonetic Cluster | Examples * Type I | Type II |
|---|---|---|
| [st] | mist, past, test | dressed, missed, passed |
| [št] | | cashed, finished, latched |
| [zd] | | amazed, composed, raised |
| [jd] | | charged, forged, judged |
| [ft] | cleft, craft, left | laughed, roughed, stuffed |
| [vd] | | lived, loved, moved |
| [nd] | band, find, mind | banned, fined, mined |
| [md] | | foamed, named, rammed |
| [ld] | cold, old, wild | called, killed, smelled |
| [pt] | adept, apt, inept | clapped, mapped, stopped |
| [kt] | act, contact, expect | cooked, cracked, looked |

\* Where there are no examples under Type I or II, the cluster does not occur under that category.[32]

The West African languages that were the progenitors of AAE generally did not add inflectional endings on verbs. This may be why past tense and past participle /t/ and /d/ are much more likely to be absent in AAE than in white nonstandard dialects.

Voiced and Unvoiced **th.** Other phonological variables produce exact homonyms in AAE. For example, unvoiced and voiced *th* show complex occurrence patterns in AAE, depending on the sounds surrounding them and their position in the word. The rules are patterned and regular, though different from those of standard English. At the beginning of words, standard /θ/ occasionally becomes /t/ (*tanks* for *thanks*) and standard /ð/ frequently becomes /d/ (*den* for *then*). If /θ/ is followed by /r/ as in *three* and *throw,* it may appear as /f/, making homonyms of *three* and *free* and *throw* and *fro.*

In the middle of words, unvoiced and voiced *th* most frequently became /t/ and /d/ respectively; /nətɨn/ for *nothing,* and /mədəh/ for *mother.* Less frequently, /θ/ and /ð/ become /f/ and /v/ respectively in medial position; /nəfɨn/ for *nothing*

[32] Adapted from Fasold and Wolfram, "Some Linguistic Features of Negro Dialect," p. 45.

and /məvəh/ for *mother.* In a few instances a medial /ð/ may disappear entirely (*mother* /məh/).

At the end of words, /f/ or /v/ are the most frequent AAE pronunciations (*Ruth* /ruwf/; *breathe* /briyv/); /f/ substitutes for /θ/, and /v/ substitutes for /ð/. But when a nasal precedes, /t/ or /d/ may appear (*tenth* /tent/) or the final consonant sound may be absent (*tenth* /ten/). Thus *Ruth* and *roof* are potential homonyms, as are *death* and *deaf,* and *tenth, tent,* and *ten.*

The following chart shows the most common substitutions for /θ/ and /ð/:

| Position | /θ/ | /ð/ |
|---|---|---|
| Initial | /t/ /tæŋks/ for *thanks* | /d/ /den/ for *then* |
| Medial | /t/ /nətin/ for *nothing* | /d/ mədəh/ for *mother* |
|  | /f/ /nəfin/ for *nothing* | /v/ /məvəh/ for *mother* |
| Final | /f/ /ruwf/ for *Ruth* | /v/ /briyv/ for *breathe* |

The pronunciation of *th* in the particular word *with* shows the AAE pattern in all its complexity. In most regions, the standard English pronunciation is /θ/ before a consonant (*with Jim*), but /ð/ before a vowel (*with Alan*). AAE has /t/ or /f/ before a consonant, and /d/ or /v/ before a vowel.

There are no voiced and unvoiced *th* sounds in the West African languages which are the progenitors of AAE. This fact may explain why AAE speakers often substitute other sounds for standard English /θ/ and /ð/.

Devoicing and Omission of /d/. In postvocalic position at the end of a word, AAE speakers often pronounce the voiced stops, *b, d,* and *g,* as the corresponding voiceless stops, *p, t,* and *k.* Thus such speakers will say /bæt/ for *bad,* /kæt/ for *cad.* Such pairs as *bat* and *bad* are not quite homophones, however, because the vowel is lengthened before an underlying voiced consonant; that is, the vowel of *bad* is longer than the vowel of *bat.* The devoicing of word-final /d/ is common in all Southern speech and can occur in standard English in the unstressed syllable of words like *salad, hundred,* and *acid.*

Sometimes final *d* is omitted altogether in AAE. This omission occurs more frequently when the next word begins with a consonant (*good man*) than when it begins with a vowel (*good idea*). The omission of *d* sometimes occurs also when the /d/ sound would represent past tense or past participle: *yesterday he play ball, he had play ball.*

Nasals. The three English nasals /m, n, ŋ/ play an important part in AAE. The use of /n/ for /ŋ/ in pronouncing the *-ing* suffix of the present participle characterizes both black and white nonstandard dialects, and is also used, though less frequently, in casual standard English.

Influence of Nasal Consonants upon Vowels. AAE speakers often use a nasalized vowel instead of a nasal consonant. This usually happens only at the end of a syllable. For example, *man* is often pronounced as /mæ̃/ (/~/ represents nasalization). The consonant /n/ is not pronounced at all, but in compensation the preceding vowel is nasalized, with the air flow issuing through the nose rather than the mouth. Thus *bam, ban,* and *bang* might all be pronounced as /bæ̃/. In AAE the nasalized vowel alternates unpredictably with the nasal consonant.

Another effect of nasals appears when *e* occurs before them, as in *ten* or *pen.* In that case the *e* is pronounced as /i/ in South Midland and Southern dialects, so that *tin* and *ten* become homonyms, as do *pin* and *pen.* This rule applies to both standard and nonstandard dialects in the regions where it occurs; it is heard as a social marker only in Northern dialect areas.

*Vowels.* There are relatively few vowel contrasts between AAE and standard English. For the most part, AAE has the same vowel patterns as Southern regional speech. We mention two of these common patterns, however, because in Northern areas such patterns are perceived as a distinguishing AAE characteristic.

Vowel Glides. In the South, the /y/ or /w/ glide is lost from the diphthongs /ay/, /aw/, and /ɔy/ so that *ride* becomes nearly homophonous with Northern *rod, proud* with Northern *prod, oil* with Northern *all.* This is a common feature of all Southern dialects; it acquires social significance only in the North, where it is perceived as a distinguishing AAE characteristic. The same is true for the addition of glides after short vowels: /klæyəs/ for *class,* /siyət/ for *sit,* and so forth.

*Intonation.* Certain stress patterns characterize Afro-American English. One pattern occurs in a small group of two-syllable words that are stressed on the second syllable in standard English: *police, July, hotel,* and so forth. The AAE speaker may stress such words on the first syllable. On the other hand, first syllables may be omitted when they are lightly stressed: *'rithmetic, 'member, 'cept,* and *'bout* for *arithmetic, remember, except,* and *about* respectively. This omission may occur in casual standard English, but there is still a distinction: for example, *supposed to* may be reduced to /powstə/ in AAE but only to /spowstə/ in standard English.

SYNTACTIC FEATURES. Other features of AAE are more clearly syntactic, although it is sometimes difficult to separate phonology from syntax. These syntactic features involve various verb forms, questions, negation, nouns, pronouns, determiners, and expletive IT.

*Verbs.* We have already seen that the reduction of consonant clusters affects the past-tense and past-participle forms of regular verbs. In addition, irregular (or strong) verbs appear in various nonstandard forms in Afro-American English. *Say* appears as both present and past, like *hit* in standard English (*he say it today; he say it yesterday*), and *was* appears for *were* (*they was here*). Afro-American English speakers frequently use nonstandard past-tense and past-participle forms of other strong verbs, too (*give* for *gave,* as in *he give it to her yesterday; did* for *done* in *he have did it*). Such nonstandard verb forms characterize all nonstandard dialects in the United States.

Perfect Constructions. In standard English, perfect constructions consist of a HAVE auxiliary followed by a past participle. For irregular verbs AAE often does not distinguish between the past-tense and past-participle forms, whereas standard English does. In AAE, the standard English past-tense form usually works for both (*he did it, he have did it*).

The perfect aspect[33] of AAE is more complex than that of standard English:

| | Standard English | Afro-American English |
|---|---|---|
| Present perfect | I have walked | I have walk(ed) |
| | I've walked | I(ve) walk(ed) |
| Past perfect | I had walked | I had walk(ed) |
| | I'd walked | |
| Completive perfect | | I done walk(ed) |
| Remote perfect | | I been walk(ed) |

---

[33] *The term* **aspect** *refers to the ongoing, continuous, or intermittent quality of an action rather than to the time of its occurrence.*

Standard English has both a full and a contracted past perfect (*I had walked, I'd walked*), whereas AAE has only the full form. The completive perfect occurs in both AAE and white nonstandard dialects, whereas the remote perfect occurs only in AAE and then, in Northern cities, only rarely. The remote aspect may be due to a West African influence, since West African languages have more aspectual categories than English. Note that to express either of the ideas in these two perfects, standard English would be forced into a wordy paraphrase something like *I have finished walking* (completive) and *I walked a long time ago* (remote). Thus the nonstandard dialects offer convenient perfects that standard English lacks.

Present tense. In standard English the third-person present tense of most verbs is set apart from all the other forms by an /s, z, ɨz/ ending (*he walks, he runs, it fizzes*). In addition, some verbs show this inflection plus some other change: *am* or *are* ∼ *is*, *have* ∼ *has, do* ∼ *does.* (Here the ∼ means "alternates with.") AAE lacks this inflection, with the result that all forms of the present tense are identical: *I walk, you walk, he walk, we walk, they walk.* The third-person singular marker is not merely omitted or forgotten; it simply does not exist as an inherent part of AAE, probably because the West African progenitor languages did not inflect verbs for person or number. Since the third-person singular inflection is not part of the AAE system, AAE speakers usually omit the regular /s/, /z/, and /ɨz/ endings and use *have* for the irregular third singular *has, do* rather than the irregular *does,* and *say* rather than the irregular *says.* If an AAE speaker becomes self-conscious about his lack of the third-person singular inflection, he may sometimes overcorrect to extend the *-s* inflection indiscriminately to all forms in the present: *I walks, you walks, he walks, we walks, they walks.* This hypercorrection is typical in the South Central states (Mississippi, Alabama, etc.), where the simple present of the verb is more often marked with /s/, /z/, and /ɨz/ for all persons (*I walks, you walks, he walks, we walks, they walks*).[34]

Future. Often future time in AAE is expressed by *gonna* (*going to*), as it is in casual standard English. In AAE, a form of BE rarely appears with this *gonna.* If the subject is other than *I,* the *gonna* /gənə/ often becomes *gon* /gõw/ in AAE, with a nasalized diphthong: /hiy gõw gow/ for *he's going to*

---

[34] *Wolfram, "On the Use of Negro Dialect in the Teaching of Reading," p. 199.*

*go.* When *I* is the subject, the *I* merges with *going to,* giving *I'mana* /ahmənə/ in AAE and even in casual standard. AAE has two other common pronunciations for *I'm going to: I'mon* /ahmõw/ and *I'ma* /ahmə/.

*Will* also expresses future but, as we have seen, when it reduces to /I/ it can disappear, so that the future seems to be expressed by the plain form of the verb: *he miss you tomorrow.*

Invariant **be.** Where standard English uses *will be, would be,* or *am, is,* or *are,* AAE may use uninflected be:

I **be** here tomorrow
　　　for
I **(wi)ll be here tomorrow**

if I was to stay longer, I **be** frozen
　　　for
**if I was to stay longer, I (woul)d be frozen**

I **be** busy
　　for
I **(a)m busy frequently**

A sentence like *I be busy* above may be three ways ambiguous in AAE. It may mean *I will be busy, I would be busy* or *I am* $\begin{Bmatrix} habitually \\ frequently \end{Bmatrix}$ *busy. I be busy* is rarely equivalent to *I am busy.* The ambiguity does not exist in the negative, where each possibility has a different auxiliary:

I **won't be** busy
I **wouldn't be** busy
I **don't be** busy

The last use is called "habituative *be*": the *be* expresses a repeated activity or state, an **habitual aspect.** This habituative *be* occurs only in AAE, not in white nonstandard dialects. Again, this difference between AAE and white dialects probably occurs because West African languages have more aspectual categories than English has.

Absence of Forms of BE. Although *am* regularly appears in AAE (almost always contracted, as in *I'm tired*), *is* and *are* often are absent, as in *he a man, we running from school, that dude bad,* as well as in *he gonna go,* as we observed above.

These absences occur in exactly the places where standard English can contract the verb to 's (*he's a man*) or 're (*we're running from school*). *Is* and *are* are not absent from sentences like *he asked who I am* or *we know where we are,* sentences in which standard English would not contract the *is* or *are:* *\*he asked who I'm, \*we know where we're.* The absences occur most often when a pronoun precedes and a participle follows: *we running from school.* The absence of *are* is common in all Southern speech, since *are* can be contracted to 'r, and an *r* is normally deleted before a following consonant.

*Questions.* Unlike standard English, AAE uses inverted word order for indirect questions:

> Standard:     I want to know **if he is going somewhere**
>                I want to know **where he is going**
>
> AAE:         I want to know **is he going somewhere**
>                I want to know **where is he going**

Many AAE speakers do not use indirect questions introduced by *it* or *whether: I want to know* **if he went somewhere,** *I want to know* **whether he went somewhere.** In fact, they seem to have difficulty in even understanding indirect questions introduced by *whether.*

*Negation.* *Ain't* occurs as a negative BE and HAVE form (*he ain't here, he ain't done it*) in nonstandard dialects throughout the United States. In some varieties of AAE, however, it also stands for *didn't,* in which case it may be misunderstood by standard speakers. For example, *he ain't touch me* can be translated not only as *he hasn't touched me* but also as *he didn't touch me.*

*Ain't* often appears in double or multiple negatives. In all nonstandard dialects, one underlying negative may be expressed at two or more points within a sentence. And even standard speakers sometimes use such "double negatives" as *can't hardly* and *didn't never,* in which a negative auxiliary is combined with a negative adverb. Some speakers use other types of double negatives (*he didn't do no work, he ain't got none*) but do not always negate all negatives within a clause: they may say *he ain't never done anything wrong* rather than *he ain't never done nothing wrong.* In AAE, all indefinites within a clause are usually negated. Thus *any* as a word or prefix almost never occurs in a clause that is negated: *any* becomes *no, anybody* becomes *nobody, anywhere* becomes *nowhere,* and so forth:

> I ain't got **no** money
> he ain't seen **nobody**
> you ain't goin' **nowhere**

Also, the adverbs *ever* and *either* become *never* and *neither: he ain't never done it, you can't go neither.*

*Nouns.* Standard English and AAE contrast in their use of possessive and plural noun forms.

Possessives. The standard possessive noun suffixes /s, z, ɨz/ (*the cat's tail, the dog's tail, the horses' tails*) are often omitted in AAE. This omission is much greater in the Eastern seaboard states than elsewhere. The absence of the possessive inflection may reflect the fact that the West African progenitor languages did not inflect nouns to indicate possession. When the suffix is omitted, the possessive relationship between the two nouns is shown by their juxtaposition: *he stole John knife, I like that boy shoes.*

Plurals. The standard plural inflections /s, z, ɨz/ may sometimes be omitted in AAE, especially in the speech of young children. This occasional absence may reflect the fact that the West African progenitor languages did not inflect nouns for plural. However, the plural ending is also often omitted in standard Northern and Southern dialects when the noun is a noun of measurement (*two foot long, three mile wide*). AAE as well as some other nonstandard dialects may also make regular plurals out of irregular ones: *two foots, three deers.* Finally AAE may form double plurals: *childrens, mens.*

*Pronouns and Determiners.* In the case of pronouns, some AAE speakers use a first-person *mines* in sentences like *this mines* for *this is mine.* This form is a regularization parallel to the other pronoun forms: *yours, ours, his, hers, its, theirs.* As we have seen in "De Cunjah Man," pronouns were formerly undifferentiated in adult AAE dialects and still are even today in the speech of some young Southern children who speak a Gullah-like AAE. This fact very likely reflects African influence, since West African languages have nearly identical subject, object, and possessive forms.

AAE, as well as white nonstandard dialects, sometimes contrasts with standard English in its use of the indefinite article. Standard English has *a* before a word beginning with a consonant and *an* before a word beginning with a vowel sound. Speakers of AAE and white nonstandard speakers do not always make this distinction, saying *a* before a vowel as well as before a consonant: *a eraser, a orange.*

*Expletive IT.* Where standard English has THERE as an expletive, AAE has IT:

for
> it's a boy in my room name Robert
> there's a boy in my room named Robert

for
> is it a Main Street in this town?
> is there a Main Street in this town?

This use is common in AAE and contrasts clearly with standard English.

A MATRIX OF CRUCIALITY.   Particularly in the North, Afro-American English is a socially stigmatized dialect. Certain features of AAE produce stronger negative reactions in hearers than other features do. Furthermore, some features are characterized by "gradient social stratification" while others are marked by "sharp social stratification." **Gradient stratification** means a progressive increase in the frequency of occurrence between social groups, without a clear difference between contiguous groups. For example, in the black community there is a gradual increase in the absence of post-vocalic *r* as we move from the upper middle-class to the lower middle-class to the upper working-class to the lower working-class. On the other hand, **sharp stratification** appears when contiguous social classes are clearly separated by a particular usage. For example, the absence of the third-person singular marker sharply differentiates upper working-class blacks from lower middle-class blacks.

The following "Matrix of Cruciality" ranks the salient markers of Afro-American English in terms of their social significance. The ones at the top are more stigmatized socially than those at the bottom. Five of the top six (multiple negation excluded) are features that probably reflect a West African influence. The bottom four features are typical of all Southern speech and therefore are socially stigmatized only in the North, where they are perceived as distinctively characteristic of AAE.

## Matrix of Cruciality [35]

| Afro-American English Feature | sharp stratification [+] / gradient stratification [-] | general rule [+] / non-general rule [-] | grammatical feature [+] / phonological feature [-] | general significance [+] / regional significance [-] | frequent occurrence [+] / infrequent occurrence [-] |
|---|---|---|---|---|---|
| -s third person singular (e.g. *he go*) | + | + | + | + | + |
| multiple negation (e.g. *didn't do nothing*) | + | + | + | + | + |
| -s possessive (e.g. *man hat*) | + | + | + | + | − |
| invariant *be* (e.g. *he be home*) | + | + | ± | + | + |
| copula absence (e.g. *he nice*) | + | + | − | + | + |
| remote aspect *been* (e.g. *he been ate the food*) | + | − | + | + | − |
| expletive *IT* (e.g. *it is a whole lot of people*) | + | − | + | + | + |
| word-medial and final /θ/ and /ð/ (e.g. /tuwf/ 'tooth') | + | + | − | + | + |
| word-final consonant clusters (e.g. /ges/ 'guest' and 'guessed') | ± | + | − | + | + |
| word-initial /ð/ (e.g. /den/ 'then') | − | + | − | + | + |
| vowel glide (e.g. /tahm/ 'time') | − | + | − | − | + |
| post-vocalic *r* and *l* (e.g. /kah/ 'car') | − | + | − | − | + |
| syllable-final *d* (e.g. /beht/ 'bed') | − | + | − | − | + |
| i/e before nasals (e.g. /pin/ 'pin' or 'pen') | − | − | − | − | − |

[35] Adapted from Walt Wolfram, "Sociolinguistic Implications for Educational Sequencing," *Teaching Standard English in the Inner City*, p. 117.

## WORKING WITH AFRO-AMERICAN ENGLISH

1. For the following words, the AAE pronunciation would differ from the formal standard English of *r*-pronouncing regions. Using Trager-Smith symbols, transcribe these words as they would be pronounced in pure AAE.

| | |
|---|---|
| guard | thanks |
| part | nothing |
| cold | with |
| help | past |
| best | this |
| dialect | breathe |
| desks | man |
| bend | den |
| tossed | unless |
| mugged | supposed to |

2. Below are the symbols of the Initial Teaching Alphabet now used in many American schools. With forty-four symbols, the alphabet establishes a nearly one-to-one correspondence between sound and symbol and is specifically for use only in the beginning stages of learning to read. By about the middle of grade two, the child is led by a series of readers and workbooks to make the transition from i.t.a. to traditional orthography. In your opinion, would it be a good idea to use this alphabet in teaching speakers of SIE and AAE to read? Why or why not?

| æ | b | c | d | εε | f | g | h | ie |
|---|---|---|---|---|---|---|---|---|
| face | bed | cat | dog | key | feet | leg | hat | fly |
| j | k | l | m | n | œ | p | ʌ | r |
| jug | key | letter | man | nest | over | pen | girl | red |
| s | t | ue | v | w | y | z | ʒ | wh |
| spoon | tree | use | voice | window | yes | zebra | daisy | when |
| ch | th | th | ʃh | ʒ | ŋ | ɑ | au | a |
| chair | three | the | shop | television | ring | father | ball | cap |
| e | i | o | u | ω | ω | ou | oi | |
| egg | milk | box | up | book | spoon | out | oil | |

**3.** The passage below is from Claude Brown's autobiographical novel *Manchild in the Promised Land,* describing Brown's early life in Harlem, from the late 1940s through the early 1960s. Claude's mother is telling his Aunt Bea how bad a child Claude is. What AAE features do you find represented in Mama's speech? Why do you suppose Brown did very little to represent the AAE phonological features that surely must have been present in his mother's speech?

|     |     |
| --- | --- |
|     | Mama said, "Lord, I sho hope nobody ain't work no roots on my child." Mama was quiet for a while, then she said, "They got some West Indian people around here who is evil enough to do |
| 5   | anything to anybody, and they always 'fixing' somebody. I always tell that boy to stop playin' and fightin' with those West Indian chillun, but he just won't listen. Who knows? Maybe he done did sumpin to one-a those kids and they people found |
| 10  | out about it and worked some roots on him. Anything might happen to that little nigger, 'cause he so damn bad. Lord, I ain't never seen a child in my life that bad. I know one thing—if I don't git that boy outta New York soon, my hair gonna be |
| 15  | gray before I get thirty years old. Sumpin gotta be wrong with the boy, 'cause nobody in my family steal and lie the way he do, and none-a his daddy people ain't never been no rogues and liars like he is. I don't know who he coulda took all |
| 20  | that roguishness at.[36] |

**4.** What nonstandard features do Spanish-influenced English and Afro-American English have in common? For each common feature, discuss whether the causes are similar (i.e., phonological in both cases, or grammatical in both cases) or different (phonological in one case, grammatical in the other).

**5.** In Charleston, South Carolina, there still exists a dialect that seems to be very close to Gullah. Compare the features of Gullah and this Charleston dialect as represented in the following books:
Gullah:
Samuel Gaillard and Gertrude Mathews Shelby, *Black Genesis: A Chronicle* (New York: The Macmillan Company, 1930).

---

[36] *Claude Brown,* Manchild in the Promised Land *(New York: New American Library Signet Book, 1965), p. 40.*

*Charleston dialect:*
DuBose Heyward, *Mamba's Daughters* (New York: The Literary Guild, 1929).


**6.** In literary works, the characters' speech is sometimes varied to show style stratification and/or social stratification of one sort or another. Analyze one or more of the works below for the type of stratification indicated.

a. *Style stratification.* Examine the speech of Gardinia in DuBose Heyward's *Mamba's Daughters* or the speech of Mama in Claude Brown's *Manchild in the Promised Land.* In what ways do these speakers shift their style to suit the occasion and/or their audience?

b. *Social stratification.* Examine the speech of the characters in Charles Gordone's play *No Place to Be Somebody.* What indications of social stratification do you find? How does the speech of the white girl Dee Jacobson compare with the speech of the black characters?

Compare the speech of the following characters in Warren Miller's *The Cool World:* "Mama" (the mother of the narrator), who is from Alabama; Royal Baron, a dealer in drugs; and Miss Dewpont, Royal's white "secretary." In what respects does their speech show social stratification?

c. *Age and social stratification.* Claude Brown's *Manchild in the Promised Land* shows the impact of education on Claude's speech as he moves from the black ghetto of Harlem to success in law school. The older and more educated a person becomes, the more his speech approaches standard English. Select three passages to demonstrate this fact: one showing Claude's speech as a child, a second showing his speech as an adolescent, and a third showing his speech as an adult. Describe the differences.


**7.** One form of Africanized English used in Africa today is Krio, the mother tongue of the descendants of freed slaves brought to Sierra Leone in the late eighteenth century. Krio is a second language for many other people in the area and is now used throughout Sierra Leone as an inter-tribal language of trade and social communication. The Krio verb system illustrates one of the ways that the structure of West African languages has influenced the structure of the English-based pidgins (and, later, creoles) spoken by Africans and their descendants. The Krio verb system shows no person/number agreement; that is, there is no distinctive third-person singular verb form. There are other differences, too, between the Krio and standard English verb systems. How do the Krio verbal phrases below compare in structure with their standard English equivalents? Judging from these examples, what similarities and what differences are there between the two systems? [37]

| | |
|---|---|
| Present: /æ dey ræyt/ | I write |
| Past: /æ ræyt / or /æ biyn ræyt/ | I wrote |
| Future: /æ gow ræyt/ | I will write |
| Perfect: /æ dɔn ræyt/ | I have written |
| Past perfect: /æ biyn dɔn ræyt/ | I had written |
| Future perfect: /æ gow dɔn ræyt/ | I will have written |
| Present progressive: /æ dey ræyt/ | I am writing |
| Past progressive: /æ biyn dey ræyt/ | I was writing |
| Future progressive: /æ gow dey ræyt/ | I will be writing |
| Past perfect progressive: /æ biyn dɔn dey ræyt/ | I had been writing |
| Future perfect progressive: /æ gow dɔn dey ræyt/ | I will have been writing |

Examples of verbal phrases involving the modals /kiyn/, *can;* /fɔ/, possibly meaning *for;* and /mɔs/, *must:*

| | |
|---|---|
| /æ biyn kiyn ræyt/ | I could write (i.e. if I wished or dared) |
| /æ biyn fɔ dɔn ræyt/ | I ought to have written *or* I would have written (i.e., by now) |
| /æ biyn fɔ mɔs dɔn rayt/ | I would (most certainly) have written |
| /æ biyn gow mɔs dɔn dey ræyt/ | I should (certainly) have been writing |

**8.** French-based Haitian Creole and English-based Jamaican Creole are both descendants of a West African pidgin language. What grammatical features do they have in common? Which of these common features may be due to a West African influence? The following references are especially useful:

> R. M. R. Hall and Beatrice Hall, "A Contrastive Haitian Creole-English Checklist." In Rodolfo Jacobson, ed., *Studies in English to Speakers of Other Languages and Standard English to Speakers of a Non-Standard Dialect.* Special anthology issue of *The English Record,* 21 (April 1971), 136–147.

---

[37] *Adapted from Eldred Jones, "Krio: An English-based Language of Sierra Leone." In* The English Language in West Africa, *ed. John Spencer (London: Longman Group Limited, 1971), pp. 83–84.*

Frederic G. Cassidy, "Teaching Standard English to Speakers of Creole in Jamaica, West Indies." In James E. Alatis, ed., *Report of the Twentieth Annual Round Table Meeting on Linguistics and Language Studies,* Georgetown Monograph Series on Languages and Linguistics, No. 22 (Washington, D.C.: Georgetown University Press, 1969), 203–214.

David Dalby, "Black Through White: Patterns of Communication in Africa and the New World." In Walter Wolfram and Nona H. Clarke, eds., *Black-White Speech Relationships* (Washington, D.C.: Center for Applied Linguistics, 1971), 99–138.

##  FOR FURTHER EXPLORATION

Bengt Loman, ed., *Conversations in a Negro American Dialect.* Washington, D.C.: Center for Applied Linguistics, 1967. Consists of actual transcriptions from interviews conducted in Washington, D.C., for the Urban Language Study, investigating the speech of school-age black children of a low socio-economic class. A tape recording of selected passages is available from the Center for Applied Linguistics.

Ralph W. Fasold and Walt Wolfram, "Some Linguistic Features of Negro Dialect." In Ralph W. Fasold and Roger W. Shuy, eds., *Teaching Standard English in the Inner City.* Washington, D.C.: Center for Applied Linguistics, 1970, pp. 41–86. The best description available of the features of Afro-American English.

Walt Wolfram and Nona H. Clarke, eds., *Black-White Speech Relationships.* Washington, D.C.: Center for Applied Linguistics, 1971. With the exception of the outdated article by Lawrence M. Davis, this collection brings together a number of valuable articles. Its major new contribution is David Dalby's excellent Hans Wolff Memorial Lecture (1970), "Black through White: Patterns of Communication in Africa and the New World," which appears in print for the first time in this volume.

J. L. Dillard, *Black English: Its History and Usage in the United States.* New York: Random House, 1972. A thorough documentation of the history of Black English in the United States.

John Spencer, ed., *The English Language in West Africa.* London: Longman Group Limited, 1971. This collection of nine essays by British and West African scholars examines how English is influencing the native languages of West Africa and being influenced by them. It is the first book to explore sociolinguistically and in depth what is happening to English where it is not the mother tongue but is widely used as a second language for social, political, economic, and literary purposes. Especially useful for the light it throws on relationships between Afro-American English and the vocabulary, pronunciation, and grammar of West African languages.

Lorenzo D. Turner, *Africanisms in the Gullah Dialect.* Chicago: The University of Chicago Press, 1949; rpt, New York: Arno Press, 1969. Turner's definitive study of Gullah clearly establishes its relationships to the West African languages which were its progenitors.

Robert A. Hall, Jr., *Pidgin and Creole Languages.* Ithaca, New York: Cornell University Press, 1966. Hall presents a world view of pidgins and creoles wherever they have developed, explaining their characteristics, function, and importance.

*The Dialect of the Black American.* Recording. Western Electric Company, Inc.: 1970. Briefly discusses some of the characteristics of Afro-American English and suggests that this dialect is a systematic and viable means of communication.

# Appendix I

## The Forms of HAVE and BE

The forms of HAVE are as follows:

*Present tense:*

**has**   Used with singular nominals, including the third singular personal pronouns *he, she* and *it,* but excluding *I* and *you:*

$$\left.\begin{array}{l} \text{my dog} \\ \text{he} \\ \text{she} \\ \text{it} \end{array}\right\}\ \textbf{has}\ \text{dandruff}$$

**have**   Used with all plural nominals and with the personal pronouns *I, we, you,* and *they:*

$$\left.\begin{array}{l} \text{my dogs} \\ \text{I} \\ \text{we} \\ \text{you} \\ \text{they} \end{array}\right\}\ \textbf{have}\ \text{dandruff}$$

*Past tense:*

**had**   Used with all nominals:
everyone **had** dandruff

*Past participle:*

**had**   Used after the HAVE auxiliary:
he **has had** dandruff
they **have had** dandruff
everyone **had had** dandruff
**having had** dandruff so long . . .

*Present participle:*

**having**   Used after the BE auxiliary:
I **am having** a fit
he **is having** a fit
they **are having** a fit
she **was having** a fit
they **were having** a fit
they had **been having** a fit
you should **be having** a fit

The forms of BE are as follows:

*Present tense:*
**am**    Used with the first singular pronoun, *I:*
        I **am** silly

**is**    Used with the third singular pronouns and with
(third    all other singular nominals except those having
singular form)    *you* as the head noun:

$$\left.\begin{array}{l} \text{my dog} \\ \text{he} \\ \text{she} \\ \text{it} \end{array}\right\} \textbf{is silly}$$

**are**    Used with all plural nominals and with all the
    other personal pronouns:

$$\left.\begin{array}{l} \text{my dogs} \\ \text{we} \\ \text{you} \\ \text{they} \end{array}\right\} \textbf{are silly}$$

*Past tense:*
**was**    Used with all singular nominals except those
    having *you* as the head noun:

$$\left.\begin{array}{l} \text{my dog} \\ \text{I} \\ \text{he} \\ \text{she} \\ \text{it} \end{array}\right\} \textbf{was silly}$$

**were**    Used with all plural nominals and with all the
    other personal pronouns:

$$\left.\begin{array}{l} \text{my dogs} \\ \text{we} \\ \text{you} \\ \text{they} \end{array}\right\} \textbf{were silly}$$

*Past participle:*
**been**    Used after the HAVE auxiliary:
        he **has been** silly
        they **have been** silly
        they **had been** silly
        **having been** silly for so long . . .

*Present participle:*
**being**    Used after the BE auxiliary:
        I **am being** silly
        he **is being** silly
        they **are being** silly
        she **was being** silly
        they **were being** silly
        they **had been** being silly

## Appendix II

### Some Latin and Some Greek
### Prefixes and Roots

## Latin Prefixes and Roots

The following set of prefixes from Latin is representative. They are given here with their literal Latin meanings, which may carry over, more or less precisely, into English.

| | | | |
|---|---|---|---|
| ad- | "to, toward" | con- | "with" |
| de- | "down" | dis- | "away" |
| ex- | "out of" | in- | "into" |
| in- | "not" | inter- | "between" |
| ob- | "against" | pre- | "before" |
| pro- | "for, forward" | re- | "again, back" |
| se- | "apart" | sub- | "under" |
| super- | "above" | trans- | "across" |

*From Paul Roberts,* The Roberts English Series: A Linguistic Program—Complete Course *(New York: Harcourt Brace Jovanovich, Inc., 1967), p. 492.*

These prefixes combine with various roots drawn usually from Latin verbs. The following table lists some familiar roots, with the form they usually take in English, and their literal Latin meaning:

| Latin Verb | Form it usually has in English | Literal meaning of verb |
|---|---|---|
| caedere | -cide | "cut" |
| claudere | -clude | "close" |
| currere | -cur | "run" |
| fidere | -fide | "trust" |
| mittere | -mit | "send" |
| pellere | -pel | "drive" |
| petere | -pet | "seek" |
| portare | -port | "carry" |
| scribere | -scribe | "write" |
| tendere | -tend | "strive" |
| cedere | -cede or -ceed | "go" |
| clinare | -cline | "lean" |
| ferre | -fer | "carry" |
| mandare | -mand | "order" |
| mutare | -mute | "change" |
| pendere | -pend | "hang" |
| plicare | -ply | "fold" |
| scandere | -scend | "climb" |
| sedere | -sede | "sit" |
| tenere | -tain | "hold" |

*From Roberts, p. 493.*

Many English verbs have used the Latin past participle form, along with or instead of the infinitive. Some of these are presented in the following set. The hypen indicates where the prefix attaches to the root and vice versa:

| Infinitive | Past Participle | Form the root usually has in English | Literal meaning of root |
|---|---|---|---|
| flare | flatus | -flate | "blow" |
| gradi | gressus | -gress | "walk" |
| jacere | jactus | -ject | "throw" |
| legere | lectus | -lect | "choose" |
| movere | motus | -mote | "move" |
| ponere | positus | -pose | "put" |
| trahere | tractus | -tract | "drag" |

*From Roberts, p. 493.*


## Greek Prefixes and Roots


English has borrowed heavily from Greek too, and continues to do so, especially in the fields of science and technology. The same Greek element may occur in one English word as a prefix and in another word as a root; therefore these Greek elements are presented here in one alphabetical list, with examples to illustrate their occurrences.

*a-, an-*(not, without): *apathy* (without feeling), *asymmetrical* (not symmetrical), *anhydrous* (without water)

*anthropo-*(man): *anthropoid* (like a man), *philanthropy* (love of man), *anthropomorphic* (having the form of a man)

*anti-*(against): *antibiotic* (against life), *antipathy* (feeling against), *antistrophe* (turning against)

*auto-*(self): *autohypnosis* (hypnosis of self), *autobiography* (writing of one's own life), *autointoxication* (self-poisoning)

*bio-*(life): *biology* (study of life), *biogenesis* (life development), *biolysis* (destruction of life)

*chron-*(time): *chronometer* (measurer of time), *synchronize* (put in time with), *diachronic* (through time)

*cracy-*(rule): *autocracy* (self-rule), *plutocracy* (rule of the wealthy), *aristocracy* (rule of the best)

*demo-*(people): *democracy* (rule of the people), *endemic* (in the people), *epidemic* (on the people)

*dia-*(through, across): *diagram* (writing through), *diagonal* (through an angle), *diameter* (measurement across)

*ge-*(earth): *geology* (earth study), *geometry* (earth measurement), *George* (worker in the earth)

*graph-, gram-*(writing): *photograph* (picture writing), *graphic* (written), *cryptogram* (secret writing)

*hetero-*(other, different): *heterogeneous* (having other forms), *heterochromatic* (having more than one color), *heterodox* (of a different opinion)

*homo-*(same): *homophone* (same sound), *homosexual* (same sex), *homotaxis* (same arrangement) *hyper-*(over, too much): *hypersensitive* (oversensitive), *hyperacidity* (too much acidity), *hyperemia* (too much blood)

*hypo-*(under): *hypodermic* (under the skin), *hypogeal* (under the earth), *hypoglossal* (under the tongue)

*mega-*(big): *megaphone* (big sound), *megalith* (big stone), *megapod* (having big feet)

*meter-*(measure): *barometer* (measure of weight), *hydrometer* (measure of water), *Nilometer* (measurer of the Nile)

*micro-*(small): *microcosm* (small world), *microbiology* (study of small life), *microphone* (small sound)

*penta-*(five): *pentagram* (five pointed figure), *pentameter* (verse of five feet), *pentarchy* (rule of five people)

*phil-*(love): *dendrophile* (lover of trees), *Anglophile* (lover of the English), *Phillip* (lover of horses)

*phob-*(hate, fear): *xenophobia* (hatred of foreigners), *Anglophobe* (hater of the English), *acrophobia* (fear of heights)

*phon-*(sound): *phonology* (study of sounds), *phonic* (pertaining to sound), *phonograph* (sound writer)

*poly-*(many): *polytechnic* (many crafts), *polymorphous* (many forms), *polydactyl* (many fingers)

*pseudo-*(false): *pseudoscience* (false science), *pseudoclassic* (false classic), *pseudomorph* (false form)

*psyche-*(mind, soul): *psychology* (study of the mind), *psychotherapy* (treatment of the mind), *psychopath* (mind sufferer)

*sym-*(with, together): *sympathy* (feeling with), *synthesize* (put together), *syndactyl* (having the toes stuck together)

*tele-*(far): *telephony* (sound sent far), *telemeter* (measurer of distance), *telelectric* (electricity sent far)

*therm-*(heat): *thermodiffusion* (spread of heat), *thermolysis* (loss of heat), *thermostat* (regulator of heat)

*zo-*(animal): *zoography* (description of animals), *zoometry* (measurement of animals), *protozoa* (first animals)

From Paul Roberts, Understanding English *(New York: Harper and Row, Publishers, 1958), pp. 373–375.*

## Appendix III

## Phonologically Conditioned Inflections

Certain noun plural forms are considered to be "irregular." The plural of *child* is *children,* for example, not *childs.* Similarly, we have irregular past tenses of verbs; the past tense of *go* is *went,* for example, not *goed.* However, there are certain predictable patterns in the way we pronounce the plurals and possessives of "regular" nouns and in the way we pronounce the third singular present, the past, and the past participle endings of "regular" verbs.

Words ending in sibilants (s, z, š, ž/) and affricates (/č, ǰ/) take a schwa or barred i̧ followed by a voiced apico-alveolar sibilant ending for noun plural and possessive and for verb third singular present. Thus the noun plural and possessive ending will be /əz/ or /ɨz/, and the third singular present tense ending will be the same. Some examples of words ending in these sibilant and affricate sounds are:

| | | | |
|---|---|---|---|
| /s/ | kiss | /č/ | march |
| /z/ | fizz | /ǰ/ | judge |
| /š/ | wish | | |
| /ž/ | rouge (for some people, this word ends in a /ǰ/ sound) | | |

Words ending in *voiceless* sounds other than the sibilants and affricates are made plural or possessive, if they are nouns, by the addition of a *voiceless sibilant,* /s/. Likewise, verbs ending in voiceless sounds other than the sibilants and affricates take /s/ as the third singular present tense ending. When such words end in a *voiced* sound other than a voiced sibilant or affricate, the plural and possessive noun ending and the third singular verb ending is a *voiced* sibilant, /z/. Some examples of words ending in *voiceless* sounds other than /s, š, č/ are:

| | |
|---|---|
| /p/ | cap |
| /t/ | bat |
| /k/ | pick |
| /f/ | laugh |
| /θ/ | teeth, unearth |

All other sounds, including all vowels, are *voiced* and take the /əz/ or /ɨz/ ending. Some examples of words ending in a voiced consonant are:

| | |
|---|---|
| /b/ | rub |
| /d/ - | pad |
| /g/ | plug |
| /v/ | love |
| /ð/ | teethe |

Verbs ending in the apico-alveolar stops /t/ and /d/ take a schwa or barred /ɨ/ plus the voiced apico-alveolar stop /d/ in the past tense and past participle forms. That is, the past tense and past participle ending for "regular" verbs ending in a /t/ sound or a /d/ sound is either /əd/ or /ɨd/. Some examples of verbs ending in /t/ and/ d/ are:

/t/    knit, wait
/d/    knot, wade

Verbs ending in *voiceless* sounds other than /t/ take the voiceless apico-alveolar, /t/, in the past tense and past participle forms. Verbs ending in voiced sounds other than /d/ take the *voiced* apico-alveolar, /d/, in the past tense and past participle forms. Some examples of verbs ending in *voiceless* sounds other than /t/ are:

/p/    cap
/k/    pick
/f/    laugh
/θ/    unearth
/s/    kiss
/š/    wish
/č/    march

All other sounds (except /t/) are *voiced*. Some examples of verbs ending in voiced consonants are:

/b/    rub
/g/    plug
/v/    love
/ð/    teethe
/z/    fizz
/ž/    rouge (?)
/ǰ/    judge

# INDEX

WH-word nominalizations, 231–232, 235, 241–242
WH-word transformation, **124, 166,** 109–110, 119–125, 177, 231–232, 241–242
WH words, **110, 121,** 109–110, 119–125, 231–232
WHAT-cleft transformation, **142–143, 165,** 142–147, 158
Williams, William Carlos, 24, 25 *fn.*
Wise, Claude Merton, 358–359
*With Aesop Along the Black Border,* 362–363
Wolfram, Walter A., 347–348, 365–367, 383

*Women in Love,* 207
Woods, John, 18
word boundary symbol, 75
word boundary transformation, **81, 85, 167,** 75
*Word Geography of the Eastern United States, A,* 339
Wright, Richard, 216

**Y**

Yeats, W. B., 220
"Yellow Chimney, The," 24–25
Yevtushenko, Yevgeny, 13

1 2 3 4 5 6 7 8 9 10 11 12 13 14 15 16 17 18 19 20 21 22 23 24 25     80 79 78 77 76 75 74 73